Promoting Independence

S/NVQ

LEVEL 3

CANDIDATE HANDBOOK

...lan

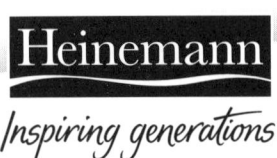

Heinemann

Inspiring generations

Heinemann Educational Publishers
Halley Court, Jordan Hill, Oxford OX2 8EJ
Part of Harcourt Education

Heinemann is the registered trademark of Harcourt Education Limited

© Yvonne Nolan, 2003

First published 2003

08 07 06 05
10 9 8 7 6 5

British Library Cataloguing in Publication Data is available from the British Library on request.

ISBN 0 435 45643 1

Designed by Wendi Watson

Typeset by Techtype

Printed and bound in Great Britain by CPI Bath

Tel: 01865 888058 www.heinemann.co.uk

Contents

Introduction

As you look through the contents of this book, and your NVQ, you will see the similarities with the units from the Care NVQ. This is because the skills and knowledge which you need are similar – it is what you do with them which is different.

If you are undertaking Promoting Independence as an NVQ, or if you are using this book to support another qualification, or even if you simply find it helpful in your day-to-day work, you are likely to be working in an environment where you are involved with people who need to learn how to adapt their environment in order to achieve their full potential and to function with maximum independence.

It is within this context that the skills and knowledge needed for Care are applied in different settings and circumstances. For all those who work in the Care field, the promotion of maximum independence is an important part of work and is a basic principle which underpins all approaches. However, in the work which you do, it is the main *purpose* and *focus* of the work and the end which you aim to achieve.

The essential skill of working alongside people in order to promote their independence lies in learning to recognise the difference between promoting people's independence and abandoning them! There is a significant gap between leaving someone to fend for themselves and doing so much for them that they lose all confidence in their own abilities. The important balance you need to reach is to find the maximum level of possible achievement for each individual and to be a major part of the environment which enables them to find the point at which they feel they are achieving the goals they have set.

Regardless of the setting in which you work, or the client group you work with, you should find that the good practice and knowledge identified in the book are appropriate to your context and will give you ideas and questions which you should discuss with your supervisor or NVQ assessor.

Working in any care setting is hugely demanding and requires a massive commitment, both physically and emotionally, if you are to develop your practice to a competent level. It is also hugely satisfying and, like most skills, the better your practice becomes the more you enjoy your work and the greater is your sense of achievement. The work required to achieve an NVQ at Level 3 means that you may find that you are facing considerable demands on your time and energy, however this is helped to some extent by your increasing levels of skill and competence which make the job easier and increase your confidence.

You have made a career choice which provides you with the unique privilege of working with people to help them reach their full potential, whatever that may be.

About this book

This handbook contains everything you need to succeed in your NVQ Level 3 Promoting Independence. The content of the units matches the NVQ specification and covers all of the mandatory units, as well as the optional units. Each unit provides you with just the right amount of theory and makes links to real-life care practice. It will also give you some practical exercises and activities to try out as part of your everyday practice and it will, hopefully, raise some questions and issues which you can give thought to and discuss with colleagues and supervisors.

Features of the book

Throughout the text there are a number of features that are designed to encourage reflection and discussion and to help relate theory into practise in a care context.

The features are:

What you need to learn	a list of knowledge points that you will have learnt by the end of the unit
Active Knowledge	an activity to encourage you to look at your work environment, research various topics, and apply the described theory to practice
Case Study	examples of 'real' situations to help link theory into practice
Did you know?	interesting 'real-world' pieces of information that illustrate how the theory works
Keys to Good Practice	a list that summarizes the key issues you have just learnt in each element or unit
Unit test	a short 10–15 question test at the end of each unit, covering all the knowledge presented in that unit

A number of experienced professionals have contributed their expertise to this book; their purpose in doing so is to support you in your chosen studies and to provide you with a firm knowledge foundation from which you can extend and develop your particular interests.

I wish you every success with your NVQ and your future career.

Yvonne Nolan

Acknowledgements

The authors and publishers would like to thank the following for permission to reproduce photographs:

Alamy – page 267
John Birdsall Photography – pages 151, 164 and 283
Robert Brook / Photofusion – page 22
Collections / Anthea Sieveking – page 160
Commission for Racial Equality – page 10
Empics – page 184
Equal Opportunity Commission – pages 13 and 26
Sally Greenhill – page 159
Science Photo Library – pages 97, 100 and 188
David Tothill / Photofusion – page 289
Crown copyright material is reproduced with the permission of the controller of HSMO.

Every effort has been made to contact copyright holders of material published in this book. We would be glad to hear from any unacknowledged sources at the first opportunity. Any omissions will be rectified in subsequent printings if notice is given to the publishers.

Dedication
To all those who give and receive care.

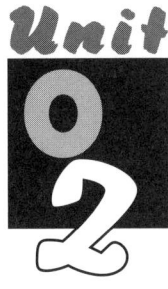

Promote people's equality, diversity and rights

This unit is one of the keys to working successfully in care at any level. You may have completed Unit O1 which is similar in content and will be referred to throughout this unit. If you have not completed Unit O1, then we strongly recommend that you read this unit in conjunction with that unit. It can be found in the book entitled *NVQ Level 2 Care*, also by Yvonne Nolan. This unit will explore the issues in more depth and will consider some broader aspects of the significance of understanding the importance of equality, diversity and rights for all people who work in the health and care sector. As in Unit O1, the confidentiality of information is explored as a vitally important component of people's rights when they are receiving a service and care.

ement 02.1 — Promote people's rights and responsibilities

WHAT YOU NEED TO LEARN

- The rights your clients have.
- How you can help people exercise their rights.

Clients' rights

Clients' rights are broadly divided into three categories. The first are basic human rights, the second are rights which are provided by legislation and the third are rights which are provided under charters, guidelines and policies. These rights are very different in their nature and in the way in which they are applied although, from October 2000 the basic human rights became law in this country for the first time. The **Human Rights Act** received the royal assent on 9 November 1998 and the majority of its provisions came into force on 2 October 2000. The effects of the Act are far-reaching and bring within UK jurisdiction the rights which were previously contained within the European charter of human rights and for the pursuit of which you had to go to the European Court of Human Rights in Strasbourg.

The Human Rights Act 1998

The Human Rights Act means that residents of the United Kingdom – this Act applies in Scotland, Wales and Northern Ireland – will now be entitled to seek redress (through the courts) in the United Kingdom if they believe that their human rights have been infringed by any public authority. The definition of public authority is very broad. It includes:

- government departments
- local authorities
- police
- benefits agencies
- the courts.

It also includes organisations which carry out any public function. The Act does not identify precisely what it means by a public function, but it is generally taken to mean:

- when an organisation performs or operates in the public domain as an integral part of a statutory system
- when it performs a duty which is of public significance
- when the rights or obligations of individuals are affected by the performance of the duty
- when a body is non-statutory but is established under the authority of government or local government
- when the body performs functions that the government or local government would otherwise perform
- when an individual may be deprived of some legitimate expectation in performance of the duty.

Organisations subject to the Human Rights Act 1998	
Residential homes or nursing homes	These perform functions which would otherwise be performed by a local authority
Charities	Again these may be providing functions which would otherwise be provided by a government or local authority
Voluntary organisations	Also in a similar capacity
Public service	This could include the privatised utilities, such as gas, electric and water companies, which will be affected by the provisions of this Act

This breadth of interpretation takes into account such bodies as the ones in the table below.

Within the health and care sector there are a great many organisations whose work will be covered by the Human Rights Act. Meals-on-wheels services, which are to a great extent provided by the voluntary sector, are likely to be seen as fulfilling part of the statutory duties of the local authority. As such they will have to ensure that they are not restricting anyone's human rights, for instance by failing to provide meals which meet somebody's religious dietary requirements. Similarly, home care services, many of which are run by the private sector, will also have to ensure that their services are provided within the requirements of the Act, and will have to ensure that all the carers are fully aware of the implications of the Act in their day-to-day work.

It is likely that anyone who works in health or care will be working within the provisions of the Human Rights Act. This Act is all about respect for, and the promotion and fostering of, the rights of individual people through all the functions of a public authority, or any organisation which is carrying out the role of a public authority. Under the Act everyone who works in a setting which is covered by the Act will have to interpret the legislation with which they work in a way which is compatible with the Human Rights Act. The workers will be required to act in accordance with the Human Rights Act. Under the Act the rights which are guaranteed are the following.

1 **The right to life.** Public authorities must not cause the death of any person and they have a positive obligation to protect life. There are particular situations where the Act defines a limited number of circumstances where it is not a contravention of the Act to take someone's life. But this only applies where the force used is no more than absolutely necessary, such as defending a person from attack or to effect a lawful arrest.

2 **The right to freedom from torture and inhuman or degrading treatment or punishment.** Torture is identified as the most serious kind of ill-treatment. Inhuman or degrading treatment is less severe than torture and may include physical assaults, inhuman detention conditions or corporal punishment. The ill-treatment relates to both mental and physical suffering. One of the factors which is taken into account under this right is the severity and duration of the torture, degrading or ill-treatment and the vulnerability of the victim.

3 **The right to freedom from slavery, servitude and forced or compulsory labour.** Slavery means that a person is owned by somebody else like a piece of property. Servitude is defined as a person not being owned by someone else but being in enforced service to them and unable to leave. There are some exceptions to this right, for example work which may be being carried out as part of a prison sentence.

4 **The right to liberty and security of person.** People have a right not to be arrested or detained except when the detention is authorised by law. This part of the Act does not just apply to police arrests but covers all aspects of detention, including for medical or psychiatric reasons. There are clearly defined circumstances under which people can be detained, such as after conviction by a court or where there are sufficient grounds to believe that they may have committed a crime.

5 **The right to a fair and a public trial within a reasonable time.** This right covers all criminal and most civil cases as well as tribunals and some internal hearings. People have a right to be presumed innocent until proven guilty and to be given adequate time and facilities to prepare their defence. The Act gives everyone a right to a trial in public so that justice can never be carried out behind closed doors.

6 **The right to freedom from retrospective criminal law and no punishment without law.** This right means that people cannot be convicted of an act which was not a criminal offence at the time it was committed, nor can they face a punishment which was not in place when the act happened.

7 **The right to respect for private and family life, home and correspondence.** This is one of the very far-reaching parts of the Human Rights Act. Public authorities may only interfere in someone's private life when they have the legal authority to do so. This covers matters such as the disclosure of private information, monitoring of telephone calls and e-mail, carrying out

searches, and imposes restrictions on entering a person's home. It also covers issues such as the right of families to live together or the right not to suffer from environmental hazards.

8 **The right to freedom of thought, conscience and religion.** Under this right people can hold whatever thoughts, positions of conscience or religious beliefs that they wish. They are guaranteed the right to manifest their religion or belief in worship, teaching, practice and observance.

9 **The right to freedom of expression.** Freedom of expression includes what is said in conversation or speeches, what is published in books, articles or leaflets, what is broadcast and what is presented as art or placed on the Internet. In fact, any means of communication.

10 **The right to freedom of assembly and association.** This includes the right of people to demonstrate peacefully and to join or choose not to join trade unions.

11 **The right to marry and found a family.** This part of the Act is particularly relevant to rules and policies concerning adoption and fostering. Public authorities will have to ensure that their policies in this regard, for example policies to do with age or race of applicants to become adoptive parents, are not contravening the Act.

12 **The prohibition of discrimination in the enjoyment of convention rights.** The Act recognises that not all differences in treatment are discriminatory, those that are discriminating are defined as those which have no objective or reasonable justification. For example, if a registry office was only to provide information about how to undertake a civil marriage in English only, then it is possible for this to be taken as affecting the human rights of someone who was unable to speak English and therefore unable to access the information they need. This could be said to be denying them the means to fulfil their human right to marry. This would probably be viewed as discriminatory because there is no objective or reasonable justification for failing to provide information in other languages. Take another case, that of a young person excluded from school and therefore unable to exercise their human right to receive an education. If it could be proved they were excluded because of their disruptive behaviour and not because of race or socio-economic circumstances, then this would not be discriminatory.

13 **The right to peaceful enjoyment of possessions and protection of property.** The Act defines many possessions as property, not just houses or cars, but things like shares, licences and goodwill. In some circumstances the right to engage in a profession can be regarded as a property right. Under the Act no one can be deprived of their property except where the action is permitted by law.

14 **The right of access to an education.** The right of access to education must be balanced against the resources available. This right may be relevant to the exclusion of disruptive pupils from schools, and may also prove to be very relevant for children with special needs.

15 **The right of free elections.** This part of the Act is about elections to whatever legislative bodies are relevant. They must be free and fair and be held at reasonable intervals. It is also likely to raise issues of participation and access and making sure that people with disabilities or those who are ill are still able to participate.

16 The right not to be subjected to the death penalty. This provision abolishes the death penalty.

What does the Human Rights Act mean in practice at work?

Under the Human Rights Act all other legislation that includes any Acts of Parliament or Regulations must be read, understood and used in a way which is compatible with the requirements of the Human Rights Act. Government advice is that this is a very strong provision and you must make every effort to interpret the legislation that you work with in a way which is compatible with the Human Rights Act. This means that if there are two possible interpretations of the provision under an Act, such as the Mental Health Act, the Children Act, or the Community Care Act, one which is compatible with the Human Rights Act and one which is not, then the one that is compatible must be followed.

Government guidance lays down that all public authorities have a positive obligation to ensure that respect for human rights is at the core of their day-to-day work. This guidance covers all aspects of activities including:

- drafting rules and regulations and policies
- internal staff and personnel issues
- administration
- decision making
- implementing policy and working with members of the public.

Active knowledge

Think about how the laws underpinning the policies and procedures in your workplace could be used better to build a culture of rights and responsibilities. This could be a useful area of discussion at a staff meeting or in a meeting with your line manager.

Quick check guide to how your work may be affected

It is unlikely that you will be involved in this area of work. This mainly concerns people who work within the law or in arranging tribunals, hearings or granting licences, making planning decisions and registering people with professional bodies. For example, when a nurse or midwife qualifies they are registered with the United Kingdom Central Council of Nurses and Midwives, and any nurse or midwife removed from this register means that they are no longer able to practise.

The nature of the health and care sector means that this provision of the Act is likely to apply to almost everything that you do. This is about the right under the Act which says that public authorities must not cause the death of any person and prohibits torture or degrading treatment. This provision is clearly very relevant when it comes to protecting and working with extremely vulnerable clients such as children or those who are confused or have learning disabilities.

The Act maintains that everyone has the right of respect to his or her private and family life, home and correspondence. This provision covers the requirements of confidentiality, and clients' rights of access to their own records and protection from intrusion into their family or private life. This could mean you cannot disclose important information about a client to their family if the client does not wish it.

This provision is largely concerned with people's rights to publish information, views and opinions and the role of the courts or other tribunals in seeking to prevent this.

This may affect the work you do. For example, the practice and policies of your organisation might prevent somebody from pursuing their religion, perhaps because you have failed to give them the assistance they need in order to observe their religion. An example would be not providing transport for an elderly disabled client to visit a Sikh temple.

This provision is mainly about those who work in situations where they could be depriving people of possessions, perhaps confiscating goods which have been gained through crime, or granting a compulsory purchase order against someone's property, or perhaps the removal of possessions, in order to satisfy a debt.

This part of the Act is an overarching clause which makes sure that you are not preventing anyone from exercising their rights through discrimination. The intention of the Act is to protect people from discrimination on any grounds, whether it be gender, race, colour, language, religion, political affiliations, national or social origin, association with a national minority, property, birth or other status. 'Other status' has been interpreted to mean sexual orientation, marital status, illegitimacy, military status and trade union status. For more details on discrimination, see page 20.

How to use the Act

If someone believes that a public authority has breached their human rights they can take the authority to court or they can use their rights under the Act in any other proceedings such as a judicial review, a criminal trial, care proceedings or housing possession proceedings.

If the court finds in favour then it can award whatever remedy seems just and appropriate. It could include damages or may simply require the public authority to correct the human right which has been breached.

Proceedings under the Human Rights Act can only be brought by the victim of a breach of the Act. This means that interest groups will not be able to bring cases directly, however, under the Act they will be able to support victims who choose to pursue the route of legal redress.

Case study

P and J are both people with profound disabilities. They met while living in residential accommodation and have a close and happy marriage. Both P and J need wheelchairs for mobility. P was severely injured in a traffic accident when she was in her late teens and is completely dependent on 24-hour-a-day carers to meet all of her needs. J has a genetic degenerative condition and, like P, requires a wheelchair for mobility and 24-hour-a-day care. When they decided to marry following long discussions with local authority and support teams, they were able to obtain a specially adapted bungalow and a full-time team of carers in order to enable them to live as independently as possible.

P and J are now both in their late 20s. Through the use of technology and the Internet P has been able to continue her career as a highly successful finance advisor and dealer and J writes popular books. The couple are financially stable and are able to afford a good lifestyle within the limitations imposed by society because of their level of disability. After considerable thought and discussion, they decided they would like to start a family. Although P is physically capable of conceiving and carrying a child, conception would have to be achieved through an IVF intervention. However, J and P have been refused IVF treatment at all the clinics, both private and NHS, they have approached. And when they discussed the possibility of adoption with their local authority, the authority also felt unable to accept them as potential adopters. They now intend to pursue legal action on the grounds that their human right to found a family is being denied to them.

1 In this situation whose rights are paramount?
2 Does the potential unborn child have any rights?
3 What are the potential implications of this for the fertility service?
4 What are the potential implications of this for the adoption service?
5 Does the financial position of P and J have any significance in this case?

Human rights are a major issue world wide. In many parts of the world people's human rights are being flagrantly abused and disregarded daily in cases of serious torture, degradation, starvation and even death. Set against these horrific abuses of human rights, it may seem that the interpretation of some of the rights afforded by the Human Rights Act are relatively minor. However, it is the development of a culture and a society which respects human rights at all levels which is likely to prove the best source of protection against any society ever becoming involved in the major abuse of human rights of large parts of its population. The Human Rights Act 1998 should provide a major innovation in ensuring that the concept of people's rights are included as an integral part of the services provided by any public authority.

Other legislation

There are a number of other Acts of Parliament which are designed to protect and promote rights and responsibilities. Depending on your area of work, you are likely to work under the requirements of at least one of the following Acts:

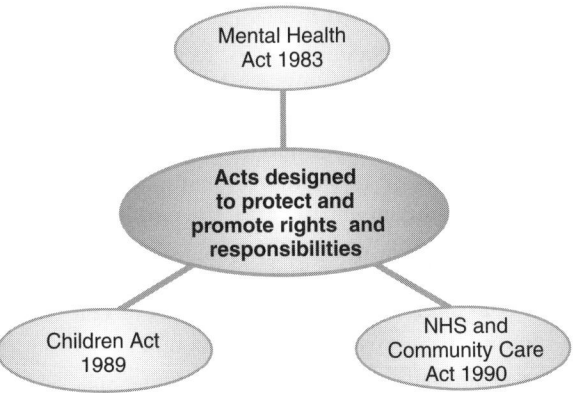

A care worker will work under conditions set down by one or more of these Acts

You will also need to know that there are provisions under a range of Acts of Parliament that protect and ensure the rights of specific groups of people. These Acts include:

Care workers need to know these Acts protect the rights of certain groups of people

For more details on these Acts, see Unit O1, in *NVQ 2 Care* .

Any work which is carried out under the provisions of Acts of Parliament is also going to be governed by the Human Rights Act. For example, under the Mental Health Act public authorities will need to consider carefully if any of their work affects the rights of patients who are compulsorily detained under the Mental Health Act or who are subject to guardianship under the Act or who are subject to any other limitations on their freedom of movement. Similarly, the Children Act will also have to be read in conjunction with the Human Rights Act to ensure that the provisions contained in that Act do not contravene the rights of people to found a family, and there may also be questions about rights of access to children. The NHS and Community Care Act covers a wide area of provision and affects the well-being, both physical and mental, of a great many people. It may also affect the way people are able to enjoy their home and possessions. It is therefore important that all public authorities consider very carefully how their work under the auspices of this Act may impinge upon human rights.

Promoting racial equality

Not all the Acts which have been designed to promote the rights of particular groups and to prevent **discrimination** are successful in doing so. There are many reasons for this, most of which are rooted in the way that society is structured and the factors which influence it and cause discrimination. For example, the Race Relations Act 1976 requires that there can be no discrimination either directly or indirectly against people in terms of employment. However, the employment figures for black and Asian people prove that the Act has not achieved its objective. For example, current figures from the Lord Chancellor's Department show that there are no black law lords or appeal court judges and only seven black circuit court judges out of a total of over 614. People from racial minorities occupy only three positions as district judges in magistrates courts out of 103.

A poster from a recent campaign run by the Commission for Racial Equality

	Black	Asian	Other	Total ethnic minority	Total in post	% Ethnic minority
Lords of Appeal in Ordinary						
Men	0	0	0	0	12	**0**
Women	0	0	0	0	0	**0**
Total	0	0	0	0	12	**0**
Heads of Division						
Men	0	0	0	0	4	**0**
Women	0	0	0	0	1	**0**
Total	0	0	0	0	5	**0**

	Black	Asian	Other	Total ethnic minority	Total in post	% Ethnic minority
Lord Justices of Appeal						
Men	0	0	0	0	33	**0**
Women	0	0	0	0	2	**0**
Total	0	0	0	0	35	**0**
High Court Judges						
Men	0	0	0	0	101	**0**
Women	0	0	0	0	6	**0**
Total	0	0	0	0	107	**0**
Circuit Judges (including judges of the Court of Technology & Construction)						
Men	0	2	3	5	554	**0.9**
Women	1	1	0	2	60	**3.3**
Total	1	3	3	7	614	**1.1**
Recorders						
Men	13	12	5	30	1161	**2.6**
Women	4	3	1	8	164	**4.9**
Total	17	15	6	38	1325	**2.9**
Recorders in Training						
Men	1	3	0	4	70	**5.7**
Women	0	0	1	1	16	**6.3**
Total	1	3	1	5	86	**5.8**
District Judges (including Family Division)						
Men	1	5	3	9	353	**2.5**
Women	0	2	1	3	80	**3.8**
Total	1	7	4	12	433	**2.8**
Deputy District Judges (including Family Division)						
Men	2	3	5	10	607	**1.6**
Women	1	2	1	4	159	**2.5**
Total	3	5	6	14	766	**1.8**
District Judges (Magistrates' Courts)						
Men	0	1	1	2	84	**2.4**
Women	0	1	0	1	19	**5.3**
Total	0	2	1	3	103	**2.9**

Note: As at 31 August 2000 all Stipendiary Magistrates became District Judges (Magistrates' Courts)

	Black	Asian	Other	Total ethnic minority	Total in post	% Ethnic minority
Deputy District Judges (Magistrates' Courts)						
Men	2	4	1	7	121	**5.8**
Women	1	0	1	2	30	**6.7**
Total	3	4	2	9	151	**6.0**

Note: As at 31 August 2000 all Stipendiary Magistrates became District Judges (Magistrates' Courts)

Source: Lord Chancellor's Department. The figures are correct as at 1 June 2002.

A similar picture occurs within the police. Despite a wide ranging and highly publicised examination of racism and its consequences within police forces, there has only been a minimal increase in the employment of black and Asian people as police officers. Between 1995 and 2001 the percentage of police officers from racial minorities only increased from 1.75 per cent to 2.3 per cent across all of the police forces in England and Wales. This represents an increase from 2,223 officers in 1995 to 2,975 officers in 2001.

However, there is a small increase in the number of black and Asian police achieving promotion within the police force, but the percentage remains tiny.

Racial minorities in senior ranks of police	1995 Out of 2,223	2001 Out of 2,975
Sergeants	158	340
Inspectors	36	83
Chief inspectors	8	24
Superintendents	1	15
Assistant chief constables	0	2

Source: Commission for Racial Equality, 2002

Recently there have been several highly publicised cases of black or Asian members of the armed forces receiving compensation because they were racially abused. Figures for 1997 show that in the armed services black and ethnic minority service personnel represented on average only about 1.3 per cent of the total. Only 13 per cent of black applicants were accepted by the Army, whereas approximately 25 per cent of white applicants were accepted. The table shows the percentage of black and ethnic recruits to each of the armed forces.

Forces	% Black and ethnic recruits
Royal Navy	1.1
Army	1.5
Royal Air Force	1.4

Source: Commission for Racial Equality, 1997

These figures show clearly that legislation alone is not sufficient to ensure that people are not discriminated against and that they are able to exercise their rights. Legislation will not be effective unless attitudes change along with it, and any change in attitude requires a long-term period of education, both formal and informal, before serious change actually occurs.

Many employers and a wide range of organisations claim to be non-racist and to have a policy of equal opportunities. However, the old saying, 'I cannot hear what you are saying, the things you do are speaking too loudly', is appropriate for many organisations in the UK today.

Active knowledge

Find out the local percentage of your population who are from black, Asian or other ethnic minority backgrounds and compare this to the number of people employed in your organisation. Check if the overall workforce reflects the makeup of your local population. Then check the number of people in senior management positions in your organisation and how many of them are from black, Asian or other ethnic minority backgrounds, and look at how this compares to the makeup of the overall work force. If your organisation compares unfavourably with the local population, what action could be taken to improve the ratio?

Promoting sexual equality

The Sex Discrimination Act 1975 makes it illegal to discriminate against particular groups. This legislation is also difficult to enforce and on its own can never achieve a truly non-discriminatory society with respect to gender. Women are particularly affected by sexual discrimination.

A campaign against sexual discrimination run by the Equal Opportunities Commission

Women tend to work in predominately low paid occupations such as clerical, catering, hairdressing, caring and other service industries. The 'glass ceiling' is an expression used to explain the barriers which exist to prevent women achieving promotion to senior positions. Many of these barriers are not obvious; they involve factors such as attitudes, working arrangements and working hours, balancing work and family, difficulties in mobility and the outdated attitude of some male senior managers.

The 'glass ceiling' is a barrier to women in the workplace

The Hansard Commission reported in 1990 on the position of women in management. At that point less than 7 per cent of senior managers were women, by 1995 that had increased to just over 10 per cent, by 2001 the percentage of women in positions as line managers and senior officials had jumped to 30 per cent. However, within the legal and judicial system, women, like black and Asian people, are under-represented. There are no women Law Lords and only two appeal court judges, and only 6 per cent of high court judges and 10 per cent of circuit judges are women. In the police force there are only two female chief constables out of 43 (just 6 per cent), there are 73 out of 11,149 superintendents (again 6 per cent), but 24 per cent of police constables are women – 19,004 out of 78,158.

Just by providing women with rights in respect of employment the Sex Discrimination Act does not necessarily change attitudes. This is a long and protracted process, as is clear from the painfully slow progress that has been made over the 25 years that this Act has been in place.

The Equal Pay Act, which also relates to women and employment, has been in force since 1970, yet there are still major inequalities in the pay which women receive. According to figures from the Office for National Statistics in 2001, women earned on average only 75 per cent of the wages earned by men. The Department for Work and Pensions figures for 1999/2000 show that women's gross individual income, including employment, pensions, benefits, investments, etc. is, on average, only 52 per cent of men's.

Employment Opportunities for women are improving, but are still limited. Women tend to work in areas which are still seen as traditionally 'women's work', for example 78 per cent of retail sales assistants are women, but only 21 per cent of sales and marketing managers are female, 90 per cent of nurses and care workers are women, as are 95 per cent of receptionists. The table from the Equal Opportunities Commission makes interesting reading and shows that there is still a strong emphasis on traditional career choices for women.

Occupational segregation 2001 – Great Britain: Selected occupations

	Employees and self-employed aged 16 or over			
	Women ('000)	% of employees	**Men** ('000)	% of employees
Taxi/cab drivers & chauffeurs	12	7	162	93
Security guards & related	12	8	140	92
Software professionals	51	16	270	84
ICT managers	34	17	169	83
Police officers up to sergeant	30	20	125	80
Marketing & sales managers	92	21	340	79
IT operations technicians	34	29	82	71
Solicitors, lawyers, judges & coroners	47	37	80	63
Sales representatives	89	37	151	63
Medical practitioners	59	38	95	62
Chefs & cooks	113	46	130	54
Shelf fillers	62	48	68	52
Secondary teachers	190	57	143	43
Sales & retail assistants	838	72	327	28
Waiters & waitresses	138	77	40	23
General office assistants & clerks	488	81	117	19
Cleaners & domestics	493	81	114	19
Primary & nursery teachers	287	86	46	14
Hairdressers & barbers	126	88	16	12
Nurses	388	90	45	10
Care assistants & home carers	485	90	55	10
Receptionists	251	95	13	5

Source: Labour Force Survey 2001 National Statistics

Case study

K is the manager of a residential facility for children and young people. There are 15 children and young people in the facility, which provides a long-term stable environment, and there is a large staff group, many of whom have been working in the setting for several years. K is very much aware that amongst her staff there is a predominance of women; out of the 30 staff, 27 are women. The deputy officer in charge is male, as is the caretaker and one other care worker. K is concerned because (a) she feels that children and young people need to be exposed to positive male role models as many of them have only experienced poor quality or abusive relationships with men, and (b) she is concerned about her liability under equal opportunities legislation and guidelines and she is not sure if the Human Rights Act could also apply in her work setting. K finds that each time she advertises a position there is a relatively small number of men who apply. Also those men who have applied have not been as suitable as women who have applied for the same post. K is wondering what steps she can take to encourage the recruitment of men.

1 What steps do you think K could take to improve male recruitment?
2 Should K attempt to improve male recruitment?
3 Are there any advantages to having a gender-balanced staff group?
4 Do you think that K could be liable under any legislation?
5 Is so, what legislation?
6 Who would benefit most from additional recruitment of male staff:
  • the children
  • the staff group as a whole
  • unemployed male care workers?

Active knowledge

Check out the number of male and female employees in your organisation and the proportions. Compare this to the number of senior managers in your organisation and see if the proportions remain the same.

Promoting equality for disabled people

The Disability Discrimination Act 1995 has put in place new rights for disabled people concerning employment, access and land, property and housing. This still leaves a great deal to be desired in terms of changing attitudes towards people with disabilities because much of the Act is advisory and may not have adequate powers of enforcement. As with discrimination on the grounds of race or gender much remains to be done in terms of changing attitudes. There is an increasing movement amongst disabled people to educate society on the disabling environment and how disability is caused by the attitudes and restrictions of society rather than a specific or individual condition. The disabled people's movement would argue that in order for disabled people to function in society without discrimination, society must adapt to meet the needs of disabled people and not the other way around. Most disabled people are able to achieve most of their goals and aspirations provided that society makes it possible rather than expecting them to limit their dreams, hopes and aspirations as a result of their disability.

Rights under charters

One way in which the rights in respect of service provision are given to users of the provision is through a **charter**. Charters mean that those who use the service and those who support them know what they can expect and know when and how to complain if the service fails to meet the standards set out in the charter.

Did you know?

Did you know the government has an entire department which now deals with charters? It is part of the Cabinet Office and is called 'Service First'.

There are currently over 20 charters in the UK which outline the levels of public service which people can expect for a wide range of services – including the tax payers charter, the customs and excise charter, the job seekers charter, a courts charter and a higher education charter. The most important charters which relate to the area of health and social care are the patients charter, which informs patients about the levels of service they can expect within the National Health Service, and the long-term care charter, which lays down the standards that must be provided for both clients and their carers in the provision of long-term care. There is also a Benefits Agency customer charter which explains the standard of service provision which claimants can expect from the Benefits Agency.

You will need to make sure that you have read and understood any charters which provide people with rights and information about service levels which cover the services in which you work. Your employer should have trained you to know what the service levels are and how they are being achieved within your organisation.

The long-term care charter

The long-term care charter lays down the values which people can expect their local services, whether they be housing, health or social services, to be based on. They are:

- Treating people with courtesy, honesty and with respect for dignity.
- Helping people achieve and sustain the maximum possible independence.
- Working in partnership with people to provide the services they need.
- Involving people in decisions and giving them enough information to make informed choices.
- Helping people to give their views through advocacy and other representative organisations.
- Treating people fairly on the basis of need and not discriminating against them on the basis of age, sex, race, religion, disability or sexual orientation.
- Making sure that people feel able to complain about the standard of services they get and are not victimised because they complain.

It is interesting to note that all those values in the long-term care charter are covered by the units in the S/NVQ at levels 2 and 3 and are incorporated into the units and elements of the national occupational standards for care. The importance of putting those values into a charter means that people have a right to complain if they do not believe that the services with which they are provided are meeting the standards set out in those value statements. It is important for you as a worker in the health and care services to understand the contents and service levels identified in charters so that you can ensure that your own practice meets those requirements. It is also important that you understand how to access information on charters for a wide range of services so that you can ensure that your clients are getting service from any agency at the best possible level and that you have sufficient information to advise and if necessary assist them to complain if those services fall short. A full range of all the charters available can be obtained from 'Service First' at *www.cabinet.gov.uk* and will also be available from the agencies providing the service.

Case study

Mrs O has been receiving support from her local authority for the past five years. She is now 85 and her mobility and general health has become increasingly poor. When she began to have home care services her needs had been limited to some shopping and some housework support. However, over the years she has been able to do less so her need for home care has increased. She now has a considerable amount of personal care and requires a morning and put-to-bed service, along with bathing and other personal care.

Mrs O has recently had her care needs assessed and has been advised that owing to financial restrictions on her local authority the amount of care she receives will have to be reduced and that she can no longer have the level of service currently provided. This means that Mrs O will not be able to continue to live in her own home, but is likely to need a move into residential care. She has made an official complaint to her local authority and has contacted her MP complaining that the level of service that she is entitled to expect under the long-term care charter has not been provided. She feels that her ability to maintain her independence is being restricted by the decision of the local authority to reduce her service. She does not feel that the local authority has worked with her or involved her in making this decision.

1 What are Mrs O's rights in this situation?
2 What are Mrs O's expectations in this situation?
3 Has the local authority failed to comply with the long-term care charter?
4 Has the local authority failed to comply with any legislation?
5 How could this have been better approached?
6 Where could Mrs O go for support to make her complaint?

Active knowledge

Find the charter which covers the services in the area you work in. Make sure that you have read it and understand the levels of service required. Check that the services are being provided to the appropriate level in the area you work in. If you believe they are not, then you could raise this with your line manager.

Policies and guidelines

Most workplaces have their own policies and guidelines which are drawn up and agreed by their organisation. This usually covers matters such as equal opportunities, staff training and development, bullying, harassment, and **confidentiality**. Whilst these policies and guidelines may not necessarily confer specific rights upon clients they will certainly indicate the way in which they can expect the organisation to behave and would provide the basis for a complaint if those standards were not met.

How you can help people exercise their rights

Many people miss out on rights which they have either because they are unaware that they exist or because they have insufficient information or because they don't know how to properly complain when things go wrong. Many other people miss out on their rights because those rights simply fail to be enforced because of attitudes and ignorance. One of the most important roles which you can play in supporting people to exercise their rights is in raising awareness about discrimination and about inequality, which so many groups of people currently suffer. You can also refuse to be a part of discrimination yourself and should ensure that in your own practice you value the diversity and difference amongst the people you care for rather than allowing them to suffer disadvantage as a result of ignorance and fear. One of your most important roles is to ensure that you have all the information about the rights which apply to your clients and the services which they currently use. If you have sufficient knowledge of the existence of their rights and know where to obtain further information then you will be able to assist your clients in ensuring that they exercise the rights which have been provided for them under legislation, charters and guidelines.

Keys to good practice

- Hold regular staff meetings and have a regular item on your agenda about rights.
- Ensure that clients are fully aware of complaints procedures and know how to follow them.
- Make sure that your workplace has a series of policies and guidelines in place which will protect and promote people's rights.
- Ensure that you are updated and that you share with your colleagues updates on any information which relates to clients' rights.
- Make sure that you advise clients of their rights.
- Support clients in obtaining their rights if necessary.
- Never participate in or encourage discriminatory behaviour.

Active knowledge

Write a case study which describes a situation that you have been involved in or are aware of where it has been difficult to reach a balance between the rights of an individual client and the responsibility of the service provider to ensure a full range of service provision for all of those who need it.

WHAT YOU NEED TO LEARN

- The causes of inequality and discrimination.
- How to challenge the causes of inequality.
- How to support those who are subjected to discrimination and oppression.
- Recording information as part of anti-discriminatory practice.

Causes of inequality and discrimination

In Unit O1 you will have learned about many of the effects of **inequality** and failure to recognise and value people's **diversity**. Before you can actively promote and encourage the equal rights of everyone for whom you provide care and to work to ensure that the diversity of individuals is valued, you will need to understand how inequalities occur and the way in which society is structured.

Structure of society

The system by which people are grouped together and given status within all societies is called **social stratification**. The way in which this happens depends on the society. For example, in the American South before the American Civil War social stratification was carried out on the basis of racial grouping, whereby black communities existed only as slaves of white plantation owners. Many societies have used religion as a means of separating groups within society. In India a caste system separates social groupings on the basis of the caste into which each individual is born.

In most modern industrial societies social stratification is not governed entirely by a preordained group into which an individual is born or only by land ownership. Broadly, people are categorised according to their socioeconomic circumstances. This relates to their occupation, disposable income and housing. In Britain the government defines people according to their occupation. For many years this classification was referred to as the Registrar Generals Social Scale, however this has recently been replaced by a new occupational scale which classifies people on a scale of 1 (top) to 8 (bottom), as follows:

Social scale classification

I Higher managerial and professional occupations

1.1 Employers and managers in larger organisations (e.g. company directors, senior company managers, senior civil servants, senior officers in police and armed forces)

1.2 Higher professionals (e.g. doctors, lawyers, clergy, teachers and social workers)

2 Lower managerial and professional occupations (e.g. nurses and midwives, journalists, actors, musicians, prison officers, lower ranges of police and armed forces)

3	Intermediate occupations (e.g. clerks, secretaries, driving instructors, telephone fitters)
4	Small employers and own account workers (e.g. publicans, farmers, taxi drivers, window cleaners, painters and decorators)
5	Lower supervisory craft and related occupations (e.g. printers, plumbers, television engineers, train drivers, butchers)
6	Semi-routine occupations (e.g. shop assistants, hairdressers, bus drivers, cooks)
7	Routine occupations (e.g. couriers, labourers, waiters and refuse collectors)
8	Those who have never had paid work and the long-term unemployed

Another way of dividing the population into different social groupings is one used by advertisers and market researchers, which is based on groupings A to E, and is divided as follows:

Group A	Professional workers – lawyers, doctors, etc., scientists, managers of large-scale organisations
Group B	Shopkeepers, farmers, teachers and white collar workers
Group C	Skilled manual workers – high grade, e.g. master builders, carpenters, shop assistants and nurses
	Skilled manual workers – low grade, e.g. electricians, plumbers
Group D	Semi-skilled manual workers, e.g. bus drivers, lorry drivers, fitters
Group E	Unskilled manual workers, e.g. general labourers, barmen, porters

It is interesting to note that this list does not include a category for those who are not in paid work or the long-term unemployed. This is primarily because advertisers and market researchers are only interested in those who are in an economic position to purchase the products that they are selling.

The government uses its scale 1 to 8 when it carries out research into the trends which are currently happening in society, and particularly once every 10 years when it carries out a count of the population in a census. This provides the government with information which it can use to plan for the services and infrastructure which it will need over the next 10 years and longer, in order to effectively meet the needs of the population.

Active knowledge

Think of two people you know of who come from the opposite ends of the occupational scale. For each, write down the main details of their socioeconomic circumstances, their likely income, housing, qualifications and education, possessions, etc. How do you think their circumstances affect their rights to equality?

Some of the most obvious effects of poverty are poor housing and a poor neighbourhood

Poverty, race, gender, disability

Many people in the lower socioeconomic group are likely to suffer hardships which are caused by **poverty**, either by living on state benefit or by working in jobs with low wages.

On a world-wide scale poverty is defined by the World Health Organisation as living on less than $1 a day. There is little doubt that in many Third World undeveloped countries there are millions of people who suffer great hardship and live in very real poverty. In a Western society, such as ours, poverty takes on a different meaning. The government definition of poverty within the UK is 'half the average income after housing costs' – this is known as the households below average income measure (HBAIM).

Individuals and families living in poverty are far more likely to experience the conditions which will lead to ill-health and a greater need for the health and care services than those higher on the occupational scale, who are likely to live in better conditions. Some of the most obvious effects of poverty are poor housing, a poor diet, the likelihood of living in a poor area or neighbourhood with poor quality local facilities. Socioeconomic factors are a major cause of inequality, as you can see from the following:

Socioeconomic factors and inequality

- Infant and childhood death rates are significantly higher amongst children whose fathers are unskilled and in social groups 7 and 8.

- Children from groups 7 and 8 are four times more likely to die in accidents as those from group 1.

- Children in poverty have poorer attendance records at school and are less likely to continue into further education – this also reduces their opportunity for social mobility.

- Highest incidents of mental health problems occur amongst people who live in poverty and are in groups 7 and 8.

- Nutrition and eating habits show that people in lower socioeconomic groups tend to eat less fruit and vegetables and less food which contains dietary fibre. There seems to be evidence that the diets of those in lower social groupings tend to lack choice and variety and often contain inappropriate foods such as crisps, sweets and soft drinks.

- Only 44 per cent of babies born to mothers in groups 7 and 8 are breast-fed compared with 81 per cent of babies born to mothers in group 1.

- Large numbers of the elderly population live on very low incomes. Over 30 per cent of pensioners entitled to higher levels of income through income support fail to claim it and as a result exist in a lifestyle of severe deprivation.

Poverty is not the only cause of inequality. It can also result from issues around race, gender or disability. For example, there are much higher rates of coronary heart disease and diabetes amongst the Asian population of the UK – the death rate from heart disease can be up to twice as high as that of the general population. There also seems to be a link between race and educational achievement. The Department for Education and Employment figures show that white and Indian students are twice as likely to obtain five or more passes at GCSE than those from Afro-Caribbean, black African, Bangladeshi or Pakistani backgrounds.

It is important that you assist in identifying within your workplace and work practice any processes or procedures which can contribute to discrimination or to reinforcing inequality.

The following table shows the number of people and children in poverty in the UK (including self-employed) – i.e. those living on 50 per cent of average income after housing costs.

	People			Children		
	Total population (m)	Number in poverty (m)	% of total population	Total population (m)	Number in poverty (m)	% of total population
1979	54	5	9	13.8	1.4	10
1994/5	55.8	13.3	24	12.7	4	31
1998/9	56.6	14.3	25	12.8	4.5	35

Source: CPAG Poverty Facts and Figures

This table shows the risk and numbers in poverty by family type (including self-employed) – those living on 50 per cent of average income after housing costs.

	% of group in poverty			Number in poverty			% of total
	1979	1994/5	1998/9	1979	1994/5	1998/9	
Pensioner couples	21	23	25	1,020	1,219	1,350	9
Single pensioners	12	32	37	520	1,376	1,554	11
Couples with children	8	23	23	2,220	4,784	4,692	34
Couples without children	5	12	12	480	1,380	1,464	10
Single with children	10	55	62	480	2,310	2,914	20
Single without children	7	23	22	530	2,231	2,178	15

Source: CPAG Poverty Facts and Figures

Socioeconomic deprivation is among the underlying causes of inequality in the UK, and makes people vulnerable to discrimination through race, sex and disability. While it is not always possible for workers in the health and social care sector to improve their clients' socioeconomic position, they can challenge discrimination and intervene actively to promote equality and diversity.

The pyramid of inequality below illustrates how inequality starts, how it is reinforced by attitudes and how it is allowed to go on.

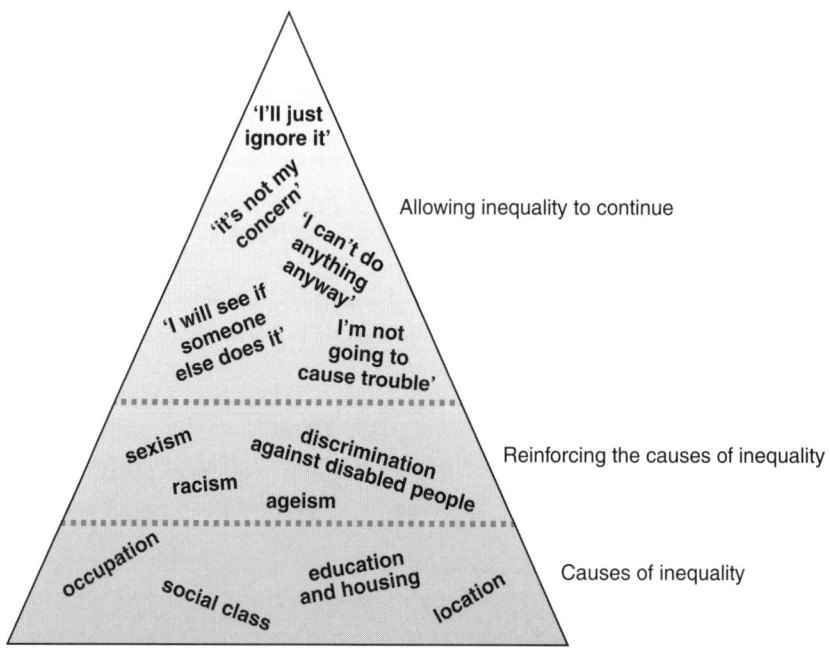

The pyramid of inequality

How to challenge the causes of inequality and discrimination

Challenging others on behalf of those who are discriminated against is often difficult and can mean confronting people about their attitudes and behaviour in a way which you may never have attempted before. The challenge is not only about individual behaviour, as you will have seen from the previous section. Inequality is caused by a great many other factors, many of which are easy to challenge on an individual basis.

However, challenging discriminatory attitudes and practices which reinforce the underlying inequalities is the responsibility of all of us who provide care and support. Although this is not easy, particularly where it involves colleagues or accepted ways of working, it is a challenge which you have a responsibility to undertake on behalf of those who are suffering from discrimination.

The following lists the types of discrimination you might encounter and ways of challenging these.

Type of discrimination	Ways to challenge
No provision for cultural or religious dietary requirements	Raise through management or in staff meetings
Inappropriate racist or sexist remarks or behaviour	Direct challenge to individual concerned. Seek support of colleagues and line manager. If necessary seek support through other channels such as supervisor or outside bodies. If behaviour results in somebody being physically at risk then the police should be contacted
Cruel or belittling and undermining behaviour or comments	Direct challenge to the individual, using the same support systems as above
Lack of knowledge amongst your work colleagues about cultural, religious or personal hygiene practices of those from ethnic minorities	Raise with your supervisor and through staff meetings and request that training is provided

Case study

G is a care worker in a residential setting for adults with disabilities. He is gay but had never discussed his sexual orientation at work or at the time of his appointment. His sexual orientation only became known when the parents of one of the residents spotted him in a picture of a gay pride event printed in a national newspaper. G had always been a popular member of staff and had an excellent work record, with appraisals which showed that his skills and abilities were developing and progressing. However, following the discovery that he was gay the atmosphere in the setting began to change. Two of the residents complained about being cared for by somebody who was gay and said they were not prepared to have G provide them with any personal care. Both these residents were young men in their late 20s. This action was supported by their parents, one of whom had spotted the photograph in the newspaper. Comments and gay jokes began to circulate within the setting, particularly when G was on duty. There would be snide comments about poofs and shirt lifters and warnings not to turn your back on him. The two residents concerned and their families had threatened to take the issue to the local press if G was not fired. The officer in charge felt that she had little choice but to ask G to leave. All the other residents, whilst they joined in with the jokes and comments about G, were happy to have their care provided by him and did not raise any objections. G felt that he was unfairly discriminated against and intended to obtain the support of his trade union.

1 What are G's rights in this situation?
2 What are his employer's rights?
3 What are the residents' rights?
4 Is the employer or the residents in contravention of any legislation?
5 How could G's trade union challenge what is happening to him?
6 What other sources of support may be available to G?

How to support those who are subjected to discrimination and oppression

In the same way as you support those who wish to make use of a complaints service and to challenge the quality and provision of services they receive, it is also important that you are able to support those who are the victims of discrimination. You have learned there are laws which provide a means of redress for those who have been discriminated against and it is essential that you ensure that you understand the broad provisions of these laws and the ways in which people may seek redress through them. This does not mean you offer legal advice, but you should be able to refer people to the right place to obtain that advice where this may be appropriate. If a client believes they have been the subject of discrimination then you should be able to advise them about the most appropriate sources of help. This could be a local advice centre, a legal aid centre or it could be a body such as the Commission for Racial Equality or the Equal Opportunities Commission. Whilst it is not your role to give detailed advice in these circumstances it is essential that you are able to give information and to support your client whilst they establish if they have any right of redress.

Not all discrimination and oppression is clear-cut, nor can all of it be acted upon through the law. Some may need to be challenged directly by the client and some may need to be referred to the police if it constitutes criminal activity. For example, an elderly person who is subject to threats and abuse from local gangs would need to be supported in making a complaint to the police.

 ## The Sex Discrimination & Equal Pay Acts   Page 2

What are my rights?

Education

Co-educational schools, colleges and universities must not discriminate in the way they provide facilities or in the way they admit students. For example, all students should have equal access to the National Curriculum. The careers service must not discriminate between boys and girls in the way they provide advice and assistance. Single-sex schools may restrict admissions to boys or girls, but they must not restrict the types of subjects they teach as a result.

Housing, goods, facilities, and services

With a few exceptions, no one providing housing, goods, facilities or services to the public may discriminate against you because of your sex. For example, you must not be discriminated against when:

- applying for a mortgage or loan
- taking part in recreational activities
- buying or renting accommodation

Advertising

Advertisements must not show that the advertiser intends to discriminate unlawfully. The Equal Opportunities Commission can take legal action against advertisers who discriminate.

Victimisation

You are protected by the law in case you are victimised for trying to exercise your rights under the Sex Discrimination or Equal Pay Acts.

What should I do first?

To help you decide whether to start a case and to gather information on your claim to present your complaint in the best way you may send a Sex Discrimination Act questionnaire to the person you believe has discriminated against you. The questions and answers in this form can be used as evidence in a court or tribunal. The form, SD.74 is available from the EOC or from your trade union, professional association, local employment office, Jobcentre or unemployment benefit office.

Where do I take my complaint?

If you feel that you have been treated unfairly because of your sex, you can take your complaint to a county court, in England or Wales, or to sheriff court in Scotland. If your complaint is about employment or equal pay you go to an employment tribunal. If your complaint is about education in a state school, college or university you must first give the Secretary of State a chance to exercise the Secretary's powers under the Education Acts.

How soon must I take action?

You must present your complaint to a tribunal not later than three months (minus one day) after the act you are complaining about took place.

You may be able to take a complaint after this time if you can show a good reason that you could not make your complaint earlier.

Complaints about unequal pay can be presented to an employment tribunal at any time while in the job to which your claim relates and up to six months (minus one day) after leaving the job. If you are taking a case to a county or sheriff court you must begin your legal action not later than six months (minus one day) after the act you are complaining about took place.

Source: Equal Opportunities Commission

The Commission for Racial Equality and the Equal Opportunities Commission provide a wide range of leaflets and reports for those who are discriminated against

Active knowledge

Find out the names and addresses of your local organisations which can advise in the case of discrimination.

Recording information as part of anti-discriminatory practice

Much of the information in this unit has come from statistics collected by a wide range of organisations, many of which are government departments or organisations concerned with specific areas of our society such as Age Concern or CPAG (Child Poverty Action Group). Collection of data and statistics about the way in which our society is made up is an important way of being able to identify issues relating to equality and diversity and to establish where people are being discriminated against.

When you record information in your workplace it will be essentially used for two main purposes. The first and most important is to record information about the individual so that appropriate services can be provided. Second, and also important, you may be asked to record information which will be used to compile statistics which in turn will inform the government or your employer or a local or regional government, or any other interested agency, about the issues which affect your client group.

For example, you are likely to be asked to record the ethnic origin of any client with whom you deal. In this way it is possible for governments and other agencies to establish the way in which individuals from ethnic minorities use the health and care services and whether or not this is likely to meet identified needs. It is normal to record the age of any individual that you are working with. From this it is possible to establish information which, for example, shows that 15 per cent of all of the population and 24 per cent of those aged 75 and over have attended a casualty or out-patient department of a hospital, or that almost half a million households each week receive home help or home care services. It is important when people are thinking about their care as they get older that they are aware that statistically 1 per cent of the population between 65 and 74 are likely to live in a care home or long-stay hospital, and that 5 per cent of those aged between 75 and 84, and 22 per cent of those aged over 85 are likely to be receiving full-time residential care. The significance of this last set of figures shows that the need for services, even amongst those aged over 85, is overwhelmingly for domiciliary and support services in their own homes. Information is essential in helping us to understand the society we live in and in making sure that we plan properly to provide the right type and level of care.

The way in which information is recorded and the way in which it is obtained also plays an important part in anti-discriminatory practice and in ensuring that you are recognising and valuing the diversity of all individuals. It goes without saying that it is necessary to record information accurately and to ensure that you have taken as many steps as possible to obtain the correct information from your client, but you also need to ensure that the information which is *about the client* is accurate *from the client's point of view*. For example, many forms look like the one on page 28.

When you are completing this kind of form on behalf of a client it is important that you ask them what ethnic minority they see themselves as being from. It is not for you to make a decision on the basis of your own observations about the ethnic origins of any individual. There are many people who may appear to be white British

Name ....
Address ....
....
....
....
Date of birth .... Age ....
Ethnic origin ☐ White British
☐ White other European
☐ Mixed heritage
☐ African Caribbean
☐ Black British
☐ Asian
☐ Chinese
☐ Other (please specify)

Example of a form which includes recording a person's ethnic identity

but who are in fact of mixed heritage and whose background, culture and experience is of African-Caribbean origin. They would rightly regard themselves as black, however an unknowing observer completing statistical information without asking may well conclude that they were white. Ethnic background is about much more than appearances, it involves culture, religion, values and the influences of the community in which an individual has grown up and developed. For example, there are many people living in the UK with Irish names but only a proportion of those would describe themselves as Irish if asked to give their racial background. The factors which are likely to influence the description will relate to family, culture and the value system of their family.

Many forms and recording requirements relate to the disability of an individual. It is essential to ask the individual concerned for their own view of their disability. It is for the individual to say whether they have a disability, or what the extent of their disability is. It is not for an observer to make those assumptions simply based on what they can see. Disability is often as much about attitude and response to disability as it is about the disability itself.

Now who is disabled?

Active knowledge

Collect together at least six different kinds of forms which are used by different agencies. You can include forms from your own workplace or from places such as the Benefits Agency, and application forms for a bank account or a mortgage or even a library ticket.

1 How many questions on each form would require you to make a judgement about somebody if you were filling it in on their behalf?
2 Think about different ways that the forms could be phrased to ensure that people's own views about themselves were included and not the images that others may have.

ement 02.3 — People's right to the confidentiality of information

WHAT YOU NEED TO LEARN

- The legislation and guidelines which govern the keeping and retrieving of information.
- How to protect confidential information and the steps to take if you are concerned that confidential information is being misused.

Legislation and guidelines

In the fields of health and social care information is recorded and stored for a great many different purposes and by many different people. The information held can range from a patient's medical records, detailed personal information about relationships, information concerning child abuse or neglect to something quite simple, such as the means of transport used to take somebody to the luncheon club or day centre.

All people working in the fields of health and social care are expected to work within the bounds of confidentiality and to follow general ethical principles which ensure that people who receive care are able to have confidence that information about them will not be shared with those who do not have a legitimate reason to have the information.

There are extensive laws in the UK to protect information held about people and they have recently been considerably strengthened and extended. There is a generally established principle called the **common law duty of confidence** which states that in general **any personal information given or received in confidence for one purpose may not be used for a different purpose or passed to anyone else without the consent of the provider of the information**. Although this has been well established in law there are still arguments about how it applies in particular circumstances. However, recent developments in legislation and guidelines should clarify much of the uncertainty around using confidential information.

The Data Protection Act 1998

The major piece of legislation which covers confidential information is the **Data Protection Act 1998.** This has replaced the previous Data Protection Act 1984, the Access to Health Records Act 1990 and the Access to Personal Files Act 1987 (this was relevant to local authority health services departments). The new Act came into force on 1 March 2000. It sets rules for processing personal information and applies to some paper records as well as those held on computers. The Data Protection Act covers all data held in respect of any individual, including credit and financial information, membership of organisations, as well as medical, health and social services records. It is extremely relevant and will have significant implications for all those who work in health and care. The Act has eight principles which apply to data. The principles are:

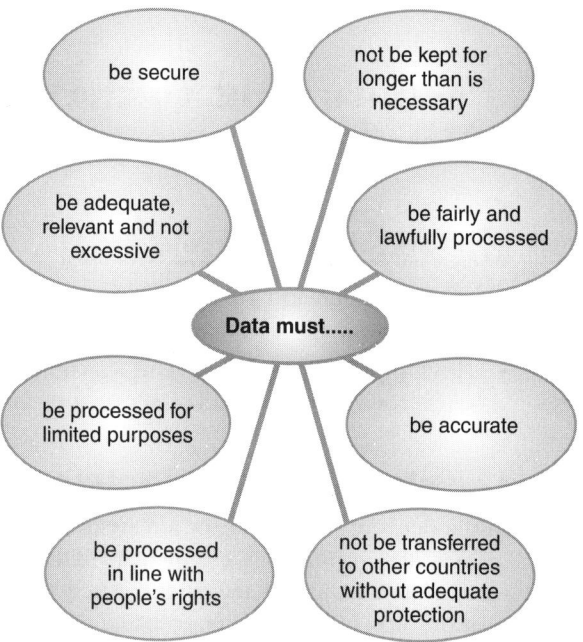

The principles of the Data Protection Act 1998

The data controllers in any organisation are required by law to work to these principles. Although the Act covers all data held by all types of organisations the implications for the National Health Service, for local authorities and for private care providers are clear. They must be able to satisfy the legal requirements in respect of keeping information.

The Data Protection Act will be further extended and is closely linked to the new Freedom of Information Bill which is currently going through the parliamentary process. When the Freedom of Information Bill becomes an Act of Parliament it will ensure that all information which is held by any public authority will, subject to certain exceptions, be available to the public. This will apply to individuals who request to see information held about themselves and there will be a provision for a 'third party access', though information will not be disclosed if that would breach the principles of data protection. It is likely that these two major pieces of legislation will make it far easier for individuals to access information contained in their own records, and the provisions should make it more difficult for information to be improperly used.

Information within the National Health Service is a huge issue. Broadly speaking the principles which apply within the National Health Service are appropriate for most other health and care settings. In 1997 the government published a report from a committee, chaired by Dame Fiona Caldecott, which had reviewed patient identifiable information within the National Health Service and which made a series of recommendations as to how this information should be handled. The recommendations of the Caldecott Committee were that each organisation should appoint an individual who would be responsible for maintaining and protecting patient information. This person has become known as a Caldecott Guardian. Every hospital and NHS organisation has to have a Caldecott Guardian. This person is normally a senior manager or a senior health professional within each organisation, however it is important that you are aware of who this person is and what their responsibilities are. The Caldecott Committee recommended a series of principles which apply to the handling of all patient identifiable information. These principles although developed for the National Health Service are sensible principles to apply in all work places.

The Caldecott Principles

Principle 1 – Justify the purpose
Every proposed use or transfer of patient identifiable information within or from an organisation should be clearly defined and scrutinised, with continuing uses regularly reviewed by an appropriate guardian.

Principle 2 – Don't use patient identifiable information unless it is absolutely necessary
Patient identifiable information items should not be used unless there is no alternative.

Principle 3 – Use the minimum necessary patient identifiable information
Where use of patient identifiable information is considered to be essential each individual item of information should be justified with the aim of reducing identifiability.

Principle 4 – Access to patient identifiable information should be on a strict need-to-know basis
Only those individuals who need access to patient identifiable information should have access to it and they should have access only to the information items that they need to see.

Principle 5 – Everyone should be aware of their responsibilities
Action should be taken to ensure that those handling patient identifiable information, both clinical and non-clinical staff, are aware of their responsibilities and obligations to respect patient confidentiality.

Principle 6 – Understand and comply with the Law
Every use of patient identifiable information must be lawful. Someone in each organisation should be responsible for ensuring that the organisation complies with legal requirements.

There are other Acts of Parliament which can affect the way in which information is used and the way in which information is shared between different organisations and agencies. For example, the Crime and Disorder Act 1998 introduces a number of measures to reduce crime and disorder, including the introduction of local crime partnerships which are based around local authority boundaries. Their role is to develop ways of reducing crime in the local area. This Act encourages exchange of information between local agencies, nonetheless it is essential that health and care agencies continue to observe the legal requirements concerning confidentiality of patient and client information. Other matters such as sexually transmitted diseases and infertility treatment are covered by specific pieces of legislation, even though the general rules on confidentiality still apply. The way in which information is used is the significant factor here. The Caldecott principles apply to patient identifiable information and similarly the Data Protection Act applies to information which can be identified as relating to a particular person.

For example, if you were to supply information which showed that Mrs Smith was receiving home help for three mornings a week because she was unable to manage

Receiving

Recording

Storing

Retrieving

Four stages of information processing

her shopping and housework and was making a financial contribution towards this because of the amount of money she had in the bank, then you would be quite rightly found to be in breach of the law. However, if you included the facts about Mrs Smith in a series of figures in a survey which showed that the home-help service in your local town was providing x number of hours per week service and y number of people were receiving that service because they were unable to cope with housework and shopping, and that z numbers of people were making a financial contribution because of their circumstances, then such information is quite legitimately allowed to be used. Mrs Smith is not identified as an individual in the survey and is simply there as one of the figures included in the report. It is also possible when compiling reports and giving information to use examples of individual circumstances provided those individuals cannot be identified. If you were providing examples as part of your survey it would be quite acceptable to say Mrs A received home-help service, and then to go on to explain Mrs Smith's circumstances provided that her identity was disguised.

How to protect confidential information

When any organisation aims to keep its information confidential one of its first considerations is to look at the ways in which information comes into the organisation. This could be from directly talking to patients or clients, it could be by letter, or fax, or telephone, or e-mail. The organisation then has to find ways to safeguard the confidentiality of the information at all the points at which it can enter the organisation. The next stage is to look at how that information is recorded, then to look at how it is stored, and the final stage is to look at how that information is retrieved from storage. At each of these stages it is possible for confidential information to be seen or heard or accessed by people who have no right or legitimate interest in knowing it.

Active knowledge

Make a list of the number of ways in which your workplace receives information on the patients or clients it cares for. You may be surprised to find out how many different ways there are to receive information. See if you can work out from your workplace procedures how information is protected at each stage.

You will have learned about the importance of not publicly discussing your clients or patients by name when the information could be overheard. You have also considered the importance of ensuring the safety and security of information which you record about individuals. But actively promoting confidentiality requires more than just being concerned about your own practice, it also requires that you are aware of the practices of your organisation and others who work inside it. You should be able to identify any potential weak points in the systems in your own workplace and raise these with your supervisor or manager.

There are several ways in which access to information can be restricted and controlled. There are physical barriers which can be placed to protect information. Medical records should always be kept in a locked room and the access to that should be limited to specific personnel. Most organisations will decide who should have access to particular information at any point in time. Access levels are very important and it should always be clear to everyone within the organisation who should have access and to what information.

Confidential information on computer can be protected by physical means

Information which is held electronically on computers is likely to require each user to have an identifier number user ID for their own use. This ensures that all activities on the computer system can be limited to the individual responsible and their access restricted by a password. Each level of access has to be carefully considered to ensure that all the procedures are within the law and within the guidelines. For example, it is not necessary for somebody who requires access to files in order to file them to have access to the contents of those files. A finance manager may need to know the numbers of people receiving a particular drug or requiring a particular type of dressing, but not necessarily any information about the individuals concerned. These types of access restrictions are probably easier to achieve with an electronic system than they are with paper files, thus allowing access at various levels through the user ID and password systems.

Another way of protecting confidential information is through a system of providing individual users with identifier numbers

Safe havens

The idea of using **safe havens** has been adopted by many organisations as a useful way to control the flow of confidential information and to restrict the number of points within any organisation where information can be obtained. Safe haven procedures mean that each workplace or site within an organisation has one point which deals with information coming into and out of that part of the organisation. This means that confidential information is only disclosed or accepted through these designated safe haven contact points. The safe haven contact point will then ensure that when information is received, the access levels which are appropriate are applied so that only the relevant staff within the organisation can have access to the information. The idea behind this exchange through safe havens is that organisations can be confident that when information goes from their safe haven point to the safe haven point in another organisation the agreed protocols will govern the use of the information from that point on.

Ownership

Another system is to have 'ownership' of information or data. This means that each set of information, whether it is in a manual file or a set of electronically held information, is assigned an owner. The organisation has an up-to-date register of owners, who have responsibility for:

* identifying all the information or data which they hold
* identifying and explaining how the information can be used
* agreeing with the person responsible about who can access the information
* what type of access each user is permitted.

Every individual within a health and care workplace has a duty and a responsibility to ensure they are extremely careful not to disclose information which is confidential. They should also contribute to the organisation having procedures in place and adhering to those procedures which minimise the risk of confidential information falling into inappropriate hands.

Personal action to safeguard confidentiality

If you have doubts about the security of patient or client information within your workplace, then it is important that you raise these with your supervisor or line manager and explain the basis of your concern. It is not acceptable to allow any deliberate misuse of patient information to go unchallenged. It is also important that where the breach of confidentiality is not deliberate, but is through thoughtlessness or carelessness of a work colleague, that you point this out to them and make clear the steps they need to take in order to ensure that the breach of confidentiality is not repeated.

If you were to become aware of some very serious misuse of information you must report it immediately. For example, if you found out that a colleague was being paid to give information to a commercial company about elderly people who are becoming disabled and may be in the market to purchase items of equipment, this would be an extremely serious matter and an entirely inappropriate use of confidential information. On the other hand, if precisely the same information is being passed to the occupational therapy service in order that they can visit to assess the need to provide aids and adaptations for the individual concerned, and you are aware that the individual has given their permission for this information to be passed on, then this is an entirely right and proper use of confidential information. This is a clear example of the first of the Caldecott principles, which is about the purpose of confidential information. In the example above the identical information was being used for two entirely different purposes, one legitimate and one not. The difference is like giving information about vulnerable people living alone to the crime prevention officer in order that they are protected and giving the same information to a gang who intend to rob them. This may seem extreme, however it serves to show how important it is to consider the purpose of the information and to always be aware of the end for which that information will be used.

Whenever you have concerns you should always report them. If your concerns turn out to be unfounded, all you will suffer will be embarrassment. However, if your concerns are justified, then you will have prevented a serious misuse of confidential information. The Data Protection Act has put in place the Data Protection Commissioner as the person responsible for investigations into breaches of Data Protection Law throughout the country. The new Freedom of Information Bill will put in place a new officer, the Information Commissioner, who will oversee both the Freedom of Information Act and the Data Protection Act. In the meantime the Data Protection Commissioner is ultimately the person responsible for ensuring that individual records are adequately maintained and for investigating and taking action in any cases where the law has not been complied with. If you work for the National Health Service the Caldecott Guardian is the responsible person within your organisation, but they too are ultimately answerable to the Data Protection Commissioner for any breaches in the law found within their own particular organisation.

Unit test

1 How are human rights protected in the UK?

2 To what extent are health and care service providers required to observe human rights?

3 What are the main changes that the Human Rights Act is likely to bring about in health and social care workplaces?

4 What are the different ways of identifying social groupings in the UK?

5 List at least four different effects of social deprivation.

6 Identify three ways to challenge discrimination.

7 What is the major piece of legislation which protects confidentiality of information?

8 What are the main areas that all organisations need to consider when looking at how to protect information?

9 Give one acceptable and one unacceptable example of the use of confidential information.

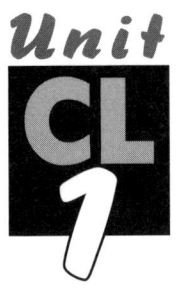

Unit CL 1

Promote effective communication and relationships

In this unit you will look at how to deal with people in a way which takes account of their individuality. When time is short and demands are high, it is often easier to treat everyone in a group in the same way, to make plans for a whole group of people or to assume that what is good for one person will be good for all. You will learn how to avoid this.

Relationships are a part of communication and communication is a part of relationships. The two are linked so closely, that it is difficult to deal with one without the other. Working in a care setting means that you work with other human beings. Being able to make relationships and to communicate with them is a very basic requirement for doing your job. Each person you care for is an individual – completely different and unique. This may sound obvious but it is so important that it is worth repeating.

You will learn how to avoid making judgments about people which are based not on knowledge and understanding of that person, but on generally accepted stereotypes, often with little truth behind them.

The work you have chosen will involve you in relationships with other people all the time. Working in caring is different from other jobs. It is not only about having good working relationships with colleagues, although good teamwork is essential, it is also about the relationships you will make with the individuals you are caring for, and it is about understanding other relationships they have, with their friends and relatives.

Element CL1.1 Develop relationships with people which value them as individuals

WHAT YOU NEED TO LEARN

- How to treat people as individuals.
- Knowing yourself and your prejudices.
- Behaviour which fails to value people.
- How to challenge unacceptable behaviour.

How to treat people as individuals

One in a million

One of the most effective ways you have of helping people is by recognising them as individuals. Learn never to make assumptions about people in groups.

Think about the number of ways in which people can be identified – they can be described by age, gender, eye colour, place of residence, job, and so on. This will remind you of the number of different aspects there are to any one individual.

The problem with 'labelling' people into particular groups for particular purposes is that it is very rarely accurate. It may be very convenient when planning care to decide that 'all individuals will want…' or 'this age group will benefit from…', but the number of individuals contained within any group means that any planning that starts with a generalisation is doomed to be unsatisfactory.

Active knowledge

Think of a way to describe yourself, starting with the most general – 'I am a woman' or 'I am a man'. So are many other people, so that does not describe you. 'I have brown hair' – so do a great many others. Continue thinking of ways to describe yourself, getting closer all the time to finding a description which is unique to you (i.e. which describes you, and no one else). Each time you think of another way to describe yourself, it will eliminate more and more people from the group, until finally you *may* (depending on how well you know yourself) come up with a description which applies to no one else but you.

Each time you are tempted to treat people as one of a group, remember how long this task took and how many descriptions you listed before you found a unique reference to you. Remember that everyone you deal with is unique – an *individual*.

You will say 'I'm not prejudiced'. Most people do, but the reality is that everyone has prejudices. They come from all kinds of previous experiences. You may be afraid of dogs because you were once bitten. Not every dog you meet is going to bite you, but that will not stop you judging all dogs from one experience. The way you have been brought up and the attitudes you grew up with will shape the kind of person you turn out to be.

What are stereotypes?

Prejudice is what makes people think in stereotypes and, equally, stereotypes support prejudice. Stereotypes are an easy way of thinking about the world. Stereotypes would suggest that all people over 65 are frail and walk with a stick, that all black young people who live in inner cities are on drugs, that all fat people are lazy, or that all families have a mother, father and two children. These stereotypes, or ways of looking at the world, are often reinforced by the media or by advertising. Television programmes will often portray violent, criminal characters as young and black.

Active knowledge

Next time you watch television, note down the number of adverts for household items that show a young, slim, white woman with one or two children, living in a nice house with a garden. This is referred to in the advertising world as the 'tart in the kitchen' scenario. The effect is to convince people that if they buy the product then they, too, will be young, slim, attractive and happy.

How many people do you know who are anything like the characters in the adverts?

How many do you know who wish they were?

What effect do stereotypes have?

The effect of stereotypes is to make us jump to conclusions about people. How many times have you felt uneasy seeing a young man with a shaved head walking towards you? You know nothing about him, but the way he looks has made you form an opinion about him. If you have a picture in your mind of a social worker or a policeman, think about how much that is influenced by the media – do they really all look like that?

1 What do you think each of these people does for a living?
2 What kind of place does each of them live in?
3 Why have you given the answers you have?

Accents can often evoke prejudice. Try to be aware of what regional accents mean – think about these stereotypes:

People from...	are known as...	are thought to be...
Liverpool	Scousers	work-shy, scroungers, funny
Birmingham	Brummies	slow, not very bright, boring
London	Cockneys	wheeler dealers, not trustworthy, clever
Glasgow	Glaswegians	aggressive, looking for a fight, drinkers
Newcastle	Geordies	warm, friendly, tough, 'salt of the earth'

The next time you find yourself making a judgement about somebody's character based on an accent, stop and think. Try to avoid a stereotype.

'*Have you heard the one about...?*'

Telling jokes at the expense of particular groups of people is similarly displaying prejudices. Stereotypes about people being mean or stupid because of their nationality fail to treat people as individuals and fail to recognise that there are individuals everywhere and that all people are different.

Active knowledge

Stop yourself every time you make a generalisation and look at the prejudice. Think about why you think the way you do, and do something about it. The next time you hear yourself saying 'Social workers never understand what is really needed', 'GPs always take ages to visit' or 'Our residents wouldn't be interested in that', stop and think what you are really doing.

It is probably quite correct that *some* social workers won't understand, maybe even all those you have met so far! But that does not necessarily apply to them all.

Perhaps most of your residents would not be interested in whatever was being suggested – a trip to the art gallery? a bike ride? or a naughty underwear party? – you cannot make that assumption. You need to ask.

Treating people as individuals

You should always consult the individual before you carry out any procedure, and explain everything you do. Even if the procedure is part of his or her plan of care and has been done many times before, you should never take a person's agreement for granted.

Everyone should be offered choices wherever possible. This may be about when, where or how their care is provided. In circumstances where a choice is not possible, either because of an individual's circumstances or a lack of resources, this should be explained.

These are examples of the kinds of choice you may be able to offer to people when you provide care:

Care service	Choices
Personal hygiene	Bath, shower or bed bath Assistance or no assistance Morning, afternoon or evening Temperature of water Toiletries
Food	Menu Dining table or tray Timing Assistance In company or alone

Clearly, the range of choices will vary depending on the circumstances, but the principal remains the same – that people should not have care imposed on them without them being able to be actively involved in the decisions about how and when care is delivered.

Did you know?

One of the fears most frequently expressed by people who need to be cared for, particularly older people whose health has deteriorated or people who have been disabled through an accident or illness, is that they will lose their independence and will no longer be regarded as a person of any value.

Part of valuing people as individuals is having respect for all of the people you deal with. Respect is usually something which develops as you form relationships. When you provide care for someone, you will get to know and talk to him or her, and a relationship will grow. This is not easy with all individuals you care for. When there appears to be no two-way communication, you may find that forming a relationship is difficult. If you work with people who do not appear to relate to you, perhaps because they are very confused, because they have a very low level of functioning or even because they are not conscious, then it is easy to forget that they are still individuals and need to be treated as such.

Keys to good practice

- Make sure that any service which you provide for someone is with their agreement. People have a right to choose the care which they receive and the way in which they receive it.
- You must make sure that each person you care for is treated in the same way, regardless of his or her ability to respond to you. This means talking to people who do not seem to understand you, and to people who may appear not to respond. You should explain everything you are doing and go through the details of any procedures you are carrying out.

Remember

- Everyone has the right to make choices about care.
- All people are different.

If you accept these points, you will never be guilty of making generalisations or making prejudiced judgements about people again.

If only it were that simple! Of course, you cannot suddenly stop doing and thinking things which you have been doing and thinking all your life, but you *can* develop an awareness of what you are doing and start to ask yourself questions about why you have acted in the way you have.

Once you realise how your own background and beliefs alter the way you think about people, you can begin to recognise the differences and see the value of other cultures and beliefs. It is inevitable that, by thinking carefully about what has influenced you, you will also consider what has influenced others with whom you come into contact.

You need to talk to people, whether they are colleagues or service users, about aspects of their culture or lifestyle you do not understand. As a care professional, it is your responsibility to make sure that you have considered the culture, beliefs and lifestyle of someone for whom you are providing care. It is not acceptable to expect that they will adapt to your set of cultural beliefs and expectations.

The diversity of the human race is what makes living in our society such a rich and varied experience. If you try to welcome this diversity, rather than resist, condemn or belittle the things you do not understand, you will find that your relationships with colleagues and service users will be much more rewarding and the quality of your care practice will be greatly improved.

Case study

H is from Somalia and is a devout Muslim. She had her first baby in hospital in the UK.

Following the delivery, H refused to get out of bed, and would press the buzzer every time she wanted anything, including asking staff to take her baby from the cot and give him to her to feed. This was in accordance with her own culture in which a new mother remains in bed for ten days after giving birth. During that time everything is done for her and her baby, and all she does is feed the baby. It is usually her mother-in-law or another female relative who takes control during this time.

The ward staff became resentful of the demands that H was making. They were not always as pleasant as they might be when they were called into her room. H became very distressed and was very agitated and nervous each time she needed assistance. She began to have problems feeding the baby and the staff were concerned about her. There was a great deal of concern about her refusal to get out of bed, and she was encouraged to do so. The midwives explained to her that she ran the risk of thrombosis or other circulatory problems if she continued to lie in bed.

A solution was eventually found by allowing her mother-in-law to remain with her in a side room to provide the care needed. But they still could not persuade her to get out of bed. As she had been provided with all the information about possible consequences, and she had made an informed choice consistent with her own beliefs, her decision to stay in bed had to be respected.

1 What were the problems presented by H's beliefs?
2 Why is this situation difficult to deal with?
3 Do you think it was handled correctly?
4 What would you have done?
5 What do you think would have happened if the situation had continued as it was?

Remember

- Stereotypes can influence how you think about someone.
- Don't rush to make judgements about people.
- Don't make assumptions.
- Everyone is entitled to his or her own beliefs and culture. If you don't know about somebody's way of life – ask.

Knowing yourself and your prejudices

'To see ourselves as others see us'

It is vital, if you are to help anyone effectively, that you understand how you affect any situation. Human beings do not react in the same way to everyone. You have all experienced meeting someone who makes you feel relaxed and at ease - you find it easy to talk to them and feel as if you had known them for a long time. Equally, there are other people you meet and find it much harder to talk to - they make you feel nervous, or unsure; you can't think of anything to say and feel generally uncomfortable. You are still the same person, but you have reacted in a totally different way to two different people. This is called **interaction** and describes what takes place between human beings. To be a good practitioner in caring, you have to learn to understand how people react to you and the way in which your own beliefs, background and prejudices will influence and alter the outcome of an interaction.

It is essential that you understand about interaction if you are working in caring. It is not always easy to understand how it works. It may help if you think about it as a fairground mirror - all of the reflections look different, some are short and fat, some long and thin, some are wavy and curved; it all depends on the mirror. You are still the same, but the mirror makes everything appear different. It is the same with people. The same person will behave in a different way - interact - depending on the person they are talking to.

Active knowledge

Try this out for yourself at work. Pick two different people and tell them both the same thing. For example, you could ask to leave early on the next shift, explain why a particular person needs a change in their plan of care, or explain where the new delivery of equipment is – in fact, anything at all. Note down how you carried out the task with each person and how you felt. Make sure you note the differences in your behaviour and feelings. Try to work out how, and why, each of them made you feel different.

Working in caring makes huge demands on people. The most important attribute you bring to the job is your own personality. This is why it is so important that you know yourself, and know what you bring to the job. You will have to learn to recognise your own prejudices and what effect they will have in the workplace.

Learning about yourself is not an easy task. Everyone thinks they know themselves so well – or do they? Often you never take the time to examine your own behaviour in depth. It is often a shock when someone else points out something you are doing, or a way you have of behaving, which you had not realised before.

Keys to good practice

- If you intend to be effective as a carer, then you will need to spend some time looking at your own behaviour and try to look in the mirror of others' reactions. You will never really know how you look in a physical way to others because you can only ever see a mirror image of yourself. If you think about looking at the world through a mirror, you will realise that it always looks slightly different to how you see it first-hand. However, you can judge how your actions and behaviour affect others by using them as your 'mirror' and being sensitive to their reactions.

Mirror, mirror on the wall...

- If you are talking to someone and he or she suddenly seems to close down the conversation, or appear unsure, try to think back to the point at which the atmosphere changed. Be honest with yourself. Did you react to something he or she said? What did you say? Was it a little thoughtless? Did you laugh? Maybe he or she thought you were laughing at him/her? Or did he or she begin to back away when you looked at your watch, or spoke briefly to someone else who wanted your attention?

- Do some individuals seem to find it easier to talk to you than others? Do you find it easier to talk to some individuals than others? Of course, there are bound to be some people you like more than others, but when you are working as a professional carer it is not enough just to acknowledge that. You have to know 'why' in order to make sure that it does not result in individuals being treated differently.

- Only you can work at examining your own behaviour. If you have a manager or colleague to work with you, that is a great help, but essentially, no one can do it for you. You will need to be able to ask yourself a series of questions, and be prepared to answer them: Which people do you find it hard to deal with? Can you work better with women than men? Do you find it hard to talk to young people? or to older people? or to people of a particular social class? or to people of particular races? or to anyone with a different accent?

- Do you find that you have less patience with some people? Can you identify which people? Is there a pattern? You may not always like the answers you come up with, but until you can work out how you behave towards others and why, you will never be able to make any adjustments to your responses.

- You will need to look at your own culture and beliefs. You may have grown up surrounded by people who believed that it was unthinkable to owe a penny to anyone, so you may find it difficult to offer empathy and support to someone who is desperate because he or she is in massive debt. If you have lived in a culture which holds older family members in high regard and accords them respect, you may find it hard to relate to the family of someone who hardly ever visits and does not appear interested in his or her welfare. Nevertheless, in your role as a carer you have to be aware of how your own background may influence you and to ensure that you include that factor in the analysis of any situation.

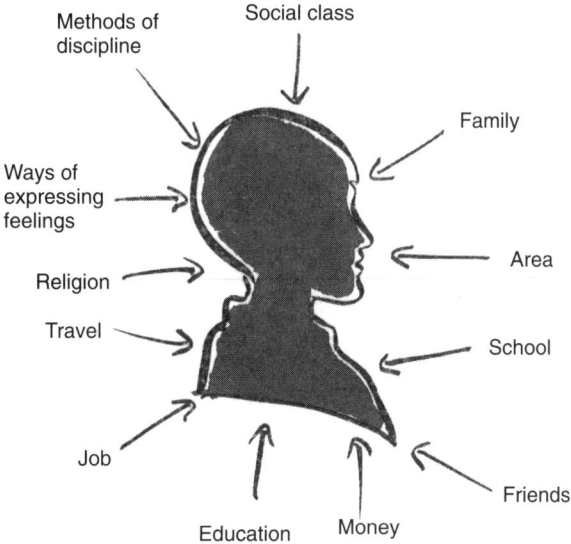

Influences on who you are

- Don't be too hard on yourself. Acknowledging your own prejudices is to go more than halfway to overcoming them. Just being able to understand *why* you behave in the way you do is more than most people achieve in a lifetime! So don't worry if it takes a while before you feel that you are really thinking about what you do and how you affect others. It may seem unlikely, but knowing how people respond to you and making allowances for that will, eventually, become second nature.

Behaviour which fails to value people

Practising a policy of equal opportunities in the workplace is one part of recognising and welcoming diversity. There are several pieces of legislation which address equal opportunities for various groups, and they are covered in depth in Unit O1 (in *NVQ Level 2 Care*), but whether or not any of those principles are put into practice is influenced by how much people are valued as individuals in any care setting.

There is little point in having legislation unless it is generally observed, and any breaches of the law are dealt with. Legislation gives rights to certain groups of people which should ensure that they are not discriminated against, but individual workers have to be prepared to defend and uphold those rights for themselves and others.

However, valuing people and welcoming the fact that everyone is diverse is about more than just upholding the law, although that is very important. Workers must be prepared to recognise when someone is subjected to behaviour which infringes their rights.

Generally you can define behaviour as unacceptable if:

- it is outside what you would normally see in that situation
- it does not take into account the needs or views of others
- people are afraid or intimidated
- people are undermined or made to feel guilty
- the behaviour is likely to cause distress or unhappiness to others.

Examples of unacceptable behaviour include:

- threatening violence
- subjecting someone to unwelcome sexual harassment
- playing loud music in a quiet area, or late at night
- verbal abuse, racist or sexist taunts
- spreading malicious gossip about someone
- attempting to isolate someone.

All of these types of behaviour are oppressive to others and need to be challenged. You can probably think of many other situations in your own workplace which have caused unhappiness. You may have had to deal with difficult situations, or have seen others deal with them, or perhaps you have wished that you had done something to challenge oppressive behaviour.

You may come across unacceptable and oppressive behaviour in your colleagues or other professionals in your workplace. Behaviour which is actually abusive is dealt with in Unit Z1. While you may see or hear a colleague behaving in a way which is not abusive as such, it may be oppressive and unacceptable. This can take various forms such as:

- speaking about clients in a derogatory way
- speaking to clients in a rude or dismissive way
- humiliating clients
- undermining people's self-esteem and confidence
- bullying or intimidation
- patronising and talking down to people
- removing people's right to exercise choice
- failing to recognise and treat people as individuals
- not respecting people's culture, values and beliefs.

In short, the types of behaviour which are unacceptable from workers in care settings are those which simply fail to meet the standards required of good quality practitioners. Any care worker who fails to remember that all people they care for are individuals and that all people have a right to be valued and accepted, is likely to fall into behaving in an oppressive or inappropriate way.

Active knowledge

Ask three colleagues in your workplace to state one behaviour that they would find unacceptable in (a) a service user and (b) a colleague. Compare the six answers and see if they have anything in common. Find out from your supervisor about the type of behaviour that is challenged in your workplace, and that which is allowed.

How to challenge unacceptable behaviour

Steps to dealing with difficult situations

Step 1 Consider all the people involved in the situation

If you have some knowledge of an individual's background, culture and beliefs, it may be easier to see why he or she is behaving in a particular way. This does not make it acceptable, just easier to understand. For example, men in some cultures, such as in Arab countries, are far more likely to touch other men (hugging and kissing as a sign of friendship), than men from the UK, where such physical contact (except between footballers!) is not generally acceptable. An individual who has been in a position of wealth or power may be used to giving people instructions and expecting to have immediate attention, and may be quite rude if it does not happen. This type of attitude is obviously not going to be tolerated, but approaching the situation with some understanding allows people to maintain their dignity whilst adapting their behaviour.

Step 2 Be aware of everyone's needs

If you are in a work situation, it can be complicated by the fact that the person whose oppressive behaviour you are challenging may also be one of your service users. In this case, it is important to ensure that you challenge the behaviour without becoming aggressive or intimidating yourself, and that you do not undermine the individual.

Step 3 Decide on the best approach

How you decide to deal with an incident of unacceptable behaviour will depend on:

- whether the behaviour is violent or non-violent – if the behaviour is violent, what the potential dangers of the situation are, who may be in danger and what needs to be done to help those in danger
- who is involved, how well you know them and know how to deal with them
- whether you need help, and who is available to help you
- whether the cause is obvious and the solution is easy to deal with.

Clearly, you will need to weigh up the situation quickly, in order to deal with it promptly. You will, no doubt, feel under pressure, as this is a stressful situation to be in, whether you are experienced or not. Try to remain calm and think clearly.

Step 4 Deal with non-violent behaviour

If the behaviour you have to deal with is not physical aggression or violence, then you will need to deal with it by ensuring that you make the challenge in a situation which provides privacy and dignity. You should challenge without becoming aggressive, remain calm and quietly state what you consider to be unacceptable about their behaviour. Do not try to approach it from various angles, or drop hints. Be clear about the problem and what you want to happen.

For example, 'Bill, you have been playing your radio very loudly until quite late each night. Other residents are finding it difficult to get to sleep. I would like you to stop playing it so loudly if you want to have it on late.' You may well have to negotiate with Bill about times, and the provision of headphones, but do not be drawn into an argument and do not be sidetracked into irrelevant discussions. For example:

Bill:'Who's been complaining? No one's complained to me. Who is it?'

You:'Bill, this is about your radio being too loud. The issue is not about who complained, but about the fact that it is upsetting residents and I want you to stop doing it.'

By the end of this discussion, Bill should be very clear about what is being required of him and be in no doubt that his behaviour will have to change.

Step 5 Attempt to calm a potentially violent situation

It is always better to avoid a violent situation than to respond to one, so you need to be aware of the signals which may indicate that violence could erupt. Be on the lookout for verbal aggression; raised volume and pitch of voice; threatening and aggressive gestures; pacing; quick, darting eye movements; prolonged eye contact.

Try to respond in ways least likely to provoke further aggression:

* Use listening skills, and appear confident (but not cocky).
* Keep your voice calm and at a level pitch.
* Do not argue.
* Do not get drawn into prolonged eye contact.
* Attempt to defuse the situation with empathy and understanding. For example, 'I realise you must be upset if you believe that George said that about you. I can see that you're very angry. Tell me about what happened.'

Be prepared to try a different approach if you find you are not getting anywhere. Always make sure that an aggressor has a way out with dignity, both physically and emotionally.

Did you know?

There is a technique which is recommended for use in situations which become violent. It is called 'Breakaway' and is approved by the Home Office for use in all types of care settings. It provides you with methods for dealing with a physical threat or attack without causing injury. Ask your employer to arrange for you to attend a course with an approved trainer.

Step 6 Deal with aggressive or violent behaviour

Be aware of the situation you are in and take some common-sense precautions: make sure that you know where the exits are, move so that the aggressor is not between you and the exit; notice if there is anything which could be used as a weapon, and try to move away from it; make sure that the aggressor has enough personal space, and do not crowd him or her.

If you are faced with a violent situation, you should try to remain calm (even though that is easier said than done!) and not resort to violence or aggression yourself.

It is often the case that a simple technique like holding up a hand in front of you, as if you were directing traffic, and shouting 'Stop' may deflect an attacker, or stop him or her long enough for you to get away. You should remove yourself from the situation as speedily as possible.

If there are other, vulnerable people at risk, you must decide whether you can summon help more effectively from outside or inside the situation.

If you decide to remain, you must summon help at once. You should do one of the following:

- Press a panic alarm or buzzer, if one is provided.
- Shout 'help!' very loudly and continuously.
- Send someone for help.
- Call the police, or security, or shout for someone else to do so.

Do not try to be a hero – that is not your job.

Active knowledge

Your workplace should have a policy on dealing with aggression and violence. Ask to see it and make sure that you read it carefully.

Remember

- Everyone is different and will react differently to each situation.
- You are the factor that makes the difference.
- Learn to know yourself before you think you can know about others.
- Each person should be valued as a unique individual.

ement CL1.2   Establish and maintain effective communication with people

WHAT YOU NEED TO LEARN

- Ways in which people communicate.
- Barriers to communication.
- How to listen.
- How to communicate clearly.

Ways in which people communicate

This element is about how people reach out to each other. Communication is much more than talking. It is about how people respond to each other in many different ways: touch, facial expression, body movements, dress, position – and this is before you start on written communication, telephone, cyberspace, message in a bottle or pigeon!

Remember

You are the most important tool you have for doing your job. Carers do not have carefully engineered machinery or complex technology – your own ability to relate to others and to understand them is the key you need!

More than talking

Any relationship comes about through communication. In order to be an effective care worker, you must learn to be a good communicator. But communication is about much more than talking to people!

People communicate through:

- speaking
- facial expression
- body language
- position
- dress
- gestures.

You will have to know how to recognise what is being communicated to you, and to be able to communicate with others without always having to use words.

Active knowledge

Do this with a friend or colleague.

1 Write the names of several emotions (such as anger, joy, sadness, disappointment, fear) on pieces of paper.
2 One of you should pick up a piece of paper. Your task is to communicate the emotion written on the paper to your partner, without saying anything.
3 Your partner then has to decide what the emotion is and say *why*.
4 Then change places and repeat the exercise. Take it in turns, until all the pieces of paper have been used. Make sure that you list all the things which made you aware of the emotion being expressed.
5 Discuss with your partner what you have discovered about communication as a result of this exercise.

Keys to good practice

When you carried out the last exercise, you will have found out that there are many things which told you what your partner was trying to communicate. It is not only the expression on people's faces which tells you about how they feel, but it is also the way they use the rest of their bodies. This area of human behaviour is referred to as **non-verbal communation**. It is very important for developing the ability to understand what people are feeling. If you understand the importance of non-verbal communication, you will be able to use it to improve your own skills when you communicate with someone.

Recognising the signals

Look at a person's facial expression. Much of what you will see will be in his or her eyes, but the eyebrows and mouth also contribute.

Notice whether someone is looking at you, or at the floor, or at a point over your shoulder. Lack of eye contact should give a first indication that all may not be well. It may be that they are not feeling confident. They may be unhappy, or feel uneasy about talking to you. You will need to follow this up.

Look at how a person sits. Is he or she relaxed and comfortable, sitting well back in the chair, or tense and perched on the edge of the seat? Is he or she slumped in the chair with the head down? Posture can indicate a great deal about how somebody is feeling. People who are feeling well and cheerful tend to hold their heads up, and sit in a relaxed and comfortable way. An individual who is tense and nervous, who feels unsure and worried is likely to reflect that in the way he or she sits or stands.

Observe hands and gestures carefully. Someone twisting his or her hands, or playing with hair or clothes is a signal of tension and worry. Frequent little shrugs of the shoulders or spreading of the hands may indicate a feeling of helplessness or hopelessness.

Case study

Mr J has just been admitted to a residential care home. He has severe arthritis and his mobility is very poor. He has some incontinence of urine. The arthritis in his hands, elbows and shoulders means that he is not able to carry out basic domestic tasks, but he can wash and dress, although he is slow and sometimes cannot manage the buttons. He had been cared for at home by his wife until last week, when she suffered a massive stroke and died. Mr J has one son who lives 200 miles away. His son came at once when his mother died, and has stayed all week with his father. However, he now has to return to work and has arranged for his father to be admitted into residential care as a matter of urgency.

1 What would you expect Mr J's facial expression to be?
2 Allowing for his physical difficulties, how do you think he would be sitting?
3 What do you think he would be doing with his hands?
4 What emotions and feelings is Mr J likely to be expressing through his body language?

Did you know?

Research shows that people pay far more attention to facial expressions and tone of voice than they do to spoken words. For example, in one study, words contributed only 7 per cent towards the impression of whether or not someone was liked, tone of voice contributed 38 per cent and facial expression 55 per cent. The study also found that if there was a contradiction between facial expression and words, people believed the facial expression.

Giving out the signals

Being aware of your own body language is just as important as understanding the person you are talking to.

Keys to good practice

- Make sure that you maintain eye contact with the person you are talking to, although you should avoid staring at them! Looking away occasionally is normal, but if you find yourself looking around the room, or watching others, then you are failing to give people the attention they deserve.
- Be aware of what you are doing and try to think why you are losing attention.
- Sit where you can be comfortably seen. Don't sit where someone has to turn in order to look at you.
- Sit a comfortable distance away – not so far that any sense of closeness is lost, but not so close that you 'invade their space'.
- Make sure that you are showing by your gestures that you are listening and interested in what they are saying – sitting half-turned away gives the message that you are not fully committed to what is being said.
- Folded arms or crossed legs can indicate that you are 'closed' rather than 'open' to what someone is expressing.
- Nodding your head will indicate that you are receptive and interested – but be careful not to overdo it and look like a nodding dog!

- Lean towards someone to show that you are interested in what they are saying. You can use leaning forward quite effectively at times when you want to emphasise your interest or support. Then move backwards a little at times when the content is a little lighter.
- Using touch to communicate your caring and concern is often useful and appropriate. Many individuals find it comforting to have their hand held or stroked, or to have an arm around their shoulders.
- Be aware of a person's body language which should tell you if they find touch acceptable or not.
- Always err on the side of caution if you are unsure about what is acceptable in another culture. Later in this chapter, and in many other places throughout the book, you will look at issues about cultures in which touch is unacceptable.
- Think about age and gender in relation to touch. An older woman may be happy to have her hand held by a female carer, but may be uncomfortable with such a response from a man.
- Ensure that you are touching someone because you think it will comfort him or her, and not because you feel helpless and can't think of anything to say.

Active knowledge

Do this with at least one other person – two or three is even better.

1 Think of an incident or situation which is quite important and significant to you. Stand still in the middle of a room and begin to tell your partner about your significant incident.
2 Your partner should start at the edge of the room and slowly move closer and closer to you.
3 At the point where you feel comfortable talking to your partner, say 'Stop'. Mark this point and measure the distance from where you are standing.
4 At the point where you feel that your partner is too close, say 'Stop'. Mark this point and measure the distance from where you are standing.
5 Change places and repeat the exercise.

You may find that you and your partner(s) will have different distances at which you feel comfortable, but it is likely to be in the range of 3–5ft.

1–2 ft
intimate zone

2–4 ft
personal zone

4–8 ft
social zone

Public zone

Remember

- You can often learn as much by observing as by listening.
- Learn to 'listen with your eyes'.
- *Your* body sends out as many messages as the person you are talking to.
- Be aware of the messages you give to others.

Barriers to communication

Not getting through?

There are many factors which can get in the way of good communication. You will need to understand how to recognise these and to learn what you can do to overcome them. Until you do this, your communication will always be less effective than it could be. It is easy to assume that everyone can communicate, and that any failure to respond to you is because of someone's unwillingness rather than inability. There are as many reasons why people find communication difficult as there are ways to make it easier.

Remember

You need to understand the things which can get in the way so you can make sure they don't!

Active knowledge

Choose two different ways in which you communicate with people, for example talking, writing, telephone – you can probably think of others. Consider the most important element in each one. For example, for talking it could be language, for telephone, hearing, and so on. Now think about how you would manage that communication without that important element. List the problems you would have and the ways you could try to overcome them. Do you begin to see how difficult it can be sometimes for people to communicate?

Thinking about the obstacles

Never assume that you can be heard and understood and that you can be responded to, without first thinking about the individual and his or her situation. Check first to ensure you are giving the communication the best possible chance of success by dealing with as many barriers as possible.

Practical difficulties

If you need to communicate with someone who has a known disability, such as hearing loss, impaired vision, mobility problems

Checklist

Practical difficulties ✓
Cultural difficulties ✓
What words mean ✗
Physical barriers ✓

Level of hearing?

Is a signer needed?

Hearing aid needs cleaning?

Hearing aid working properly?

or speech impairment, you must consider the implications for your communication.

If someone is profoundly deaf, you will need to establish what sort of assistance he or she needs. If he or she communicates by signing, you will need to have a sign language interpreter available. Do not assume that you can do this yourself – it is highly skilled and people train for a long time to do this. If someone uses a hearing aid, consider that it may not be operating efficiently if you seem to be having communication problems.

Consider the level of someone's hearing. Many people are hard of hearing, but this may not be a profound hearing loss. It can mean that they have difficulty hearing where there is background noise and other people talking.

If someone has a physical disability, you will need to consider whether this is likely to affect his or her non-verbal communication. Also, his or her body language may not be what you would expect.

Facial expressions may seem inappropriate

Hand and arm gestures may not be possible

Body posture may not give out the messages you would expect

Someone with a physical disability may be unable to communicate in the expected non-verbal way

Case study

Mr T lives alone. For many years he had been well known in the neighbourhood. He was never particularly chatty, but always said a polite 'Good Morning' on his way to the shops, and had a smile and a kind word for the children. His wife died about fifteen years ago. They had only had one son, and he was killed in the war. Recently, however, Mr T's health has begun to deteriorate. He has had a bad winter with a chest infection and a nasty fall in the snow. This has seemed to shake his confidence, and he has accepted the offer of a home care assistant twice a week.

Neighbours began to notice that Mr T no longer spoke to them, and he failed to acknowledge the children. His outings to the shops became less frequent. Jean, his home care assistant, was worried that he hardly responded to her cheerful chat as she worked. She realised that Mr T's hearing was deteriorating. After medical investigations, Mr T was provided with a hearing aid. He began to be much more like his old self – he spoke to people again, smiled at the children and enjoyed his visits to the shops.

1 How do you think Mr T felt when he began to have problems hearing people?
2 Why do you think he reacted in the way he did?
3 What other factors might Jean have thought were causing Mr T's deterioration?
4 How are people likely to have reacted to Mr T?

Individuals who have visual impairment to any significant degree will need to be addressed with thought and care. Do not rely on your facial expressions to communicate your interest and concern – use words and touch where appropriate. Remember to obtain any information they may need in a format they can use. Think about large print books, braille or audio tapes. If you need any further information, the Royal National Institute for the Blind (RNIB) will be able to advise you about local sources of supplies.

Speech bubble: Good morning, Ralph. It's Sue. How are you?

Speech bubble: Hello. I'm Jeff and I'm going to be the person who is mainly responsible for looking after you while you are in here...

The way you address people who have sensory impairment needs to be done with thought and care

Make sure that you know what language an individual is comfortable with – do not assume it is the same as yours without making certain! Find out if you need to provide any translation facilities, or written information in another language. If translation is needed, your team leader or manager should be able to help you to arrange it. Your local social services department will have a list of interpreters, as will the police or the consulate or embassy of their country. Many organisations provide information about where specialised assistance can be obtained.

Did you know?

The Benefits Agency produces a catalogue of its leaflets, posters and information. This lists which items are available in other languages, braille, large print or on audio tape. Many other agencies and organisations do the same. Always make sure you ask if information is available in the format your client needs. Being given information in an accessible format is far better than having to receive it 'second-hand'.

Cultural difficulties

You will need to be aware of cultural differences between you and the person you are talking to. For example, using first names or touching someone to whom you are not related, or a very close friend, can be viewed as disrespectful in some cultures. Talking familiarly to someone of a different gender or age group can be unacceptable in some cultures. For example, some young Muslim women believe they should not talk at all to men to whom they are not related.

Many older men and women consider it disrespectful to address people by their first names. You will often find older people with neighbours they have known for fifty years, who still call each other 'Mrs Baker' or 'Mrs Wood'.

Remember

The golden rule when you are communicating with someone from a different culture is to *find out*. Do not assume that you can approach everyone in the same way. It is your responsibility to find out the way to approach someone.

What words mean

Be aware that the words you use can mean different things to different people and generations – words like 'web', 'chip' or 'gay'. Be aware of particular local words which are used in your part of the country, which may not mean the same to someone from another area.

Think carefully about the subject under discussion. Some people from particular cultures, or people of particular generations, may find some subjects very sensitive and difficult to discuss. These days, it is not unusual amongst a younger age group to discuss personal income levels. However, people of older generations may consider such information to be highly personal.

Physical barriers

Communication can be hindered by physical and environmental factors. This may seem obvious, but they need to be considered when planning communication.

Always provide a private situation if you have personal matters to discuss. It is rarely the case that the best which can be arranged is to pull the curtains around a bed.

You need to think about the surroundings. People find it difficult to talk in noisy, crowded places. A communal lounge with a television and other people is not going to produce good communication.

Remember the temperature – make sure that it is comfortable. Think about lighting. Is it too dark or too bright? Is the sun in someone's eyes? Make sure that you do not sit with your face in shadow. It is very disconcerting not to be able to see someone's face when talking to him or her – remember the previous section on non-verbal communication.

It is important when communicating with someone that they see your face and that you hear what they are saying

Remember

- Never take communication for granted.
- Not everyone communicates in the same way.
- It is *your* responsibility to ensure that the individual is able to communicate.
- As far as possible, plan ahead and think what you will need to take into account.

How to listen

So far you have looked at some of the factors which assist effective communication, and some of the barriers which can hinder it. Now it is time to look at the key areas of listening and talking. You may think that this comes naturally to most people. Not so. You can learn some basic skills which will improve your communication significantly.

Remember

- To hear what someone is really telling you, you have to be a *good listener*.
- To help someone understand what you are saying and tell you what he or she wants to say, you have to be a *good communicator*.

Active listening

Active listening is about doing much more than simply hearing the words which an individual is speaking. It is the way you encourage someone to talk to you, the way you let him or her know that you are interested, concerned and supportive, and the way you allow him or her the space, time and attention to express feelings and concerns.

Active knowledge

This really needs to be done with a friend or colleague. Begin to tell your partner about something simple and straightforward – about your holiday, what you did last Saturday, a planned shopping trip – anything at all. Your partner's job is to look around the room, to look at you but not nod or make any sound, to examine his or her nails – in short to fail to respond to you in any way. You should stop talking when you feel uncomfortable. Then change places. During this exercise you will begin to see how difficult it is to keep talking when you do not get a positive response.

The way in which you listen to someone can make all the difference to how easy he or she finds it to talk to you. When someone is talking to you, keep encouraging him or her by responding – nodding and 'mm' or 'I see' are often all that is needed. There is nothing worse than talking to someone who gives you no response.

Sometimes people find it difficult to express what they want to say and need some encouragement. You can help by repeating back to them what they have been saying, not in a 'parrot style', but in an encouraging way, such as:

Client: 'My family are very busy, I don't see them much, they all have important jobs…' [silence].

You: 'So your children don't have much time to come here because they all work so hard…'

Paraphrasing what someone has told you can also be a useful way of showing that you have understood what he or she is saying. In paraphrasing you take what someone has been saying and repeat it in a slightly different way.

This can be used effectively to clarify what someone has said. For example, if an individual has just told you about feelings ranging from sadness and anger to relief at coming into residential care, a reply of something like 'so your feelings are very mixed – that's very understandable' demonstrates that you have heard what he or she said and also offers reassurance that this reaction is normal and only to be expected.

How to communicate clearly

How you talk to someone matters a great deal. You can ask 'open' or 'closed' questions. Which questions you use makes a difference to the response you will get:

- Closed questions are those which allow people to answer 'Yes' or 'No'. For example, 'Are you worried about the tests tomorrow?' This may get only a one-word response. If you then want to find out any more, you have to ask another question. If you are not careful, individuals can then end up feeling like they are on 'Twenty Questions'.
- Open questions are those which do not allow a one-word response. So, if you rephrase the previous question it becomes 'How do you feel about tomorrow's tests?' The difference is obvious, and there is a far greater chance that the person you are talking to will feel able to express his or her feelings.

Advice

There will be occasions when you are asked to give advice. Sometimes this is appropriate. If, for example, someone asked whether he or she would be able to carry on claiming a particular benefit whilst in residential care, it would be pretty silly to say 'Well, do you think that you will continue to need that benefit?' Clearly, there are three possible answers: 'Yes', 'No' or 'I'm not sure, but I'll find out'. These sorts of request for factual advice are quite different from a situation where someone is dealing with personal or emotional issues.

What you say

Make sure that you are not the one doing all the talking. Be careful not to tell someone what *you* think and keep giving *your* opinions. Telling someone 'If I were you I would...' is not good practice and is not good communication.

Do not *ever* say 'That's silly' or 'Oh you shouldn't feel like that'. That effectively dismisses people's feelings or tells them that they have no right to feel that way.

How you say it

Think about the speed and volume of what you say. We often fail to realise how quickly we speak. It can often be difficult for someone who has some impairment of hearing or poor eyesight to catch what you say, if you speak too fast.

Think about your accent, and the individual you are talking to. Local accents can be difficult to understand, if they are unfamiliar.

Active knowledge

You may not know how strong your own accent is. Try making a tape recording and listening to yourself. Or ask a friend or colleague to advise you honestly about the strength of your accent and the speed at which you talk.

Volume is also important. There is no need to shout – it simply distorts what you say and plays havoc with your facial expression! You should, however, make sure that you speak clearly and at a reasonable level. Generally, speaking too softly can make it hard for you to be understood.

There are some occasions when you may have to balance the volume of what you say with the need to maintain someone's privacy. It may be worth having to repeat yourself a few times, if it helps to keep a discussion private.

Stages of an interaction

As you spend time in communication with someone, the nature of the interaction will go through changes.

- *Stage 1:* Introduction, light, general. At first, communication may be light and general with very little content of any significance. This is the stage at which both parties decide if they want to continue the discussion, and how comfortable they feel. Body language and non-verbal communication are very important at this stage.
- *Stage 2:* Main contact, significant information. The middle of any interaction is likely to contain the 'meat' and this is where you will need to use active listening skills to ensure that the interaction is beneficial.
- *Stage 3:* Reflect, wind up, end positively. People often have the greatest difficulty in knowing how to end an interaction. Ending in a positive way where all participants are left feeling that they have benefited from the interaction is very important. You may find that you have to end an interaction because of time restrictions, or you may feel that enough has been covered – the other person may need a rest, or you may need a break!

At the end of an interaction you should always try to reflect on the areas you have covered, and try to offer a positive and encouraging ending, for example, 'I'm glad you have talked about how unhappy you have been feeling. Now we can try to work at making things better.'

Even if the content of an interaction has been fairly negative, you should encourage the individual to see the fact that the interaction has taken place as being positive in itself.

If you get called away before you have had a chance to properly 'wind up' an interaction with an individual, make a point of returning to end things in a positive way. If you say 'I'll be back in a minute', make sure that you do go back.

Written communication

Written communication may not be something you do very frequently. You may not write many formal letters, but as a care worker you will have to write information in records which could prove to be of vital importance.

The golden rule of good communication is to consider its *purpose*. If you are completing a care plan or record for an individual, then that information needs to be there in order to inform the next carer who takes over.

Think about the sort of information you would need to know. What things are important when handing over care?

You need to record accurately any distress or worries you have tried to deal with, any physical signs of illness or accidents. You may need to record fluid balances or calorie intake charts. It may be important to record visitors, or any medical interventions. The purposes of records and the systems are dealt with in detail in Unit CU5, but the importance in this context is the usefulness of what you write in terms of communication.

Written communication is useless unless it is legible. There is no point in scribbling something unreadable in someone's notes. It is actually worse than not writing anything, because colleagues waste time trying to decipher what is there, and have to deal with the concerns raised by the fact that there was clearly something worth recording, but they have no idea what it was.

You also need to convey the message in a clear and concise way. People do not want to spend time reading a lengthy report when the main points could have been expressed in a paragraph. Equally, you need to make sure that the relevant points are there. Often bullet points can be useful in recording information clearly and concisely. Look at the examples on page 62.

> *Mrs P had a bad night.*

Too little information

> Mrs P had a bad night. It began when I found her crying about 10 p.m. She said she had been thinking about her husband. I thought she seemed a bit hot, so I made her a cup of tea and got her to sit in the lounge for a while before she went to bed. After about half an hour, I managed to get her to go to her room and I went with her . . .

Too much irrelevant information

> Mrs P had a bad night because:
> a) she was distressed about her husband
> b) she wandered out of her room about 2 a.m. crying again
> c) unable to settle despite further cocoa
> d) wandered into Mr W's room at 5.30 believing he was her husband
> She will need to be closely observed today. Any further confused episodes should be logged.

Clear, helpful. Gives a short picture of problems overnight, and suggests action for next day

Records should be accurate, clear and concise

Remember

- Communication is a two-way process.
- Barriers have to be removed for communication to work.
- You have to recognise the barriers before you can remove them.
- Communication is about more than talking.

Unit test

1. How can your personality affect how you work?
2. Is there any point in talking to someone who clearly doesn't understand you? Give reasons for your answer.
3. How does society reinforce stereotypes?
4. Why do you have to challenge oppressive behaviour?
5. Why is body language important?
6. What factors can affect the way people will respond to you?
7. List some examples of unacceptable behaviour and say how you would challenge each.
8. Name three possible barriers to communication. How would you deal with each of them?
9. What environmental factors do you need to consider when planning communication?
10. What is the difference between an open question and a closed question? Name situations where you would use each type of question.

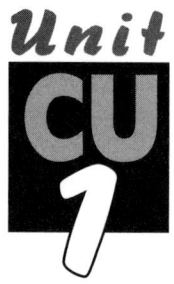

Unit CU1 Promote, monitor and maintain health, safety and security in the workplace

This unit is about the way you can contribute to making your workplace a safe, secure and healthy place for people who need care. Workplace, in this unit, means a home environment or any other facility which provides a health or care service. In the first element you will need to learn about what needs to be done to ensure a safe workplace environment. In the second element you will be looking at how you may need to adapt the way you work and become more safety conscious. The third element in this unit is about how to respond in an emergency.

Element CU1.1 | Monitor and maintain the safety and security of the work environment

WHAT YOU NEED TO LEARN

- How to maintain safety.
- How to maintain security.
- The legal framework.
- Dealing with hazardous waste.

How to maintain safety

It sounds very simple and straightforward: make sure that the place in which you work is safe and secure. However, when you start to think about it – safe for whom? from whom? safe from tripping over things? or safe from hazardous fumes? safe from infection? safe from intruders? safe from work-related injuries? You can begin to see that this is a wide and complex subject. It may help if you think about safety and security in respect of the areas of responsibility shown in the table on the next page.

Responsibilities for safety and security in the workplace

Employer's responsibilities	Employee's responsibilities	Shared responsibilities
Planning safety and security Providing information about safety and security Updating systems and procedures	Using the systems and procedures correctly Reporting flaws or gaps in the systems or procedures when in use	Safety of individuals being cared for Safety of the environment

Safety of the environment

You share the responsibility with your employer for the safety of all the people in your care. There are many hazards which can cause injury to people, even more so if they are old, ill or disabled. You need to be aware of:

- *environmental hazards,* such as:
  - wet or slippery floors
  - cluttered passageways or corridors
  - re-arranged furniture
  - worn carpets or rugs
  - electrical flexes

- *hazards to do with equipment and materials,* such as:
  - faulty brakes on beds
  - worn or faulty electrical or gas appliances
  - worn or damaged lifting equipment
  - worn or damaged mobility aids
  - incorrectly labelled substances, such as cleaning fluids
  - leaking or damaged containers
  - faulty waste disposal equipment

- *hazards connected with people,* such as:
  - visitors to the building
  - handling procedures
  - intruders
  - violent and aggressive behaviour.

Your responsibility to contribute to a safe environment is more than simply being aware of these potential hazards. You must take steps to check and deal with any sources of risk.

You can fulfil your role in two ways:

- by dealing directly with the hazard, which means that you have taken individual responsibility. This will probably apply to obvious hazards such as:
  - trailing flexes – roll them up and store them safely
  - wet floors – dry them as far as possible and put out warning signs
  - cluttered doorways and corridors – remove objects and store them safely or dispose of them appropriately. If items are heavy, use assistance or mechanical aids

- visitors to the building – challenge anyone you do not recognise. 'Can I help you?' is usually sufficient to establish whether a person has a good reason to be there or not
- fire – by following the correct procedures to raise the alarm and assist with evacuation

• by informing your manager, which means that it becomes an organisational responsibility. This applies to hazards which are beyond your role and competence to deal with, such as:
- faulty equipment – fires, kettles, computers, etc.
- worn floor coverings
- loose or damaged fittings
- obstructions too heavy for you to move safely
- damaged or faulty aids – hoists, bed brakes, bathing aids, etc.
- people acting suspiciously on the premises
- fire.

Manual handling

Handling and moving clients is dealt with in detail in Unit Z7, but the implications for the safety of both the care worker and the client are examined in this unit.

Did you know?

Lifting and handling individuals is the single largest cause of injuries at work in health and care settings. One in four workers take time off because of a back injury sustained at work.

The Manual Handling Operations Regulations 1993 require employers to avoid all manual handling where there is a risk of injury 'so far as it is reasonably practical'. Everyone from the European Commission to the Royal College of Nurses has issued policies and directives about avoiding lifting.

There is almost no situation in which manual lifting and handling could be considered acceptable.

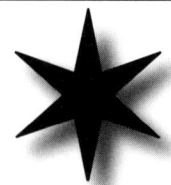

Remember

• Always use lifting and handling aids.
• There is no such thing as a safe lift.
• Use the aids which your employer is obliged to provide.

On the rare occasions when it is still absolutely necessary for manual lifting to be done, the employer has to make a 'risk assessment' and put procedures in place to reduce the risk of injury to the employee. This could involve ensuring that sufficient staff are available to lift or handle someone safely, which can often mean that four people are needed.

Use the aids which your employer is obliged to provide

Remember

- Many workers in care still lift people manually – it seems quicker and easier than going to all the trouble of using a hoist – *it isn't*.
- Manual lifting is now actively discouraged throughout the profession.
- Manual lifting presents unnecessary and unacceptable risks to the client and to you.
- Don't forget, a back injury can end your career. It's not worth the risk.

Your employer should arrange for you to attend a lifting and handling course. You must attend one each year, so that you are up-to-date with the safest possible practices.

Fire safety

Your workplace will have procedures which must be followed in the case of an emergency. All workplaces must display information about what action to take in case of fire. The fire procedure is likely to be similar to the one shown below.

Fire Safety Procedure

1 Raise the alarm.

2 Inform telephonist or dial 999.

3 Ensure that everyone is safe and out of the danger area.

4 If it is safe to do so, attack fire with correct extinguisher.

5 Go to fire assembly point (this will be stated on the fire procedure notice).

6 Do not return to the building for any reason.

- Make sure that you know where the fire extinguishers or fire blankets are in your workplace, and that you know where the fire exits are.
- Your employer will have installed fire doors to comply with regulations – *never* prop them open.
- Your employer should provide fire lectures each year. You must attend and make sure that you are up-to-date with the procedures to be followed.

Which for what?

There are specific fire extinguishers for fighting different types of fire. It is important that you know this. You do not have to memorise them as each one has clear instructions on it, but you do need to be aware that there are different types and make sure that you read the instructions before use.

Did you know?

All new fire extinguishers are red. Each one has its purpose written on it. Each one also has a patch of the colour previously used for that type of extinguisher.

| Powder ABC | Powder BC | Water | Carbon dioxide | Foam | Foam spray |

Remember

- Read the fire extinguisher instructions before tackling the fire. The extra few seconds will be well spent making sure you are using the correct equipment. This is even more important with the new extinguishers which are predominately red.
- Check that you have the right extinguisher for the blaze you are tackling. Check the colour labels:
  - red – water, used for paper, wood and general fires
  - cream – foam, used for liquid oil fires, fat, petrol, oil, etc.
  - blue – dry powder, used for fuel oil, and can be used on electrical fires
  - black – carbon dioxide, used for electrical, wiring fires
  - green – BCF, used for electrical and most other fires, but not used in most workplaces because of high cost.
- Only tackle a fire if you can do so safely – otherwise leave the building and wait for help to arrive.

Evacuating buildings

You may be involved in evacuating buildings if there is a fire, or for other reasons, such as:

- a bomb scare
- the building has become structurally unsafe
- an explosion
- a leak of dangerous chemicals or fumes.

The evacuation procedure you need to follow will be laid down by your workplace. The information will be the same whatever the emergency is: the same exits will be used and the same assembly point. It is likely to be along the following lines:

- Stay calm, do not shout or run.
- Do not allow others to run.
- Organise people quickly and firmly without panic.
- Direct those who can move themselves and assist those who cannot.
- Use wheelchairs to move people quickly.
- Move the bed with the person in, if necessary.

How to maintain security

Most workplaces where care is provided are not under lock and key. This is an inevitable part of ensuring that people have choice and that their rights are respected. However, they also have a right to be secure. Security in a care environment is about:

- security against intruders
- security in respect of their privacy and decisions about unwanted visitors
- security against being abused
- security of property.

Security against intruders

If you work for a large organisation, such as an NHS trust, it may be that all employees are easily identifiable by identity badges with photographs. Some of these even contain a microchip which allows the card to be 'swiped' to gain access to secure parts of the building. This makes it easier to identify people who do not have a right to be on the premises.

In a smaller workplace, there may be a system of issuing visitors' badges to visitors who have reasons to be there, or it may simply rely on the vigilance of the staff.

Keys to good practice

- Be aware of everyone you come across. Get into the habit of noticing people and thinking, 'Do I know that person?'
- Challenge anyone you do not recognise.
- The challenge should be polite. 'Can I help you?' is usually enough to find out if a visitor has a reason to be on the premises.

If a person says that he or she is there to see someone:

- Don't give directions – escort him or her.
- If the person is a genuine visitor, he or she will be grateful. If not, he or she will disappear pretty quickly!

The more dependent individuals are, the greater the risk. If you work with babies, high-dependency or unconscious patients, people with severe learning difficulties or multiple disabilities or people who are very confused, you will have to be extremely vigilant in protecting them from criminals.

Remember

If you find an intruder on the premises, don't tackle him or her – raise the alarm.

Protecting people

If very dependent individuals are living in their own homes, the risks are far greater. You must try to impress on them the importance of finding out who people are before letting them in. If they are able to use it, the 'password' schemes from the utilities (water, gas and electricity companies) are helpful. Information record cards like those provided by the 'Safe as Houses' scheme can be invaluable in providing basic information to anyone who is involved in helping in an emergency.

Remember

- Every time you visit, you may have to explain again what the individual should do when someone knocks on the door.
- Give the individual a card with simple instructions.
- Obtain agreement to speak to the local 'homewatch' scheme and ask that a special eye is kept on visitors.
- Speak to the local police and make them aware that a vulnerable individual is living alone in the house.

People also have a right to choose who they see. This can often be a difficult area to deal with. If there are relatives or friends who wish to visit and an individual does not want to see them, you may have to make this clear. It is difficult to do, but you can only be effective if you are clear and assertive. You should not make excuses or invent reasons why visitors cannot see the person concerned. You could say something like: 'I'm sorry, Mr P has told us that he does not want to see you. I understand that this may be upsetting, but it is his choice. If he does change his mind we will contact you. Would you like to leave your phone number?'

Do not allow yourself to be drawn into passing on messages or attempting to persuade – that is not your role. Your job is to respect the wishes of the person you are caring for. If you are asked to intervene or to pass on a message, you must refuse politely but firmly: 'I'm sorry, that is not something I can do. If your uncle does decide he wants to see you, I will let you know right away. I will tell him you have visited, but I can't do anything else.'

Abuse is dealt with in depth in Unit Z1, but it can never be repeated often enough that individuals have a right to be protected from abuse, and you must report immediately any abuse you see or suspect.

Active knowledge

You need a colleague or friend to try this. One of you should be the person who has come to visit and the other the care worker who has to tell him or her that a friend or relative will not see them. Try using different scenarios – angry, upset, aggressive, and so on. Try at least three different scenarios each. By the time you have practised a few times, you may feel better equipped to deal with the situation when it happens in reality.

If you cannot find anyone to work with you, it is possible to do a similar exercise by imagining three or four different scenarios and then writing down the words you would say in each of the situations.

Security of property

Property and valuables belonging to individuals in care settings should be safeguarded. It is likely that your employer will have a property book in which records of all valuables and personal possessions are entered.

There may be particular policies within your organisation, but as a general rule you are likely to need to:

- make a record of all possessions on admission
- record valuable items separately
- describe items of jewellery by their colour, for example yellow metal not 'gold'
- ensure that individuals sign for any valuables they are keeping, and that they understand that they are liable for their loss
- inform your manager if an individual is keeping valuables or a significant amount of money.

Active knowledge

Find out where the property book is in your workplace, and how it is filled in. Check who has the responsibility to complete it. If you are likely to have to use the book at any time, make sure you know exactly what your role is. Do you have to enter the property in the book, then give it to someone else to deal with the valuables? Do you have to make sure the valuables are safe? Do you have to give the individual a copy of the entry in the book? Ask the questions in advance – don't leave it until you have to do it.

It is always difficult when items go missing in a care setting, particularly if they are valuable. It is important that you check all possibilities before calling the police.

Action stages when property goes missing

The legal framework

The settings in which you provide care are generally covered by the Health and Safety at Work Act 1974 (HASAWA). This Act has been updated and supplemented by many sets of regulations and guidelines, which extend it, support it or explain it. The regulations most likely to affect your workplace are shown in the diagram on page 73.

The effect of the laws

There are many regulations, laws and guidelines dealing with health and safety. You do not need to know the detail, but you do need to know where your responsibilities begin and end.

The laws place certain responsibilities on both employers and employees. For example, it is up to the employer to provide a safe place in which to work, but the employee also has to show reasonable care for his or her own safety.

Employers have to:
- provide a safe workplace
- ensure that there is safe access to and from the workplace
- provide information on health and safety
- provide health and safety training.

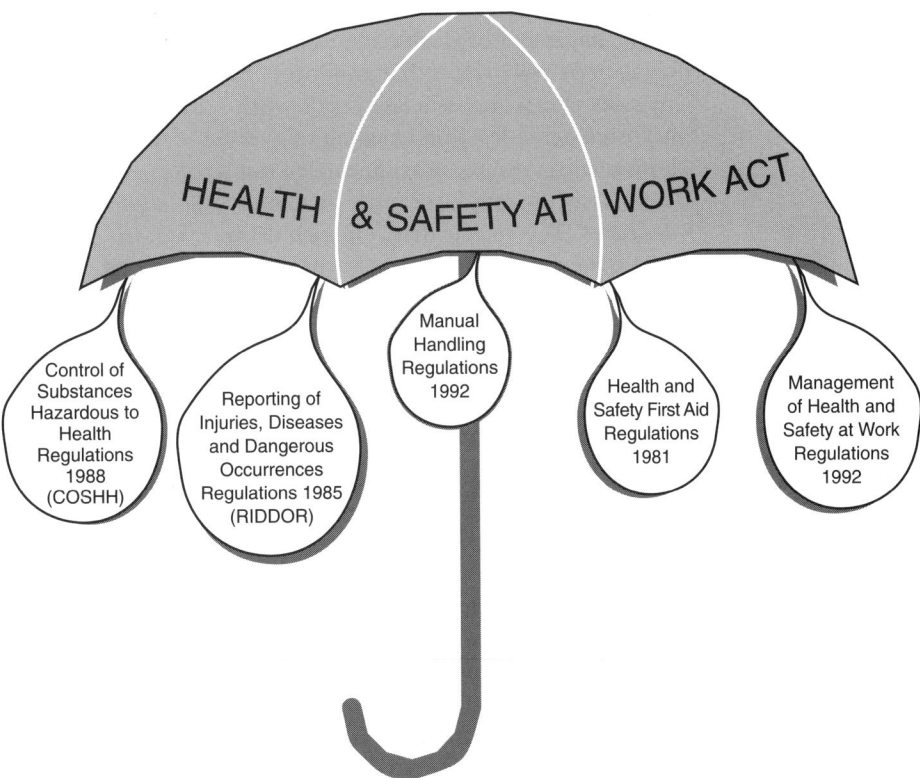

The Health and Safety at Work Act is like an umbrella.

Workers must:
- take reasonable care for their own safety and that of others
- co-operate with the employer in respect of health and safety matters
- not intentionally damage any health and safety equipment or materials provided by the employer.

Both the employee and employer are jointly responsible for safeguarding the health and safety of anyone using the premises.

Each workplace where there are five or more workers must have a written statement of their health and safety policy. The policy must include:
- a statement of intention to provide a safe workplace
- the name of the person responsible for implementing the policy
- the names of any other individuals responsible for particular health and safety hazards
- a list of identified health and safety hazards and the procedures to be followed in relation to them
- procedures for recording accidents at work
- details for evacuation of the premises.

Active knowledge

Find out where the health and safety policy is for your workplace and make sure you read it.

Risk assessment

The Management of Health and Safety at Work Regulations 1992 states that employers have to assess any risks which are associated with work activities. This means *all* activities, from walking on wet floors to dealing with violence. Having carried out a risk assessment, the employer must then apply *risk control measures*. This means that actions must be taken to reduce the risks, for example alarm buzzers may need to be installed or extra staff employed, as well as steps like extra training provided for staff or written guidelines produced on how to deal with a particular hazard.

Risks in someone's home

Of course, the situation is somewhat different if you work in an individual's own home. Your employer can still carry out risk assessments and put risk control measures in place, such as a procedure for working in twos in a situation where there is a risk of violence. What cannot be done is to remove environmental hazards such as trailing electrical flexes, rugs with curled up edges, worn patches on stair carpets or old equipment. All you can do is to advise the person whose home it is of the risks, and suggest how things could be improved. You also need to take care!

Remember

- It may be your workplace, but it is the person's home. If you work in an individual's home or long-term residential setting, you have to balance the need for safety with the rights of people to have their living space the way they want it.
- Both you and the individuals receiving care are entitled to expect a safe place in which to live and work, but remember their rights to choose how they want to live.

Control of Substances Hazardous to Health (COSHH)

What are hazardous substances? There are many substances hazardous to health – nicotine, many drugs, even too much alcohol! In this context, however, COSHH applies to substances which have been identified as being toxic, corrosive or irritant. This includes cleaning materials, pesticides, acids, disinfectants and bleaches. Workplaces may have other hazardous substances which are particular to the nature of the work carried out.

Every workplace must have a COSHH file. This file lists all the hazardous substances used in the workplace. It should detail:

- where they are kept
- how they are labelled
- their effects
- the maximum amount of time it is safe to be exposed to them
- how to deal with an emergency involving one of them.

Hazardous substances are not just things like poisons and radioactive material, they are also substances like cleaning fluids and bleach.

Active knowledge

Ask to see the COSHH file in your workplace. Make sure you read it and know which substances you use or come into contact with. Check in the file what the maximum exposure limits are. Your employer must include this information in the COSHH file.

If you have to work with hazardous substances, make sure that you take the precautions detailed in the COSHH file – this may be wearing gloves or protective goggles, or it may involve limiting the time you are exposed to the substance or only using it in certain circumstances.

The COSHH file should also give you information about how to store hazardous substances. This will involve using the correct containers as supplied by the manufacturers. All containers must have safety lids and caps, and must be correctly labelled.

Never use the container of one substance for storing another, and *never* change the labels.

These symbols, which warn you of hazardous substances, are always yellow.

The symbols above indicate hazardous substances. They are there for your safety and for the safety of those you care for. Before you use *any* substance, whether it is liquid, powder, spray, cream or aerosol, take the following simple steps:

- Check the container for the hazard symbol.
- If there is a hazard symbol, go to the COSHH file.
- Look up the precautions you need to take with the substance.
- Make sure you follow procedures, which are intended to protect you.

If you are concerned that a substance being used in your workplace is not in the COSHH file, or if you notice incorrect containers or labels being used, report it to your supervisor. Once you have informed your supervisor, it becomes his or her responsibility to act to correct the problem.

Reporting of Injuries, Diseases and Dangerous Occurrences (RIDDOR)

Diseases

There are certain diseases and groups of infections which are 'notifiable'. In other words, you must report them to the appropriate authorities, usually the Environmental Health Department of your local council. The list of notifiable diseases and infections is a long one, ranging from food poisoning and measles to rabies and yellow fever. Your employer, or an individual's own doctor, will have procedures in place for making the notification, but it is useful for you to know what the more common ones are, and if there is any role you have to play, such as recording or passing on any information.

The most common notifiable diseases are:

acute encephalitis	malaria	smallpox
acute poliomyelitis	measles	tetanus
anthrax	meningitis	tuberculosis
cholera	mumps	typhoid
diphtheria	plague	viral hepatitis
dysentery	rabies	whooping cough
food poisoning	rubella (German measles)	yellow fever
leprosy	scarlet fever	

Injuries and dangerous occurrences

You are, however, much more likely to be involved in reporting and recording accidents or dangerous incidents which occur in your workplace. If accidents or injuries occur at work, either to you or to an individual you are caring for, then the details must be recorded. For example, someone may have a fall, or slip on a wet floor. You must record the incident regardless of whether there was an injury.

Your employer should have procedures in place for making a record of accidents, either an accident book or an accident report form. This is not only required by the RIDDOR regulations, but also, if you work in a residential or nursing home, by the Registered Homes Inspectors.

Make sure you know where the accident report forms or the accident book are kept, and who is responsible for recording accidents. It is likely to be your manager.

You must report any accident in which you are involved, or have witnessed, to your manager or supervisor.

Any medical treatment or assessment which is necessary should be arranged without delay. If an individual has been involved in an accident, you should check if there is anyone he or she would like to be contacted, perhaps a relative or friend. If the accident is serious, and you cannot consult the individual – because he or she is unconscious, for example – the next of kin should be informed as soon as possible.

Complete a report, and ensure that all witnesses to the accident also complete reports. You should include the following in any accident report (see the example on the next page):

- date, time and place of accident
- person/people involved
- circumstances and details of exactly what you saw
- anything which was said by the individuals involved
- the condition of the individual after the accident

- steps taken to summon help, time of summoning help and time when help arrived
- names of any other people who witnessed the accident
- any equipment involved in the accident.

Date: *24.3.01*   Time: *14.30 hrs*   Location: *Main lounge*

Description of accident:

PH got out of her chair and began to walk across the lounge with the aid of her stick. She turned her head to continue the conversation she had been having with GK, and as she turned back again she appeared not to have noticed that MP's handbag had been left on the floor. PH tripped over handbag and fell heavily, banging her head on a footstool.

She was very shaken and although she said that she was not hurt, there was a large bump on her head. P appeared pale and shaky. I asked J to fetch a blanket and to call Mrs J, deputy officer in charge. Covered P with a blanket. Mrs J arrived immediately. Dr was sent for after P was examined by Mrs J.

Dr arrived after about 20 mins and said that she was bruised and shaken, but did not seem to have any injuries.

She wanted to go and lie down. She was helped to bed.

Incident was witnessed by six residents who were in the lounge at the time: GK, MP, IL, MC, CR and BQ.

Signed: _   Name: _ _ _ _ _ _ _ _ _ _ _ _ _ _ _ _

An example of an accident report

Active knowledge

Your manager has asked you to design a new incident/accident report form for your workplace. She has asked you to do this because the current form does not provide enough information. The purpose of the new form is to provide sufficient information to:

- ensure the individual receives the proper medical attention
- provide information for treatment at a later date, in case of delayed reactions
- give information to any inspector who may need to see the records
- identify any gaps or need for improvements in safety procedures
- provide information about the circumstances in case of any future legal action.

Think about how you would design the new report form and what headings you would include. Use the list above as a checklist to make sure you have covered everything you need.

Dealing with hazardous waste

As part of providing a safe working environment, employers have to put procedures in place to deal with waste materials and spillages. There are various types of waste, which must be dealt with in particular ways. These are summarised in the table below.

Types of hazardous waste and methods of disposal

Type of waste	Method of disposal
Clinical waste – used dressings	Yellow bags, clearly labelled with contents and location. This waste is incinerated.
Needles, syringes, cannulas ('sharps')	Yellow sharps box. *Never* put sharps into anything other than a hard plastic box. This is sealed and incinerated.
Body fluids and waste – urine, vomit, blood, sputum, faeces	Cleared and flushed down sluice drain. Area to be cleaned and disinfected.
Soiled linen	Red bags, direct into laundry, bags disintegrate in wash. If handled, gloves must be worn.
Recyclable instruments and equipment	Blue bags, to be returned to the Central Sterilisation Services Department (CSSD) for recycling and sterilising.

Remember

- Other people will have to deal with the waste after you have placed it in the bags or containers.
- Make sure it is properly labelled and in the correct containers.

Active knowledge

Look carefully around your workplace. Try to identify six potential hazards, or risky activities. When you have chosen them, check through the Health and Safety Manual and find the risk control measures and provisions made for each of them. If you believe that you have noticed a potential risk which your employer has not covered, you should discuss it with your manager or supervisor immediately.

ement CU1.2 Promote standards of health and safety in working practice

This element is about what you *do* when you are working. In the previous element, you looked at the procedures and policies which have to be put in place to protect workers and people who use the service, and the laws which govern health and safety. Now you need to learn about the steps you should be following to ensure that the laws and policies actually work in practice.

WHAT YOU NEED TO LEARN

- How to promote a safe work environment.
- How to contribute to infection control.
- How to maintain personal safety.
- How to lift and handle safely.

How to promote a safe work environment

It is important that you develop an awareness of health and safety risks and that you are always aware of any risks in any situation you are in. If you get into the habit of making a mental checklist, you will find that it helps. The checklist will vary from one workplace to another, but could look like the one below.

Checklist for a safe work environment	
Hazards	*Check*
Environment	
Floors	Are they dry?
Carpets and rugs	Are they worn or curled at the edges?
Doorways and corridors	Are they clear of obstacles?
Electrical flexes	Are they trailing?
Equipment	
Beds	Are the brakes on? Are they high enough?
Electrical or gas appliances	Are they worn? Have they been safety checked?
Lifting equipment	Is it worn or damaged?
Mobility aids	Are they worn or damaged?

Checklist for a safe work environment (*cont.*)

Hazards	Check
Substances such as cleaning fluids	Are they correctly labelled?
Containers	Are they leaking or damaged?
Waste disposal equipment	Is it faulty?
People	
Visitors to the building	Should they be there?
Handling procedures	Have they been assessed for risk?
Intruders	Have police been called?
Violent and aggressive behaviour	Has it been dealt with?

One of the other factors to consider in your checklist may be what your colleagues do about health and safety issues. It is very difficult if you are the only person following good practice. You may be able to encourage others by trying some of the following options:

- always showing a good example yourself
- explaining why you are following procedures
- getting some health and safety leaflets from your trade union or environmental health office and leaving them in the staffroom for people to see
- bringing in any information you can about courses or safety lectures
- asking your supervisor if he or she can arrange a talk on health and safety.

What you wear

You may not think that what you wear has much bearing on health and safety, but it is important. Even if your employer supplies, or insists on you wearing, a uniform, there are still other aspects to the safety of your work outfit.

There may be restrictions on wearing jewellery or carrying things in your pocket which could cause injury. This can also pose a risk to you – you could be stabbed in the chest by a pair of scissors or ball-point pen!

Many workplaces do not allow the wearing of rings with stones. Not only is this a possible source of infection, but they can also scratch people or tear protective gloves.

High-heeled or poorly supporting shoes are a risk to you in terms of foot injuries and very sore feet! They also present a risk to individuals you are helping, because if you overbalance or stumble, so will they.

What you wear in the workplace has an important bearing on health and safety. What problems can you see in this picture?

Key to good practice

Simple precautions can often be the most effective in reducing the risk. Always look for the risk and take steps to reduce it.

THINK RISK⟶ ASSESS ⟶ REDUCE ⟶ AVOID

How to contribute to infection control

The very nature of work in a care setting, means that great care must be taken to control the spread of infection. You will come into contact with a number of people during your working day – an ideal opportunity for infection to spread. Infection which spreads from one person to another is called 'cross-infection'. If you work in the community, cross-infection is difficult to control. However, if you work in a residential or hospital setting, infection control is essential. There are various steps which you can take in terms of the way you carry out your work (wherever you work), which can help to prevent the spread of infection.

You do not know what viruses or bacteria may be present in any individual, so it is important that you take precautions when dealing with everyone. The precautions are called 'universal precautions' precisely because you need to take them with everyone you deal with.

Wear gloves

- *When?* Any occasion when you will have contact with body fluids (including body waste, blood, mucus, sputum, sweat or vomit), or when you have any contact with anyone with a rash, pressure sore, wound, bleeding or any broken skin. You must also wear gloves when you clear up spills of blood or body fluids or have to deal with soiled linen or dressings.
- *Why?* Because gloves act as a protective barrier against infection.
- *How?* Check gloves before putting them on. Never use gloves with holes or tears. Check that they are not cracked or faded. Pull gloves on, making sure that they fit properly. If you are wearing a gown, pull them over the cuffs. Take them off by pulling from the cuff – this turns the glove inside out. Pull off the second glove whilst still holding the first so that the two gloves are folded together inside out. Dispose of them in the correct waste disposal container and wash your hands.

Wash your hands

- *When?* Before and after carrying out any procedure which has involved contact with an individual, or with any body fluids, soiled linen or clinical waste. You must wash your hands even though you have worn gloves. You must also wash your hands before you start and after you finish your shift, before and after eating, after using the toilet and after coughing, sneezing or blowing your nose.
- *Why?* Because hands are a major route to spreading infection. When tests have been carried out on people's hands, an enormous number of bacteria have been found.
- *How?* In running water, in a basin deep enough to hold the splashes and with either foot pedals or elbow bars rather than taps, because you can re-infect your hands from still water in a basin, or from touching taps with your hands once they have been washed. Use the soaps and disinfectants supplied. Make sure that you wash thoroughly, including between your fingers.

Wear protective clothing

- *When?* You should always wear a gown or plastic apron for any procedure which involves bodily contact or is likely to deal with body waste or fluids. An apron is preferable, unless it is likely to be very messy, as gowns can be a little frightening.
- *Why?* Because it will reduce the spread of infection by preventing infection getting on your clothes and spreading to the next person you come into contact with.
- *How?* The plastic apron should be disposable and thrown away at the end of each procedure. You should use a new apron for each individual you come into contact with.

Tie up hair

- *Why?* Because if it hangs over your face, it is more likely to come into contact with the individual you are working with and could spread infection. It could also become entangled in equipment and cause a serious injury.

Clean equipment

- *Why?* Because infection can spread from one person to another on instruments, linen and equipment just as easily as on hands or hair.
- *How?* By washing large items like trolleys with antiseptic solution. Small instruments must be sterilised. Do not shake soiled linen or dump it on the floor. Keep it held away from you. Place linen in proper bags or hampers for laundering.

Deal with waste

- *Why?* Because it can then be processed correctly, and the risk to others working further along the line in the disposal process is reduced, as far as possible.
- *How?* By placing it in the proper bags. Make sure that you know the system in your workplace. It is usually:

  clinical waste – yellow
  soiled linen – red
  recyclable instruments and equipment – blue.

Take special precautions

- *When?* There may be occasions when you have to deal with an individual who has a particular type of infection that requires special handling. This can involve things like hepatitis, some types of food poisoning or highly infectious diseases.
- *How?* Your workplace will have special procedures to follow. They may include such measures as gowning, double gloving or wearing masks. Follow the procedures strictly. They are there for your benefit and for the benefit of the other individuals you care for.

Active knowledge

Make notes of three ways in which infection can be spread. Then note down three effective ways to reduce the possibility of cross-infection.

There is always an element of risk in working with people. There is little doubt that there is an increase in the level of personal abuse suffered by workers in the health and care services. There is also the element of personal risk encountered by workers who visit people in the community, and have to deal with homes in poor states of repair and an assortment of domestic animals!

However, there are some steps which you can take to assist with safety.

Keys to good practice

- If you work alone in the community, always leave details of where you are going and what time you expect to return. This is important in case of accidents or other emergencies, so that you can be found.
- Carry a personal alarm, and use it if necessary.
- Ask your employer to provide training in techniques to combat aggression and violence. It is foolish and potentially dangerous to go into risky situations without any training.
- Try to defuse potentially aggressive situations by being as calm as possible and by talking quietly and reasonably. But, if this is not effective, leave. There is more detail on how to deal with potentially violent situations in Units CL1 and Z1.
- If you work in a residential or hospital setting, raise the alarm if you find you are in a threatening situation.
- Do not tackle aggressors, whoever they are – raise the alarm.
- Use an alarm or panic button if you have it – otherwise yell – very loudly.

Case study

K was a home-care assistant on her first visit to a new client, Mr W. She had been warned that his house was in a poor condition and that he had a large dog. She also knew that he had a history of psychiatric illness and had, in the past, been admitted to hospital compulsorily under the Mental Health Act.

When K arrived on her first morning, the outside of the house was in a very poor state – the garden was overgrown, and it was full of rubbish and old furniture. The front door was half open and she could see that half the floor boards in the hallway appeared to be missing – there were simply joists and a drop into the cellar below. Mr W's dog was at the top of the hallway growling and barking, and Mr W was at the top of the stairs shouting 'Who are you? You won't get me out of here – I'll kill you first!'

1 **Q** What should K do?
  A Leave! She should leave the house at once and report the situation to her manager.
2 **Q** When should she go back?
  A Only after a risk assessment has been carried out.
3 **Q** What sort of risks need to be assessed?
  A **a** Mr W's mental health and whether any treatment or support is required.
  b The safety of the house. Mr W will have to be consulted about whether he is willing for his house to be made safe and the floorboards repaired.
  c The dog and whether it is likely to present a risk of attack on a visitor to the house.

4 Q If Mr W refuses to allow a risk assessment, or his house to be repaired, should K go back in anyway?

A No. K's job is to provide care, but not at the risk of her own safety.

5 Q Who should carry out the risk assessment?

A K's employer.

How to lift and handle safely

In the previous element you found out about the regulations which govern lifting and handling. Unit Z7 will give you detailed information about using lifting and handling equipment safely.

You will know that your employer is required to carry out a risk assessment of any lifting and handling which is necessary and to supply the necessary equipment, and sufficient people, to carry out the lift.

All lifting and handling should be carried out using appropriate aids and sufficient people. Manual lifting is not something to be undertaken in the normal course of events and you should use mechanical lifting aids and hoists wherever possible.

Remember

Your employer has a statutory requirement to install lifting equipment, but it is your responsibility to use the equipment that is there.

If you do have to lift, what should you do?

Encourage all individuals to help themselves – you would be surprised how much 'learned helplessness' exists. This is largely brought about by care workers who find it is quicker and easier to do things themselves rather than allowing a person to do it for him or herself! Does this sound familiar?

There is more detailed information in Units Z6 (in *NVQ Level 2 Care*) and Z7 about maintaining mobility and helping people to move themselves.

Keys to good practice

On the rare occasions when you have to lift, take the following precautions:

- Never lift without an assessment and the right number of people.
- Never lift alone.
- Never lift a dead weight.
- Never lift someone vertically from the floor.
- Always keep your back straight.
- Bend your knees and lift with the weight on your legs.
- Never lift with your spine twisted.
- Never stretch and lift.
- Never lift with your arms outstretched.
- Attend a lifting and handling course – your employer should allow you to do this every year, as part of your workplace manual handling policy.

Minimise the risks arising from health emergencies

This element is about first aid, and helping you to understand the actions you should take if a health emergency arises. This is not a substitute for a first aid course, and will only give you an outline of the steps you need to take. Reading this unit will not qualify you to deal with these emergencies. Unless you have been on a first aid course, you should be careful about what you do, because the wrong action can cause more harm to the casualty. It may be better to summon help.

WHAT YOU NEED TO LEARN

- What you can safely do.
- How you can help the casualty in a health emergency.
- Other ways to help.
- How to deal with witnesses' distress – and your own.

What you can safely do

Most people have a useful role to play in a health emergency, even if it is not dealing directly with the ill or injured person. It is also vital that someone:

- summons help as quickly as possible
- offers any assistance to the competent person who is dealing with the emergency
- clears the immediate environment and makes it safe – for example, if someone has fallen through a glass door, the glass must be removed as soon as possible before there are any more injuries
- offers help and support to other people who have witnessed the illness or injury and may have been upset by it. Clearly this can only be dealt with once the ill or injured person is being helped.

Remember

Only attempt what you know you can safely do. Do not attempt something you are not sure of. You could do further damage to the ill or injured person and you could lay yourself and your employer open to being sued. Do not try to do something outside your responsibility or capability – summon help and wait for it to arrive.

How you can help the casualty in a health emergency

It is important that you are aware of the initial steps to take when dealing with the commonest health emergencies. You may be involved with any of these emergencies when you are at work, whether you work in a residential, hospital or community setting. Clearly, there are major differences between the different work situations:

- If you are working in a hospital where skilled assistance is always immediately available, the likelihood of your having to act in an emergency, other than to summon help, is remote.

- In a residential setting, help is likely to be readily available, although it may not necessarily be the professional medical expertise of a hospital.
- In the community you may have to summon help and take action to support a casualty until the help arrives. It is in this setting that you are most likely to need some knowledge of how to respond to a health emergency.

This section gives a guide to the recognition and initial action to be taken in a number of health emergencies:

- severe bleeding
- cardiac arrest
- shock
- loss of consciousness
- epileptic seizure
- choking and difficulty with breathing
- fractures and suspected fractures
- burns and scalds
- poisoning
- electrical injuries.

Severe bleeding

Severe bleeding can be the result of a fall or injury. The most common causes of severe cuts are glass, as the result of a fall into a window or glass door, or knives from accidents in the kitchen.

Symptoms

There will be apparently large quantities of blood from the wound. In some very serious cases, the blood may be pumping out. Even small amounts of blood can be very frightening, both for you and the casualty. Remember that a small amount of blood goes a long way, and things may look worse than they are. However, severe bleeding requires urgent medical attention in hospital. Although people rarely bleed to death, extensive bleeding can cause shock and loss of consciousness.

Aims

- To bring the bleeding under control.
- To limit the possibility of infection.
- To arrange urgent medical attention.

Action

1 You will need to apply pressure to a wound that is bleeding. If possible, use a sterile dressing. If one is not readily available, use any readily available absorbent material, or even your hand. Do not forget the precautions (see 'Protect yourself' below). You will need to apply direct pressure over the wound for ten minutes (this can seem like a very long time) to allow the blood to clot.

2 If there is any object in the wound, such as a piece of glass, *do not* try to remove it. Simply apply pressure to the sides of the wound.

3 Lay the casualty down and raise the affected part if possible.

4 Make the person comfortable and secure.

5 Dial 999 for an ambulance.

Lay the casualty down and raise the affected part

Protect yourself

You should take steps to protect yourself when you are dealing with casualties who are bleeding. Your skin provides an excellent barrier to infections, but you must take care if you have any broken skin such as a cut, graze or sore. Seek medical advice if blood comes into contact with your mouth, nose or gets into your eyes. Blood-borne viruses (such as HIV or hepatitis) can be passed only if the blood of someone who is already infected comes into contact with broken skin.

- If possible, wear disposable gloves.
- If possible, wash your hands thoroughly in soap and water before and after treatment.
- If this is not possible, cover any areas of broken skin with a waterproof dressing.
- Take care with any needles or broken glass in the area.
- Use a mask for mouth-to-mouth resuscitation if the casualty's nose or mouth is bleeding.

Cardiac arrest

Cardiac arrest occurs when a person's heart stops. Cardiac arrest can happen for various reasons, the most common of which is a heart attack, but a person's heart can also stop as a result of shock, electric shock, a convulsion or other illness or injury.

Symptoms

- No pulse.
- No breathing.

Aims

- To obtain medical help as a matter of urgency.
- It is important to give oxygen, using mouth-to-mouth resuscitation, and to stimulate the heart, using chest compressions. This procedure is called cardio-pulmonary resuscitation – CPR. You will need to attend a first aid course to learn how to resuscitate – you cannot learn how to do this from a book. On the first aid course you will be able to practise on a special dummy.

Actions

1 Check whether the person has a pulse and whether he or she is breathing.
2 If not, call for urgent help from the emergency services.
3 Start methods of resuscitation *if* you have been taught how to do it.
4 Keep up resuscitation until help arrives.

Mouth-to-mouth resuscitation (a) and chest compressions (b)

Shock

Shock occurs because blood is not being pumped around the body efficiently. This can be the result of loss of body fluids through bleeding, burns, severe vomiting or diarrhoea, or a sudden drop in blood pressure or a heart attack.

Symptoms

The signs of shock are easily recognised. The person:

- will look very pale, almost grey
- will be very sweaty, and the skin will be cold and clammy
- will have a very fast pulse
- may feel sick and may vomit
- may be breathing very quickly.

Aims

- To obtain medical help as a matter of urgency.
- To improve blood supply to heart, lungs and brain.

Actions

1 Call for urgent medical assistance.
2 Lay the person down on the floor. Try to raise the feet off the ground to help the blood supply to the important organs.
3 Loosen any tight clothing.
4 Watch the person carefully. Check the pulse and breathing regularly.
5 Keep the person warm and comfortable, but *do not* warm the casualty with direct heat, such as a hot water bottle.

Do not:

- allow casualty to eat or drink
- leave the casualty alone, unless it is essential to do so briefly in order to summon help.

Raise the feet off the ground and keep the casualty warm

Loss of consciousness

Loss of consciousness can happen for many reasons, from a straightforward faint to unconsciousness following a serious injury or illness.

Symptom

A reduced level of response and awareness. This can range from being vague and 'woozy' to total unconsciousness.

Aims

- To summon expert medical help as a matter of urgency.
- To keep the airway open.
- To note any information which may help to establish the cause of the unconsciousness.

Action

1 Make sure that the person is breathing and has a clear airway.
2 You need to maintain the airway by lifting the chin and tilting the head backwards.

Open the airway

3 Look for any obvious reasons why the person may be unconscious, such as a wound or an ID band telling you of any condition they may have. For example,

many people who have medical conditions which may cause unconsciousness, such as epilepsy or diabetes, will wear special bracelets or necklaces giving information about their condition.

4 Place the casualty in the recovery position (see below), *but not if you suspect a back or neck injury*, until the emergency services arrive.

Do not:

- attempt to give anything by mouth
- attempt to make the casualty sit or stand
- leave the casualty alone, unless it is essential to leave briefly in order to summon help.

The recovery position

Many of the actions you need to take to deal with health emergencies will involve you in placing someone in the recovery position. In this position a casualty has the best chance of keeping a clear airway, not inhaling vomit and remaining as safe as possible until help arrives. This position should *not* be attempted if you think someone has back or neck injuries, and it may not be possible if there are fractures of limbs.

1 Kneel at one side of the casualty, at about waist level.
2 Tilt back the person's head – this opens the airway. With the casualty on his/her back, make sure that limbs are straight.
3 Bend the casualty's near arm as in a wave (so it is at right angles to the body). Pull the arm on the far side over the chest and place the back of the hand against the opposite cheek (**a** in diagram opposite).
4 Use your other hand to roll the casualty towards you by pulling on the far leg, just above the knee (**b** in the diagram). The casualty should now be on his or her side.
5 Once the casualty is rolled over, bend the leg at right angles to the body. Make sure the head is tilted well back to keep the airway open (**c** in diagram).

(a)

(b)

(c)

The recovery position

Epileptic seizure

Epilepsy is a medical condition that causes disturbances in the brain which result in sufferers becoming unconscious and having involuntary contractions of their muscles. This contraction of the muscles produces the fit or seizure. People who suffer with epilepsy do not have any control over their seizures, and may actually do themselves harm by falling when they have a seizure.

Aims

- To ensure that the person is safe and does not injure him or herself during the fit.
- To offer any help needed following the fit.

Action

1 Try to make sure that the area in which the person has fallen is safe.
2 Loosen all clothing.
3 Once the seizure has ended, make sure that the person has a clear airway and place in the recovery position.
4 Make sure that the person is comfortable and safe. Particularly try to prevent head injury.
5 If the fit lasts longer than five minutes, or you are unaware that the casualty is a known epileptic, call an ambulance.

Do not:

- attempt to hold the casualty down, or put anything in the mouth
- move the casualty until he or she is fully conscious, unless there is a risk of injury in the place where he or she has fallen.

Choking and difficulty with breathing (in adults and children over 8 years)

This is caused by something (usually a piece of food) stuck at the back of the throat. It is a situation which needs to be dealt with, as people can quickly stop breathing if the obstruction is not removed.

Symptoms

- Red, congested face at first, later turning grey.
- Unable to speak or breathe, may gasp and indicate throat or neck.

Aims

- To remove obstruction as quickly as possible.
- To summon medical assistance as a matter of urgency if the obstruction cannot be removed.

Action

1 Try to get the person to cough. If that is not immediately effective, move on to step 2.
2 Bend the person forwards. Slap sharply on the back between the shoulder blades up to five times (**a** in diagram on page 92).
3 If this fails, stand behind the person with your arms around him/her. Join your hands just below the breastbone. One hand should be in a fist and the other holding it (**b** in the diagram).
4 Then sharply pull your joined hands upwards and into the person's body at the same time. The force should expel the obstruction.
5 You should alternate backslaps and abdominal thrusts until you clear the obstruction.

(a) (b)

Dealing with an adult who is choking

Fractures and suspected fractures

Fractures are breaks or cracks in bones. They are usually caused by a fall or other type of injury. The casualty will need to go to a hospital as soon as possible to have a fracture diagnosed correctly.

Symptoms

- Acute pain around the site of the injury.
- Swelling and discoloration around the affected area.
- Limbs or joints may be in odd positions.
- Broken bones may protrude through the skin.

Action

1 The important thing is to support the affected part. Help the casualty to find the most comfortable position.
2 Support the injured limb in that position with as much padding as necessary – towels, cushions or clothing will do.
3 Take the person to hospital or call an ambulance.

Do not:

- try to bandage or splint the injury
- allow the casualty to have anything to eat or drink.

Support the injured limb

Burns and scalds

There are several different types of burn; the most usual are burns caused by heat or flame. Scalds are caused by hot liquids. People can be burned by chemicals or by electrical currents.

Symptoms

- Depending on the type and severity of the burn, skin may be red, swollen and tender, blistered and raw or charred.
- Usually severe pain and possibly shock.

Aims

- To obtain immediate medical assistance if the burn is over a large area (as big as the casualty's hand or more) or is deep.
- To send for an ambulance if the burn is severe or extensive. If the burn or scald is over a smaller area, the casualty could be transported to hospital by car.
- To stop the burning and reduce pain.
- To minimise possibility of infection.

Action

1 For major burns, summon immediate medical assistance.
2 Cool down the burn. Keep it flooded with cold water for 10 minutes. If it is a chemical burn, this needs to be done for 20 minutes. Ensure that the contaminated water used to cool a chemical burn is disposed of safely.
3 Remove any jewellery, watches or clothing which are not sticking to the burn.
4 Cover the burn if possible, unless it is a facial burn, with a sterile or, at least, clean dressing. For a burn on a hand or foot, a clean plastic bag will protect it from infection until it can be treated by an expert.

Cool the burn with water

5 If clothing is on fire, remember the basics: *stop*, *drop*, *wrap* and *roll* the person on the ground.

Do not:

- remove anything which is stuck to a burn
- touch a burn, or use any ointment or cream
- cover facial burns – keep pouring water on until help arrives.

Remember

If a person's clothing is on fire, STOP – DROP – WRAP – ROLL
- *Stop* him or her from running around.
- Get him/her to *drop* to the ground – push him/her if you have to and can do so safely.
- *Wrap* him/her in something to smother the flames – a blanket or coat, anything to hand. This is better if it is soaked in water.
- *Roll* him/her on the ground to put out the flames.

Poisoning

People can be poisoned by many substances: drugs, plants, chemicals, fumes or alcohol.

Symptoms

Symptoms will vary depending on the poison.
- The person could be unconscious.
- There may be acute abdominal pain.
- There may be blistering of the mouth and lips.

Aims

- To remove the casualty to a safe area if he/she is at risk, and it is safe for you to move him/her.
- To summon medical assistance as a matter of urgency.
- To gather any information which will identify the poison.
- To maintain a clear airway and breathing until help arrives.

Action

1 If the casualty is unconscious, place him/her in the recovery position to ensure that the airway is clear, and that he/she cannot choke on any vomit.
2 Dial 999 for an ambulance.
3 Try to establish what the poison is and how much has been taken. This information could be vital in saving a life.
4 If a conscious casualty has burned mouth or lips, he or she can be given small frequent sips of water or cold milk.

Do not try to make the casualty vomit.

Electrical injuries

Electrocution occurs when an electrical current passes though the body.

Symptoms

Electrocution can cause cardiac arrest and burns where the electrical current entered and left the body.

Aims

- To remove the casualty from the current when you can safely do so.
- To obtain medical assistance as a matter of urgency.
- To maintain a clear airway and breathing until help arrives.
- To treat any burns.

Action

There are different procedures to follow depending on whether the injury has been caused by a high or low voltage current.

Injury caused by high voltage current

This type of injury may be caused by overhead power cables or rail lines, for example. What you need to do.

1 Contact the emergency services immediately.
2 *Do not* touch the person until all electricity has been cut off.
3 If the person is unconscious, clear the airway.
4 Treat any other injuries present, such as burns.
5 Place in the recovery position until help arrives.

Injury caused by low voltage current

This type of injury may be caused by powered kettles, computers, drills, lawnmowers, etc. What you need to do.

1 Break the contact with the current by switching off the electricity at the mains if possible.
2 It is vital to break the contact as soon as possible, *but* if you touch a person who is 'live' (still in contact with the current) you too will be injured. If you are unable to switch off the electricity, then you must stand on something dry which can insulate you, such as a telephone directory, rubber mat or a pile of newspapers, and then move the casualty away from the current as described below.
3 Do not use anything made of metal, or anything wet, to move the casualty from the current. Try to move him/her with a wooden pole or broom-handle, even a chair.
4 Alternatively, drag him/her with a rope or cord or, as a last resort, pull by holding any of the person's dry clothing which is *not* in contact with his/her body.
5 Once the person is no longer in contact with the current, you should follow the same steps as with a high voltage injury.

Move the casualty away from the current

Other ways to help

Summoning assistance

In the majority of cases this will mean telephoning 999 and requesting an ambulance. It will depend on the setting in which you work and clearly is not required if you work in a hospital! But it may mean calling for a colleague with medical qualifications, who will then be able to make an assessment of the need for further assistance. Similarly, if you work in the residential sector, there should be a medically qualified colleague available. If you are the first on the scene at an emergency in the community, you may need to summon an ambulance for urgent assistance.

If you need to call an ambulance, try to keep calm and give clearly all the details you are asked for. Do not attempt to give details until they are asked for – this wastes time. Emergency service operators are trained to find out the necessary information, so let them ask the questions, then answer calmly and clearly.

Follow the action steps outlined in the previous section whilst you are waiting for help to arrive.

Assist the person dealing with the emergency

A second pair of hands is invaluable when dealing with an emergency. If you are assisting someone with first aid or medical expertise, follow all his or her instructions, even if you don't understand why. An emergency situation is not the time for a discussion or debate – that can happen later. You may be needed to help to move a casualty, or to fetch water, blankets or dressings, or to reassure and comfort the casualty during treatment.

Make the area safe

An accident or injury may have occurred in an unsafe area – and it was probably for precisely that reason that the accident occurred there! Sometimes, it may be that the accident has made the area unsafe for others. For example, if someone has tripped over an electric flex, there may be exposed wires or a damaged electric socket. Alternatively, a fall against a window or glass door may have left shards of broken glass in the area, or there may be blood or other body fluids on the floor. You may need to make the area safe by turning off the power, clearing broken glass or dealing with a spillage.

It may be necessary to redirect people away from the area of the accident in order to avoid further casualties.

Maintain the privacy of the casualty

You may need to act to provide some privacy for the casualty by asking onlookers to move away or stand back. If you can erect a temporary screen with coats or blankets, this may help to offer some privacy. It may not matter to the casualty at the time, but he or she has a right to privacy if possible.

Make accurate reports

You may be responsible for making a report on an emergency situation you have witnessed, or for filling in records later. Concentrate on the most important aspects of the incident and record the actions of yourself and others in an accurate, legible and complete manner.

How to deal with witnesses' distress – and your own

People who have witnessed accidents can often be very distressed by what they have seen. The distress may be as a result of the nature of the injury, or the blood loss. It could be because the casualty is a friend or relative or simply because seeing accidents or injuries is traumatic. Some people can become upset because they feel helpless and do not know how to assist, or they may have been afraid and then feel guilty later.

You will need to reassure people about the casualty and the fact that he or she is being cared for appropriately. However, do not give false reassurance about things you may not be sure of.

You may need to allow individuals to talk about what they saw. One of the commonest effects of witnessing a trauma is that people need to repeat over and over again what they saw.

Witnessing accidents is often distressing

What about you?

You may feel very distressed by the experience you have gone through. You may find that you need to talk about what has happened, and that you need to look again at the role you played. You may feel that you could have done more, or you may feel angry with yourself for not having a greater knowledge about what to do.

There is a whole range of emotions which you may experience. Unit Z1 covers in detail the different ways to cope with these feelings, but you should be able to discuss your feelings with your supervisor and use any support provided by your employer.

If you have followed the basic guidelines in this element, you will have done as much as could be expected of anyone at the scene of an emergency who is not a trained first aider.

? Unit test

I Name three aspects of safety which you could deal with in your workplace: List the actions you would take in each of the three situations you have identified.

2 Look at the picture on page 97. How many possible hazards and risks can you find in the picture?
    a List at least six.
    b Which of these are the responsibility of the employer?
    c Which should you do something about?

3 What are the employer's responsibilities in respect of hazardous substances? What are the employee's responsibilities for hazardous substances?

4 What should you do if you see someone in your workplace whom you do not recognise?

5 What are the different ways of disposing of waste?

6 What should you do if you find an intruder on the premises?

7 You should always attempt first aid because it is always better to do something. True or false? What is the single most important act for an untrained person to do in a health emergency? List three tasks you can carry out at the scene of an emergency which do not necessarily involve first aid.

8 How would you talk to a casualty while you waited for help? What would you say to others who had witnessed the incident?

9 Imagine you are just about to start work in a new day-care facility for older people.
    a What kinds of substance would you expect to see in the COSHH file?
    b Which tasks would you expect to find in the risk assessment file?
    c Would you expect to see any specialised care equipment in the centre?
    d What type of equipment?
    e What basic precautions will you expect to follow?
    f Do you think there will be an expectation about how you dress? What do you think it will be?
    g What training courses would you expect to undertake?
    h List at least three security precautions you think the setting may take.

10 Now imagine that you are about to start working in a residential setting for young people. Answer the same questions. Which of your answers are different and which remain the same?

Unit SC8

Contribute to the development, provision and review of care programmes

Services are provided by a wide range of agencies in many different ways. These could be as different as providing a hospital bed for somebody who is acutely ill, providing residential accommodation for a homeless young person or providing large print books for somebody who has visual impairment. One of the most important aspects of the provision of service is to ensure that it is meeting the needs of the client.

Clients' needs are not about what the agency or the care worker believes is needed, they are about what the client understands their own needs to be. One of the most important roles of a care worker is to find out from the client about the type of service they need and then to work alongside them and with their family, and any other carers, to ensure that the maximum effective level of service is provided and that it meets the needs of all those concerned. It is also important that the worker understands the limitations of the service that is provided by their own agency. Sometimes it is necessary to explain this to the client, even though it may be disappointing not to provide them with exactly what they had hoped for.

In this unit you will learn about the best ways to ensure that you have the maximum possible information about your client, about how you can work with them and make sure that they are happy about the service they are getting. You will also learn about the importance of continually looking at the service which is provided for your client together them to make sure that it continues to meet their needs.

ement SC8.1 Obtain information about clients and their needs

WHAT YOU NEED TO LEARN

- How to understand and explain the role that you play in the assessment process.
- How to obtain information from the client.
- How to obtain information about the client from other sources.
- How to organise recorded information for easy access.

Your role in the assessment process

Your role is to ensure that you find out what your client needs and wants, always making sure that every option for maintaining or increasing independence is explored.

Many different care workers undertake the role of obtaining information about clients and what services they need. You could be assessing people for domiciliary services while they remain in their own homes, you could be assessing the needs which people may have once they leave a hospital or a residential care setting, you could be talking to a teenager or a young person about the needs they have either for residential or other support services – the possibilities are very broad. However, whatever role you have as a worker and regardless of which agency you are working for and the kind of services that your agency provides, there are some basic principles which apply to the work you will do. One of these is that you must carefully explain to

One of your roles as carer is to discuss with the client their need for independence and how that can be achieved

the client your role in the whole process. However, before you can clearly explain your role to someone else in a way that they can understand, you must ensure that you understand your own role.

In these circumstances it is not necessarily your role to speak on behalf of your client.

Your role is to ensure that:

- what your client wants and needs is clearly explained to those providing the service

- as much information as possible is obtained from the client

- you also provide the client and their carers and family with as much information as you can about the nature of the service that will be provided.

This helps to avoid misunderstandings which can occur through lack of information and through lack of clear explanation about exactly what a client can expect from the agency that is providing the service.

There are also other matters you need to deal with in your role in providing a care service.

1 You will also need to explain to a client exactly what service your agency provides. It can sometimes be helpful to explain how your agency is funded and what the limitations may be on the types of services that can be provided.

2 You might find that clients or their families have an unrealistic expectation and will ask for services which are simply not available – either because of lack of funding or other resources or lack of trained personnel, or simply that this service is not one which is currently available in your area or through your agency. Explaining this can be difficult to handle. You may feel as if you have 'let down' the client, and in some way that it is your responsibility.

3 It is important to realise that it is not your personal responsibility or any personal failing of yours if your agency is unable, through lack of funding or any other resources, to provide a specific service at the level or with the frequency that a client is looking for.

4 You should not let this influence or affect the way in which you are able to relate to the client, neither should you over-commit your agency or make promises that simply cannot be fulfilled. It is far worse for a client to feel let down and disappointed because you told them or led them to expect that something can be provided which later proves to be impossible.

Before visiting a client it may be helpful to make a list of exactly what your role is and the limitations of that role. You can then check off the points on the list, either on the list, or in your head, and in that way be sure that you have covered all the important information points.

Remember

- To give all possible information about your role and the role of your agency.
- That you may have to repeat this several times if there are several family members or other people who are involved in your client's care.
- That if your client has hearing, understanding, or learning difficulties you may have to repeat the information or write it down or make it available in some other accessible format.
- That information is very important and that it empowers people. You will fail to properly empower your client to make informed choices if you fail to give them sufficient information.

How to obtain information from the client

Developing a relationship with the client

The importance of the relationships which you develop with your clients cannot be stressed enough. There is no substitute for an effective worker/client relationship in the assessment delivery and review of services. In Unit CL1 you will have learned the basic communication skills involved in building working relationships with clients and you will need to use all those skills when you are working with clients in order to establish their needs and expectations of a service. The information that you gather should be based on much more than the answers your client has supplied to a set of questions. It should also include your observations, what you know about your clients' values and beliefs and the factors which have influenced their development. All of these are important in assessing the kind of service which will be appropriate for any particular individual. It is through using effective communication skills to develop a working relationship with your client that you will be able to best contribute towards providing a service which will meet their individual needs.

A good working relationship with a care worker should increase rather than reduce a client's level of independence. It is often the case that people will feel more confident to attempt new challenges if they know that they have support they can fall back on if they need to.

Case study

Elizabeth G is 85 years old. She lives alone and has recently become increasingly frail. She has no memory difficulties but finds shopping, cooking and coping with housework increasingly difficult. Elizabeth had never married and during her professional life had been head teacher of a large primary school. She has one brother, who emigrated to New Zealand over 50 years ago and never returned to live in England. Since her retirement she enjoyed travelling abroad and visited many countries, including New Zealand to see her brother. She always travelled alone, or occasionally with another teacher from her school. Elizabeth had never been particularly religious and attended her local Anglican church only on formal occasions, such as the marriage of friends, baptisms or funerals. She has always enjoyed gardening but recently been unable to do it, so her once lovely garden had now become overgrown.

Elizabeth reluctantly contacted social services to ask for help with the preparation and cooking of meals and some basic housework. She no longer had the money to pay for the private provision of any of these services, and she was aware she felt it inappropriate for her to be asking for help from social services. The help provided was in the form of a home help once a week to do some shopping. The person carrying out the assessment of Elizabeth's needs also decided she needed some company. It was decided that the best way for her to get a regular meal and some company would be to attend a local luncheon club. The worker dealing with Elizabeth arranged transport for her to do this, in the hope that Elizabeth would enjoy socialising with the others at the luncheon club. Elizabeth attended the luncheon club once. When transport arrived for her the following day she told them that she would not be going again and then contacted social services to cancel all the other arrangements that had been made for her. She said that she had re-thought her needs and decided that she could manage quite well and that there was no need for them to take up services which could be of more use to someone else.

1   From what you know of Elizabeth's background would you expect her to be happy with a group of strangers?

2   Given her background what would you expect her interests to be?

3   What sort of social situations would you expect Elizabeth to feel comfortable in?

4   What do you know about Elizabeth's feelings about asking for help?

5   What do you think Elizabeth's reaction would be to any problems in the provision of her service?

6   How do you think Elizabeth's feelings about asking for help should be approached?

7   Do you think that the services provided were appropriate for Elizabeth?

8   If not, why not?

9   Were Elizabeth's background and influences taken into account?

10 What services would be appropriate provision for Elizabeth?

11 What would you do to re-establish contact with Elizabeth?

12 How could Elizabeth's need for independence have been taken into account?

In addition to considering the cultural and developmental influences on your client you should never forget the influence that your presence and your relationship has on the way in which your client will describe their own needs. It is always extremely difficult for us to assess what affect we have on others, however it is possible to take this into account when you are considering someone's response. If you have done some of the exercises in Unit CL1, where you began to look at the affect you have on others, then you should apply what you learned from those exercises to the situation of establishing client needs and expectations. Remember that if a client believes you expect them to minimise their complaints and to always be cheerful, then they are less likely to tell you the true extent of their needs and are far more likely to minimise their requirements. It is normal for any of us to seek approval from others by doing what they expect us to do.

You need to think carefully about the way you can influence clients. It is not only your own personal style of communication which influences them, it is also the way you explain the possibilities of service provision. So you will need to be aware of pushing clients and their families into a particular solution, simply because you happen to believe that it is the best one. Clients will ask for your advice and will ask the question 'What would you do?' You will have to learn to avoid answering the client directly, as it is not for you to give direct advice about a course of action that a client can take, nor is it for you to explain what you would do if you were them. You are not them, you are not in their circumstances and never will be, therefore it is not possible for you to answer in any helpful way the question, 'What would you do if you were me?'

What you can usefully do is provide information about the services and empower your client to make their own decisions. However, you should be very careful not to direct or influence your client in making those decisions, simply provide unbiased,

It is really important that you give the client a chance to make up their own mind about what they want

accurate and clear information and then follow that by supporting them to achieve the outcome of the decision they have made.

Putting clients in control

Throughout the process of obtaining information you should make sure you constantly check back with the client that they are fully aware of everything that is happening and feel they are in control of the process. One of the problems with the way services are provided, regardless of whether they are services for health, for social care provision or provision for children and young people, is that many clients feel they play only a passive role in the services they receive. It is easy to see how this can happen. Agencies and service providers have well-organised systems which can often involve filling in a great many forms, attending meetings and working through the bureaucracy. If you work regularly for such an organisation these things are a day-to-day part of your working life. They do not represent a threat to you and they do not represent something which is frightening, confusing or difficult to understand. However, you need to remind yourself that many of the clients you deal with will not be as familiar with all of the workings of your agency and that they may not feel confident enough to question or to challenge what is happening. There are several steps you can take at each stage of the process to ensure that clients feel that they are in charge of providing the information that is required for their service.

1 Clients should make clear who needs to be involved in the process of thinking about and planning their service provision.

You may need to prompt your client to think about the people that they would like to be involved. Sometimes it is helpful to make some suggestions or to ensure that your client has considered all the possibilities. For example, you could ask 'What about your neighbour Mrs S, the one who pops in with your dinner. Might it be a good idea to ask her?' Or, 'You know your niece Susan, she might have some ideas about the sort of services that you could use.'

If you are meeting your client for the first time and you have little knowledge of their background or family, you will need to ask some questions to establish the people who are significant in their lives and who should be involved in planning

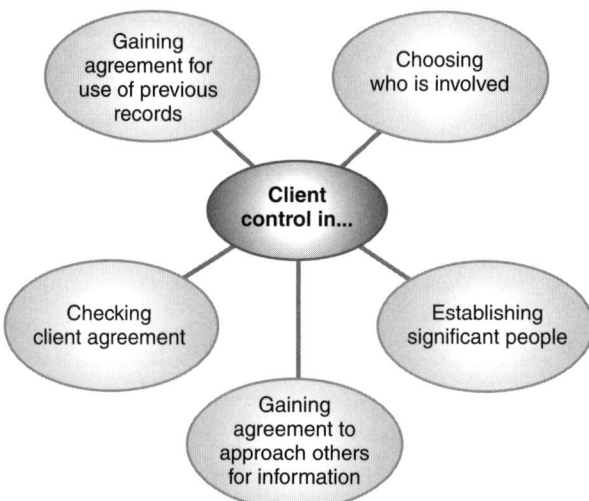

You need to make sure that the client is involved and feels in control of what is happening in the provision of services to them

their care. You could prompt your client by asking, 'Is there anyone else who pops in to see you? Does anyone help with your shopping or take you out? Is there anyone amongst your friends, family or neighbours who helps with cooking or providing meals?'

2 At each stage of the process you should check with the client that they are in agreement with the steps which have been taken so far. You should do this by using the means of communication which is most effective with your client and to go over what you have already discussed with them and any arrangements which you have put in hand. For example, if your normal means of communication is to talk to your client, then you could have a regular review with them where you would explain, 'Right Mr F... so far you have decided that you would like a home-help and I have arranged for that to start next week. And you said that you would like to have meals on wheels delivered. They will be able to start next Thursday. Is this alright with you, or do you want anything different?' Alternatively, if you have a client who has any form of hearing impairment then your means of communication may be written. If this is the case you could provide a short list of what has so far been arranged and check that they are still happy with that.

3 The use of any additional sources of information, for example previous records or other agencies who may be involved with your client, must be agreed with the client in advance before you approach the sources for the information.

4 It is important you do not take this agreement for granted and that you establish an agreement with your client and make sure that they understand. You will need to explain exactly what it is you intend to do so your client is clear what they are agreeing to.

You should make sure that you record your client's agreement to approaching other people for information. Many agencies will require written confirmation of your client's agreement to provide information about them. You will need to establish this at the agency concerned and if necessary complete their authorisation form with your client, ensuring that you explain to them what the implications of signing the form are. If at any point during your initial assessment and checking of information your client withdraws their consent for you to approach a particular agency or individual, then you must respect that and not pursue that particular source of information.

It is important that your client understands exactly what they are agreeing to

How to obtain information from other sources

We have already looked at the information you can obtain directly from the clients themselves and also considered the information which you will gain by observing your client and from what you know about their background, culture and beliefs, however there are other sources of information which are extremely useful. Once you have ensured you have your client's agreement to do so, you may wish to consider accessing a range of other sources to complete the picture you have of your client and the way in which they can most benefit from the services that your agency provides. Examples of to the sources are:

A care worker may need access to other sources of information to get a fuller picture of what services a client needs

Bear in mind that information that you gain, particularly from other professional sources, may be restricted by:

- the bounds of confidentiality under which that professional operates
- the legal restrictions as to how information may be passed on.

Most professionals are bound by principles of confidentiality in respect of their clients. You will know that there are limits to the information that you can and should share with others about your client, so you must expect that other professionals from whom you are seeking information will also be bound by the same restrictions of confidentiality regarding your client. Information can be protected under a range of different legislation, as shown below.

Type of information	Relevant legislation
Medical information/hospital records	Data Protection Act 1998
Information relating to children and young people	Children Act 1989
Information relating to people with mental health problems	Mental Health Act 1983
Information relating to people with a disability	Disability Discrimination Act 1995
Any information stored on a computer and some manual records	Data Protection Act 1998

All these Acts work on the basic principle that personal information which is given or received, in what is understood to be a confidential situation and for one particular purpose, may not be used for a different purpose. They also contain the proviso that information may not be passed to anyone else without the agreement of the person who provided the information. **The Access to Medical Records Act** ensures the individual has access to their own records but that these are not available to anyone else unless the individual gives express permission. This applies even after death where an individual has expressly forbidden any information to be passed to anyone else or to a specific individual.

The Data Protection Act relates specifically to information which is stored by computer. This also meets the broad proviso about the purpose which information has been supplied and also contains the requirement that information may not be passed on to others without the express consent of the person to whom it relates.

You should always take great care that you are not contravening any laws when you are accessing information from other agencies in respect of your client.

Family and friends

Family and friends are an invaluable source of information about a client and the needs they have. However, you must be sure before you discuss anything with family or friends that this is being done with the express consent of the client. It is easy to make assumptions that because someone is a relative or close friend that the client will have no objections to them being involved in talking to you and giving information. Always confirm with the client that they have no objection to you discussing their case with family or friends.

How to organise recorded information for easy access

When you have gathered information that you need about your client, it is important that it is readily accessible for all those who are going to be involved in the planning and delivering of the services. Your agency is likely to have a specific form that you need to complete. This will describe your client's needs and will also contain your assessment of the best way in which those needs can be met.

The way in which this information is recorded is important if you are to provide an effective service for your client. It must be recorded in a way which those who need can easily access it. Those who may need to access the information will vary depending on your client and their circumstances. They could be:

Those who may need to access recorded information about clients

The information that you obtain during this initial stage will be vital in its contribution to the next stage of the process, which is planning the service provision for your client, which you will have a vital role in contributing to.

Keys to good practice

1 Ensure that your client understands your role and the role and limitations of what your agency can provide.

2 Make sure that you keep your client informed at all times so that they can make informed choices about the service they need.

3 Use all sources of information that you are able to locate but ensure that you have the client's agreement to do so.

4 Organise and record the information in a way which is clear and easily accessible for all others who may need to make use of it.

Active knowledge

Try preparing a record sheet which you will use for all clients about whom you have to gather information. This should include the basic factual information which is required by your agency, however make sure you add to it information which you have obtained through your own observation or through your understanding of the client's values, beliefs and culture. You could organise this as a checklist so that you can use it whenever you work with clients in obtaining information. Check your list against any forms which are already provided by your agency and see how many additional aspects you have included. This should give you some indication of the importance of obtaining information on all aspects of your client, not just the basic factual information which is often all that is required on agency forms.

Element SC8.2 Contribute to planning how clients' needs can best be met

WHAT YOU NEED TO LEARN

* Your role in planning for service provision.
* How to involve the client in planning the provision.
* How to record the decisions about meeting a client's needs.

Your role in planning for service provision

You may be involved in a care planning meeting. This may be because your agency is the main provider or commissioner of services for the particular client and you have been involved in collecting information and making the initial assessment of the client's needs. Or you may be involved because you are one of the other service providers and you need to plan and agree the services which your agency will provide. If you are responsible for carrying out the initial information gathering and assessment of needs, you must make sure that you provide all the information to the participants in the meeting as early as possible. People need time to read and consider background information before coming to a meeting. This way they are most likely to be able to make firm decisions about the services which should be provided. If they only receive information when they arrive at the meeting it may not be possible for a decision to be made on the spot. This can result in delays, causing frustration and disappointment for your client, and may, depending on their circumstances, increase risk.

The responsibility for organising the meeting may lie with you or it may be someone else in your agency or in another agency. You must ensure that you contact whoever is responsible for the meetings and provide all your information as soon as possible so that the meeting may proceed smoothly.

Health and care workers may need to meet to plan the services a client needs

The following table provides a list of care workers and what their responsibilities are.

Worker	Responsible for
Social worker	Managing and coordinating the delivery of service provision for an individual client
Domiciliary services organiser	Managing and delivering domiciliary support services, such as home help, and for assessing service level requirements
Voluntary coordinator	Coordinating and organising volunteers who provide a wide range of support services to clients in the community
Support worker	Providing direct support to a wide range of clients in their own homes or in hostel accommodation. This support enables people with a range of different types of needs to maintain an independent or supported living situation
Health visitor	Works with GP practice and provides help with monitoring review and promotion within the community
Occupational therapist	Assesses needs for aids and adaptations to enable independent or supported living

How to involve the client in planning the provision

Meetings held between health care professionals can be very intimidating for clients and they may feel that they do not have the confidence to participate. It is important that you work to encourage the client, and their family and any friends they wish to be involved in the process, to feel able to make an active and effective contribution to the meeting. The meeting is about the client and they are the most important person. It is easy to lose sight of this and to allow the client to feel that their role is purely a passive one. There are a range of actions that you can take prior to the meeting to help the client feel they have a useful and important contribution to make to the meeting. You should:

1 Go through the procedure of the meeting with them so that they know exactly who will be there, what will happen, in what order matters will be discussed and the type of contributions that all of those present at the meeting will make.

2 Help them to decide what they want to say and to work out the best way to present it. This could be in a written form or they could prepare some notes in advance to ensure that they cover all the points they want to make.

3 Make sure they know the different results which could come from the meeting so that they will not be surprised by any of the decisions which could be made. Explain to them that there could be a range of options for the meeting to consider.

4 Where necessary make practical arrangements for them to attend. This could include ensuring the client's accessibility to the meeting, providing transport where necessary, or providing linguistic translation or other communication assistance.

Putting the client's views

Your client may feel confident and well able to put across their own point of view. If so your role is simply to support and encourage them in doing so. However, if your client does not feel able to put their own views across adequately, or if they have done so and there is either a misunderstanding or a difference of opinion within the care planning meeting as to how this client's needs are best met, then your role is to ensure that the client's views are clearly represented and understood. This is particularly important when the client cannot communicate for themselves, because the client is a young child or because they have learning or communication difficulties or because they suffer from dementia or some other condition which may inhibit communication.

Active knowledge

Try to remember a situation where you have felt you were not in control and that other people held the power. This may have been a medical situation, for example where you were a patient and felt that you were unable to ask all the questions that you wanted to because the doctor simply did not seem to have time to answer them. It may have been one which involved lawyers or other professionals, or it could have involved your child's teacher or head teacher who had made you feel you were lacking in the skill and ability to put across what you really wanted to say. Remember how you felt in those situations, and choose one of them to act as your 'trigger' to recall those feelings whenever you are in a care planning meeting, or any other situation, with a client. This should remind you to encourage your client to put across their views if they are having difficulty doing so. Think how much easier it might have been if somebody had been acting as a support for you.

It is important not only for the accuracy of the views, but also to make sure the client knows that it is their views which are being represented and not the carer's own views, and that they are the person who is actually in control of what is happening to them

There is a fine balance between representing the client's point of view and putting across your own views about what you think may be best for them. You will need to be careful that it is the client's viewpoint that you represent and not your own, even if you think their views are not the most appropriate. When you are making contributions at a meeting you should always ensure that you begin with, 'Mr X has told me that', or 'Mrs Y has explained to me that she would prefer', rather than, 'I think that' or 'In my opinion the best course of action would be.' It is important not only for the accuracy of the views, but also to make sure the client knows that it is their views which are being represented and not your own, and that they are the person who is in control of what is happening to them.

Difficult situations

You can find yourself in a difficult position when your client's views and expectations of the service that they need are different from the views of the other professionals at the care planning meeting, or from the client's own relatives or carers, and particularly if they differ from the views of your own agency. Your role is to represent the views of your client. However you should not get drawn into the role of attempting to manipulate the meeting to ensure that your client achieves their desired outcome. Neither should you get involved in arguments with other professionals, you should simply ensure that the client's views are clearly expressed. You may also wish to add your own views as a professional and these will be based on your client's needs and wishes, however it is not necessary for you to act beyond

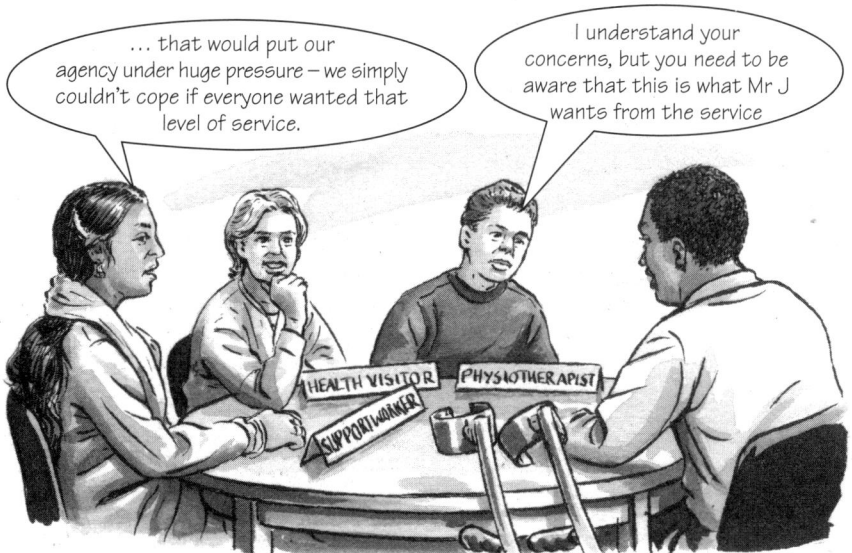

You need to look after your client's interests in any discussion to determine what services are available, particularly those that enable them to look after themselves as much as possible.

the limits of this role. Your own agency may have a particular view on the type of service which can be provided, and this may be based on resource limitations or agency policy and guidelines. For example, you may have a client who wants a regular home help but refuses to accept a home help of a particular race or gender and wishes to specify the race or the gender of the home help. If your agency has an equal opportunities policy in respect of its employees it may not be prepared to comply with that request. In these circumstances you would simply have to make the views of your client known. However, you would be bound in your professional actions by the equal opportunities policy under which you work with your agency.

You will also need to be aware of the potential for the stereotyping or labelling of your client at the care planning meeting, and be ready to counteract any such attitudes towards your client. Be aware that assumptions may be made about the abilities of your client. For example, in the case of clients with learning difficulties, it is not uncommon for assumptions to be made which underestimate their abilities based on a generalisation of what can be achieved by those who have learning difficulties. There is also a very commonly held belief that people with Alzheimer's disease need round-the-clock protection. However, this is not always the case and many people who suffer from Alzheimer's are capable of achieving a great deal of independence, provided the environment in which they live is suitably adapted. You need to be aware of the assumptions being made about clients and you should refer back to Unit CL1 for details of the ways in which stereotyping and labelling can affect individuals.

Case study

G is a 30-year-old man with Down's syndrome. His mother had just died and his father had died two years previously. G had always lived at home and attended a local day care facility. He also enjoyed socialising at a club which was organised by Mencap on two evenings each week. G often complained that he was restricted by the very protective attitude of his parents and wanted to have a more independent existence and to be able to participate in a wide range of sporting and social activities. His parents had always felt he would be placing himself at risk if they agreed to his plans to join in this sort of activity. G has an older brother and two older sisters who had always been supportive of his parents during G's upbringing, but none were able to accommodate him full time within their own families. Following the death of their mother they were heavily involved in discussions with the social services department and voluntary agencies about the most appropriate solution to meet the long-term needs of G.

G was most insistent to the key worker that he wished to live completely independently and to remain in his own home. He felt that he was extremely capable of living in this way and that he intended to now take up some of the activities, such as hang-gliding and parachute jumping, which his mother had never allowed him to become involved in. He believed that he was capable of meeting all of his own needs and was unwilling to listen to the concerns of his brother and sisters. His family felt that G needed to be in residential care. They had found a residential facility with a vacancy which was only a few miles from their home town and would enable G to continue attending his regular day centre and his twice-weekly social club. They felt this was the only way in which they could ensure that G would be properly cared for and that his safety would be ensured. The family fully intended to continue their regular contact with G and were enthusiastic at the prospect of him moving into the residential facility. The family were supported in their view by the GP and the staff from the day care facility, which was linked to the residential accommodation. However, the staff from the social club were supportive of G's wishes to extend his independence.

The key worker proposed that G accompany her to look at a supported living situation where six people with a certain degree of learning difficulty shared a house and were responsible between them for shopping, cooking and meeting their own needs. However, they had daily access to a support worker and received a visit each day to provide an agreed level of assistance. This living situation would, within reason, allow G to increase his level of independence and to introduce more risk and challenge into his life. G and the family (although they had reservations) accepted this as a useful way forward, so G moved and settled in happily. He was finally dissuaded from hang-gliding and parachute jumping but did become involved in sand yachting, at which he was highly competitive and quite successful, and he also frequently assisted as navigator for one of the drivers in the local car rally club.

1   Why do you believe the family felt as they did about G?

2   What may have been the basis for the GP's views in this situation?

3   Examine your own feelings about a young man with learning difficulties living in the way G wished to. What is your initial response? What is your response after consideration and reflection on the issues?

4   What was the potential if either solution, that proposed by the family or that proposed by G himself, had been followed?

5   Whose views were of paramount consideration in this situation?

6   Which of the professionals involved is likely to have the best knowledge of G?

7   What other factors may influence the views of both professionals?

8   Do you consider this situation was resolved satisfactorily?

9   If so, identify the needs of all of the parties involved and how they were met by this solution.

10 If not, what alternative solution would you propose?

Case study

Mr J is 72 years old. His wife has recently died and although he has children they do not live locally. He is insisting that he wishes to go into residential care. Mr J is not confused, nor is he physically frail. He is a fit and healthy 72-year-old, but he is very lonely following the death of his wife and he finds it impossible to carry out domestic tasks. He never did any domestic tasks within the house as his wife did everything, and he has no idea how to cook, clean or shop. However, he is still able to maintain his garden, which he has always done, and is happy to carry out physical tasks around the house. The key worker has suggested that services be provided for Mr J in his own home and that it would be possible for him to have support to learn how to cook simple meals and how to maintain the cleanliness of his house. However, Mr J has refused these offers of help, saying that he does not believe that it is a man's role to carry out these tasks and that he needs to be in residential care so that he can have women who will look after him.

1 Identify Mr J's needs.

2 Do you consider that his needs will be met by residential care?

3 What are the alternatives which could be considered?

4 Do you think that Mr J's demands mask other needs?

5 There are three suggested outcomes to this situation. Select which one you consider to be most appropriate or develop one of your own.

Outcome 1

Mr J's request for residential care is agreed to and he is admitted into full-time care. All of his physical needs are met, he has his own room and appears to be very content with the way in which care is provided for him. He spends his days reading the newspapers and watching TV. He is gradually becoming more and more confused but appears happy in the residential setting.

Outcome 2

The key worker has another client a few streets away whose husband died about nine months ago. She is very lonely and is finding that the physical upkeep of her house is increasingly difficult for her to manage. She has little idea how to maintain the garden and has never undertaken jobs around the house. She also misses having meals to cook and a man to look after. The key worker introduces the two and they develop a friendship and share the tasks of daily living between them. Mr J maintains the gardens and houses, and she cooks, shops and does the washing and cleaning for both of them. Both appear to be very happy with the arrangement.

Outcome 3

Mr J's request for residential care is refused. However, the key worker introduces him to a cookery course at his local college which also includes the basics of home management, shopping and cleaning. He attends very reluctantly but realises that he has little choice. As a result of his attending college he finds out about other courses which are available, he has bought himself a computer and discovered the Internet. He has also joined his local over-50s swimming club, which he found out about whilst at college, and goes there three mornings a week, as well as attending college two other days each week. He spends his time at home surfing the Internet and 'chatting' to a wide range of people from all over the world.

6 List the advantages and disadvantages of each of these solutions. If you are curious, outcome 2 was what actually happened in this particular situation.

How to record the decisions about meeting a client's needs

The outcomes of any meeting to discuss care and meeting a client's needs must be recorded. The needs which clients are likely to have could include:

- **Educational**. For example, selection of appropriate school or college provision, access to information about services or systems or access to information relating to their current circumstances.
- **Recreational**. This could include identifying activities and opportunities to pursue interests.
- **Financial**. This could include identifying needs for budgeting or obtaining additional income.
- **Legal or advocacy**. This would involve identifying or enabling access to advice and support services or to solicitors or barristers via the legal aid system if necessary.
- **Emotional**. The need for love and close relationships.
- **Social**. Access to company and friends.
- **Physical**. This can be a wide range depending on the client's circumstances, but they need to be met in order for clients to survive.

Recording the outcomes of meetings is essential in order to avoid the possibility of confusion and misunderstanding. It is likely that your agency will have a specific format for recording decisions. If not, then very careful minutes must be taken of the meeting and all of the conclusions reached must be recorded. It is important that the discussions which were undertaken at the meeting are briefly recorded. This enables the people who have taken part in the meeting to check that their contribution and views have been noted, but the key is to have a clear record of all final decisions. The form which your agency has, or any documents which you subsequently develop, may look something like this:

Record of care planning decisions
Client name
Date of meeting
Those present at meeting
Main points of discussion
Decisions   (Please show each decision with a separate number, e.g. 1,2,3, a,b,c, etc.)

It will be important to make sure, either through you directly or through whoever organises it within your agency, that the information recorded from the care planning meeting is circulated to all those who were present. There may be also be those who were not present at the meeting but who would still have an interest in knowing the outcome. The most important person who must receive a copy of this information is the client, regardless of whether or not they were present at the meeting. The information about decisions should also go to any carers or relatives whom the client wishes to be involved, and to the relevant health or other care professionals who are involved with the client. You must ensure that your client is aware of the fact that this information will be circulated and you must take their views into account if there are particular people who they do not wish to receive this information.

WHAT YOU NEED TO LEARN

- How to communicate the care options to the client.
- How to ensure your client's agreement.
- How to keep all parties informed.
- How to record decisions.

How to communicate the care options to the client

If a care planning meeting has gone well and there is sufficient information on which to base the plans, then you should be able to present the client with a proposal that they are able to consider, and hopefully one which has met their original needs and expectations. You may find that you need to explain in detail the options which are available. Even if your client and their family and friends have been present at the care planning meeting, you may find that you need to go over again the information that was discussed and the decisions which were reached. It is extremely important that you provide the client with a written or other form of accessible record of the decisions taken at the planning meeting so that there is no misunderstanding about the options which they have for service provision.

It is also important that you do not present a *fait accompli* to your client and that you do not, by your behaviour, discourage them from commenting on the proposals. It is sometimes easy to give a client the impression that everything is organised and agreed and that they do not have the option to disagree or possibly even reject the proposals which are made. You can often do this unwittingly, so you should check against your own method of communicating information to ensure that you are giving your client the opportunity to comment on any proposals. For example, you should always check that:

- you are not suggesting these are the only options and that if the client did not agree to them the service could not be provided at all
- you are not 'selling' the proposal by making it sound so ideal that the client feels that they will disappoint you if they reject it
- you are not making the client feel guilty if they are dissatisfied with the proposals by implying that there are a great many others who would be grateful for the level of service which is being suggested for them.

Being aware of how you come across to your client is an important part of working in a reflective way, as is being aware always of the effect which your actions are having on others. You can never afford to make assumptions that your client will agree with your perspective or that of your agency.

How to ensure your client's agreement

Any proposals which have resulted from the planning meeting must receive the agreement of your client. It is important that you seek out confirmation of this agreement even if your client has been present at the planning meeting. This is important for two reasons:

1 They have had time to reflect and think things over since the planning meeting and their views may have changed.

2 They might not have felt confident enough to express any reservations that they may have had during the meeting.

You will need to make sure you give them the opportunity to express any doubts or concerns they have at this stage. It is always more helpful to establish concerns before service provision has begun than to have to adapt and change the service during its provision. With the client's agreement you should also ensure that those who are involved with their care, such as friends and family, are also given the opportunity to comment on the proposals and the extent to which they consider the service will meet the client's needs and the needs of those who are involved in providing informal care. There may be disagreements between a client and members of their family or close friends about the way in which services should be provided. It may be useful to provide your client and any of their friends or family who are involved with a list of the decisions which were taken with space for them to make notes about whether they agree or disagree with the proposals and make any comments that they have. If they can have this in advance of you seeing them, it will give them a chance to discuss and consider in their own time whether or not they feel that the proposed services are appropriate.

Planning Meeting

Client's name: _____

Address: _____
_____
_____
_____

Phone no: _____

Present at the meeting _____
_____

Proposals from planning meeting

1 _____
_____
_____

2 _____
_____
_____

3 _____
_____
_____

4 _____
_____

Contact name: _____

Phone no: _____

I am available each day between .... and ....

It is useful to provide a list of decisions with space for notes

---

Dealing with a client whose choice is limited

There are some circumstances in which proposals for service provision can be imposed upon a client. These do happen but are rare. This could be as a result of the client being:

- the subject of an order made by the court
- the subject of a compulsory admission to hospital under the Mental Health Act
- the subject of a compulsory admission to hospital or residential care under the National Assistance Act
- the subject of a guardianship order under the Mental Health Act
- the subject of an order made under the Children Act.

When service provision is imposed on a client, it is considerably more difficult to work with that client and to assist them to feel that they do have a contribution to make to the planning process. Obviously, because of the compulsory nature of the service provision, there are some aspects over which they have no choice. However, where this is the case you should encourage your client to exercise choice in the areas where it is possible for them to do so. Simply because they are living in a particular setting or in receipt of a particular service as a result of compulsion, does not remove their rights to exercise choice within the limitations of the setting in which they find themselves. You should ensure that where possible clients are able to exercise choice, however limited those options may be.

How to keep all parties informed

One of your key roles in this process is to provide information to your client and those who are involved in the process with them about precisely the services which are proposed. You cannot expect your client to agree to a service, for example that 'day care will be provided', unless they have all the information needed to make a choice. This will include information about:

- the exact nature of the day care proposed
- the location of the day care
- the type of care offered
- the general atmosphere and ethos of the facility
- the number of people who attend
- what the transport arrangements will be.

These are just a few of the questions which a client or their family may have about services which will be provided. Informed choice must be made with full information. It is not sufficient to simply tell your client that the proposal is for day care. If necessary you should offer to assist your client or to make arrangements for your client and those who are supporting them to visit any establishments which are part of the proposal for care services.

We all have the right to make informed choices about all aspects of our lives. For example, you would not purchase a house simply because the estate agent said 'Oh, I have got a nice house for you.' You would want a great deal of information about the house, you would want to visit the house for yourself and to carry out extensive planning and questioning before you finally made that decision. Similarly, you would not buy a holiday or a car simply because somebody said to you, 'I have got a nice holiday here that I am sure would suit you.' You would want to ask questions about where, when, how much, what type of accommodation, and so on. If you always ask yourself the question, 'Does the client have sufficient information to make this decision?', then you should never fall into the trap of failing to provide them with everything they need to make an informed choice.

The key word in the whole process is agreement. What has been proposed at the care planning meeting as a result of your initial information gathering is simply a proposal and it requires the client's agreement in most circumstances.

How to record decisions

Once you have obtained the agreement of the client to the proposals, and any changes have been discussed with all the relevant people involved, then you should ensure that those decisions are recorded in a way that all of those involved with the process can access them readily. You may want to consider using a similar form to that used for recording the outcomes of the planning meeting (see page 115) and to simply add to it any subsequent changes made and agreed with the client.

Keys to good practice

1 Communicate all information to your client clearly and in a way they can understand.

2 Make sure their views are clearly represented to any forum where decisions are being taken or proposals being formulated.

3 Support the client to put forward their own views wherever possible.

4 Clearly record information and planning proposals and ensure that all the relevant people involved receive them.

5 Make sure your client and those involved with them receive the planning proposals in a form they can access and understand.

6 Ensure the client and those involved with them have the opportunity to comment in their own time on the proposals and in an atmosphere where they feel able to make adverse comments if necessary.

7 Ensure that all final proposals for care provision have the agreement of your client and those who are involved with them.

8 Always provide your clients with the information they need to make informed choices, even if those are restricted by their circumstances.

9 Ensure that all of those involved with the process are kept informed of any changes and updates made to the proposals.

Active knowledge

Think about a client you are currently working with. Consider all your actions in respect of the client and whether or not the client was given a choice in the services provided for them. If you believe they were given every possible choice then list the ways in which you ensured that was the case. If you believe their choice was restricted in some way, identify the reasons why this happened and the steps you can take to ensure it is not repeated.

WHAT YOU NEED TO LEARN

- How to monitor provision.
- How to identify changes in needs and services.
- How to implement changes in provision.
- How to record the review process.

How to monitor provision

Once an agreed programme of care has been put into place for your client, you should not assume that this will now continue indefinitely. All situations change on a regular basis and the change can be brought about by a wide range of factors. Therefore it is important to monitor the service which a client receives on an ongoing basis and to periodically review the service to see if any changes are needed.

Active knowledge

Look at yourself and your circumstances over the last 10 years and make a list of the ways in which your circumstances have changed. For example, you may have more children than you had 10 years ago, or you may have some children who have left home and moved away. Members of your family may have died or been born in the last 10 years, you could be living in a larger house or a smaller house, you could have more money or less money, you could be doing the same job or a different job. All these are major changes which have taken place in your life in just the short period of 10 years. Listing the changes will help you see the sorts of situations which change and affect people's lives.

Then take a much shorter period, for example the last year, and look at much smaller changes which may have happened to you during that time. They could be changes in your finances and your job role, you could now be undertaking a qualification, you may be driving a different car, you may have acquired digital television – any number of small changes which have affected the way you are living your life. Again, make a list of these changes and consider the impact each of them has had. Although the second list may have had a smaller impact than some of the big changes you listed in your first reflection, they will nonetheless have combined together to illustrate some quite large changes in your lifestyle. Consider the results of this exercise when you are thinking about how you will monitor the care programmes which are in place for your clients.

Many changes can take place in a client's life that affect the provision of care

Monitoring a care programme

At the start of the service delivery of a care programme, you should establish with your client a process for **monitoring** the care programme. This can be done on an ongoing basis and you should encourage your client to keep a record, especially about problems or difficulties or about the service no longer meeting their changed needs. You should plan regular contact with your client in order to participate in the monitoring process. Ideally this should involve visiting the client so that you can observe for yourself any conditions which may be changing. At the very least there should be contact by letter or telephone or other suitable means, so that you can provide your client with the opportunity to inform you of any changes. It will also allow you to review the adequacy of the service that has been provided and whether or not it is meeting the client's needs in the way that was anticipated at the planning stage.

Methods of monitoring

There are two main aspects of the care programme which need to be monitored. The first is the client's situation and any changes which could alter their needs, and the other is the service provision itself and any changes which may be required in the nature of the provision or the way in which it is delivered. You will need to ensure that your monitoring process enables you to keep a regular check on both aspects of the care programme. You can do this through either:

- devising a checklist which you would go through with your client on a regular basis

or

- providing the client and the service provider with a form or checklist that enables them to record any changes they have noticed that need to be made in the provision of the service.

How to identify changes in needs and services

You will have a key role in being the contact between the client and the agency providing the service. It will be your role to ensure the client is aware of any changes in agency policy or in the resources that may alter the way in which their service is provided, and you will need to ensure that the agency providing the service is aware of any changes in your client's circumstances. If you have provided your client with, or if you use a regular checklist, this will be a useful way of keeping a record of the information so that you can pass it on as appropriate.

Client checklist		
Changes in circumstances	YES	NO
Are my living circumstances the same	☐	☐
Do I still have the same support from family/friends/neighbours	☐	☐
Are my finances the same	☐	☐
Has my physical condition changed	☐	☐
Has my medical condition changed	☐	☐

Agency/organisation checklist		
	YES	NO
Is the level of service provided still appropriate	☐	☐
Is it still possible to provide this service within current resources	☐	☐
Have agency policies changed in respect of the provision of this service	☐	☐

Examples of checklists to identify changes in clients' needs and care provision

Case study

K is a woman in her early 50s. She has Parkinson's disease, her level of mobility has been decreasing gradually over the past three years, and she has recently begun to fall frequently. She lives with her two sons aged 19 and 25 years, and her only contact with health and care provision so far has been through her hospital consultant and the primary care team. Her service requirements have been mainly medical with regular support from a physiotherapist. Her increase in falling has coincided with a major change in her circumstances. Her younger son has just been offered a place at an excellent university and her older son has been headhunted for a 'once in a lifetime' chance of his dream job in the United States for two years. K does not want either of her sons to miss the opportunities they have been offered – so she now wants to discuss the ways in which she can arrange support which will allow her to remain as independent as possible.

1 Who should be the first professionals K holds discussions with?

2 Who else should be involved in planning?

3 How would you ensure that K retained control of the process?

4 What feelings would you anticipate K would have about her change in circumstances?

5 What steps would you take to make sure that K remains independent?

How to implement changes in provision

There is little point in monitoring the service to a client unless there is a procedure in place to then review that service and to make any changes which are necessary. This could take the form of recalling the original planning meeting, although in many agencies the process of review is undertaken on a much smaller scale, given that it is unlikely that all the people who attended the original meeting would be free or available to attend review meetings on a regular basis.

The most likely composition of a review meeting will consist of the key worker, the client, any supportive members of the family or friends, and the main agency who is providing the service. This group should be able to review on a regular basis the effectiveness of the service currently being provided and should be able to put forward ideas and proposals for any changes needed. It is important that the client is involved directly in the process of monitoring and review and that any of the changes proposed are agreed by the client and clearly understood.

This is likely to be an easier process if changes occur as a result of requests from the client. However, there may be occasions when service provisions have to be changed because of changes within the agency or because of a reduction in the availability of resources. This will have to be explained to the client and plans made for alternative services or other support which can be used to make up for the short-fall in service provision. This can be difficult for clients to accept and understand, and they may feel that they have been let down by a service on which they have relied. This can be a difficult situation to manage. You will need to use good communication skills to ensure the client has the opportunity to express their feelings about any changes in their service. They should also be made to feel they can question and make suggestions as to how you can move things forward in a positive way to maintain and support them within their present circumstances.

Case study

Miss P is aged 73. She lives alone and is a retired millinery buyer from a local large department store. She has had support from the home help and mobile meals service since her mobility deteriorated with the increasing severity of her arthritis over the last five years. She was a fiercely independent lady who had always refused to accept any benefits or support in addition to her state pension. After finally getting her agreement to review her finances her key worker had identified that she had some additional benefits due to her from her company pension scheme. This had increased Miss P's monthly income considerably and had eased her financial situation. However, this change in circumstances had also put her income above the payment threshold for home-help service and she now had to pay for the service that she had previously received at no charge. Miss P is angry at this and is considering cancelling the home-help service, although she would find it extremely difficult to manage without it.

1 How would you explain this situation to Miss P?

2 What are the skills you would need in order to successfully encourage Miss P to continue using support services?

3 How do you think Miss P is likely to feel?

4 Should this potential problem have been foreseen by the key worker in pursuing additional finances?

5 Should it have been discussed with Miss P in advance of obtaining her agreement to review her finances?

How to record the review process

As with all parts of the care programme planning process, it is essential that any changes agreed at a review are recorded and copies of this are provided to all of those who are involved with the client. This should include any of the agencies involved in providing any part of the client's programme of care, as well as the client and whoever else is involved in their support. This will reduce the possibility of confusion or misunderstanding about the way in which the service should be delivered.

If there is disagreement at a care review meeting this is usually resolved by consensus following discussion. It is rare that such decisions are taken on a vote, but it has occurred in exceptional circumstances. Normally, changes to a care programme are agreed by all parties concerned even if the discussion has been lengthy and lively. Even those parties present or involved in the review who have not supported the changes will comply with the review decisions. It is the responsibility of the key worker for the client to record review decisions and to briefly record the discussions which took place. This will need to be kept as part of the client's record and circulated to all those concerned.

The records can be fairly short, however they need to include full details of any changes and who is responsible for the implementation of them. The record forms can vary depending on the agency, however each one is likely to contain information which will identify what decisions were made and who is responsible for ensuring that they are carried out.

Keys to good practice

As a key worker in the planning and delivery of care programmes there are basic principles which you can follow which are likely to provide your client with the best possible service and the best possible care programme in order to meet their needs.

1   Always ensure that you have information about all of the client's circumstances, using observation as well as direct questioning.

2   Make sure you have the client's agreement to use any of the information you have acquired.

3   Ensure that all those who are involved in planning the care provision have access to all the relevant information about the client and their circumstances.

4   Support the client in making a direct contribution to the process of planning their own care programme.

5   Make sure that proposals made by professional agencies meet with the agreement of the client before starting any programme of care.

6   Make arrangements to regularly monitor provision of the service.

7   Set up regular arrangements for reviewing the service and make sure that the client is involved throughout the process.

8   Keep all the relevant agencies and individuals who are involved in the programme of care informed about any changes which are made.

Unit test

1   What factors do you need to take into account when dealing with a client whose programme of care is being provided with their consent?

2   What factors do you need to take into account when dealing with a client whose programme of care is being provided without their consent?

3   Why is it important to provide information at each stage of the process to the client and to their family and friends who may be involved in supporting them?

4   What is the value of involving all agencies and professionals who may be involved with a client in a care planning meeting?

5   What is the purpose of regularly monitoring and reviewing a programme of care?

6   What are the potential changes to a client's circumstances which could alter their care provision. How could the level of care provision be altered by changes in circumstances at the providing agency?

7   What factors must the key worker take into account when balancing issues such as risk and challenge against protection and safety for a client?

8   To what extent can information about a client be shared with other agencies?

9   Why is it important that clients agree to the programme of care which is being provided for them?

10   What is the main skill needed by a key worker when informing clients of changes in their care programme?

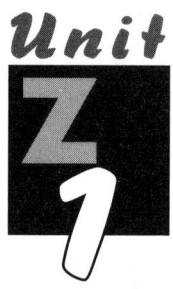

Unit Z1

Contribute to the protection of individuals from abuse

In this unit you will look at some of the most difficult issues that you will face as a care professional. You need to know how society handles abuse, how to recognise it, and what to do about it. It is a tragic fact that almost all disclosures of abuse are true – and you will have to learn to *think the unthinkable*. If you can learn always to consider the possibility of abuse, always to be aware of potentially abusive situations and always to *listen* and *believe* when you are told of abuse, then you will provide the best possible protection for people in your care.

This unit refers to 'children and young people', and deals with children between 8 and 18 years. Work with very young children (under 8 years) is not covered by the NVQ Care qualification. If this is the age group you work with, you should look at an NVQ in Early Years Care and Education.

Element Z1.1 — Contribute to minimising the level of abuse in care environments

WHAT YOU NEED TO LEARN

- What is meant by abuse in care environments.
- How the law affects what you do.
- How you can contribute to the minimising of abuse.
- How to report and to record information.

What is meant by abuse in care environments

What is a care environment?

The obvious answers are residential care and hospitals, but people are cared for in many other situations: children are cared for by their parents, by a childminder, in school, in a youth group or in foster homes. Vulnerable adults can be cared for in supported living schemes, at home with informal carers or professional carers, with relatives and in day care, as well as in residential or nursing homes.

What is abuse?

Abuse is more than being hit or sexually assaulted. Of course, they are the most violent and obvious forms of abuse, and they may be the ones which are easier to identify. But there are other ways in which people can be abused, as the diagram on the next page shows.

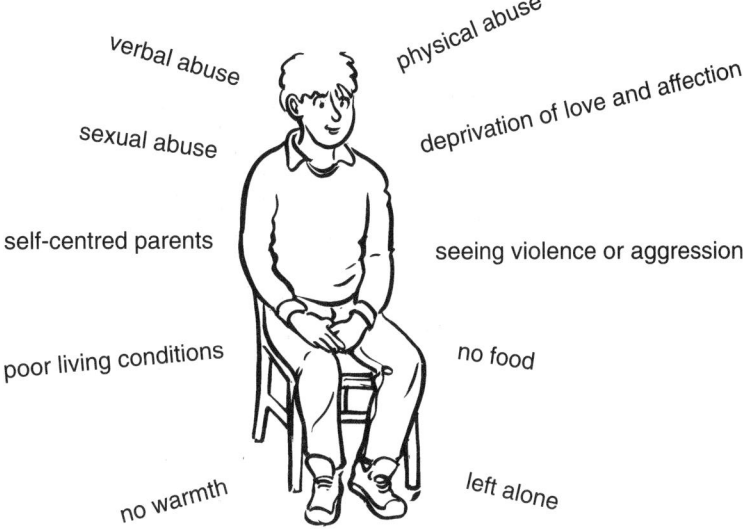

verbal abuse

physical abuse

sexual abuse

deprivation of love and affection

self-centred parents

seeing violence or aggression

poor living conditions

no food

no warmth

left alone

Ways in which children can be abused

Children can be abused:

- emotionally, by being deprived of love or physical contact
- verbally, by being constantly shouted at
- by having to witness violent or aggressive scenes at home
- by being parented by people who are unable to put their child's needs before their own
- by being physically neglected, by living in filthy conditions
- by being deprived of food, warmth or shelter
- by being left without adult protection, to fend for themselves
- at the hands of other children, by being bullied at school or in the local neighbourhood.

Remember

Child abuse can be:
- physical
- sexual
- emotional
- neglect.

Did you know?

About 10,000 calls are made each day to Childline, the helpline for children who are being abused. Of those, only around 3,000 actually get through because the lines are so busy.

no medical attention

harassment

physical abuse

no food

cold

isolated

financial exploitation

humiliation

Ways in which older people can be abused

Abuse of older people is described in the government guidelines 'No Longer Afraid' as:

> 'physical, sexual, psychological or financial: intentional or unintentional or the result of neglect; causing harm or distress to the older person either temporarily or over a period of time.'

This definition could be usefully applied to abuse of all adults, not just older people. As with children, abuse of older people can take many forms:

- physical – hitting, slapping, pushing, restraining
- psychological – blaming, swearing, humiliating or harassing
- neglect, where people are deprived of food, warmth, comfort or medical attention
- forcible isolation, where a carer may deny someone access to the outside world
- sexual
- financial – theft of money or property, or exploitation.

Abuse can also be self-inflicted, for example through the use of substances or self-harming behaviours. Individuals in such a position may also be regarded as at risk.

Remember

Adult abuse can be:

- physical
- sexual
- psychological
- financial
- neglect
- isolation.

Active knowledge

How many types of abuse does your workplace have guidelines to deal with? Look at the policy and procedures for dealing with abuse. See how many types of abuse are listed and what the procedures are. Ask your supervisor if you cannot find any information.

Who can abuse?

Abuse can take place at home or in a formal care setting. At home, it could be an informal carer who is the abuser, although it could be a neighbour or regular visitor. It can also be a professional care worker who is carrying out the abuse. This situation can mean that abuse goes undetected for some time because of the unsupervised nature of a carer's visits to someone's home.

In a formal care setting, abuse may be more likely to be noticed, although some of the more subtle forms of abuse, such as humiliation, can sometimes be so commonplace that it is not recognised as abusive behaviour.

Abuse is not only carried out by individuals; groups, or even organisations can also create abusive situations. It has been known that groups of carers in residential settings can abuse individuals in their care. Often people will act in a different way in a group than they would alone. Think about teenage 'gangs' which exist because people are prepared to do things jointly which they would not think to do if they were by themselves.

Abuse in a care setting may not just be at the hands of members of staff. There is also abuse which comes about because of the way in which an establishment is run, where the basis for planning the systems, rules and regulations is not the welfare, rights and dignity of the residents or patients, but the convenience of the staff and management. This is the sort of situation where people can be told when to get up and go to bed, given communal clothing, only allowed medical attention at set times and not allowed to go out.

No dear, you can't go out now, you nearly slipped last time. You can't go on your own and I don't have anyone to send with you – can't you see how busy we all are?

Remember

Abusers can be:
- individuals
- groups
- organisations.

Case study

Meadow View was a 40-bed EMI (Elderly Mentally Infirm) unit. The residents were all suffering various forms of dementia – some wandered, many were aggressive and several residents were violent. Over 75 per cent of the residents were incontinent. There was no formal continence management programme, but staff would toilet residents at regular intervals throughout the day. Following a regular visit from the Registered Homes Inspector, the staff were surprised to find that they were considered to have been abusive towards their residents. The inspector reported that she had heard staff talking loudly to residents in the lounge with such phrases as 'Come on Mary, time for a tinkle or we'll have another puddle like we did this morning' and 'Oh Charlie, my little pooh machine – you've done it again!'

1 Do you agree that the behaviour of the staff amounted to abuse?
2 If you do, why was it abusive?
3 If you do not think that this was abusive, why not?
4 How could Mary and Charles have been treated differently?

Up to this point, consideration has been given to abuse by carers, whether parents, informal or professional. But, do not forget that in residential or hospital settings, abuse can occur between residents or patients, and it can also happen between visitors and residents or patients. People can also abuse themselves.

As a carer whose role is to reduce the risk of abuse wherever you can, you need to be very much aware of abuse between individuals you are caring for and to take action whenever you suspect that this is happening. Bear in mind the types of behaviour which are abusive and be alert to any signs of those behaviours.

Visitors can also behave abusively, and if the care team considers that they pose a risk to the health or well-being of an individual, then a plan will be developed for how the visitor should be dealt with. You must ensure that you follow the plan of care, and always check with your supervisor if you are unsure about access.

Did you know?

Some of the most difficult places to make secure are hospitals and residential homes. The large number of visitors makes it almost impossible to have a secure system of identifying everyone on the premises at any given time.

The one abuser it is very hard to protect someone from is him or herself. Individuals who self-harm will be identified in their plan of care, and responses to their behaviour will be recorded. You must ensure that you follow the agreed plan for provision of care for someone who has a history of self-harm. It is usual that an individual who is at risk of harming him or herself will be closely supported and you may need to contribute towards activities or therapies which have been planned for the individual.

How the law affects what you do

Much of the work in caring is governed by legislation, but the only group where legislation specifically provides for protection from abuse is children. Older people, people with learning difficulties, disabilities or mental health problems have service provision, restrictions, rights and all sorts of other requirements laid down in law, but no overall legal framework to provide protection from abuse. The laws which cover your work in the field of care are summarised in the table below.

There are, however a number of sets of guidelines, policies and procedures in respect of abuse for client groups other than children, and you will need to ensure that you familiarise yourself with policies for your area of work and particularly with those policies which apply in your own workplace.

Active knowledge

Ask your supervisor about the procedures in your workplace for dealing with abuse. There should be a written policy and guidelines to be followed if abuse is suspected. Ask if there are any laws or guidelines which are related to the way you work. Check with experienced colleagues about situations they have dealt with and ask them to tell you about what happened.

A summary of the laws you work with

Client group	Laws which govern their care	Protection from abuse?
Children	Children Act 1989	Yes
People with mental health problems	Mental Health Act 1983	No
Adults with learning difficulties	Mental Health Act 1983	No
Adults with disabilities	Chronically Sick and Disabled Persons Act 1986 Disability Discrimination Act 1995	No
Older people	National Assistance Act 1948 NHS and Community Care Act 1990	No

Government guidelines

The most influential set of government guidelines which lay down practices for inter-agency co-operation is called 'Working Together'. It was published along with the Children Act 1989, and forms the basis for present child protection work. This guideline ensures that information is shared between agencies and professionals, and that decisions in respect of children are not taken by just one person.

There is a similar set of guidelines published by the government about older people, called 'No Longer Afraid'. These guidelines state that older people have specific rights, which include being treated with respect, and being able to live in their home and community without fear of physical or emotional violence or harassment.

What does the law say about protecting children?

The Children Act 1989 requires that local authority social services departments provide protection from abuse for children in their area. This Act gives powers to social services departments to take legal steps to ensure the safety of children.

What happens in an emergency?

In an emergency, a social worker, or an NSPCC officer, can apply to a magistrate for an order to look after a child. This is an Emergency Protection Order (known as an EPO). The police are also able to take immediate steps to protect children in an emergency situation. (This is a Police Protection Order, or PPO.) These orders require evidence which shows that there is reasonable cause to believe that a child may suffer 'significant harm'. They are short-term orders, usually for 3–7 days, and are followed by a court hearing where more detailed evidence is produced and the parents are represented.

Not all investigations into abuse are emergencies, and not all involve legal proceedings. Some abusive, or potentially abusive, situations are dealt with by working with the family, usually by agreeing a 'contract' between social services and the family.

The three agencies able to protect children

What does the law say about protecting older people?

The Acts of Parliament which are mainly concerned with provisions for older people are the National Assistance Act 1948 and the NHS and Community Care Act 1990. They do not specifically give social services departments a 'duty to protect' but, of course, older people are protected by the law. If an older person is abused and that abuse is considered to be a criminal offence, then the police will act. It is sometimes thought that because someone is confused, that a prosecution will not be brought – this is not so. One of the rights specified in 'No Longer Afraid' is the right to have an advocate or representative to act on behalf of the older person, if necessary.

Some older people suffer abuse in residential or hospital settings. These settings are ultimately controlled by legislation. Hospitals have complaints procedures and arrangements for allowing 'whistleblowers' who have concerns about abuse to come forward. Residential homes and nursing homes have to be registered either with social services or with the health service. Both run registration and inspection units which will investigate allegations of abuse and can ultimately close an unsatisfactory residential home or nursing home.

What happens in an emergency?

Many social services departments now have procedures in place similar to those for protecting children. There will be an investigation of the alleged or suspected abuse, followed by a case conference where information will be shared between all the professionals concerned and a plan of action worked out. The older person concerned and/or a friend or advocate will also be invited to take part in the conference if he or she wishes.

What does the law say about adults with mental health problems or learning difficulties?

The Mental Health Act 1983 forms the framework for service provision for people with mental health problems and people with learning difficulties. There are provisions within this legislation for social services departments to assume responsibility for people who are so 'mentally impaired' that they are not able to be responsible for their own affairs. This is called guardianship. However, like all other adults, there is no overall duty to protect people from abuse.

What does the law say about adults with disabilities?

Whilst the Chronically Sick and Disabled Persons Act and the Disability Discrimination Act provide disabled people with rights, services and protection from discrimination, they do not provide any means of comprehensive protection from abuse.

As with all vulnerable groups, there is a long and tragic history to the physical and emotional abuse suffered by people with disabilities and learning difficulties. The public humiliation and abuse of those with mental health problems is still visible today, so it is hardly surprising that abuse on an individual level is still all too commonplace.

These vulnerable groups have not benefited from the high level of public awareness of child abuse, or the growing recognition of abuse of older people. Few workplaces will have specific procedures in place, although exactly the same guidelines should apply.

What if a professional carer abuses?

There are special procedures in place for investigating abuse which is inflicted by care workers or foster carers. It is investigated by an outside agency and immediate steps are taken to remove the suspected abuser (often called the 'perpetrator') from contact until the investigation has been completed.

These issues are well publicised at the moment as many cases of systematic and long-term abuse by care workers are coming to light. Later, this unit will make sure that you know how to deal with a situation where you know, or suspect abuse in your workplace.

How you can contribute to the minimising of abuse

One of the key contributions you can make towards limiting abuse is to be aware of where abuse may be happening. It is not easy to accept that abuse is going on, and it is often simpler to find other explanations.

Be prepared to *think the unthinkable*. If you know about the circumstances in which abuse has been found to occur most frequently, then you are better able to respond quickly if you suspect a problem.

It is not possible accurately to predict situations where abuse will take place – a great deal of misery could be saved if it were. It is possible, though, to identify some factors which seem to make it more likely that abuse could occur. This does not mean that abuse will definitely happen – neither should you assume that all people in these circumstances are abusers – but it does mean that you should be aware of the possibility when you are dealing with these situations.

Situations when child abuse can happen

Child abuse can happen in situations where:

- parents are unable to put a child's needs first
- parents or carers need to show dominance over others
- parents or carers have been poorly parented themselves
- parents or carers were abused themselves as children
- families have financial problems (this does not just mean families on low incomes)
- families have a history of poor relationships or of use of violence.

Situations when adults may be abused at home

Adults may be abused at home in situations where:

- carers have had to change their lifestyles unwillingly
- the dependent person has communication problems, has had a personality or behaviour change, such as dementia, rejects help or is aggressive
- there is no support from family or professional carers
- carers are becoming dependent on drugs or alcohol
- carers have no privacy
- the dependent person is difficult and inconsiderate.

Case study

S is 48 years old. She has Parkinson's disease which has recently begun to develop very rapidly. Her mobility has become very limited and she cannot be left alone because she falls frequently. The number of personal care tasks she can carry out has decreased significantly, and she is almost totally dependent on her husband for care. They have two grown up sons who live and work considerable distances away. They both visit as often as they can, but are not able to offer any regular caring support. S's husband has given up his career as a ranger in the local country park, which he loved, in order to look after S. She is very reluctant to go out because she feels people are looking at her. She is very angry about the way Parkinson's has affected her, and has alienated many of the friends who tried to help initially, by being unco-operative and refusing much of the help they offered.

1 Are there any 'warning bells' in this situation which would make you aware of the possibility of abuse?
2 If so, what are they?
3 How would you try to alleviate the pressures in this situation?

Active knowledge

Think about the clients you deal with. Make a list of how many of them fit into the circumstances outlined. Now resolve to keep a particular eye on those clients and watch for any signs that abuse may be happening. Be prepared to *think the unthinkable*.

Situations when abuse can happen in a care setting

Abuse can happen in a care setting when:

- staff are poorly trained or untrained
- there is little or no management supervision or support
- staff work in isolation
- there are inadequate numbers of staff to cope with the workload
- there are inadequate security arrangements
- there is no key worker system and good relationships are not formed between staff and residents.

Active knowledge

Look at your workplace. Do any of the above points apply? If any of these are the case in your workplace, you need to be aware that people can be put under so much stress that they behave abusively. Remember that abuse is not just about physical cruelty. If none of these things happen in your workplace, then try to imagine what work would be like if they did. Sit down with a colleague, if you can, and discuss what you think the effects of any two of the items in the list would be. If you cannot do this with a colleague, you can do it on your own by making a list.

If you want to be effective in helping to stop abuse you will need to:

- believe that abuse happens
- recognise abusive behaviour
- be aware of when abuse can happen
- understand who abusers can be
- know the policies and procedures for handling abuse
- follow the individual's plan of care
- recognise likely abusive situations
- report any concerns or suspicions.

Your most important contribution will be to be *alert*. For example, an individual's plan of care or your organisational policy should specify ways in which the individual's whereabouts are constantly monitored – and if you are alert to where a vulnerable person is, and who he or she is with, you can do much to help avoid abusive situations.

Remember

Either in a care setting or in an individual's own home, it is important to establish that callers are genuinely entitled to see the individual. Any doubts about rights of access should be cleared up immediately.

There are many factors involved in building protection against abuse

How to report and record information

Information about abuse you suspect, or situations you are working with which are 'high risk', must be recorded after being reported to your supervisor. Your supervisor will be responsible for passing on the information, if necessary.

Sometimes your information may need to be included in a client's plan of care or personal records, particularly if you have noticed a change in the way he or she is cared for, or if his/her behaviour could be an 'early warning' that the care team need to be especially observant. Your workplace may have a special report form for

> P. was visited by her son this afternoon. She was very quiet over tea, did not join in conversation or joke with anyone. Just said she was tired when asked what was wrong. Went to her room without going into lounge for the 'seconds evening'. Said she thought the clothes were too expensive and she couldn't afford them. Unusual for her. Similar to incident about a month ago when she said she couldn't afford the hairdresser - again after a visit from her son.
>
> Needs to be watched. Is he getting money from her? For discussion at planning meeting.

An example of a written report on possible abuse

recording 'causes for concern'. If not, you should write your report, making sure you include the following:

- what happened to make you concerned
- who you are concerned about
- whether this links to anything you have noticed previously
- what needs to happen next.

Discuss your report and your concerns with your supervisor and colleagues.

You must report anything unusual that you notice, even if you think it is too small to be important. It is the small details which make the whole picture. Sometimes, your observations may add to other small things noticed by members of the team, and a picture may start to emerge. Teamwork and good communication are vitally important.

Case study

One family support worker had a nickname – he was known as 'Cecil', short for Cecil B. de Mille the film director. Cecil was known for regularly phoning the schools, social workers and GP surgeries of the families he visited every time there was any event, incident or change with the families he visited. Cecil always started his conversation with 'I'm just keeping you in the picture' hence the nickname! However, with the G family, it was thanks to being 'kept in the picture' by Cecil that the social worker was made aware of the mother's new boyfriend. When his details were checked out, it was discovered that he had lived with another family where the children were on the Child Protection register. When this information was put together with the teacher noticing that one of the children had become much quieter recently, alarm bells began to ring and the children were carefully monitored, both at home and school.

1 What was Cecil doing which was important?
2 What might have happened if the information had not been passed on?
3 Why was Cecil in a good position to keep everyone informed?

Keeping professional carers informed of possible abuse is important

Did you know?

If you were to take one piece from a jigsaw puzzle, it would be very difficult to guess from it what the complete picture is – if not impossible. It would be easy to guess wrongly! You would need quite a few pieces before you could begin to draw a conclusion. The same applies to identifying the true picture in cases of abuse.

Remember

- Care environments are not just in residential homes and hospitals.
- Abuse is about far more than physical or sexual assault.
- Vulnerable adults and children can be abused by carers, other patients or service users or by organisations.
- Children are the only client group specifically protected by the law.
- You need to be alert to the situations where abuse can occur.
- You must share information.
- You must record information clearly and accurately.

Element Z1.2   Minimise the effects of abusive behaviour

WHAT YOU NEED TO LEARN

- Indications of abuse.
- How to respond to disclosure of abuse.
- How to deal with abusive behaviour.
- The effects of abuse on all those concerned.

Indications of abuse

This is not a comprehensive list of all the indicators of abuse. It is not possible to be exhaustive, neither does the existence of one of these signs mean that abuse has definitely occurred. Each is an *indicator,* which needs to be used alongside your other skills, such as observation and listening. It is a further piece of evidence – often the conclusive one – in building a complete picture.

Physical signs of abuse in children

- Bruising, or injuries which the child cannot explain.
- Bruises in the shape of objects – belt buckles, soles of shoes, etc.
- Handmarks.
- Bruises in lines.
- Injuries to the frenulum (the piece of skin below the tongue), or between the upper and lower lips and the gums.
- Black eyes.
- Bruising to ears.
- Burns, particularly small round burns which could have come from a cigarette.
- Burns or scalds to buttocks and backs of legs.
- Burns in lines, like the elements of an electric fire.

Emotional signs of abuse in children

- Sudden change in behaviour, becoming quiet and withdrawn.
- Change to overtly sexual behaviour, or an obsession with sexual comments.
- Problems sleeping or onset of nightmares.
- A sudden unwillingness to change clothes or participate in sports.

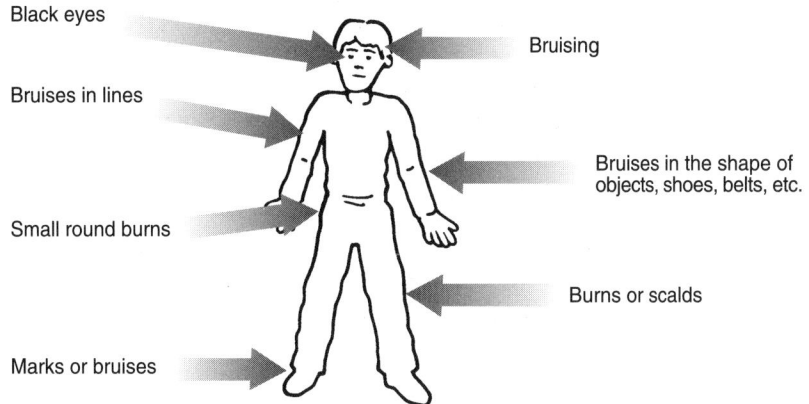

Physical signs of abuse in children

- Complaints of soreness or infections in the genital/anal area.
- Frequent complaints of abdominal pain.
- Deterioration of personal hygiene.
- Finding excuses not to go home.
- Appearing tense or frightened with a particular adult.

Physical signs of abuse in adults

- Series of unexplained falls or injuries.
- 'Pepperpot' bruising – a covering of small bruises, usually on the chest and caused by poking with a finger or tightening of clothing.
- Finger marks.
- Bruising in unusual areas, such as inside arms or thighs.
- Burns in unusual areas.
- Marks to wrists, arms or legs which could show use of physical restraint.
- Ulcers or bed sores, rashes caused by wet clothing.
- Unusual sexual behaviour.
- Recurrent genital infections.
- Blood or marks on underclothes.

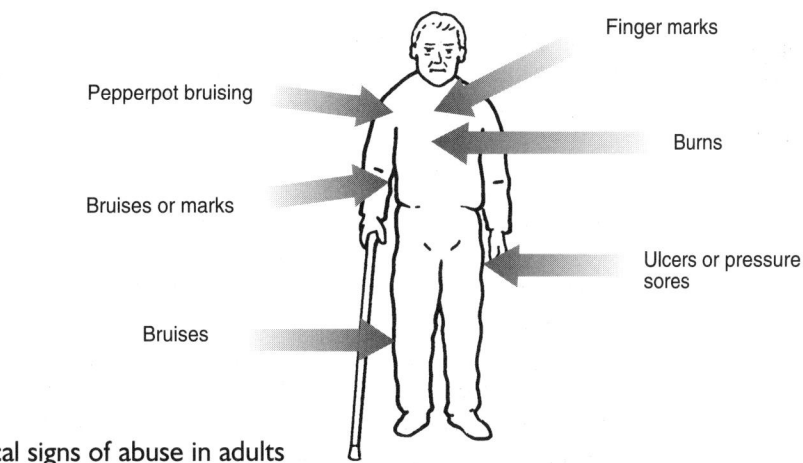

Physical signs of abuse in adults

Emotional signs of abuse in adults

- Changes in behaviour, becoming withdrawn or anxious.

- Unusually expressing feelings of hopelessness and depression.
- Change in eating pattern, loss/gain in weight.
- Sleep problems.
- Fear of making decisions or choices.
- Difficulty for care professionals to gain access to individual – be concerned if there is always a reason why the person cannot be seen.
- Sudden apparent change in financial circumstances.
- Disappearance of bank account records or pension books.
- Unusual level of interest by carer or others in finances and assets.
- Financial arrangement which the individual has not understood or has not willingly agreed to.
- Excessive requests for repeat prescriptions.
- Insistence by carer on being present at interviews.
- References to the dependent person in a derogatory way by the carer.

Active knowledge

Think of three clients you have worked with in the past month. Look carefully at the list of indications of abuse, and write down any which could apply to the clients you have selected. If there are none, that is fine. If you have noticed any signs, the first thing to do is to report this to your supervisor. Then go back to the previous element and look at the list of *circumstances* in which abuse is likely to occur. Do any of those fit? If so, you should also discuss this with your supervisor and develop a plan to monitor the situation.

How to respond to disclosure of abuse

If abuse is disclosed to you by someone you are caring for, you should deal with it in the same way whether it is a child or adult. First you must *listen* and *believe*. Make sure that you communicate, both by words and by body language, that you believe the person.

Did you know?

Being abused is terrible, and not being believed makes that abuse ten times worse. Don't be the second abuser – always *listen* and *believe*.

Do not ask any questions which could possibly be leading questions, for example 'and then did he hit you again?' The only questions you should ask should be to prompt the individual to continue his or her disclosure, such as 'and then what happened?'

You may well be asked to promise not to tell anyone – *never make that promise,* as it is not one you can keep. If you are asked 'If I tell you something, will you promise not to tell anyone?' you must always make it clear that you cannot make that promise. You must say something like, 'I can't say that until I know what you are going to tell me'.

Following disclosure, you must make it clear that you have to tell others about what you have been told, but you should also make it clear that the information is confidential within the group of people who need to know in order to protect. The answer to 'I don't want people to know' is to say something like 'The only people who will know are those who will make you safe'.

Remember

- People who disclose abuse do so because they want to be protected.
- They tell you because they want the abuse to stop.
- You are the first step to that protection.
- You have a responsibility to ensure that the information is passed on.

How to deal with abusive behaviour

Most of the time, your role in dealing with abuse will be the vital one of being aware of the possibility of abuse, reporting and recording any concerns you have, or reporting any disclosure made to you.

However, there may be occasions when you have to intervene in order to prevent an abusive situation developing. The abuse can be physical, verbal or behavioural. This is most likely to happen in a hospital, residential or day-care setting between patients or service users. If you work in the community, you could be in the situation of having to deal with abusive behaviour from a carer. If you do have to act directly to prevent abuse, you need to take the following steps:

- Always prevent a situation if you can. If you know, for example, that two people regularly disagree violently about everything from politics to whether or not it is raining, try to arrange that they are involved in separate activities and, if possible, have seats in separate lounges! Alternatively, you may decide to deal with the situation by talking to them both, and offering to help them to try to resolve their disagreements.
- Deal with abusive behaviour in the same way as aggression – be calm and be clear. Do not get drawn into an argument and do not become aggressive, but make it very clear that abusive behaviour will not be tolerated.
- You should only intervene directly if there is an immediate risk. You will need to use your communication skills to ensure that you handle the situation in a way that does not make things worse and will ensure that you protect the person at risk.
- If there is not an immediate risk, you should report the incident and get assistance as soon as possible.
- If you do have to intervene in an abusive situation, you will need to behave assertively. Do not shout, panic or get into an argument. State firmly and clearly what you want to happen – 'Mary, stop hitting Enid now!' You can deal with the consequences a little later, but the key action is to stop the abuse – 'Lee, stop calling Mike those names and move away from him now!' There must be no mistake about what has to happen. This is not the time to discuss it, this is the time to stop it – the discussion comes later.
- If you have witnessed, or intervened in, an act of abuse which may constitute a criminal offence, you must *not* remove any possible evidence until the police have examined the scene.

Rules for dealing with
abusive behaviour
1 Avoid it if possible.
2 Try to get people talking.
3 Keep calm. Be clear.
4 Be assertive, never
aggressive.

Active knowledge

Think of a situation where you have had to act to stop abuse or likely abuse. Make a note of how you handled it. Could you have dealt with it in a better way? What else could you have done? Would it have turned out differently? If you have never had to act in such a situation, ask an experienced colleague to tell you about an incident he or she has had to deal with.

Then answer the same questions, based on what your colleague has told you. Remember – your colleague may not want to hear the answers you come up with!

Once the immediate risk has been averted, you must then report the incident to your manager, and the correct procedures for dealing with abuse must be followed. You are not in a position to take a decision about what is and what is not serious enough to be followed up. That is a decision which will be taken after discussion between the agencies involved.

Where there are injuries, or the possibility of physical evidence, as in sexual abuse, then a medical examination must be carried out. If an adult has been abused, he or she must consent to an examination before one can be carried out. In the case of a child, the parents must consent, unless they are the suspected abusers.

Recording an incident

It is also important that you write a report of the incident as soon as possible. You may think that you will never forget what you saw or heard, but details do become blurred with time and repetition. Your workplace may have a special form or you may have to write a report. If there is a reason why writing a report is not possible, then you should record your evidence on audio tape. It is not acceptable practice to pass on the information verbally – there must be a record which can be referred to. Your evidence may be needed by the social workers who will investigate the situation. It may be useful for a doctor who will conduct an examination, or it may be needed for the case conference or for court proceedings.

Active knowledge

Think about the children's game of Chinese Whispers. The players sit in a circle and a message is whispered from one person to the next around the circle. The last player speaks the message aloud. It has usually changed quite a lot as it has been passed around the circle!

So it is easy to see how verbal information can become distorted, or messages lose their emphasis, as they are retold. Always make sure you record information as soon as you can.

When risk situations occur in the community, you may be in a position to intervene directly or to report to your supervisor and offer suggestions about ways to reduce risks.

No one can guarantee to prevent abuse from happening – human beings have always abused each other in one form or another. However, using the information you have about possible abusive situations, you are now able to work towards preventing abuse by recognising where it can happen.

Try to ensure that people in potentially abusive situations are offered as much support as possible. A carer, whether of a child or an adult, is less likely to resort to abuse if he or she feels supported, acknowledged and appreciated. Showing caring and understanding of a person's situation can often defuse potential explosions. A care worker could express this by saying, 'It must be so difficult caring for your mother. The demands she makes are so difficult. I think you are doing a wonderful job.' Such comments can often help a carer to feel that he or she does have someone who understands and has some interest in supporting him or her. So many times the focus is on the individual in need of care and the carer is ignored.

Did you know?

There is a saying that 'The best way to keep on caring *about* someone is not to have to care *for* them'. There are many thousands of carers looking after relatives who would testify to the truth of that saying.

Some situations require much more than words of support, and giving practical, physical support to a carer or family may help to reduce the risk of abuse. The extra support provided by a professional carer can do this in two ways: firstly, it can provide the additional help which allows the carer to feel that he or she is not in a hopeless never-ending situation; and secondly, it can provide a regular opportunity to check an individual where abuse is suspected or considered to be a major risk.

When resources are provided within the community rather than at home, this also offers a chance to observe someone who is thought to be at risk. Day centres, training centres, schools, after school clubs and youth centres also provide an opportunity for people to talk to staff and to feel that they are in a supportive environment where they can talk about any abuse they have suffered and they will be believed and helped.

Remember
- Preventing abuse is better than dealing with it.
- Support may make all the difference to a carer under stress.
- Only intervene directly if there is an immediate risk.
- Act assertively to stop any abusive behaviour.

The effects of abuse on all those concerned

Abuse devastates those who suffer it. It causes people to lose their self-esteem and their confidence. Many adults and children become withdrawn and difficult to communicate with. Anger is a common emotion amongst people who have been abused. It may be directed against the abuser, or at those people around them who failed to recognise the abuse and stop it happening.

One of the greatest tragedies is when people who have been abused turn their anger against themselves and blame themselves for everything which has happened to them. These are situations which require expert help, and this should be available to anyone who has been abused, regardless of the circumstances.

In an earlier section of this chapter you learned about the indications of abuse. Some of the behaviour changes which can be signs of abuse can be almost permanent, or certainly very long-lasting. There are very few survivors of abuse whose personality remains unchanged, and for those who do conquer the effects of abuse, it is a long, hard fight.

The abuser, often called the 'perpetrator', also requires expert help, and this should be available through various agencies depending on the type and seriousness of the abuse. People who abuse, whether their victims are children or vulnerable adults, receive very little sympathy or understanding from society. There is no public recognition that some abusers may have been under tremendous strain and pressure, and abusers may find that they have no support from friends or family. Many abusers will face the consequences of their actions alone.

Case study

J is now 18 years old and had been sexually abused by her father from the age of 8 years until she was 16. The abuse only stopped when she disclosed it to her teacher when her father began abusing her younger sister too. Her father was eventually imprisoned for the abuse, but the family never recovered and the girls and their two brothers went to live with an aunt. J has never spoken much about the abuse and its effect on her, she has always found it hard to relate to others, and does not have any friends with whom she socialises. She has her hair cropped, will only wear jeans and shirts or high neck jumpers, and has had several admissions to psychiatric hospital following episodes of self-harm, usually involving cutting her arms. J is receiving therapy and her therapist is encouraging her to go to a survivors group. She is considering this but is reluctant because she feels that the others will not like her and she will not make friends.

Did you know?

Prisoners who are serving sentences for child abuse, or for abuse of vulnerable adults, have to be kept in separate areas of the prison for their own safety. If they were allowed to mix with other prisoners, they could be seriously assaulted or even killed.

Care workers who have to deal with abusive situations react in different ways. There is no 'right way' to react. Everyone is different and will deal with things in his or her own way. If you have to deal with abuse, these are some of the ways you may feel, and some steps you can take which may help.

- You may feel quite traumatised by the abusive incident. It is quite normal to find that you cannot get the incident off your mind, that you have difficulty concentrating on other things, or that you keep having 'flashbacks' and re-enact the situation in your head. You may also feel that you need to keep talking about what happened.
- Talking can be very beneficial, but if you are discussing an incident outside your workplace, you must remember rules of confidentiality and *never* use names. You will find that you can talk about the circumstances just as well by referring to 'the boy' or 'the father' or 'the daughter'. This way of talking does become second nature, and is useful because it allows you to tell others about things which have happened at work whilst maintaining confidentiality.
- These feelings are likely to last for a fairly short time, and are a natural reaction to shock and trauma. If at any time you feel that you are having difficulty, you must talk to your manager or supervisor, who should be able to help.
- Alternatively, the situation may have made you feel very angry, and you may have an overwhelming urge to inflict some serious damage on the perpetrator of the abuse. Whilst this is understandable, it is not professional and you will have to find other ways of dealing with your anger. Again, your supervisor or manager should help you to work through your feelings.
- Everyone has different ways of dealing with anger, such as taking physical exercise, doing housework, punching a cushion, writing feelings down and then tearing the paper up, crying or telling your best friend. Whatever you do with your anger in ordinary situations, you should do the same in this situation (just remember to respect confidentiality if you need to tell your best friend – miss out the names). It is perfectly legitimate to be angry, but you cannot bring this anger into the professional relationship.
- The situation may have made you distressed, and you may want to go home and have a good cry, or give your own children or elderly relatives an extra hug. This is a perfectly normal reaction. No matter how many years you work, or how many times it happens, you may still feel the same way.
- Some workplaces will have arrangements in place where workers are able to share difficult situations and get support from each other. Others may not have any formal meetings or groups arranged, but colleagues will offer each other support and advice in an informal way. You may find that work colleagues who have had similar experiences are the best people with whom to share this type of experience.
- There is, of course, the possibility that the situation may have brought back many painful memories for you of abuse you have suffered in your own past. This is often the most difficult situation to deal with, because you may feel as if you should be able to help because you know how it feels, but your own experience has left you

without any room to deal with the feelings of others. There are many avenues of support now available to survivors of abuse. You can find out about the nearest support confidentially, if you do not want your workplace colleagues or supervisor to know.

- There is no doubt that dealing with abuse is one of the most stressful aspects of working in care. There is nothing odd or abnormal about feeling that you need to share what you have experienced and looking for support from others. This is a perfectly reasonable reaction and, in fact, most experienced managers would be far more concerned about a worker involved in dealing with abuse who appears quite unaffected by it, than about one who comes looking for guidance and reassurance.

Remember

- Feeling upset is normal.
- Talk about the incident if that helps.
- Being angry is OK, but deal with it sensibly – take physical exercise, do the housework, cry.
- Do not be unprofessional with the abuser.
- If you are a survivor of abuse and you find it hard to deal with, ask for help.

Element Z1.3 Contribute to monitoring individuals who are at risk from abuse

WHAT YOU NEED TO LEARN

- How to share information.
- Ways of assessing risk.
- What to do if you suspect abuse in your own workplace.

How to share information

Sharing information between different agencies and organisations can often be a vital way of ensuring that people at risk are protected.

There are often several care and other professionals involved with any child or adult considered to be at risk. One of the most important features of work with people at risk is co-operation between agencies.

Teamwork is vital, both with other involved professional care workers and within your own team. Information is always clearer and more comprehensive when it is shared, and you may find that different members of the team have observed slightly different aspects and so the picture will become more complete.

It may also be possible that people will have different views on any allegations or incidents which have taken place. It is important that all these views are taken into account. Some of the professionals involved may be working with the person alleged to be the abuser and they may have a different perspective to add to any discussions. Remember that there is always more than one story to be told, even though it may not always be easy to take account of the alleged abuser's perspective.

Did you know?

Every report (called Fatal Case Inquiry) into child deaths from abuse in the past twenty-five years has highlighted the need for agencies to co-operate, work together and share information.

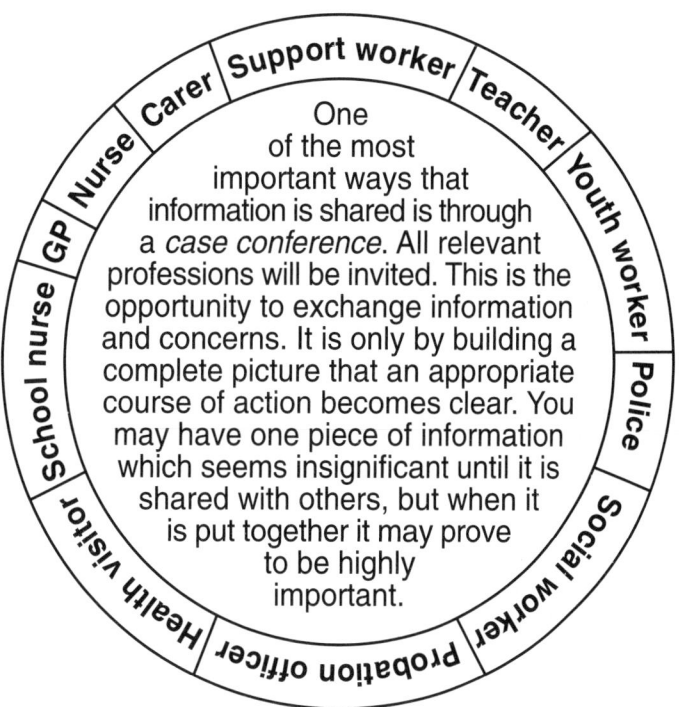

One of the most important ways that information is shared is through a *case conference*. All relevant professions will be invited. This is the opportunity to exchange information and concerns. It is only by building a complete picture that an appropriate course of action becomes clear. You may have one piece of information which seems insignificant until it is shared with others, but when it is put together it may prove to be highly important.

Sharing information

Each local area has an Area Child Protection Committee (ACPC), which includes representatives of all relevant professionals: social workers, health professionals, teachers, police, and so on. The ACPC meets to lay down procedures which must be followed where child abuse is suspected or confirmed. It also ensures that a register of children who have been abused, or are at risk of abuse, is maintained by the social services department.

The Child Protection Register is a record of all the children about whom there are concerns. The register is held and maintained by social services, but the information can be shared with other relevant professionals. There are four main categories in the register: physical abuse, sexual abuse, neglect and emotional abuse.

There is no similar register for adults considered to be at risk.

Did you know?

Anyone, including a child, who has been abused by someone who has been tried in court and found guilty, can receive Criminal Injuries compensation. It is also possible for cases to be brought even where there is no criminal trial. It is vital that anyone who has been abused in any way should have a solicitor to act in his or her interests.

Ways of assessing risk

Decisions about abuse of adults are different from those about children because, ultimately, it is the adult him or herself who will make the decision about how to proceed. Clearly there are some situations where this is not possible, but such circumstances are provided for under the law. If an adult has been abused, but he or she decides to remain in the abusive situation, then there are generally no legal steps which can be taken to prevent that.

Case study

Mrs C is 75 years old. She is quite fit, although increasingly her arthritis is slowing her down and making her less steady on her feet. She has been a widow for fifteen years and lives with her only son, R, who is 51. When R was 29, he was involved in a motorcycle accident which caused brain damage, from which he has never fully recovered. His speech is slow and he sometimes has problems in communication. His co-ordination and fine motor skills have been affected, so he has problems with buttons, shoelaces and writing. R also suffers from major mood swings and can be aggressive. Mrs C is R's only carer. He has never worked since the accident, but he goes to a day centre three days each week. Mrs C takes the opportunity to go to a day centre herself on those three days because she enjoys the company, the outings and activities.

Recently, Mrs C has had an increasing number of injuries. In the past two months she has had a grazed forehead, a black eye, a split lip and last week she arrived at the day centre with a bruised and sprained wrist. She finally admitted to the centre staff that R had inflicted the injuries during his periods of bad temper. She said that these were becoming more frequent as he became more frustrated with her slowness.

Despite being very distressed, Mrs C would not agree to being separated from R. She was adamant that he didn't mean to hurt her. She would not consider making a complaint to the police. Finally, Mrs C agreed to increasing both her and R's attendance at their day centres, and to having some assistance with daily living.

1 What do you think Mrs C should have done?
2 Can she be left with R?
3 Why do you think Mrs C will not take any action against R?

workers, but there are limits on the legal powers to intervene and there is no justification for removing Mrs C's right to make her own decisions.

Care workers faced with an abusive situation which cannot be resolved must assess the risks and work out ways of minimising the likelihood of further abuse. A 'risk assessment' will be carried out. Your workplace will have procedures about the way in which a risk assessment is carried out and how decisions are made. Many workplaces will have a system where decisions about level of risk are taken by a case conference. In others, decisions may be made by a team manager, who would need to be in possession of all the available facts. At no time would any worker be expected to make such judgements and decisions alone, or to accept full responsibility for this type of assessment.

Did you know?

This type of shared responsibility and decision-making has only developed over the past twenty years or so in the case of children, and far more recently in the case of adults. Prior to that, workers were often left to make decisions without any support, and took the full weight of blame if things went wrong.

A risk assessment will consider all the elements in a situation and try to reach a judgement about potential dangers and what can be done. Clearly, the options are far more limited in respect of adults, because there is no overall legislation offering protection. It is also very rarely possible to act against the will of an adult, even where it may be in his or her best interests.

What to do if you suspect abuse in your own workplace

Blowing the whistle

One of the most difficult situations to deal with is when you believe that abuse is happening in your workplace. It is often hard to accept that the people you work with would abuse, but if you have evidence or good grounds for concern, then you will have to take action.

- The first step is to report the abuse to your manager.
- If you suspect that your manager is involved, or will not take action, you must refer it to the most senior manager who is likely to be impartial.
- If you do not believe that it is possible to report the abuse to anyone within your workplace, you should contact social services (or the NSPCC, if you prefer, for children).
- If you work for the NSPCC, social services or the health service and you are concerned about abuse, you should still follow the same steps, although you may need to contact a senior manager who is not directly involved with your workplace.
- There are organisations which provide helplines offering support and advice to workers concerned about abuse. You may find that a good starting point.
- You could also contact your trade union if you belong to one.

Remember

- Consider all possibilities when there are any suspicions about the care of a vulnerable person.
- Abuse may be the last thing you would expect in a particular situation.
- Think the unthinkable – *listen* and *believe*.
- That does not just mean listening to what you are told: *listen* to what you see and *believe* what you feel.

Keys to good practice

- Always listen and believe those who tell you they have been abused.
- Be prepared to accept the possibility of abuse where you don't expect it.
- Know the procedures and follow them strictly.
- Never underestimate the importance of sharing information.
- Protecting the vulnerable is your first priority.
- Never allow abusive behaviour to go unchallenged.
- Remember that people who disclose abuse want it to stop.
- You could make the difference – always be aware of the possibility of abuse.
- Do not try to deal with abuse alone.
- Use the support available for those who work with abusive situations.

The last word

Much of this unit may sound as though the field of dealing with abuse is full of rules and procedures. It is – and for very good reasons. Abuse is very serious – it is potentially life-threatening. Systems and rules have been developed by learning from the tragedies that have happened in the past. Many of these tragedies occurred because procedures were either not in place, or were not followed. You must make sure that you know what the procedure is in your workplace and follow it to the letter.

Unit test

1 Abuse can happen when people are being cared for. Name the circumstances which make this more likely.
2 Look back to the case study on page 130. Write a report on this situation, making sure you include the main information points.
3 Make a list of the people in your workplace with whom you would need to share information. Say why each of them is on your list.
4 Make notes about the way you would behave if someone told you he or she had been abused.
5 If you consider an abusive incident to be minor and unimportant, what should you do?
6 What effects might abuse have on a child?
7 What reactions would you expect to see in a care worker who had dealt with an abusive situation?
8 What should you do if you suspect abuse in your workplace?
9 Are there different factors to consider when dealing with abuse of adults or children? If so, what are they?
10 What are the two key things to do when someone discloses that he or she has been abused?

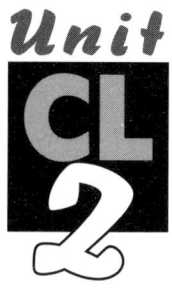

Promote communication with individuals where there are communication differences

Communicating in normal circumstances is dealt with in Unit CL1. This unit deals with communication where there are differences between the worker and an individual which can cause problems.

It is important that you, as a health or care worker, understand how to communicate with people even though the differences may make that quite difficult. Communication is not just about talking to people when it is easy, it is also about managing to make contact with those people for whom it is much harder.

There are many ways in which you can help to make communication more effective, not just by talking, but by the actions that you take in making the environment better for communication or by making sure that communication is handled appropriately for the particular individual and that proper records are kept on the best way of communicating with each individual for whom you provide care.

The way you communicate with people in your care can help them be more independent

Determine the nature and scope of communication differences

WHAT YOU NEED TO LEARN

- What communication differences are and their effects.
- How to find out about likely communication problems.
- How to record information.

What communication differences are and their effects

Communication differences

Communication differences include:

- people speaking different languages
- either the worker or the individual having a sensory impairment
- distress, where somebody is so upset that he or she is unable to communicate
- a physical illness or disability, such as a stroke or confusion
- cultural differences.

Language

Where an individual speaks a different language from those who are providing care, it can be an isolating and frustrating experience. The individual may become distressed and frightened as it is very difficult to establish exactly what is happening and he or she is not in a position to ask or to have any questions answered. The person will feel excluded from anything happening in the care setting and will find making relationships with carers extremely difficult. There is the possibility that confusion and misunderstanding will occur.

Hearing loss

A loss or reduction of ability to hear clearly can cause major differences in the ability to communicate.

Communication is a two-way process, and it is very difficult for somebody who does not hear sounds at all or hears them in a blurred and indistinct way to be able to respond and to join in. The result can be that people become withdrawn and feel very isolated and excluded from others around them. This can lead to frustration and anger. People may present some quite challenging behaviour.

Profound deafness is not as common as partial hearing loss. People are most likely to suffer from loss of hearing of certain sounds at certain volumes or at certain pitches, such as high sounds or low sounds. It is also very common for people to find it difficult to hear if there is background noise – many sounds may jumble together, making it very hard to pick out the voice of one person. Hearing loss can also have an effect on speech, particularly for those who are profoundly deaf and are unable to hear their own voices as they speak. This can make communication doubly difficult.

Visual impairment

Visual impairment causes many communication difficulties. Not only is an individual unable to pick up the visual signals which are being given out by someone who is speaking, but, because he or she is unaware of these signals, the person may also fail to give appropriate signals in communication. This lack of non-verbal communication and lack of ability to receive and interpret non-verbal communication can lead to misunderstandings about somebody's attitudes and behaviour. It means that a person's communications can easily be misinterpreted, or it could be thought that he or she is behaving in a way that is not appropriate.

Physical disability

Depending on the disability, this can have various effects. People who have suffered strokes, for example, will often have communication difficulties, not only in forming words and speaking, but they often also suffer from dysphasia, which is the inability to understand and to express meaning through words. That is, they lose the ability to find the right words for something they want to say, or to understand the meanings of words said to them. This condition is very distressing for the individual and for those who are trying to communicate. Often this is coupled with a loss of movement and a difficulty in using facial muscles to form words.

In some cases, the communication difficulty is a symptom of a disability. For example, many people with cerebral palsy and motor neurone disease have difficulty in controlling the muscles that affect voice production, and so speaking in a way which can be readily understood becomes very difficult. Other disabilities may have no effect at all upon voice production or the thought processes that produce spoken words, but the lack of other body movements may mean that non-verbal communication may be difficult or not what you would expect.

Learning difficulties

These may, dependent upon their severity, cause differences in communication in terms of the level of understanding of the individual and his or her ability to respond appropriately to any form of communication. This will vary depending on the degree of learning disability of the individual, but broadly the effect of learning disabilities is to limit the ability of an individual to understand and process information given to him or her. It is also likely that individuals will have a short attention span, so this may mean that communications have to be repeated several times in an appropriate form.

Dementia/confusion

This difficult and distressing condition is most prevalent in older people and people who suffer from Alzheimer's disease. The confusion can result ultimately in the loss of the ability to communicate, but in the early stages it involves short-term memory loss to the extent of being unable to remember the essential parts of a conversation or a recent exchange. It can necessitate the constant repetition of any form of communication.

Cultural differences

People's communication differences can result from differences in culture and background. Culture is about more than language – it is about the way that people live, think and relate to each other. In some cultures, for example, children are not allowed to speak in the presence of certain adults. Other cultures do not allow women to speak to men they do not know.

Some people may have been brought up in a background or in a period of time when challenging authority by asking questions was not acceptable. Such people may find it very hard to ask questions of doctors or other health professionals and are unlikely to feel able to raise any queries about how their care or treatment should be carried out.

Remember

Communication differences can result as much from differences in attitude as they can from differences in language.

Active knowledge

Try renting a video in a language other than your own, or watch a subtitled film on TV, covering the lower half of the TV screen where the subtitles are. Try to make sense of what is shown in the film. Note how difficult it is to understand what is happening and how frustrating it is. Notice how quickly you lose interest and decide that you will not bother to watch any more. Imagine how that feels if you are ill or in need of care, and everyone around you is speaking in a language you do not understand.

General effects of communication differences

The most common effect of communication differences is for the person receiving care to feel frustrated and isolated. It is an important part of your job to do everything in your power to reduce the effect of communication differences and to try to lessen the feelings of isolation and frustration that people experience.

Case study

D is from a small town just outside Athens. He speaks little English. While in England on an exchange visit to a university, he has been involved in a road accident. As a result of the accident, he has spinal injuries and is likely to be in hospital for several weeks. His injuries mean that his movements are limited and he is restricted to lying flat. The other students in his group visited during the first two weeks of his hospitalisation, but they have now all returned to Greece. His family cannot afford to travel to England to visit him.

1 How do you think D is feeling?
2 What would you do as a first step to communicating?
3 If you were D's key worker, who else would you involve?
4 What effect could a lack of communication have on his overall condition?

How to find out about likely communication problems

You can discover likely communication problems by simply observing an individual. You can find out a great deal about how a person communicates and what the differences are between his or her way of communicating and your own.

Observation should be able to establish:

- which language is being used
- if the client experiences any hearing difficulties or visual impairment
- if there is any physical illness or disability
- if there are any learning difficulties.

Any of these factors could have a bearing on how well a person will be able to communicate with you, and what steps you may need to take to make things easier. Observation will give you some very good clues to start with, but there are other useful sources of information for establishing exactly what a particular individual needs to assist communication. You may consider:

- asking the individual where this is possible – he or she is likely to be your best source of information
- discussing with colleagues who have worked with the individual before and who are likely to have some background information and advice
- consulting other professionals who have worked with the individual and may have knowledge of means of communication which have been effective for them
- reading previous case notes or case histories
- finding out as much as you can about an individual's particular illness or disability, where you have been able to establish this – the most useful sources of information are likely to be the specialist agencies for the particular condition
- talking to family or friends. They are likely to have a great deal of information about what the differences in communication are for the individual. They will have developed ways of dealing with communication, possibly over a long period of time, and are likely to be a very useful source of advice and help.

How to record information

There would be little point in finding out about effective means of communication with someone and then not making an accurate record so that other people can also communicate with that person.

You should establish your employer's policy on where such information is to be recorded – it is likely to be in the client's case notes.

Be sure that you record:

- the nature of the communication differences
- how they show themselves
- ways which you have found to be effective in overcoming the differences.

Information recorded in notes may look like this:

Mr P has communication difficulties following his stroke. He is dysphasic, with left side haemaplaegia. Speech is slurred but possible to understand with care. Most effective approaches are:

a) allow maximum time for communication responses
b) modify delivery if necessary in order to allow understanding
c) speak slowly, with short sentences
d) physical reassurance (holding and stroking hand) seems to help while waiting for a response
e) can use flashcards on bad days (ensure they are placed on the right-hand side)

Keys to good practice

- Check what the differences in communication are.
- Remember they can be cultural as well as physical.
- Examine the effects of the communication differences for a particular individual.
- Use all possible sources to obtain information.

Element CL2.2 Contribute to effective communication where there are communication differences

- How to communicate appropriately.
- How to respond to communication and check understanding.

How to communicate appropriately

Overcoming language differences in communication

Where you are in the position of providing care for someone who speaks a different language from you, it is clear that you will need the services of an interpreter for any serious discussions or communication.

- Your work setting is likely to have a contact list of interpreters.
- Social services departments and the police have lists of interpreters.
- The embassy or consulate for the appropriate country will also have a list of qualified interpreters.

You should always use professional interpreters wherever possible. It may be very tempting to use other members of the family – very often children have excellent language skills – but it is inappropriate in most care settings. This is because:

- their English and their ability to interpret may not be at the same standard as a professional interpreter and misunderstandings can easily occur
- you may wish to discuss matters which are not appropriate to be discussed with children, or the individual may not want members of his or her family involved in very personal discussions about health or care issues.

It is unlikely that you would be able to have a full-time interpreter available throughout somebody's period of care, so it is necessary to consider alternatives for encouraging everyday communication.

Be prepared to learn words in the individual's language which will help communication. You could try to give the person some words in your language if he or she is willing and able to learn them.

There are other simple techniques that you may wish to try which can help basic levels of communication. For example, you could use flashcards and signals, similar to those which you would use for a person who has suffered a stroke. This gives the person the opportunity to show a flashcard to indicate his or her needs. You can also use them to find out what kind of assistance may be needed.

Some of the flashcards you may use

The suggestions shown above are not exhaustive and you will come up with many which are appropriate for the individual and for your particular care setting. They are a helpful way of assisting with simple communication and allowing people to express their immediate physical needs.

The most effective way of communication with a person who speaks a different language is through non-verbal communication. A smile and a friendly face are understood in all languages, as are a concerned facial expression and a warm and welcoming body position.

However, be careful about the use of gestures – gestures which are acceptable in one culture may not be acceptable in all. For example, an extended thumb in this culture would mean 'great, that's fine, OK', but in many cultures it is an extremely offensive gesture. If you are unsure which gestures are acceptable in another culture, make sure that you check before using any which may be misinterpreted.

Overcoming hearing difficulties in communication

- Ensure that any means of improving hearing which an individual uses, for example a hearing aid, is working properly and is fitted correctly, that the batteries are fresh and working, that it is clean and that it is doing its job properly in terms of improving the individual's hearing.
- Ensure that you are sitting in a good light, not too far away and that you speak clearly, but do not shout. Shouting simply distorts your face and makes it more difficult for a person with hearing loss to be able to read what you are saying.

Some people will lip read, while others will use a form of sign language for understanding. This may be BSL (British Sign Language) or MAKATON, which is a simplified form of sign language. They may rely on a combination of lip reading and gestures.

Remember

If you are able to learn even simple signing or the basic rules of straightforward spoken communication with people who have hearing loss, you will significantly improve the way in which they are able to relate to their care environment.

Other services which are extremely helpful to people who have hearing difficulties are telecommunication services, such as using a minicom or typetalk service. These allow a spoken conversation to be translated in written form using a form of typewriter, and the responses can be passed in the same way by an operator who will relay them to the hearing person. These services have provided a major advance in enabling people who are hard of hearing or profoundly deaf to use telephone equipment. For people who are less severely affected by hearing impairment there are facilities such as raising the volume on telephone receivers to allow them to hear conversations more clearly.

Did you know?

Although humans use language to communicate, most forms of life have some means of communication. Bees dance in a particular pattern to show each other where the nectar is; elephants communicate with sounds which are so low pitched that humans cannot hear them; monkeys and chimpanzees are thought to use body language to communicate.

Overcoming visual difficulties in communication

One of the commonest ways of assisting people who have visual problems is to provide them with glasses. You need to be sure that these are clean and that they are the correct prescription. You must make sure that people have their eyes tested every two years and that their prescription is regularly updated. A person whose eyesight and requirements for glasses have changed will obviously have difficulty in picking up many of the non-verbal signals which you will be giving out when you are communicating with him or her.

For people with more serious loss or impairment, you will need to take other steps to ensure that you minimise the differences that will exist in your styles of communication.

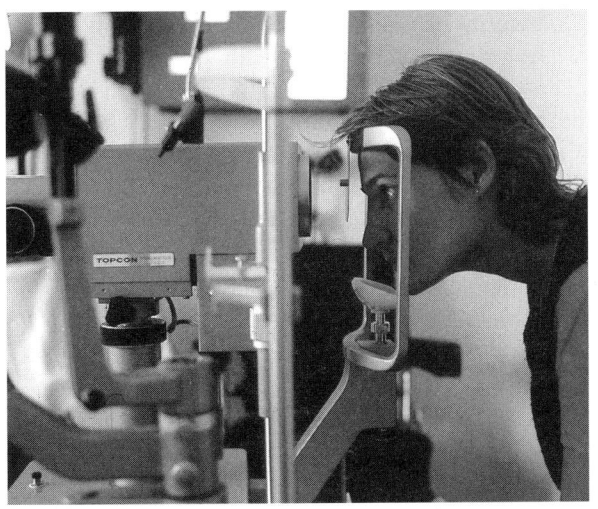

Everyone, and in particular your clients, should have regular eye tests (every two years) to make sure they can see well enough to live their lives as independently as possible

Keys to good practice

When communicating with people who have visual impairment:

- Do not suddenly begin to speak to someone without first of all letting him or her know that you are there by touching and saying hello.
- Make sure that you introduce yourself when you come in to a room. It is easy to forget that someone cannot see. A simple 'Hello John, it's Sue' is all that is needed so that you don't 'arrive' unexpectedly.
- You may need to use touch more than you would in speaking to a sighted person, because the concerns that you would normally be expressing through your face and your general body movements will not be seen. So, if you are expressing concern or sympathy, it may be appropriate to touch someone's hand or arm, at the same time that you are saying you are concerned and sympathetic.
- Ask the individual what system of communication he or she requires – do not impose your idea of appropriate systems on the person. Most people who are visually impaired know very well what they can and cannot do, and if you ask they will tell you exactly what they need you to do.
- Do not decide that you know the best way to help. Never take the arm of somebody who is visually impaired to help him or her to move around. Allow the person to take your arm, to ask for guidance and tell you where he or she wishes to go.

Overcoming physical learning disabilities in communication

Physical disability or illness has to be dealt with according to the nature of the disability or the illness. For example, if you were communicating with somebody who had a stroke you would have to work out ways of coping with his or her dysphasia. This is best dealt with by:

- using very simple, short sentences, speaking slowly and being prepared to wait while the individual processes what you have said and composes a reply

- using gestures – they are helpful in terms of making it easier for people to understand the idea that you are trying to get across
- using very simple, closed questions which only need a 'yes' or 'no' answer. Avoid long, complicated sentences with interrelated ideas. For example, do not say 'It's getting near tea time now, isn't it? How about some tea? Have you thought about what you would like?' Instead say, 'Are you hungry? Would you like fish? Would you like chicken?' and so on, until you have established what sort of meal the individual would prefer.

Other illnesses, such as motor neurone disease or cerebral palsy, can also lead to difficulties in speech, although not in comprehension.

- The individual will understand perfectly what you are saying to him or her but the difficulty will be in communicating with you.
- There is no need for you to speak slowly, although you will have to be prepared to allow time for a response owing to the difficulties that the individual will have in producing words.
- You will have to become familiar with the sound of the individual's voice and the way in which he or she communicates. It can be hard to understand people who have illnesses which affect their facial, throat or larynx muscles.

Many people with learning disabilities are able to communicate on a physical level more easily than on a verbal level

Overcoming learning disabilities in communication

Where people have learning disabilities, you will need to adjust your methods of communicating to take account of the level of disability that they experience. You should have gathered sufficient information about the individual to know the level of understanding that he or she has – and how simply and how often you need to explain things and the sorts of communication which are likely to be the most effective.

Many people with learning disabilities respond well to physical contact and are able to relate and communicate on a physical level more easily than on a verbal level. This will vary between individuals and you should be prepared to use a great deal of physical contact and hugs when communicating with people who have learning difficulties.

Overcoming cultural differences in communication

Communication is about much more than words being exchanged between two people – it is influenced by a great many things. The way in which people have been brought up and the society and culture that they live in has a great effect on the way in which they communicate.

For example, some cultures use gestures or touch much more than others. In some cultures it is acceptable to stand very close to someone, whereas in others people feel extremely uncomfortable if others stand too close. You need to find out about the person's background when you are thinking about how you can make communication work for him or her. To find out the information you need, you could:

- look in the person's records
- speak to a member of the family or a friend, if this is possible
- ask someone else from the same culture, either a colleague or through the country's cultural representatives (contacting their embassy or consulate and asking for the information) – alternatively you could try a local multicultural organisation
- use reference books, if necessary.

It is also important that you communicate with people at the correct intellectual level. Make sure that you communicate with them at a language level which they are likely to understand, but not find patronising. For example, older people and people who have disabilities have every right to be spoken to as adults and not patronised or talked down to. One of the commonest complaints from people with physical disabilities is that people will talk to their carers about them rather than talk to them directly – this is known as the 'does he take sugar' approach.

Never treat disabled people as if they are incapable of being talked to

Active knowledge

Find out the policy in your workplace for checking on people's cultural preferences. Ask who establishes the information about the cultural background of people who use your service, and what the policies are to ensure their needs are met.

Case study

A Russian teacher accompanied a group of students on a visit to England. All of the party were staying with host families and the teacher was placed with a woman of similar age (early forties) who was a single parent with a teenage son. Neither woman spoke any of the other's language.

On the first morning the organiser of the trip spoke to the host family on the telephone and asked how the two women had got on the previous evening. He was amazed to be told that, despite not speaking a word of each other's language, they had spent the evening sitting either side of the fire with a bottle of wine and that both knew each other's life stories. They had managed to tell each other of their marriages, divorces and problems with their children. They had laughed and cried together, and had achieved all of this by using family photographs, gestures and facial expressions, and by speaking in their own language had managed to communicate their entire life histories. The two women had ended the evening firm friends and this continued throughout the rest of the visit.

1 How do you think the women managed to communicate?
2 What methods of communication would you have used if you were in that situation?
3 Do you think it is significant that they were both middle-aged women with no disabilities? Why?
4 Can you think of a situation in your workplace which has any similarities to this?

How to respond to communication and check understanding

Although it is unacceptable to talk down to people, it is pointless trying to communicate with them by using so much jargon and medical terminology that they don't understand anything you have said. You must be sure that your communication is being understood. The most straightforward way to do this is to ask someone to recap on what you have discussed.

You could say something like: 'Can we just go over this so that we are both sure about what is happening – you tell me what is happening tomorrow', or you can rephrase what you have just said and check with the individual that he or she has understood. For example:

> 'The bus is coming earlier than usual tomorrow because of the trip. It will be here at eight o'clock instead of nine – is that OK?'
>
> 'Yes.'
>
> 'So, you're sure that you can be up and ready by eight o'clock to go on the trip?'

Communication through actions

For many people, it is easier to communicate by actions than by words. You will need to make sure that you respond in an appropriate way by recognising the significance of a touch or a sudden movement from somebody who is ill and bedridden, or a gesture from somebody who speaks a different language. A gesture can indicate what his or her needs are and what sort of response the person is looking for from you. You may be faced with a young person with challenging behaviour who throws something at you – this is a means of communication. It may not be a very pleasant one, but nonetheless, it expresses much of the person's hurt, anger and distress. It is important that you recognise this for what it is and respond in the same way you would if that person had been able to express his or her feelings in words.

Remember

If you are planning communication with somebody who has a sensory impairment or who has a learning disability, you will need to take account of this and adjust your communication so that it is at a level he or she is are able to understand and make sense of. The single most important factor in communicating is that you are understood.

Encouraging communication

The best way to ensure that somebody is able to communicate to the best of his or her ability is to make the person feel as comfortable and as relaxed as possible. There are several factors to consider when thinking about how to make people feel confident enough to communicate. They are summarised in the table below.

Ways of encouraging communication

Communication difference	Encouraging actions
Different language	<ul><li>Smile</li><li>Friendly facial expression</li><li>Gestures</li><li>Use pictures</li><li>Warmth and encouragement – repeat their words with a smile to check understanding</li></ul>
Hearing impairment	<ul><li>Speak clearly, listen carefully, respond to what is said to you</li><li>Remove any distractions and other noises</li><li>Make sure any aids to hearing are working</li><li>Use written communication where appropriate</li><li>Use signing where appropriate and understood</li><li>Use properly trained interpreter if high level of skill is required</li></ul>
Visual impairment	<ul><li>Use touch to communicate concern, sympathy and interest</li><li>Use tone of voice rather than facial expressions to communicate mood and response</li><li>Do not rely on non-verbal communication, e.g. facial expression or nodding head</li><li>Ensure that all visual communication is transferred into something which can be heard, either a tape or somebody reading</li></ul>
Confusion or dementia	<ul><li>Repeat information as often as necessary</li><li>Keep re-orientating the conversation if you need to</li><li>Remain patient</li><li>Be very clear and keep conversation short and simple</li><li>Use simple written communication or pictures where they seem to help</li></ul>
Physical disability	<ul><li>Ensure that surroundings are appropriate and accessible</li><li>Allow for difficulties with voice production if necessary</li><li>Do not patronise</li><li>Remember that some body language may not be appropriate</li></ul>

Communication difference	Encouraging actions
Learning difficulties	• Judge appropriate level of understanding • Make sure that you respond at the right level • Repeat things as often as necessary • Remain patient and be prepared to keep covering the same ground • Be prepared to wait and listen carefully to responses

If you can communicate using sign language, this will make a huge difference to the independence of those clients who need to communicate in this way

Active knowledge

Take some of the ideas from the table on pages 163–164 and discuss them with your supervisor. Ask him or her to give you other ideas and methods which have been found to be effective in your workplace.

Key to good practice

The single most important thing that you need to remember is that you must tailor your response to the individual not the condition.

Unit test

1 What would you expect to be the effects of partial hearing loss on someone's style of communication?

2 What sort of steps could you take to improve communication with someone following a stroke? List three.

3 What would you expect to be the cultural differences between an 80-year-old woman brought up in an industrial town and the 25-year-old son of an Indian consultant cardiac surgeon, who is working as a care assistant in the care home she lives in?

4 What is one of the most important ways of communicating with someone who speaks a different language?

5 An inability to communicate will not affect the rate of recovery or standard of physical care. True or false?

6 What factors would you take into account when judging the best way to communicate with somebody from a different country?

7 What common mistake is made in talking to older people?

8 What do you need to do to encourage somebody with visual impairment to feel confident about communicating?

9 What is the most important purpose of communication?

10 Collect information about different cultures and the gestures which are used in communication.

11 Imagine you have to devise methods of communicating with:
- a blind French teenage girl
- an older man from Pakistan who is hard of hearing.

a What would be the problems you would expect to face?

b What are the likely differences in their communication needs?

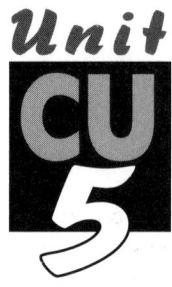

Unit CU5

Receive, transmit, store and retrieve information

Giving and receiving accurate information is vitally important for any care setting. The information could be about an individual who is being cared for in your workplace, a relative or friend, or it could be to do with the organisation itself, about or for somebody who works there, or for administrative purposes. The information could come to you in a range of ways:

- verbally, for example, in a conversation either face-to-face or on the telephone
- on paper, for example in a letter, a client's health record or instructions from a health professional
- electronically, by fax or on a computer.

Whatever the purpose of the information, it is important that you record it accurately. It is also important that you pass on any information correctly, in the right form and to the right person. Recording information is essential in health and care services, because the services that are provided are about *people* rather than objects, so it is vital that information is accurate, accessible and readable. The information that is held in health and care records can seriously affect people's lives. The methods storage and access to records are also important for the smooth and efficient running of the organisation that carries out the caring. Loss of files or records can cause serious delays in providing a service, can cause people to spend hours of time searching or could, in fact, have very serious consequences if services are provided or procedures carried out without proper records being available.

Element CU5.1 Receive and transmit information

WHAT YOU NEED TO LEARN

- Why the accuracy of information is important
- Ways of receiving and passing on information
- Restrictions on information giving
- Choosing the best way to pass on information

Why the accuracy of information is important

All kinds of different information will come into the place where you work. It could be messages for somebody who works there, information about appointments, information for somebody's records, dates of meetings, notices about outcomes of meetings or messages for a resident. The information could be minor or it could be very serious and important. However, it is not always possible to judge the importance of information unless you know all of the circumstances. You may consider a piece of information to be fairly trivial, but unless you know the reason why it is needed you are not in a position to make that decision, so you should pass on information as quickly as you can and make sure it is absolutely accurate. Look at these two examples:

- A message is received from the office supplies wholesaler saying that the computer printer cartridges will not be in until Friday. Failure to pass this on immediately could mean that a vital report for a case conference is written but cannot be printed, so verbal information will have to given at the conference. Lack of information means that a full picture is not available to everyone present, and particularly to those unable to attend. A wrong decision could be made.
- The meat supplier calls to say that the mince ordered for Thursday cannot be delivered until Friday afternoon. Failure to pass this message on could mean the planned menu for Thursday is not changed, so alternative meals have to be provided at very short notice. This could cause great difficulty in providing for some of the special diets and religious requirements, resulting in very disgruntled catering staff!

Check it out

Find out what kinds of information come into your workplace. Make a list of the different types of information under different headings, for example information about clients, information about the organisation, information about supplies, etc.

Keys to good practice

Don't try to judge for yourself whether a mesaage is important. Treat *all* messages as important and pass them on accurately and immediately to right person.

Ways of receiving and passing on information

Today within health and care there are many ways in which information is circulated between agencies, colleagues, other team members, individuals receiving care, carers, volunteers and so on. The growth of electronic communication has meant a considerable change in the way that people receive and send information, in comparison to only a few years ago where information sharing was limited to either face-to-face meetings, telephone calls or posted letters.

Telephone

One of the commonest means of communication is the telephone. It has advantages because it is instant, straightforward and is a relatively safe and accurate way of communicating and passing on information. However, there are some disadvantages to the telephone in that it can often be difficult to ensure that you have clearly understood what has been said, partly because there can be problems with telephone lines which cause crackling and technical difficulties. It is also possible to misinterpret somebody's meaning when you cannot pick up other signals from them, such as facial expression and body language. If you regularly take or place messages on the telephone, there are some very simple steps that you can take to ensure that you cut down the risk of getting a message wrong.

- Make sure that you check the name of the person who is calling. If necessary, ask the person to spell his or her name and be sure that you have it right. Repeat it to make sure. It is easy to mix up Thomas and Thompson, Williams and Wilkins, and so on. You may also need to take the person's address, and again it is worthwhile asking him or her to spell the details to ensure that you have written them correctly.

- Always ask for a return telephone number so that the person who receives the message can phone back if necessary. There is nothing more infuriating than receiving a message on which you have some queries and no means of contacting the person who has left it for you. You should read back the message itself to the person who is leaving it just to check that you have the correct information and that you have understood his or her meaning.

Incoming post

If it is part of your role to open and check any incoming post, you must make sure that you:

- open it as soon as it arrives
- follow your own workplace procedures for dealing with incoming mail – this is likely to involve stamping it with the date it is received
- pass it on to the appropriate person for it to be dealt with or filed. Check the next section for advice on how to deal with confidential information.

Faxed information

The steps for dealing with an incoming fax message are as follows.

- Take the fax from the machine.
- Read the cover sheet – this will tell you who the fax is for, who it is from (it should include a telephone and fax numbers) and how many pages there should be.
- Check how many pages there should be and make sure that they have all been received. If a fax has misprinted or has pages missing then you should contact the telephone number identified on the cover sheet and ask for the information to be sent again. If there is no telephone number, then send a fax immediately to the sending fax number asking them to resend the fax.
- Follow your organisation's procedure for dealing with incoming faxes. Make sure the fax is handed to the appropriate person as soon as possible.

Check in the next section for information about dealing with confidential information which comes in by fax.

E-mail

If you have access to e-mail in your workplace, there is likely to be a procedure within your agency for dealing with it. This will probably involve either printing out the e-mail or sending a message to a particular individual to alert him or her to check the e-mail box.

Outgoing mail

If you have to write information to send to another organisation, whether it is by letter or by fax, you should be sure that the contents of your letter are clear, cannot be misunderstood and are to the point. Do not write a rambling, long letter which obliges recipients to hunt for the information they need.

It is likely that, within most organisations, you will need to show any faxes or letters to your supervisor or manager before they leave the premises. This safeguard is in place in most workplaces for the good reason that information being sent on behalf of your employer must be accurate and appropriate. As your employer is the person ultimately responsible for any information sent out, he or she will want to have procedures in place to check this.

Restrictions on information giving

Computer-based information

If you hold any information on computer, whether it is about staff or people who are cared for in your workplace, it is governed by the Data Protection Act 1998. There are more details about this in Unit O2, page 30. The Act essentially protects all information which is held on computer about anybody. It restricts the purposes for which it can be used and it also gives people the right to know what is being held about them and to change any information that is incorrect. The information you hold about anybody on a computer record or database can only be used for the purpose for which it was collected. This means that, if the reason for getting the information was to provide care for someone, it cannot then be used as information for outside people, for example the police, the media, relatives or friends, who have not been authorised by the individual to have that information.

Remember

- Access to information held on a computer is restricted.
- The person the information is about has a right to see it, but noone else has that right.
- It can only be used for the purpose for which it was obtained, for example to provide care.

Personal records

The Access to Personal Files Act 1987 also allows people to see their health records or other records which are held about them from the date of the Act. It does not, however, allow for that information to be given to anyone else whom the individual has not authorised. This means that you have to be careful when you are being asked for information about somebody your organisation cares for, and be very sure that you are not contravening the law, or acting against the principles and guidelines on confidentiality of your own workplace.

See the section 'How to refuse to give information' on page 172.

Keys to good practice

The basic rule when you are asked for information is:

Do not give any information without seeking the consent of the individual concerned, unless you know that the caller has a right to have that information and a need to know it.

Written records

The confidentiality of written records is also extremely important. You will need to make sure that, when you receive information in a written form (perhaps intended for somebody's file or a letter concerning somebody you are caring for), the information is not left where it could be easily read by others.

Do not leave confidential letters or notes lying in a reception area, or on a desk where visitors or other staff members might see it. You should ensure that the information is filed, or handed to the person it is intended for, or that you follow your agency procedure for handling confidential information as it comes in to the organisation.

You may need to stamp information which is confidential with a 'Confidential' stamp so that people handle it correctly.

Do not leave confidential material lying around in public areas

Telephone

It may be that you will have a telephone request for information, or that you are involved in taking messages over the telephone which concern confidential matters.

- You must be very sure that you do not hand out confidential information over the telephone without first checking the identity of the caller.
- If necessary, ask for a telephone number and agree to ring the caller back. Just because somebody says that he or she is a social worker, or from a doctor's surgery, or from another care organisation, does not necessarily mean that is the case.
- You have a duty to check a person's identity and his or her rights to any information before you hand it out.
- A great deal of information about individuals which ought to be confidential is inadvertently handed out over the telephone to unauthorised people simply because they have claimed to work in a particular setting or claimed to have a right to the information.
- If you are unsure as to how much you should tell someone, take the telephone number and offer to call back, then check with your supervisor.

Faxes

Fax machines have presented a new type of problem in terms of confidentiality of information coming into any work setting. Many agencies and organisations will have a fax machine in a central point. This can often mean that incoming faxes are received in a very public area and can be left lying in the fax tray or can be read by anybody who happens to be standing in the office.

Check it out

Your organisation should have a policy for dealing with incoming faxes. It is important that you check what this policy is and discuss it with your supervisor. Ensure that you follow whatever guidelines are in place for maintaining confidentiality of faxed information.

Organisational information

Obviously, there is some information which callers may ask for which is generally available to the public, such as visiting times, directions to your place of work, and so on.

In most places of work this sort of information is readily available and given to anyone who asks. However, if you worked in a women's refuge, for example, then certainly the address or telephone number would not be given out to anyone who asked for it. So there are always considerations to take into account before passing on information, and you should always check if you are unsure.

Keys to good practice

- Always check before giving out any information concerning an individual.
- Never leave confidential information in a place where it can be seen.
- Make sure that confidential information is marked as such.

Did you know?

Many large organisations have systems of linked computers called networks. The information held in a network is protected by 'firewall' – this is the name given to a system which limits access to just those people authorised to use the network. *You need to be a 'firewall' for information about your clients.*

The dos and don'ts of dealing with information

Type of Information	Do	Don't
Telephone calls incoming	Check the identity of the caller	Give out any information unless you are sure who the caller is
Telephone calls outgoing	Make sure that you are passing on information which the caller is entitled to	Give out details that the individual has not agreed to
Written information	Check that it goes immediately to the person it is intended for	Leave written information lying around where it can be read by anyone
Faxed information	Check your organisation's procedure for dealing with faxed material. Collect it as soon as possible from any central fax point	Leave it in a fax tray where it could be read by unauthorised people
Sending faxed material	Ensure that is clearly marked 'Confidential' and has the name on it of the person to whom it should be given	Fax confidential material without clearly stating that it is confidential and it is only to be given to a named person If in doubt, do not use a fax to send confidential information

How to refuse to give information

It can be quite hard to refuse to give information to someone, especially if he or she is insistent. It is also hard if the person is known to you, perhaps as a relative or friend of a client. If you are placed in this position, try to remember some simple facts:

- The law is on your side.
- You must act in your client's interests, no matter how much you sympathise with the person asking for information.
- Be polite, but firm – never allow yourself to be bullied.
- If someone becomes rude or aggressive, do not argue – offer to arrange for him or her to speak to a more senior member of staff.
- Try saying something like 'I'm sorry, I'm afraid I can't give you that information. Only [name of client] can give permission for that information to be passed on.'

Choosing the best way to pass on information

Sometimes the method of communication is dictated by the circumstances. If the situation requires an immediate response, or you need to find essential information urgently, then you are unlikely to sit and write a long letter, walk down to the post office, put it in the post and wait until next week to get a reply! You are far more likely to pick up the telephone and see if you can contact the person that you need to speak to. Or you may choose to fax your request, or fax information in response to a telephone request from someone else. Both methods are fast, almost instant, and relatively reliable for getting information accurately from one place to another.

There may be other occasions when, on the grounds of confidentiality, something is sent through the post marked 'Strictly confidential' and only to be opened by the

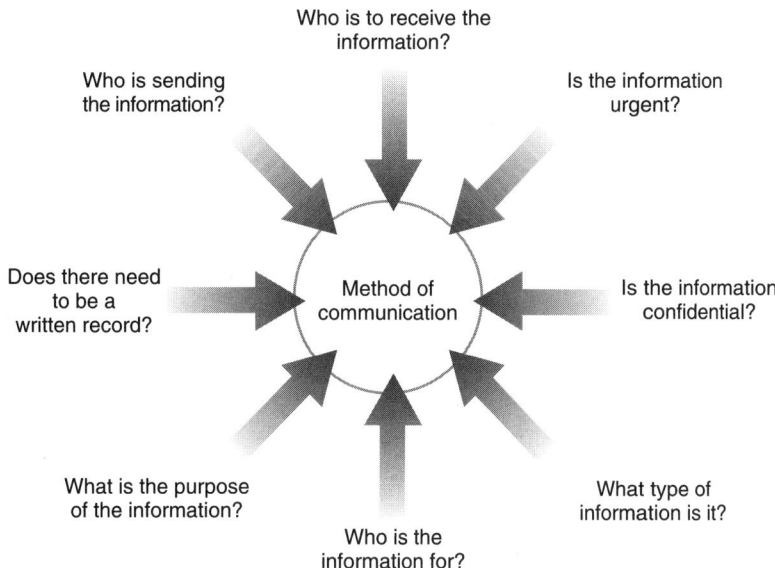

Factors to consider when choosing a method of communication

person whose name is on the envelope. This method may be entirely appropriate for information which is too confidential to be sent by fax and would be inappropriate in a telephone conversation.

You will have to take a number of factors into account when deciding which method to use, as the diagram above shows.

Types of information

The types of information you wish to convey can vary from the simplest day-to-day information to the most complicated and detailed information on somebody's history, background, diagnosis and prognosis.

Simple information

You may simply wish to communicate to a colleague that an individual you are caring for is probably not well enough to go out for a walk today. However, you have agreed with the colleague that you will go in with a cup of tea and see how she is feeling. You do not wish to shout the information in public, thus making the individual the object of general interest, and you have agreed with your colleague that you will check the situation and give her a nod or a shake of the head to let her know. This is a very simple example of the way that information can be sent from one person to another by physical signals, without the need for words.

Two-way exchange

The information that you have to share may be of a kind that requires a conversation with a colleague or relative or the individual him or herself. The advantage of a verbal exchange of information is that it can be two-way, and you can receive information at the same time as you are sharing what you know.

Written information

Other information is of a nature that requires it to be written down. This could include detailed records on someone, or information that may need to be shared with more than one person and may be for inclusion in a person's health or care records. In this case you would probably choose to write the information and send it by fax, by post or by e-mail.

Making a decision between these three means of communicating written information may be based on:

- availability of fax or e-mail
- the nature and level of confidentiality of the information.

The person receiving the information

One of the factors you must consider when choosing the best method of passing on information is the person who is going to receive it.

- Make sure that the method is appropriate for the person who will receive it.
- Do not send a letter to a person who is visually impaired unless you know he or she has a method of having it read.
- Do not attempt to pass on information by telephone to someone with hearing loss unless you are using an adapted telephone system.
- Use language which is at the right level for the person receiving it.

Case study

Mrs H was a long-term resident in a residential care home. She had been unwell for some time, and had been treated for a bad dose of flu. Her heart was failing and it was known that her death was a possibility. One morning, the staff went in to find that she had died in her sleep. The information was passed on to various people involved in the following ways.

To the GP:
'Hello, this is Redcroft. A patient of Dr Williams, Mrs H, has just died. Could we have someone out to certify, please? Dr Williams saw her only yesterday. He was expecting this.'

To the funeral director
'Hello, this is Redcroft. One of our residents, Sarah H, died this morning. Dr Williams from the health centre will be out to do the certificates. Can you call later this morning? Thank you.'

To the social worker:
'Hello, Gill, this is Sue from Redcroft. Just to let you know that Sarah H died this morning. I know you were fond of her, so I wanted to let you know straightaway. We went in to see her just before handover, and she had died. As you know from yesterday, it wasn't unexpected – I just wish one of us had been with her.'

To her niece:
'Hello, Mrs Johnson? This is Sue from Redcroft. I'm afraid I have some sad news about your aunt. She passed away a short while ago. It was very peaceful, she just slipped away in her sleep – she didn't suffer at all. I know you were expecting it, but it's still upsetting isn't it? As you asked, we've put all the arrangements in hand. You don't have to worry about anything, but there will be papers for you to sign later on if you feel up to calling in.'

1 Which different styles of giving the same information can you identify?
2 Why do you think all those people were spoken to in a different way?
3 How would the niece have felt if she had been spoken to like the doctor?
4 How would the doctor have felt if he had been spoken to like the niece?

Check it out

Keep a record for a week of the types of information that come into and go out of your workplace. Note the methods used for different types of information. Ask people why they have chosen to pass on information in a particular way.

Test yourself

1 Describe three different methods of sending and receiving information.
2 What would be an appropriate way of passing on the records of a case conference or case meeting?
3 What are the safeguards that need to be taken about faxed material?
4 What are the steps that you can take to maintain accuracy with telephone information?
5 In what sorts of situation would the verbal exchange of information be appropriate?

ement CU5.2 Store and retrieve records

WHAT YOU NEED TO LEARN

- The purpose of keeping records
- How to record information
- Methods of storing and retrieving records

The purpose of keeping records

In any organisation records are kept for a variety of different purposes. The type of record that you keep is likely to be dictated by the purpose for which it is required. It could be:

- information that is needed for making decisions
- information to provide background knowledge and understanding for another worker
- information about family and contacts of people who are important to an individual
- information to be passed to another professional who is also involved in providing a caring service
- information to be passed from yourself to a colleague over a short space of time to ensure that the care that you provide offers an element of continuity.

The kind of information that you may record to pass on within your own organisation may well be different from the types of record that you would keep if you were going to send that information to another agency or if it was going into somebody else's filing system.

> *Sally*
>
> **Mary Johnson**
>
> Please could you make sure that you check on Mrs Johnson several times during the next shift. Nothing I can put my finger on, nothing that could go on the handover record, but she just doesn't seem herself. Please keep an eye on her.
>
> See you tomorrow.
>
> *Sue*

An informal note like the one above is often used to pass on information which is not appropriate for a formal file or record sheet, but it is nevertheless important for a colleague to take note of. This is different from information which has to go outside the organisation – it would need to be formally written, and typed using a very structured format.

Medical records

One of the very common means of transmitting information and keeping records that you will come across in health and care is an observation chart recording temperature and blood pressure, like the one on page 177.

This is done in a very simple form on a graph so it is easy to see at a glance if there are any problems. The purpose of this record is simply to monitor a person's physical condition so that everybody who is caring for him or her is able to check on the person's well-being.

If you were to put a written record into someone's case notes or to write a report for another agency or another professional, it is unlikely that you would include the actual charts. It is far more likely that you would include a comment or an interpretation of the information on the charts similar to the one below.

> Mrs J has shown no significant abnormalities in terms of raised temperature or blood pressure for the past week. It would seem to indicate her infection has now cleared up and her temperature has returned to normal after the very high levels of ten days ago.

Other types of record

Information which is likely to be used in making decisions about someone is very important. It may concern a child or older person who has been the subject of a protection conference, or a young person who has been in trouble with the law and

An observation chart

A10b 94

is the subject of a report for the courts, or someone with mental health problems where a background report is being provided to assist in decisions about how to best treat him or her.

Where such records are being kept for the purpose of assisting with decision-making, it is important that reports are not written in such a way that people have to read through vast amounts of material before finding the key important points. It may be necessary to include a significant amount of information in order to make sure that all of the background is there, but a summary at the beginning or the end that covers the main points is always useful for a reader in a hurry.

Check it out

Find out how many different types of record are kept in your workplace. There may be reports, charts, notes, index cards… these are just a start. Check how many there are and note what each is used for.

How to record information

If you think about the purpose for which the information is to be used, this should help you to decide on the best way to record it. There would be little point in going to the trouble of typing out a piece of information that you were simply going to pass over to a colleague on the next shift. Alternatively, if you were writing something which was to go into somebody's case notes or case file and be permanently recorded, then you would need to make sure that the information is likely to be of use to colleagues, or others who may need to have access to the file.

Check it out

Find out if your organisation has a policy about record-keeping and about where different types of information should be recorded and kept. Check whether there are clear guidelines on what should be handwritten and information that needs to be typed or wordprocessed.

You must make sure that you follow the guidelines and provide information in the format that your organisation needs. If you are unsure about how you should produce particular kinds of records, ask your supervisor or manager.

Keys to good practice

There are certain golden rules which are likely to be included in any organisation's policy about keeping records and recording information:

- All information needs to be clear.
- It needs to be legible (particularly if you are handwriting it) – there is nothing more useless than a piece of information in a record file which cannot be read because somebody's handwriting is poor.
- It should be to the point, not ramble or contain far more words than necessary.
- Any record should cover the important points clearly and logically.

There is a great deal more information about how to record things effectively in Unit CL1.

Methods of storing and retrieving records

Imagine going into a record shop which has thousands of CDs stored in racks but in no recognisable order; they are not filed by the name of the artist, nor by the title of the album. Imagine how much time it would take to trace the particular album that you are looking for. Anything from REM to the Rolling Stones to Mantovani would be all jumbled together! This is exactly what it is like with a filing system – unless there is a system that is easily recognisable and allows people to trace files quickly and accurately, then it is impossible to use.

Records are stored in filing systems. These may be manual or computerised. All organisations will have a filing system, and one of the first jobs you must undertake is to learn how to use it.

Remember

Someone who uses an organisation's filing system incorrectly can soon cause chaos!

Some organisations have people who deal specifically with filing, and they do not allow untrained people to access the files. This is likely to be the case if you work for a large organisation, such as an NHS Trust. Smaller agencies are likely to have a general filing system which everybody in the organisation has access to and uses directly. This is exactly the kind of situation where files and records are likely to go missing and to be misplaced.

If you learn to appreciate the importance of records and the different systems that can be used for their storage, then you can assist rather than hinder the process of keeping records up-to-date in the right place and readily accessible when people need them.

Manual systems

In a manual filing system the types of file used can vary. The most usual type of life is a brown manila folder with a series of documents fastened inside. Other types include ring binders, lever arch files and bound copies of computer printouts.

All of the files have to be organised (indexed) and stored in a way which makes them easily accessible whenever they are required.

Alphabetical system

If there are not too many files, they can be kept in an alphabetical system in a simple filing cabinet or cupboard. In this sort of system, files are simply placed according to the surname of the person they are about. They are put in the same order as you would see names in a telephone directory, starting with A and working through to the end of the alphabet, with names beginning *Mc* being filed like *Mac* and *St* being filed as *Saint*.

GP's patient records are usually kept using an alphabetical system.

An alphabetical card index

Numerical systems

Where there are large numbers of files an alphabetical system would not work. Imagine the numbers of M. Johnsons or P. Williams who would appear as patients in a large hospital! In that situation an alphabetical filing system would become impossible to manage, so large organisations give their files numbers, and they are stored in number order. Clearly, a numerical system needs to have an index system so that a person's name can be attached to the appropriate number.

A hospital is likely to give a patient a number which will appear on all relevant documentation so that it is always possible to trace his or her medical notes. However, there still needs to be an overall record to attach that person's name and address to that particular set of case notes, and these days this is normally kept on a central computer.

Other indexing systems

It could be that, instead of files being organised alphabetically, they may be organised according to the different services an agency offers. For example, they could be kept under 'Mental health services', 'Care in the community services', 'Services for children' and so on. Within these categories files would be kept in alphabetical order. In a similar way, files may be organised under geographical areas.

Computerised systems

If your organisation uses a computerised system, there will be very clear procedures which must be followed by everybody who accesses the system. The procedures will vary depending on the system used, but usually involve accessing files through a special programme, which may well have been written either especially for your organisation, or is one which is specifically about record-keeping in health and care.

You are unlikely to be able to delete or alter any information which is in someone's file on a computer. It is possible that you will only be able to add information in very specific places, or it could be that files are 'read only' and you cannot add any information to them. This process, because it will not allow people to change or alter files, does have the advantage that information is likely to remain in a clear format. It is less likely to become lost or damaged in the way that manual files are. After all, it is really not possible to leave a computer system on a bus!

A computerised system enables organisations to keep a great deal more information in much less space. Although they are expensive initially to install and to set up, the advantages outweigh the disadvantages in the long run. It also means that everybody in the organisation has to learn how to operate the system and how to use the computer – this is a new skill for a great many people! It is, however, a skill worth learning if it enables you to record and use information more accurately and effectively.

Check it out

Find out about the filing system used in your workplace. Check how much information is kept in files, and how much on computer. Find out if the system is alphabetical or numerical, and ask someone who understands it to show you how to use it.

Other types of records

Other parts of the organisation will also need a filing system. It will be necessary to store information for the day-to-day running of the organisation, for personnel files, information about suppliers, accounts information, and so on. There could be a useful filing system of advice and information about support services and help in your local area.

All of this information needs to be available and is likely to be lost or forgotten if it is simply piled in a heap on a shelf or a window sill, or on the top of someone's filing cabinet.

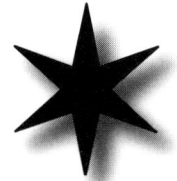

Remember

Filing systems can work extremely well if they are properly run. They work efficiently and effectively in most organisations as long as a few basic rules are followed by everyone who uses them (see the table below).

Some basic rules about filing

Do	Don't
Leave a note or card (or something similar) when you borrow a file.	Remove an index card from a system
Return files as soon as possible	Keep files lying around after you have finished with them
Enter information clearly and precisely	Alter or move around the contents of a file and don't take out or replace documents which are part of somebody's file

Unit test

1 Name the two main ways of storing information.

2 What are the main disadvantages of a manual filing system?

3 Name two different ways of indexing files in a manual system.

4 Name two advantages of a computerised filing system.

5 If you were passing information to a colleague on the next shift, would you:

   a type it?

   b handwrite it?

   c ask someone to pass on a message?

6 If you were providing some information for your supervisor who wanted to take it to a conference about one of your clients, would you:

   a handwrite it?

   b phone her and tell her about it?

   c type a report?

7 You have to tell six people that there has been a change in time for a meeting next week – a colleague from a similar workplace to yours, the client's social worker, the client's GP, an officer-in-charge from another care home, the client's mother who is very deaf and the client's friend who has poor literacy skills.

   a How you would contact each person?

   b How would you record your contacts?

   c Why would you record your contacts?

8 You receive a telephone call from someone who says she is your client's niece. She asks for details about her aunt's condition and well-being. You have never heard your client mention a niece, and to your knowledge she has never visited her aunt. How would you deal with this telephone call? Give reasons for your answer.

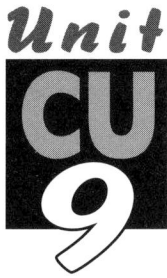

Unit CU9
Contribute to the development and effectiveness of work teams

Most of the work that is done in caring for others involves working as part of a team. You will either be working as part of a team within a residential establishment, within a hospital, or within a supported living environment, or you could be working as part of a more broadly based team if you support people in the community. In order for your clients to benefit from the best quality care that you can provide you need to work effectively as part of your team and a team needs to be clear about the service it is providing and the best way of organising to provide it.

This unit is designed to be generally applicable to anyone who works as part of a team but does not carry overall responsibility for the functioning of the team and is not in a management role.

Element CU9.1 Contribute to effective team practice

WHAT YOU NEED TO LEARN

- How to communicate constructively with other team members.
- How a team can work effectively.
- How to help resolve issues or difficulties that arise in the team.

How to communicate constructively

You will have developed good communication skills through your work in Units CL1 and CL2, but communicating well and working effectively in a team means that you need to develop those communication skills even further. Teams are essentially groups with a purpose and, as such, people communicate within teams in the same way as they do in groups. So you will need to use your group communication skills and to recognise the way your team is operating within those identified ways in which groups perform.

Teams and groups form for many different purposes. It could be to form:

- a family group
- a group of friends
- a support group
- a group with a common interest, such as a club
- an educational group.

Groups and teams form for many different purposes

The list of groups is large. The circumstances in which groups can form are almost endless. However, if a group has a specific aim, objective or range of aims and objectives which it is setting out to achieve, then that group becomes a team. For example, a group of friends who are a group because they all drink in a particular pub become a team when they enter the annual tug-of-war contest and attempt to win. This is the way a quiz team develops or a football team develops.

A team, however it is formed, is a group which shares the same aims and objectives

A team = a group with a purpose

In order to work well and effectively and communicate constructively in a team you need to understand how it operates. Two of the most important key things that you need to understand about a team are its **aims** and **objectives**.

The aims and objectives of a team can be:

- set by the organisation which employs the team
- decided by the members of the team
- focused on those who receive the service provided by the team.

Hopefully any of these aims and objectives will be shared by all those involved. Where they are different, serious problems can arise in the effectiveness and the working of the team.

A team is more likely to be effective if the members share the same aims and objectives

Active knowledge

Make three lists.

1 The aims and objectives of the organisation you work for. This should be contained in your organisation's mission statement or policy documents or possibly a public plan or charter that your organisation has developed.

2 Make a list of your own aims and objectives in your work. Although they may appear to be different from those of your organisation, they may include things like wanting to give the best possible service to people, wanting to be of use to the people you provide a service for, or possibly wanting to improve your skills and understanding of the area you work in. When you have completed this list you should check how well it fits with the aims and objectives of your organisation. Do not compare simply the words on the list but look at the overall effect of what it is you want to achieve and your organisation wants to achieve and see how far they match.

3 Ask the service users what they want from the service and what their aims are in terms of their own achievement and how they see the service that you provide can assist them.

When you have completed all three lists compare them and see to what extent they match in what they are setting out to achieve.

Communication in teams

If you work on the basis that a team is simply a group with a purpose, then you need to understand how groups operate. Some understanding of this will help you to see how communication works inside a team. There are many theories about communication in groups, the roles of individuals within groups and how people respond to group situations in very different ways. One of the major theories about groups and their formation and behaviour is that they go through certain stages of development in their lifetime.

These are:

Forming

Storming

Norming

Performing

Forming

The forming stage, as you might expect, is the early stage of the group. It occurs when a team has just begun to work together. New teams can be formed from scratch, out of reorganisation, or when team members have changed. You need to remember that a change in team members produces a new team, even though some members are still part of it. A different member makes a different team.

During the forming stage people are getting to know each other, getting to understand the way in which each other works and establishing what the team is about. It is during this stage that teams need to work out what their aims and objectives are and to make plans for the way in which they will work together. This is when the team plans work rotas and off duty periods, how the work is allocated and when individuals assume particular roles within the team. The roles within a team are not just those which are allocated by an employer. The employer may decide the job description and working tasks of the individuals in the team, however there are other roles which people will take up depending on their individual personality.

For example:

- There may be a *natural organiser*, who may take a lead role in planning and organising the team.
- There is likely to be someone who is a *peace maker*, who is always keen to settle disagreements and arrange for people to compromise.
- Someone else may take on the role being a *team jester*, keeping everyone amused and always seeing the funny side of things.
- Somebody else may be the *finisher*, who makes sure the group achieves the tasks it sets out to complete.
- The team may have a *bully*, somebody who is aggressive and challenges others constantly.
- There may be someone who is an *innovator*, who always thinks up new plans and new ideas and makes sure that the team stays up to date.

There are a wide range of different roles that people will assume in the team. If you take time to look at the way in which your team operates, you may be surprised to find that particular roles are not necessarily fulfilled by the people who hold the job titles for those roles.

Active knowledge

Think about the team you work in. If you work in a hospital or residential setting it is far easier to think about a work team. If you work in the community as a support worker where you spend much of your time working alone with clients, then your team may not be as close. However you should think about the colleagues with whom you have regular contact and the way in which that team is structured and how it operates. Make a list of the roles that people have assumed within your group. You can call them any names you wish (try not to use rude ones!). The names should describe the way in which they behave in the team. When your list is complete you should be able to see how each individual within your team assumes a particular role. Do this immediately following a team meeting when you have had a chance to observe people's behaviour in the meeting.

Storming

The second stage of the development of effective teams is the storming stage. This is when teams seem to do nothing but argue. This is because after the first stage the team members feel more confident with each other and each individual fights to establish what they believe to be the best way forward for the team. This is when you may see particular individuals engaging in what may seem to be a power struggle, where one or two people may be fighting to take control of the team. This can be a distressing and worrying stage for many people in the team as they feel that everything is going wrong and that every team meeting involves conflict and disagreement.

Arguing with one another is part of the storming stage of team development

Storming is part of the development of a strong and effective team and can be valuable in establishing the way in which the team will operate and in the forming of strong bonds and relationships between the members. However, it is important at the storming stage that debate, discussion and argument within the team does not become destructive. Whilst challenge and disagreement are a normal part of this stage, this should not degenerate into aggression, bullying, intimidation or an attempt to split and divide the team. If the team becomes aware of individuals who are becoming potentially destructive in their behaviour, then this should be openly challenged at a team meeting. Alternatively, the issues could be raised with a manager or whoever is responsible for running team meetings, who would be asked to raise the issues at meetings. Storming is a valuable and important stage of developing a strong team, however it is also the most potentially dangerous time, when a team can degenerate into cliques and factions who are each following their own aims and objectives. If it is used constructively to air issues and to plan a way forward in a robust and mature way then storming has achieved its purpose.

Norming

Norming is when the team begins to settle down and people firmly adopt the roles identified in the forming stage. The points at which these different stages occur will vary greatly, depending on the individuals in the team, the way it is structured, how often it meets and the way it is managed. The transaction from one stage to the next may almost be unnoticeable unless you are carefully charting the progress of your particular team. You are 'norming' as a team when you have stopped the storming stage and people have settled down and are working together, beginning to accept each others' roles, and becoming more tolerant of them. This can happen almost before you realise it and it may be only on reflection that you will recognise this stage of development.

This stage of team formation also establishes the rules for behaviour in the group and the general acceptance of the way people will behave towards each other and to the clients. The sets of rules that were considered at the forming stage and battled over at the storming stage have by the norming stage begun to settle down and be accepted as the 'normal' ways of behaving within that particular team. By the time the team is norming, the team members should be effectively working together. They should be able to openly share ideas, constructive criticism and suggestions at team meetings. Any unacceptable behaviour should be openly challenged and be established within the norms of group behaviour as unacceptable.

Performing

The ultimate aim of any team development is that after progressing through the first three stages, the team finally reaches the stage where it is delivering an effective service – that is, performing. This is the stage of team development which is the most satisfactory because the aims and objectives should be being achieved, people should be gaining satisfaction from their own roles in the team and the client group that you provide a service for should be feeling the benefits. If

The performing stage is when aims and objectives should be being achieved

there are no changes to team members then teams can reach the performing stage and remain there for a considerable period of time. There is no reason why a team which works well when it first begins to perform effectively should not continue to do so, provided all of the factors remain the same. But there are many things which influence a team's ability to continue to perform: change of team members, change of workplace or work practices, change in the level of resources available to the team. All these have the potential to affect the team's ability to perform. It is important to be aware of the changes that can be brought about by any of these factors and the way in which they can influence the behaviour of your team. If teams are aware of the changes and the way that this can affect their ability to deliver a service, then it is more likely that a well formed strong team will be able to discuss the effects of the changes and to plan for how they will meet them without an overall deterioration in performance.

How a team can work effectively

One important way to maintain good team performance is to keep the team motivated. Much research has been carried out on the **motivation** of people at work. Clearly, in industry and manufacturing the profitability of companies depends on the motivation of the employees. This has led to a considerable amount of work being done by industrial psychologists in examining the concept of motivating people at work.

Having a purpose and new challenges

The first stage in motivating any team, and maintaining that motivation, is to make sure that the team has a purpose and that it is one that meets each member's personal aims and objectives. This takes us back to the exercise on aims and objectives on page 185. In many ways this is the same as the concept of purpose. Every so often you should look at whether your role is continuing to provide you with the sort of purpose which meets your own wants, needs and aspirations. Sometimes when the team appears to be losing its motivation and people are becoming disheartened and demoralised it can help to set a smaller challenge – a purpose within a purpose in your own work setting. For example, your overall purpose, aim and motivation may be to provide a caring service for the young people with disabilities who are in the residential establishment you work for, or it may be to provide support, personal care and protection for the group of frail, confused, elderly residents that you care for. However, these broader aims alone may not be sufficient to maintain good team performance because they may not maintain people's

To be motivated, the team and each member of it must have a purpose

motivation. So your team may decide to undertake a new and specific task for the benefit of the client group you work with. This could take the form of developing a new type of service or developing further the skills and abilities of some of the team members. This approach helps to maintain motivation and also provides challenges, another key factor in maintaining a sense of purpose and providing a challenge. Research has shown that the teams which tend to be most effective are those which continually set themselves new challenges.

However, teams do not want to face challenges every day – many who work in caring services say that this is a sufficient challenge for anyone! But challenges are important as even the most difficult job can become hum drum eventually. As individual team members become more skilled and confident in their own area of work the challenge decreases, so it is important that the team recognises when this stage is being reached and that all members share and contribute in developing new ideas and innovative ways of working.

Camaraderie

One of the other keys to successful team performance is the way team members relate to each other. The camaraderie of team members and the support that they give each other are vital components in the continuous quality performance of a successful team. The ways in which team members relate to each other can often be the difference between a successful and an unsuccessful team. In all the best teams there is a genuine warmth, concern and caring between team members. They are loyal to each other and to the team and genuinely care about and like each other. Of course, it is not possible to like every individual with whom you come into contact, neither is it possible to work only with people who share your own interests, values and beliefs. However, applying all the principles you have learned about valuing individuals, recognising the effects on individuals of their background, culture and beliefs, will encourage the workings of a successful team if each member of the team is genuinely respected and valued.

Camaraderie is one of the keys to a successful team

Active knowledge

Make a list of members in your team and honestly make a note of those you like and those you dislike. This is unlikely to be straightforward, as there are always degrees in who you like or dislike, and other considerations. You will find that there are people who you consider to be perfectly pleasant but with whom you have nothing in common, and there will be others who you genuinely like and would be happy to form a personal friendship with. There may be others in the team you find extremely difficult to deal with and whose attitudes and beliefs you find unpleasant or totally opposed to yours. It is important that you are aware of these feelings and that you take time to consider what may be behind them and how you can approach them.

Responsibility

One of the other factors likely to maintain the motivation, and therefore the performance, of a team is responsibility. Responsibility for the outcome of the team's work is often a very important factor in motivating the team. If you have developed challenges and plans for your own team and are able to see and be responsible for the outcome of this, rather than have to hand over responsibility to another level in the management chain, then this is far more likely to provide the team members with the challenge and motivation necessary to maintain good team performance. For your team to be able to accept responsibility for its actions it will also need to have the authority to carry out the plans it has made. The team may need to approach management in order to gain this authority, and it may only be for specific events or plans that this is possible. However, the research evidence into effectively performing teams shows that those with both responsibility and the authority to carry out their plans and actions tend to maintain motivation over longer periods of time.

Responsibility, however, can be demotivating if the consequences of error or failure are too great. For example, if the organisation has a history of punishing mistakes then the giving of responsibility could be viewed as a negative factor in the performance of the team. The short-term performance may be good (fear is a motivator), but long-term motivation is likely to be difficult to sustain because it is hard for teams to maintain a good performance over a period of time when the major motivation is the fear of the consequences of failing to deliver.

Personal development

The other major influencing factor in helping teams to perform well is the development of the individual within the team and the team as a whole. When people feel that they are moving forward in their own personal career goals, learning new concepts, adding to their skill base and stretching their minds, motivation is likely to remain high. Personal growth enhances self-

Major factors that contribute to the good performance of teams esteem and self-worth, and a team member who is feeling self-confident and believes that their own personal goals are being achieved is likely to contribute effectively to the work of the team.

How to help resolve issues and difficulties

When you start considering your relationship with the individuals in your team you will need to work out how you will deal with any problem relationships. It's inevitable that some members in any team will not get on with each other. Bear in mind that a working relationship does not require the same commitment, sharing of ideals, values and understanding as a personal friendship. In order to work with someone it is sufficient that you recognise and value their contribution to the team performance and that you always communicate effectively and courteously when working with them. It is not necessary that you socialise with your work colleagues, although many team members do socialise with one another. However, this is not an essential requirement for a successful team. The loyalty and camaraderie which is built up amongst good team members can be purely based on their performance at work and does not involve their personal lives. It is not uncommon to hear the comment, 'I can't stand the women personally but you have to hand it to her she is brilliant at her job'. The important part of this statement is the valuing of people's contribution to the work of the team. This is an essential part of developing the loyalties which are the characteristics of effective teams.

Thinking positively checklist

If you have to work with people with whom you feel you have little in common try following the guidelines in this checklist in order to view them in a more positive light.

1 Tick off all the positive things and only the positive things about your colleague. For example:

- Do they have a nice smile? ☐
- Are they very good with the clients? ☐
- Do they have a particular skill in one area of practice? ☐
- Are they good in a crisis? ☐
- Are they willing to accommodate swaps in rotas? ☐
- Are they good at organising? ☐
- Do they make good coffee? ☐

2 Make a positive comment to your colleague at least once each day. This could range from 'Your hair looks nice today' to 'I have learned such a lot from watching you deal with Mrs.'

3 Ask questions about your colleague and try to find out more about them. This does not have to be on a personal level. Questions could be about their professional skills. You could try something like, 'Where did you learn to move patients so well?' Or take the trouble to find out their opinions on current issues. Perhaps you could ask, 'What do you think about the new set of proposals for the shift rotas?'

4 Pick up on any comments which may lead to areas of common interest. For example, your colleague may comment about something they have done over the weekend, or they may make a reference to reading something or seeing a film or a play that you know something about. You should follow up on any of these potential leads which may allow you to find out more about the individual.

5 Learn what you can about your colleague, either by listening to others or by asking questions about the person's background, and look at where their ideas and influences have come from. If you understand their culture, their beliefs and values it will be easier to see how and why they hold the opinions and views that they do.

6 Make a list of the positives that this particular colleague brings to the team.

Active knowledge

After looking at your list of team members and those who you like and dislike, it will be useful to set out an action plan of how you will tackle the issues raised by those team members that you find it more difficult to relate to. You may decide that you will concentrate on looking at the quality of their work and appreciating and valuing their contribution, or you may consider their personal circumstances and develop an understanding of why they may act as they do. If your team has reached the stage where you feel confident enough to openly share your concerns about the behaviour of another, then you should do so in a team meeting, provided that you can do this in a constructive way.

Be careful before you share views about somebody's personal behaviour that you are not making statements which can be hurtful and destructive. Make sure that any aspects of behaviour that you challenge is behaviour which genuinely affects the quality of the work or the functioning of the team. You do not have a right to challenge somebody's behaviour simply because you personally do not like it. You should only challenge behaviour which is damaging others or the work of the team.

Communication styles

So how can you contribute towards the self-confidence and success of your team?

Everything which you have learnt so far about the development of teams makes it clear that without good communication it is not possible to have an effective team. Each team member may have a different style of communication but it is important that all the team members are able to relate to each other, even if the style of communication is different. Some people communicate openly and are happy to share their feelings and concerns with others, but others may find it harder to discuss feelings and will need encouragement and support within the team to enable them to do that. The different styles of communication that you may see amongst team members could be:

- Open, sharing and clear.
- Secretive, unwilling to share information.

Individual style of communication can have an effect on the performance of the team

- Aggressive, dominating, wanting to override the views of others and to impose their own views on the workings of the team.

- No confidence, someone who finds it difficult to express any of their views, who is unassertive and although they may have ideas and suggestions which are valuable they are unable to share them with the team.

- Manipulative, someone who may try to control the team in a less obvious way than the aggressive person.

- Negative, someone who can only see the problems in every situation, who is never able to offer a constructive idea or suggestion but simply identifies the problems.

You will need to recognise the value of each different style of communication within your team and to appreciate that every team member, regardless of the way in which they communicate, will have something valuable to bring to team meetings. It will be important for the effectiveness of the team that your meetings and communications take account of the range of ways in which people function within the team. Also you need to make sure that information is shared in a way that each different member is able to use it best and that all members of the team are able to make a contribution in the way in which they feel comfortable. For example, if the team is discussing ideas for a new project or how a particular event will be organised and take place, then contributions should be asked for from team members in a way which is going to allow everyone to contribute.

If there are people in the team who tend to be unassertive and quiet in team meetings, then the request for ideas and contributions could be posted on the staff notice board some days before. Contributions and suggestions could be asked for in writing or at the meeting. This will give an unassertive team member the chance to make some notes which can then be circulated to other team members.

If there is a team member who tends to be dominant and take over group discussions, then this will have to be challenged if it is damaging the functioning of the team. Remember that not all teams are damaged by having a dominant member. It may suit the structure of some teams, and there may be team members who are happy to allow someone else to take that leading role and to make their own contribution to the work of the team in other ways. However, this is unusual and in most teams the attempted domination by an individual is unlikely to be welcome. Similarly, any aggressive behaviour in team meetings must be challenged.

In the work you did for Unit Z1 you learned about challenging inappropriate and unacceptable individual behaviour. However challenging this in a group situation can be far more threatening and more difficult to achieve. Conversely, if you are confident that you have the support of other team members it can be easier than making a challenge on a one-to-one basis, as you know that you will be supported by other members. Challenges to the behaviour of an individual in a team must be made in a constructive way. These are some ways to do it:

Team member	Response
Dominant team member	'Carol, you have some brilliant ideas for how we can run this event but it would be really helpful if you could give the rest of us a chance to comment on them and to see what we have got to add to your ideas.'
Aggressive/rude/bullying team member	'Jim, I don't think there is any need to be so aggressive to make your point. We all appreciate what you are saying, you don't need to shout.'
Unassertive – unwilling to contribute team member	'Leslie, could you explain to the rest of the team those ideas you were telling me about over coffee the other day.'
Manipulative team member	'Nancy, are you intending to make everyone feel guilty or hadn't you realised what you were doing?'

The Apollo syndrome

One of the greatest difficulties in team operation arises when there is more than one dominant individual or when teams are composed of a group of high-powered, often highly intelligent members. It is often assumed that if you form a team of real high flyers that they will achieve great things. This situation, known as the **Apollo syndrome**, is often not the case. In fact it is often the reverse and the teams with the highly intelligent, high-flying members often achieve far less than other teams.

Too many high-flyers in a team can make it impossible for the team to perform effectively

The Apollo syndrome was identified in 1981 by Dr Meredith Belbin, who has done a great deal of research into team development and team building. What he established in his identification of the Apollo syndrome was that teams formed of people with high mental ability showed the following characteristics:

- They spent excessive time in abortive or destructive debate trying to persuade other team members to adopt their own view and demonstrating a flair for spotting weaknesses in others' arguments.
- They had difficulties in decision making and the decisions they did reach lacked coherence.
- They tended to pursue their own interests without taking account what other members were doing, so effectively they worked as a group of individuals and not as a team.
- They are likely to be people or individuals who have an overly important view of their own role within a team.

This work has been extremely useful in helping to identify the sorts of problems which can arise within teams and helps to clarify the view that everybody working at the same time is not necessarily the same thing as everybody working together.

Case study

Tom, Jane, Rose and Natalia were all members of the support worker team at a small mental health hostel. Sue had just arrived as a new team member to fill a long-standing vacancy. Jane was the senior support worker and had been in the post for about four months. Tom, Rose and Natalia had all worked at the hostel since it opened six years previously.

The first staff meeting following Sue's appointment was to discuss new rotas and the staff development programme planned for the coming year. Jane announced the first item on the agenda, which was the new staff rotas. She began by briefly outlining the hours which they had now been asked to cover and the number of staff who would need to be available on sleep-in cover. At this point Tom said that he had organised the rotas and produced a chart showing when everybody would be working. He said that he had explored all the options and had discussed them with one of the senior managers. He had also contacted workers in other hostels to ask how they had adapted the new system, but he felt that the system he had developed was probably the one which would work most effectively. Sue was a little surprised that there was no discussion about the issue and that the other members of staff and herself did not appear to have been consulted about whether or not these rotas were suitable, but she did not feel that she could make a stand, given it was the first item of her first staff meeting.

Jane then moved on to the next item on the agenda, which was the staff development plans for the coming year. She explained the budget which had been allocated for staff development for mental health support workers. At this point Tom interrupted to say that he had been speaking to the staff at the local university who were running some excellent courses which he felt were entirely appropriate for the staff to attend. He had accordingly booked people to attend a series of courses which reflected the needs of the particular hostel and the skill mix that people had. He said that he had the information pack with details of the courses and he would leave it in the staff room for people to look at. At this point Sue said that she felt that the selection of training courses should be a matter for the individual members of staff and not have the choice made on their behalf by a colleague. She said that she would welcome the opportunity to look at the pack and when she had done so she would advise Jane if she was interested in any of those courses. She added that she would also bring in some information she had about courses which were being run by a local voluntary organisation, and which were extremely relevant to the needs of the workers in the mental health hostel.

1 How do you think Tom will react to Sue's intervention?

2 How would you expect Rose and Natalia to react?

3 What are Jane's feelings likely to be?

4 Who should have resolved this situation?

5 How should it have been approached?

6 What alternatives are there for Tom to behaving in this way?

7 Suggest what Sue's feelings may be following the meeting.

Keys to good practice

To be a team member in a successful team you will need to check that you are contributing to the following:

- ☐ Agreeing and sharing a common purpose, aims and objectives.
- ☐ Working on building relationships which value and respect all team members.
- ☐ Contributing to the planning process for all the team activities.
- ☐ Making sure that all team members are involved in decision making.
- ☐ Respect and value the diversity of each team member.
- ☐ Value working together and recognise the difference between working at the same time and working together.
- ☐ Support the goals which have been agreed by the team.
- ☐ Praise and give credit to the work of all team members.
- ☐ Use your communication skills effectively when working with other members of the team.
- ☐ Ensure the team has dialogue and not debate.
- ☐ Work to identify and resolve conflicts within the team.
- ☐ Examine the way the team is operating and don't be afraid to initiate constructive and supportive criticism.
- ☐ Contribute to the growth and development of the team as a whole, the members of the team and yourself as an individual.

Active knowledge

Teams are good for us?

The *Lancet* medical journal reported that research showed that people who work in effective teams have a lower risk of coronary heart disease. The research found that people who had low control felt frustrated and unhappy, were not motivated in their work setting, and were more likely to suffer coronary heart disease than those who were able to exert more control over their working environment. One of the ways of achieving more control is by working in an effective team.

Element CU9.2 Contribute to the development of others in the work team

WHAT YOU NEED TO LEARN

- How to support other members of your team effectively.
- How to communicate in a way that increases understanding.
- How to disseminate information to other team members.

How to support team members

Supporting people is a very general term and it can mean a great many things depending on the context and the purpose for which the support is offered. In the context of supporting a work colleague in a team, support could mean:

- Recognising when somebody is having difficulty in a particular area of work.
- Recognising when somebody is having difficulty in their personal life which may be affecting their work.
- Recognising and acknowledging when a colleague has worked particularly well.
- Noticing when people are overloaded with jobs to do and offering to lend a hand.
- Telling colleagues about information you have discovered or something you have seen or read which you know would be of interest to them.
- Making sure colleagues know of opportunities for training courses which you think are likely to interest them.
- Noticing when a colleague is nervous or unsure of a new task or procedure and offering help and encouragement.
- Noticing if a colleague is being made uncomfortable by the way in which they are being spoken to or treated by another colleague or client and offering to help if it is needed.

This list and any additional items which you can add to it will make a contribution towards the support and development of other members of your team. If your team is working well, your colleagues will be doing the same thing for you and supporting you in your development.

Active knowledge

Keep a calendar for a week or two or even a month. On each day draw a stick figure which represents yourself and at the end of each working shift draw arrows out from you for support which you have given to others in your team and draw inward facing arrows for the occasions when support has been offered to you. None of the support may be major, however a series of small actions of support are what is likely to contribute most effectively to

successful teams. At the end of each week count up the arrows inward and the arrows outward. They should be in proportion to the people who work on the team and you should be giving and receiving support in equal measure. If there are more arrows in than out then you need to explore for yourself additional ways in which you can support colleagues. If there are more arrows out than in then this is an item that could be placed on the agenda for discussion at a team meeting.

Ways to offer support

Giving support to other team members can sometimes be misinterpreted. So you will need to ensure that you use all your communication skills in order to offer the support, advice or encouragement in a way which is not seen as patronising or implying some kind of criticism of your colleague. Every team is different in nature, some are quite formal in the relationships between team members, others are very casual and relaxed. The communication style of your team should always be the approach which you use when you are offering support to any colleagues. If your team works on a casual, friendly basis and you notice a colleague struggling, it would be normal practice to cheerfully say, 'Want a hand?' However, if your team has a more formalised relationship, with lines of responsibility and seniority carefully observed, then the same kind of offer of help would be approached quite differently. Perhaps, 'You look busy Mrs M…, can I help with that?' The way in which help is offered can often be the key to whether or not it is accepted. If you are offering advice, support or information with a genuine desire to assist your colleagues then you are unlikely to offend.

Case study

Sandy Court is a large purpose-built day centre which caters for 60 older people with varying ranges of mobility and levels of confusion. Most of the staff have worked in the day centre for the past three years since it was opened. Val is the officer in charge, Sharan is the deputy officer in charge and Margaret, Maureen and Hyacinth are the care team. Elaine and Louise, who is a trainee, work in the kitchen and a new member of staff, Sarah, has just started work at the centre. Margaret has been asked to look after Sarah and support her during her first few weeks. She has introduced Sarah to all the regular users of the centre.

On the second day, Sarah went to join one of the groups after lunch and suggested that they may begin to do some story telling and to recall the things that used to go on in the local area in the past. Margaret was quick to explain that this group was the card-playing group and that talking was not something that they wanted to do, or would have enjoyed. She carefully explained to Sarah that it wasn't her fault, it was just that she was new and obviously she would get to know these things as she gained more experience. Later that same afternoon Sarah was assisting Mrs B to the toilet when Margaret came across and said, 'Oh, it's much better to put Mrs B in a wheelchair, she gets there a lot quicker that way and we don't have any accidents. Don't worry Sarah, you will soon get used to it, it just takes a bit more knowledge.'

At the end of Sarah's first fortnight, Val, the officer in charge, spoke to Margaret to ask her views about how Sarah was progressing. Margaret said that she was sure that the girl had potential, but she didn't seem to know very much and that she wasn't sure how quickly she was learning things because she still seemed not to be able to undertake any tasks for herself.

1 What do you think Sarah's response will be when Val asks her how she has got on in her first two weeks?

2 What is the possible motivation behind the way Margaret is dealing with Sarah?

3 Are there any advantages for Sarah in this kind of approach?

4 Are there any advantages for Margaret in this kind of approach?

5 Can Sarah do anything to improve this situation, if so what?

6 What should Val do?

7 What should the rest of the team do?

How to communicate in a way that increases understanding

Every group of people has its own way of communicating. This is particularly true of teams who work in particular settings. It is also true in many situations in life, as in the case of people in a particular age group or class who use certain phrases and terminology common to their age group or class and which identifies them to others.

For example, you would be advertising yourself as coming from fairly high up the social ladder if you were to refer to:

You need to communicate to others in a way they will understand

- a sitting room or drawing room rather than a lounge.
- a napkin rather than a serviette.
- a toilet rather than a loo or lavatory.

You would be clearly identified as being of an older generation if you were to use such phrases as: 'Before the war we may not have had much money, but we did see life'; and 'We had a wireless.'

Terminology can also define people's occupational background. For instance, if you heard somebody saying that they had a 'nasal discharge' rather than a 'runny nose', you might be likely to assume that that person worked in the medical field. If you were to overhear somebody explaining that their 'galanthus nivalis had looked wonderful under the ilex aquifolium', then you would be correct in assuming that this was a gardener telling you that their snowdrops had looked wonderful under the holly bush.

This is no less true of people who work in the care sector. For example, if you were to read a set of medical case notes and a set of case notes for a child being looked after by the local authority you may find the initials B/O in both of them. In the medical notes it would mean 'bowel open', in the child's case notes it would refer to the child being 'boarded out', that is placed with foster parents. Similarly, if you talked about CPD in a social work or early year setting, people would understand you to be talking about 'continuous professional development'. In other words, ensuring that their practice was current and up to date. On the other hand, if you were part of a team working in a maternity unit, this would refer to 'cephra pelvic disproportion', which means that a woman has a pelvis which is too small to fit a baby through.

The words used by this person identifies him as someone with specialised knowledge of computers

It is always important to check that the terminology that you are using is the terminology which your work colleagues use and that you all understand to mean the same thing. This is particularly important if you are working in a multi-disciplinary team, or have moved to a new team in a slightly different setting.

Active knowledge

Translate the following paragraph and rewrite it or explain it verbally to a brand new member of staff.

'I'm not happy about signing off this NVQ. I am not convinced that the PCs have been covered and I don't think the IV has assessed it yet. It is going to have to be ready for the EV and I think I will ask her advice. If you look at the latest QCA guidance it seems to argue and say the opposite to the guidance from DfEE. But I saw information the other day from the NTO that indicated that not all the PCs on the EARS had to be recorded, so I want some guidance before I make a decision.'

If you have a problem with translating this ask your assessor and your internal verifier for help. If you have had a problem, think about how you felt and remember how new members of staff feel when jargon is being used which they may not understand.

How to disseminate information

One of the valuable roles of all team members is to share information they have. This may be information that you picked up from a meeting or a training day that you attended, or it may have come from a documentary that you saw on TV, or an article you read, or information that you found on the Internet. One of the important contributions that you can make to your team and to the development of all the team members is to make sure that such information is shared and that you do not keep it to yourself and fail to let others know about it. There is an old but true saying 'that knowledge is power', and there are people who will hold onto information in the hope that it will give them an edge or an advantage over their own team members. This means they are not functioning well as members of their team and having difficulty in accepting the basic requirements of contributing to team effectiveness.

If there is a member of your team who tends to behave in this way then the team will need to consider some strategies to deal with that person. One effective way might be to suggest that at each team meeting a different team member makes a presentation about some new or emerging information they know about which will be of value to others. It could be suggested that the team member who is causing difficulties is the first one to make this presentation and the team could then praise and encourage them for the valuable contribution they have made. This might help the team member to see that there is more to be gained from sharing information with others than keeping it to oneself.

There is little point in sharing information and updates with your colleagues unless you do it in a way they can understand and accept. Placing an interesting article on a notice board may be one way of letting people see it, however notice boards tend to be like wallpaper, in that people don't always notice what's on them. Also, it isn't easy to stand and read a whole article if it is pinned on a notice board. If you have an interesting article which you would like to share with team members, the best way

Information   knowledge

In organisations information and knowledge can 'cascade' to others might be to ask your manager if you can photocopy the article and distribute it to team members. If you have been to a particularly valuable or useful meeting or training day you may want to copy and share any of the handouts with your colleagues. Or it may be possible to arrange a short presentation at a team meeting so you can share the information you have gained. This is called '**cascading**' and is used by many organisations as a cost-effective way of sharing information across a wide range of staff.

Active knowledge

Think of an occasion when some useful or interesting information was passed on to you by a fellow team member. How did it make you feel?

Element CU9.3   Develop oneself in own work role

WHAT YOU NEED TO LEARN

- How to make a development plan.
- How to make use of feedback.
- How to monitor and evaluate your own development.

How to make a development plan

Development plans can take many forms, the best ones likely to be those developed in conjunction with your manager or the workplace supervisor. You need to carefully consider your 'areas of competence' and understand which you need to develop for your work role. You will have to make judgements about yourself in respect of those. You need to identify each one as either an area in which you feel fully confident, or one where there is room for improvement and development, or where you have very limited current ability. In the table below the headings in the columns are suggestions only, however if you do this exercise yourself the headings will need to broadly reflect those three different areas.

Once you have completed your table you can then identify the areas on which you need to concentrate. You should set some goals and targets and your line manager should be able to help you ensure they are realistic. For example, if you were to decide that you needed to achieve competence in managing a team and you were to identify your goal as being fully competent in six months time, this would be unrealistic and unachievable. You would inevitably fail to meet your target and would therefore be disappointed and likely to become demoralised and demotivated. Alternatively, if your target was to attend a training and development programme on team building during the next six months and to lead perhaps two team meetings by the end of the next six months, those goals and targets would be realistic and you would be likely to achieve them.

Only in conjunction with your line manager can you examine the areas of competency and skills which you need to achieve. There are no rights or wrongs, this is very much a personal development programme for you, and you must be sure it reflects not only the objectives of your organisation and the job roles they may want you to fulfil, but also your own personal ambitions and aspirations. After you have identified the areas in which you feel competent and have chosen your target areas for development, you will need to include other pages in your personal development log which will enable you to keep a record of your progress in achieving your goals. The pages can be put together in any way that you find effective, however the suggestions in the table below of things to include may be helpful.

The types of things you may wish to include can be as varied as developing a particular skill, for example learning sign language or learning a particular technique for working with clients with dementia. Or it could be developing your skills as a potential manager, for example, learning about organisational and human resources skills. It could also include some areas of personal professional development, such as time management and stress management. All these are legitimate areas for inclusion in your own personal and professional development plan.

Development plan

Development area:	Goals
Time management and workload organisation	Learn to use computer recording and information systems
Skills development, including time scale and how skill improvement has been measured	
Action plan: Attend two-day training and use study pack. Attend follow-up training days. Use computer instead of handwriting reports	Improvement
Review date: 3 months	
Professional development – priorities My priorities for training and development in the next 6 months are:	IT and computerised record systems.
My priorities for training and development in the next 6-12 months are:	As above and NVQ assessor training.
Repeat this exercise in 6 months and review the areas of competency and priorities.	

How to make use of feedback

Feedback is one of the most valuable ways of ensuring that you are continuing to work towards your targets. If some of the targets you have set yourself involves the acquisition of particular skill levels you will not know whether or not you have achieved them if you do not receive feedback from colleagues and line managers. You should make arrangements to include feedback from your line manager at the review stages of your personal development plan and you should also set aside time to ask colleagues and, if appropriate, clients to provide you with some feedback on your progress. When you have received feedback you should make sure that you make good use of it. You could use it to improve the skills and practice you are intending to develop.

How to monitor and evaluate your own development

Use your personal and professional development plan as a means of recording ongoing monitoring of your progress towards your goals and targets. If you find that you are moving too slowly towards your target, you will need to consider whether you have set your goal or target too high, or if there is anything that you can or should be doing in order to speed up progress.

Many things can get in the way of achieving goals, for example your employer may have reduced the resources available for training and development and so your plans to attend a particular number of training days may no longer be possible. Where you meet this type of difficulty you should explore alternative means of obtaining the information that you would have had, such as using textbooks, the Internet and gathering information from colleagues and others who have previously attended such training days.

The review and evaluation process is essential to the successful progress and achievements of your own career goals. Your development plan should be a working document which you use on an ongoing basis year on year, and each time you review and evaluate you should update your targets and alter them to fit any changed circumstances or changed ambitions or aspirations which you may develop. A development plan can move with you if you change job roles or settings and you will need to undertake a major review at that point.

If you value your own career development sufficiently to take the time and effort to ensure that you plan it and follow the plan to achieve your goals then you are more likely to be an effective and valuable member of a team. You will also better understand the importance of supporting and encouraging others to achieve their own goals, aspirations and ambitions and thus contribute to a team which performs enthusiastically and well and provides a high-quality service for those for whom you care.

Unit test

1   What are the stages of development of teams?

2   Identify the characteristics of each of the stages?

3   What is the Apollo syndrome?

4   How can you deal with the Apollo syndrome?

5   What are the main characteristics of effective teams?

6   What steps can you take to ensure that your team is effective?

7   Suggest three different sources of information which could be shared with the team?

8   Consider likely methods of disseminating information to team members.

9   What is the importance of a personal development plan?

10   What are the important elements to be included in a personal and professional development plan?

Unit SC3 Contribute to the monitoring and review of care packages

Keeping all provided care services under a process of monitoring and regular review is absolutely essential in the provision of an effective service, both for the individual and their family and for ensuring best value for the funders and commissioners of the services. If you have any role in supporting an individual who is receiving services or who is in receipt of direct payments to obtain their own services, then you will need to be able to monitor and review the services provided in an effective way. Throughout the process of both monitoring and review the individual and their carers must be involved and should be the main participants in the process. Clearly, where direct payments are concerned your role will simply be to ensure that the individual does not need any additional help or support to manage and commission their services.

Monitoring and review are different processes, but both are essential and contribute to the overall evaluation of the services provided. Monitoring is a process of regular checks against a clearly defined set of criteria that services are continuing to meet the needs for which they were provided; a review is an opportunity to reassess circumstances, needs and the services to ensure that the provision being made is still the most appropriate. Both of these processes lead into a final evaluation as to the quality and appropriateness of the services being provided.

The principles of effective monitoring, review and evaluation apply regardless of whether you are working through a care management process for services being delivered to individuals via social care agencies, or through a care programme approach (CPA) for clients in receipt of mental health services through the health service.

ement SC3.1   Contribute to monitoring and evaluating the effectiveness of care packages

WHAT YOU NEED TO LEARN

- Why monitoring is important.
- Ways of monitoring.
- How to ensure the involvement of individuals and their carers.
- How to evaluate care packages.
- How to identify significant changes which affect the care package.

Why monitoring is important

The major and most straightforward reason why monitoring is important is that it is essential to ensure that any package of care provision is continuing to meet the same needs that it was designed to meet in the first place. However, there are also other aspects of monitoring which are important and which have to be considered. When a package of care was originally assessed, planned and put in place it would have been to meet a particular set of circumstances. The original assessment should have:

- involved the individual
- involved the individual's carers and family
- assessed their levels of need
- assessed the level of provision which was available
- planned for monitoring and review

That all of this was done at the time of setting up the original care package does not mean that it will still be appropriate six months or a year into the future. Neither does it mean that care packages which were set up, even with the most thorough assessment and with careful planning and contracting of service providers, will necessarily continue to provide services at the quality or at the level originally expected. Monitoring may sound a complex process but its principles are very simple. For example, most of us monitor many things in our lives on a regular basis without realising it.

Active knowledge

If you were to go to the same butcher every week to buy meat, you would not do it for very long if the meat was always tough, stringy and inedible. Your weekly visit to the butcher is a case of monitoring on a regular basis the quality of the meat you are buying, and you would decide whether to go on buying your meat from the butcher according to the quality of the meat you were getting. Think about other examples of monitoring you do in your everyday life and make some notes. Then, think about those things you monitor at work, and make notes about how and why you monitor.

According to the Department of Health over 1.6 million people have services provided for them through care packages. Approximately 1.3 million of those are community services and 0.3 million are residential services. Almost 600,000 packages of care are reviewed every year and about half of these result in a new or amended care plan. This shows that people's circumstances and needs change and therefore the services provided must be able to respond to those changes in needs.

Monitoring of care services needs to pick up changes in the circumstances of those receiving the services, their carers and the service provider. The original care plan will use forms of care and support that reflect the client's needs at the time. For example, somebody recently discharged from hospital following treatment for mental health problems may have received quite extensive support under the care programme approach, which may have consisted of day care, community psychiatric nurse visits, and access to a support group of carers. However, monitoring that individual's progress may show their mental health problems have improved to the point that day care is no longer needed on the previous level and that an alternate service, such as support in finding employment but with back-up support when needed, is now far more appropriate. A service which is constantly or frequently monitored is likely to be one which is responsive to the needs of the individual, and is also an effective use of the resources of the health service or social services department responsible for funding.

Resources

Monitoring resources can also be important if changes in the availability of those resources means that a care package will have to be altered in some way. A reduction in available funding or an increase in demand for a particular resource may mean that adjustments in the level of service provision will have to be made. Regular monitoring makes it easier to be aware of where resources are being used and where changes need to be made.

Monitoring resources enables providers to determine what services they can provide

Legislation and guidelines

Depending on an individual's circumstances, the services provided under their package of care may be covered by legislation or specific guidelines. For example, the Mental Health Act 1983 covers the service provision to anyone receiving treatment from the health service, regardless of the setting in which they receive that treatment – i.e. whether it is in the community or in a hospital setting.

Carers

Regular monitoring should cover the needs of carers, to make sure the provisions are still meeting those needs. Carers should be included in monitoring the service. They are also, in many cases, a very useful source of feedback about the provision of services, and this can be built into any plans for monitoring. Regular feedback from a carer, and the knowledge that they will contact you if circumstances change, can be reassuring and can be taken into account when monitoring. However, it is not appropriate or reasonable to put the onus on a carer to notify you when changes take place.

Ways of setting up feedback from carers

Carers cope with tremendous demands on their time and energy, both physical and emotional. Whatever systems you agree in order to keep up to date with feedback from carers, you must make sure you are not placing even more demands on their time. The following are useful methods for obtaining feedback:

- Agree a regular time (and stick to) for you to telephone.

- Make sure the carer knows the times when you are most likely to be available.

- Try to be contactable for a specific period each day, e.g. 9–10am or 4–5pm or a specific time each week – say Friday afternoon.

- Organise a written feedback sheet – perhaps with tick boxes or space for short comments. This could be posted, or collected by a service provider if they are making regular calls.

- If the carer has Internet access, you could set up a regular e-mail contact.

Ways of monitoring

Whatever approach you take to monitoring it is important to decide at the outset how a particular care package will be monitored and that the methods you choose to use are agreed with the individual and their carers. A monitoring process should be devised which involves the following key people:

- the individual receiving the service
- their carers or family
- other health care professionals
- the service provider – who will have their performance monitored.

In addition to the monitoring carried out by the care manager/co-ordinator, each of these people has an important role to play in monitoring, to a greater or lesser extent depending on the individual's circumstances.

Monitoring by the individual

Obviously the most important person in any monitoring process is the individual. So, they must be clear as to how they can record and feed back information on how well their care package is working for them. This can be through:

- completing a checklist on a regular basis (weekly or monthly)
- maintaining regular contact with the care manager/co-ordinator, either by telephone or through a visit
- using an electronic checking and monitoring form which would be e-mailed on a regular basis to the care manager/co-ordinator
- recording and reporting any changes in their own circumstances or changes in the provision of the care package.

The following is an example of the sort of form that can be used to obtain feedback from an individual in care.

Have there been any changes in your health since the last report? If so, please say what.	*Not really - much the same*
Have there been any changes in your circumstances since the last report? If so, please say what.	*My sister has come to live a few roads away*
Are the services you receive still giving the support you need?	*Yes, still very good, but don't need day centre on Thursdays now as my sister takes me out every Thursday*
How would you like the services to change what you receive?	*Cancel Thursday at the day centre, but everything else is fine*

Monitoring by carers and families

Carers and families are likely to participate in monitoring a care package in similar ways. You will need to make sure that carers are willing to participate in monitoring and they do not feel you are adding yet another burden to their lives.

Monitoring by other health care professionals

Maintaining contact between reviews with other professionals who may be involved with the individual is an essential part of your role. The most effective method of doing this is to agree the sorts of changes which will trigger contact. For example:

- You could agree with the GP that they will notify you of any significant health changes or hospital admissions.
- You could agree with the district nurse that they will notify you of any problems in compliance with treatment, or changes in the individual's ability to administer their own medication, or changes in home conditions.
- You could agree with the physiotherapist that they will notify you of any significant changes in mobility.

There may be other professionals, such as occupational or speech therapists, involved depending on the circumstances of the individual, however the principles of monitoring remain the same.

Monitoring of the service provider

Monitoring the performance of service providers is very important. It is likely your organisation will have systems and criteria which apply to all service providers who are contracted to provide a service. The performance indicators to which service providers have to perform may have been determined centrally within your organisation. Performance indicators are important. They are an essential tool for monitoring how well a service is being provided. If you have a standard a service provider has to work to, then you are able to monitor whether or not they are working to that standard. The performance indicators will vary depending on your agency and the nature of the service, but indicators are likely to cover items such as:

- Reliability of provision
- Timekeeping
- Feedback from service user
- Presentation of care staff.

As a care manager/co-ordinator or key worker you will have information about the performance indicators that you need to measure service providers/contractors against. Written contracts with service providers can be a very useful way of providing measures to monitor against. Contracts based on outputs or results, rather than inputs or descriptions of tasks, provide useful measures against which service providers/contractors can be judged. For example, a contract which simply says that 'The Fairways Day Centre will provide day care facilities on 5 days per week for Mr J.' is more difficult to monitor than a contract which states 'The output required of the Fairways Day Centre under this contract are:

- The provision of confirmation of attendance records for 5 days per week for Mr J.
- Production of evidence of day centre participation in multi-disciplinary case reviews.
- Evidence of Mr J's participation in multi-disciplinary case reviews.
- Completion of Mr J's preparation for work course.
- Completed carer liaison record demonstrating links with carer and family.'

… and so on.

The second form of contract provides clear outputs which give a starting point for monitoring. Each of the requirements that the service provider (Fairways Day Centre) has to achieve is clearly stated in the contract. The care manager/co-ordinator or key worker has a starting point for monitoring the performance of the service provider/contractor. This information contributes to regular measurements of the progress of the individual and the standard of the work of the service provider.

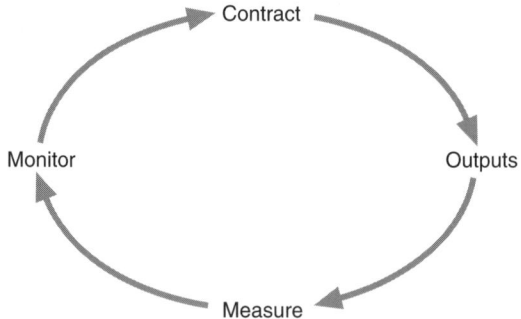

Steps in monitoring a service provider

How to ensure the involvement of individuals and their carers

The involvement of all those concerned with any package of care is essential in the process of monitoring. The relationship between you, as the care manager/co-ordinator or key worker, and a service provider is likely to be relatively straightforward, although you will always be in the position of being the commissioner and purchaser of services so should always be able to assume that as the 'customer', you are 'always right!'. However, this can change in periods or areas of scarce resources where several commissioners are competing for the limited resources. This puts the provider of services in a much stronger position. However, regardless of the nature of the relationship between you, the commissioner and purchaser of services, and the provider, it is essential the provider remains an active participant in the monitoring process.

Involving individuals and their carers

The individual receiving the service and their carer/s are the most important people involved in the monitoring and evaluation process. As the care manager/co-ordinator or key worker you must make sure you do not create any barriers to their access to this process. You will need to ensure that you use all your communication skills so that both the individual and their carers understand how the process works and what their role is; but you will also need to check out any possible barriers and make sure these are overcome. The kind of barriers which can prevent individuals becoming involved in monitoring their own care packages are:

- Using jargon and complex professional language.
- Making the process complicated and difficult to understand.
- Having an attitude which intimidates and alienates individuals.
- Designing a monitoring system using methods which the particular individual would find hard or impossible to use, e.g. a written monitoring system for monitoring a care package for somebody with a profound visual impairment.

Individuals and their carers should be involved at every stage of the assessment implementation monitoring review and evaluation of care packages, and you should use a checklist at the different stages of the process to ensure that you have made adequate arrangements for those involved. Try the following care package checklist to make sure that you have involved individuals and their carers at each stage.

Care package checklist

1 Does the individual have enough information to know what their care package will offer them, how you will keep information about the individual and their package and who will share that information?

2 Do they know who is responsible at each stage of the process for providing them with support, e.g. initial contact, assessment, monitoring, review and evaluation? Do they know who to contact in an emergency?

3 Has their needs been assessed with their involvement and the involvement of their carers or family?

4 Do they have a care plan which gives them a clear statement of how they will be supported and how all the people concerned will be involved in the process of monitoring any changes in their circumstances?

---

5   Do they have a package of care which meets their individual needs and allows them to make an active contribution to the development of those services?

6   Does the individual know that the people who care for them will be involved in a review process when their needs change or on a regular basis regardless of changes in circumstances?

7   Does the individual have a plan agreed and discussed with them and their carers to deal with any emergencies which may arise?

8   Is the individual given opportunities to feed into the development of services through using the complaints procedures, through being asked for contributions to staff training, and through being given access to any audit or inspection procedures?

9   Does the individual have as wide a choice of levels of service as possible?

10 If there are changes because an individual has moved or because of reorganisations or changes of service provider does the individual have the opportunity to meet with all of those involved in the current and in the new arrangements to agree the next care plan?

11 Are the individual's carers involved in the process and are their needs assessed?

Active knowledge

Is a checklist like the one above available in your workplace? If so, check what is in it and see if you think anything needs to be changed. If not, why not create one.

Direct payments

The traditional role of a social services department and the health service has always been to place the individual receiver of services in a position where the care manager/co-ordinator or key worker has power over the individual receiving the services, because they are the person with access to and control over the resources. The development of direct payments has changed this situation dramatically.

Direct payments are made by social services departments directly to the individual concerned, who then becomes responsible for contracting and managing their own service provision. This approach is being used by many local authorities throughout the country and its use is being encouraged and is on the increase. Direct payments are not appropriate for everyone and not all individuals want to take on the responsibility for their own services, but it has transformed the lives of a great many people and has enabled them to take control, very often for the first time, of the way in which their lives are structured.

Where direct payments are made and the individuals are responsible for arranging their own package of care, they may choose to contract the services from whoever a social services department or health authority already has arrangements with. However, they can advertise, recruit and employ their own carers and establish their package of care as they wish. A care manager/co-ordinator or key worker still has a responsibility to liaise with the individual to make sure that they are receiving all the care and support that they need, and that their needs as originally assessed are being met by the provision that they have.

For many individuals in receipt of direct payments for the first time, the prospect of recruiting and managing their own service provision may be liberating and exciting, but also a little daunting. Training is often provided by the social services departments who are making the direct payments. After undergoing the training, which will cover matters such as advertising, employment law, contracting and managing the quality of provision, many individuals do feel confident enough to effectively take control of the way in which their needs are met. This changes their lives. From always having to be dependent on a care manager/co-ordinator and local authority they now have the power to decide the level and type of support that they will have.

How to evaluate care packages

The evaluation is the end result of a process of monitoring and review. The evaluation is the final judgement in respect of a care package as to whether or not it continues to meet the needs of the individual and their current circumstances. Making judgements is the central process of evaluation. The evidence you should use to make those judgements is the evidence you have gathered from the process of monitoring and from the discussions held during a review. The criteria which you have set out during monitoring, such as:

- the service provider must show evidence of meeting all of the outputs,
- changes in individual circumstances must be taken into account, and so on,

should be used to pull together the evidence which you will use to make your judgement or evaluation about how effective the care package is in achieving what it originally set out to do.

The steps to evaluation are very simple.

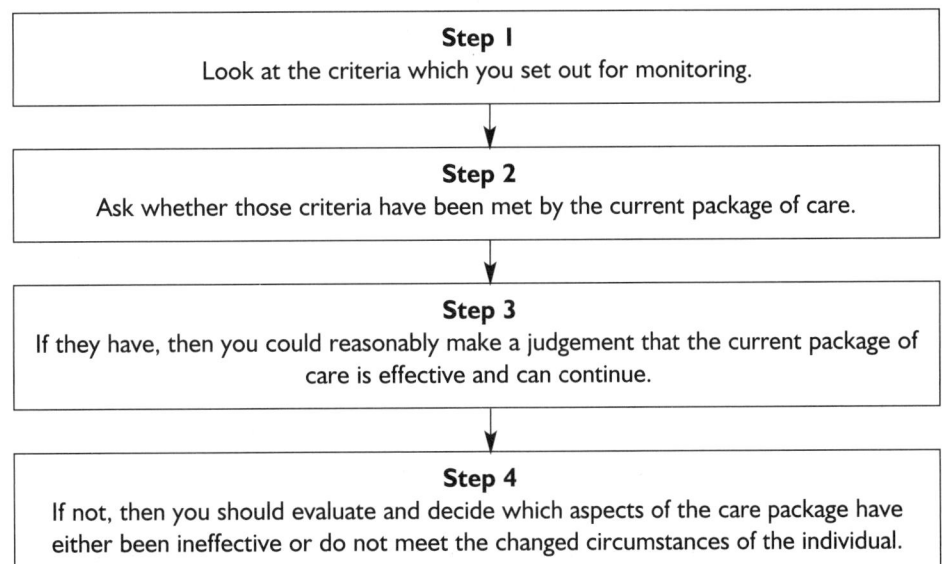

Step 1
Look at the criteria which you set out for monitoring.

Step 2
Ask whether those criteria have been met by the current package of care.

Step 3
If they have, then you could reasonably make a judgement that the current package of care is effective and can continue.

Step 4
If not, then you should evaluate and decide which aspects of the care package have either been ineffective or do not meet the changed circumstances of the individual.

Step 5
Having established what needs to be changed, you can complete the evaluation by identifying the parts of the package which are no longer effective in meeting needs and identifying the ways in which those now need to be amended.

Active knowledge

Think about a situation in your workplace where you have undertaken evaluation. Did you follow the steps outlined above? If you have not been involved in evaluating care packages, look at other situations where you evaluate progress or development for individuals – think about the steps you take to complete the evaluation. You may be surprised at how broadly similar the evaluation process is.

You should always ensure that the individual and their family are aware of the role which you have in the process of monitoring and evaluation. Depending on the way in which the organisation you work for is structured, you may have a quite extensive role in relation to the monitoring and evaluation of care packages and may deal with some of the broader more strategic aspects of commissioning and contracting within your organisation. Alternatively, you may have a role which is limited to the particular individuals with whom you work, and that information and feedback which could influence wider decisions is something which you provide as information and records to your line managers through an information system. It is important that everyone is clear about the extent of your role so that unrealistic expectations are not raised. For example, an individual who provides feedback saying, 'That day centre was hopeless, I hope you can get it closed down', will need to be advised of the steps you can take in informing the necessary inspection and quality monitoring teams within your organisation about any possible poor performance of a particular contractor. You also need to tell them that your ability to single-handedly close a poorly performing facility is somewhat limited!

Any information that a contractor or service provider is not meeting expected standards or is offering a poor quality service should be fed back to the relevant inspection or registration unit within your organisation. Your organisation is likely to have procedures in place to ensure that this happens and you should check what they are and make sure that the necessary information is passed on accurately, clearly and without delay. If you have concerns about the quality of the service being provided you should make sure that you pass on:

- The name of the service provider.
- The date and length of the contract.
- The service they were contracted to provide.
- The way in which your evaluation has identified a problem with their performance.
- The circumstances under which they were delivering a service to the individual concerned.
- Your contact details for a further discussion.
- A file reference where records of the review and evaluation may be obtained.

This is a general list, so each organisation is likely to have something similar in place.

How to identify significant changes which affect the care package

Throughout any monitoring and evaluation process you are looking for and responding to change. It is important you are clear about the sort of changes which require action and the sort that are simply a part of everyday life and do not involve a major re-think of a care package! For example, an individual who inherits £50,000 will experience significant change, whereas someone who receives a £1.20 per week increase in their Income Support will not! Both, however, have experienced a change in their financial circumstances. Similarly, someone who changes from working two days each week to a full-time job experiences a significant change which will involve changes in the care package they receive. Whereas someone who changes from working two days each week as a telephonist to working the same two days as a receptionist is unlikely to need significant changes in any care package.

Case study

B has a long history of mental health problems which she has experienced since her late teens; she is now in her early forties. She experiences episodes of elations and disinhibition, at other times she will experience depressive episodes. B has regular medication which controls her mental health most of the time and she has a comprehensive care programme, with her community psychiatric nurse as her care co-ordinator. She lives in a hostel and receives support from hostel-based support workers and the staff at the day centre she attends each day. B's family have lived in a town about 10 miles away from B – her mother, who died last year, was a lone parent, and B has a married sister who has two children. Following the death of her mother, B's sister decided to move to be nearer to B. They have always been close and her sister has always encouraged B to maintain her treatment regime and to make use of support services. B's sister moved into a new house in the same area as the hostel a few weeks ago.

1 Is this change significant for B?
2 If so, why?
3 If not, why not?
4 What could be the benefits for B?
5 Are there any potential disadvantages?
6 How could B's care programme be affected?
7 What would you think if you were B's co-ordinator?

Element SC3.2   Contribute to reviewing the effectiveness of care packages

WHAT YOU NEED TO LEARN

- The purpose of review.
- Who is involved in the review process.
- How to manage the review process.
- How to record the review process.

The purpose of review

Reviews are essential because care situations very rarely remain the same for long periods of time. As circumstances change the package of care may need to be reviewed in the light of those changes. At agreed intervals all of the interested and involved parties should come together to reflect on whether or not the package of care is continuing to do the job that it was initially set up to do. If there were no reviews then the arrangements in place would continue for years regardless of whether they were still meeting the care needs.

Reviews of care needs are essential for finding out how those needs may have changed

A review will gather together all the information known about the circumstances of the individual, the service provided, the service provider, and will provide all those involved and concerned with the care of the individual the opportunity to express their opinions and to be involved in a discussion about how effective the current care provision has been and what are the most appropriate changes, if any, that need to be made.

Who is involved in the review process

Any review should attempt to obtain the views and participation from as many as possible of those who are involved in the care of the individual. The most important people at the review are the individual and their carers or family. The key worker or care manager/co-ordinator is also central to the review process, as is the organisation/s or individual/s providing the care. It is also important that others with an interest in the care of the individual also have the opportunity to participate in a review. For example, a GP, health visitor, community psychiatric nurse, community OT, physiotherapist, speech therapist, welfare rights support worker, representative of a support group, or anyone else who has been a significant contributor to the life and care of the individual concerned should be involved if at all possible. The status of all the participants should be equal in that everyone has the opportunity to give a view and to contribute to the discussion, however the key person who must agree to any review decision is the individual concerned.

How to manage the review process

If you are the care manager/co-ordinator or key worker you are likely to be the person responsible for organising the review itself and making sure that it takes place at the time it is supposed to. If the individual receiving care is in receipt of direct payment, they are likely to take responsibility for initiating a review if they feel it is necessary. Where direct payments are involved your role is very different; it is simply one of being there to provide support and assistance if it is required by the individual, and you would only become involved in a review if that was requested by the individual.

If you are responsible for managing the review you may want to go through the following checklist to make sure that you are meeting the needs of all of the participants in a review, but most importantly those of the individuals concerned.

Review checklist

1   Does the individual understand what a review is?

2   Do the individual's carers also understand what a review is and its purpose?

3   Is the review arranged at an appropriate time to check the progress?

4   Is it at least once a year or have the individual's circumstances changed?

5   Does the review cover whether the individual continues to need the same level of support and services, whether there have been any changes, what the original care plan intended, and the results of the monitoring?

6   Has the individual been asked when and where would be convenient for the review?

7   Has it been explained to the individual what decisions the review is able to take in respect of their continuing care provision and the development of a new care plan?

8   Has the individual been offered an advocate in order to help them prepare for the review, to support them at the review, or to speak for them at the review?

9   Does the individual know who is responsible for making sure that the review meeting is managed?

10   Does the individual know all of the people who will be at the review?

11   Can all of the participants contribute either in writing or verbally to the review?

12   Do all the participants in the care plan know that they can request a review?

13   Have carers been consulted about the appropriate time and location for the review?

14   Have crèche facilities been offered for anyone who needs them so that they can attend the review?

15   If you represent the sole profession supporting the individual is there an independent person to oversee the review?

During the review everyone should be given a chance to contribute verbally and you should use your communication skills to ensure it is possible for everyone to feel they can contribute their views. If the individual receiving care has chosen to use an advocate to present their point of view, then you should ensure they have every opportunity to contribute on the individual's behalf. If some choose to communicate in writing or by some other means, such as e-mail, then you should make sure that those comments are taken into account. If there have been any changes in your organisation's policies or access to resources, or changes in the circumstances of the service provider, these are also key matters and should be fed into the review for consideration. It is your responsibility to ensure that everyone feels that they have had an adequate opportunity to participate and you should check carefully with the individuals who are present that this is the case.

This is, of course, particularly important for the individual receiving the services. You may need to support the individual to recognise the impact of significant change and to identify the differences between important and insignificant change. You may wish to use a prompt such as:

> *'B, your sister coming to live nearby is something which has happened to you since the last review isn't it? Do you think things will change much for you?'*

> *'J, have you found that your new job has made much of a difference to you?'*

> or

> *'M, has having an extra afternoon at the centre made the difference you hoped for at the last review?'*

Making decisions

Once all the information has been gathered and all contributions have been made, those taking part in the review will then need to make a decision about any changes which are needed to the care plan and the care package for the next period of time. Decisions should be clearly based on the monitoring of evidence and should particularly take account of contributions from the individual and their carers. A review should not take a decision in respect of changing provision with which the individual receiving care fundamentally disagrees. If the circumstances which have changed relate to a change in the level of available resources and result in a reduction in service to the individual, then it may be that such a decision is inevitable. However, it is important that the alternative which will be in place is acceptable to the individual. If they are dissatisfied at the end of the review, then it is important they are informed of the complaints procedure and of the process for asking for a further review of the resources available to them. Full access should be ensured by offering advocacy or any other support services which may be required for individuals to take full advantage of any complaints system or any further routes to changing decisions, e.g. approaching decision makers or accessing pressure groups.

At the end of each review it is essential that the date is set for the next review and that all the participants, particularly the individual and their carers, are happy with the date, both in terms of their own availability and the length of time before the next review is due to take place. All reviews must be undertaken at least once a year and if an individual is receiving a care package under the care programme approach system through the mental health services, then any admission to hospital must generate a review within a month of discharge.

A review is made after information has been gathered from various sources

How to record the review process

Keys to good practice: Recording a care package review

All reviews must be recorded in the individual's records and they must include:

- Written reports from each care service included in the care package.

- There should also be a record that all relevant staff have been invited to the review or to participate in the review if they are doing so in writing.

- There should be a record showing how the individual has been prepared for the review and the access that they have had to an advocate if they wish to use one.

- There should be evidence that relevant carers and others who offer support have been invited to contribute.

- There should be a record of all those who attended or who contributed.

- Any changes must be carefully recorded and the revised care plan should be recorded as a separate document.

All organisations have their own documentation and they are all likely to contain most or all of the above points. It is important that all those who have contributed, even if they have not yet been present at the review, are informed of the outcome and that they know of any changes to the care plan for the individual. If the review has raised concerns about quality of provision, then this must be cross-referenced to the relevant registration and inspection service, and all such concerns must be clearly documented and drawn to the attention of your line manager.

The revised care plan and any changes to existing contracts should be drawn up using the procedures and documentation required by your organisation.

Recorded reviews contribute to the overall quality of the service your organisation offers and they are likely to be included in any file audit undertaken during most inspection processes. The review process, if it is well conducted, provides a vital opportunity for individuals to contribute and to make choices about the care package which they receive. Reviews which are sloppy, badly prepared and carelessly undertaken rob individuals of the opportunity to take decisions which affect their lives significantly, and they also contribute to an ineffective use of scarce and valuable resources.

Unit test

1 What is the process of monitoring?

2 Why is monitoring important in respect of maintaining quality of service provision?

3 Why is monitoring important to promoting the independence of individuals in receipt of care packages?

4 How can individuals contribute to the monitoring process?

5 How can contracts be used to provide information for monitoring?

6 Who are the people who need to be involved in the review process?

7 Name three key differences for individuals in receipt of direct payments in the way their care packages are managed?

8 How does the receipt of direct payments alter the relationship between care managers/co-ordinators and the individual receiving services?

9 Why is it important to accurately record reviews?

10 What changes should be documented after a review?

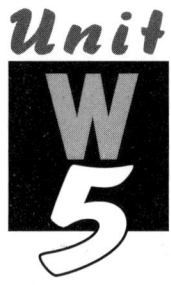

Unit W5 Support clients with difficult or potentially difficult relationships

This unit is important for the work that you will do in supporting your clients in the way they deal with relationships in their lives. Not all relationships are straightforward or easy to deal with and there can be situations where clients will need your help and support to deal with awkward, unpleasant or difficult situations. You will need to develop and use a range of skills in order to provide this support. The communication skills you have used in your work with clients will be particularly important here, and you may find you are having to use basic counselling skills in order to deal with more difficult situations. You will also need to understand how difficult situations can develop and know the steps to take to ensure your client is able to decide the level of support and help they need from you and to have enough information to make choices about the best ways to handle their own relationships.

ement W5.1 Support clients in their decisions regarding relationships

WHAT YOU NEED TO LEARN

- Different types of relationships.
- Features of relationships.
- Difficulties which can surround relationships when they go wrong.
- How to support clients in making decisions about relationships.
- Issues around contact with others.

Different types of relationships

Everyone has a wide range of relationships with different people in different aspects of their lives. Relationships range from family to work colleagues. Each of the different types of relationship is important and plays a valuable role in contributing to the overall well-being of each of us as an individual. However, the needs and demands of different types of relationships are varied, as are the effects that relationships can have on an individual's view of themselves and the confidence with which they deal with the world. Some of the different relationships are listed below.

Types of relationships	Features of relationship
Family relationships	These are relationships with parents, grandparents, siblings and children. Depending on the type of family they can be close or distant.
Sexual relationships	These relationships can be long or short term, can be with a spouse or permanent partner or can be shorter term non-permanent relationships. The impact of sexual relationships is different from family relationships and more intense than the demands of a friendship.
Friendships	Friendships can be long term or can be short term but quite intense. Most people have a few close friends and a much larger circle of friends who are not quite so intimate or close. These may be friends who are part of a wide social circle but perhaps not close enough to share intimate details of someone's life. Close friends on the other hand are often the ones who are an immediate source of support in times of difficulty and the first person with whom good news is shared.
Working relationships	These can be relationships with employers or with work colleagues. Some may stray over the boundaries into friendships but for most people the colleagues with whom they work are related in a different way to the way they would relate to friends. For example, work colleagues may share very little information about someone's personal life even though they may have very close and regular day-to-day contact. In fact it is perfectly possible to spend a great deal more time with work colleagues than with friends, but not be as close.

Family relationships

Family relationships are usually those that influence people most. For most children the type of relationship they have within the family where they grow up influences the rest of their lives and the kind of people they become. Primarily it is the relationship with their parents or main carers that is the most influential during childhood. For a growing child, relationships with parents and other extended family members, such as grandparents and siblings, provide the emotional security which is important in establishing a positive self-image and in developing confidence. As children grow through adolescence and into early adulthood, family relationships become less dominant as an influence, however they remain significant for most people throughout their lives. It is notable that most major occasions in people's lives, such as weddings, christenings, coming of age birthdays, are regarded as 'family concerns', when members of the immediate and extended family are usually involved and invited to join the celebrations.

Sexual relationships

Most people who have a long-term sexual relationship would probably view that as being the most significant relationship in their lives. Even short-term sexual relationships can have a huge effect on individuals and how they regard themselves and their general health and well-being. The physical closeness involved in a sexual relationship means that the dynamics involved are significantly different from other family relationships. Sexual partners are often close emotionally as a result of their intimate physical relationship. Sexual relationships can be long or short term, can be with an opposite or same sex partner, and can be exclusive – with just one partner – or non-exclusive – where partners also have sexual relationships with others. These types of sexual relationships will obviously have different effects and will meet the needs of different individuals, possibly at different stages in their lives. For example, many teenagers and young adults have short-term and non-exclusive sexual relationships with quite a number of partners, but many will eventually develop a long-term exclusive relationship with one partner with whom they may remain for many years.

Friendship

Friends become increasingly significant as children grow. For very young children, pre-school individual friendships with other children are relatively insignificant as influences on their lives. Their relationships with other members of their family or their main carer are far more important. As children progress through school and into adolescence their friendships become more important and have a huge influence on their behaviour. The ability to form friendships with others is an important skill and is a need which most human beings have. An inability of a child or young person to make friends or to be in a situation in which they feel they do not have friends, or are being bullied or excluded by others with whom they had hoped to be friends, can be extremely distressing and have a serious effect on the child's self-image and self-confidence. Adults too find it difficult to cope with being excluded and being unable to relate to others as friends. Most people, regardless of circumstances, need to have a close relationship with another person, through which they can share confidences, worries and joy.

Working relationships

Effective working relationships are extremely important both to individuals and to the organisations for whom they work. Businesses do use techniques designed to

We all develop relationships that are important to our lives

encourage work colleagues to work well and effectively together. Usually, establishing good working relationships with colleagues requires an effective use of communication skills and a recognition of the value and significance of work undertaken by colleagues. For most people, having a good working relationship with colleagues is important as it contributes significantly to overall job satisfaction.

Family structures

As recently as the early part of the last century, family structures were very different than they are now. Less than a hundred years ago the most common family structure was an extended family with mother, father, grandparents, aunts and uncles living close to one another, if not in the same house. Children would move between different members of the family regularly and would be equally at home being cared for by a range of relations. Fifty years ago the most common family structure was a nuclear family, with mother, father and children living in the same house but not necessarily living close to other members of their family. Whilst both nuclear and extended families are still quite common, there is now a much wider range of family structures and as a result a wider range of relationships and patterns of communication within families. The following are family structures and relationships within them.

Type of family	Features
Traditional extended family	Parents, grandparents, aunts, uncles, sisters, brothers, children, nieces, nephews living together or in close proximity.
Traditional nuclear family	Two parents and children living together. May or may not be close contact with other members of the family but less likely than in an extended family.
Reconstituted family	Parents both with children from previous relationships.
Step-parent family	Families where one parent has children from a previous relationship and the other takes a step-parenting role.
Lone parent family	One parent bringing up children without a partner.
Cohabiting family	Unmarried partners who may also come into any of the categories above.
Same sex family	Same sex partners with or without children.

As family life has changed so have the roles and relationships within families. As a result, the way in which people understand relationships and the way in which they view themselves has changed. Working patterns in families have changed considerably and the roles are now less clear cut. At one time the work force was largely male, mainly undertaking physical labour, although not exclusively. Traditionally, women had the roles of caring for children and running a household. The decline of manufacturing and heavy industry meant the decline of manual work, once the traditional occupations of men. Technology and service industries have grown and there are now more women in employment, many of them in high-tech and service industries.

One of the consequences of increased career opportunities for women has been a change in the patterns of childcare, with many women choosing to start their families at a later stage in their lives and more children being cared for by professional carers rather than a parent. Children now are less likely to have regular contact with members of their extended family than children 50 or 100 years ago.

All of these factors contribute to how children learn to form relationships and the way in which they relate to others. For example, children who have only experienced relationships with their own parents, their parents' friends and other children may have no idea how to relate to older people. Children who have had the experience of growing up in a family where there is regular contact with family members of different generations will feel much more comfortable in relating to people across a wide age range.

Active knowledge

Think about a family you know well; it could be your own. Look at the family structure and list the relationships and work roles within it. Talk to family members about what sort of relationships and work roles were evident in the family 50 years ago. Go back even longer if you can find someone to talk to. Compare the difference in relationships and work roles now and 50 years ago.

Traditional extended family

Traditional nuclear family

Step-parent family

Reconstituted family

Lone parent family

Cohabiting family

Same sex family

The different family structures

Features of relationships

Relationships are characterised by certain features. Some may be:

- Supportive
- Sharing
- Equal
- Demanding

- Abusive
- Violent
- Damaging

Some off these features are positive and some are very negative. It is important to establish the features of a relationship and determine whether or not it is positive or negative.

Active knowledge

Think about three relationships which you have. First of all describe the type of relationship, then look at the features of the relationship and finally identify whether it is positive or negative for you. Try to work out why you feel that it is a positive or a negative relationship and make a note of how you came to that conclusion.

Effects of relationships

Relationships have a significant effect on the development, health and well-being of all individuals. Most people want to be liked and tend to feel happy when they are part of a group, or feel that they have friends and they are considered a friend by others. Very few people are content to be excluded from groups and to live their life in isolation, never having any significant close relationships with others. Generally, humans are sociable creatures who have always lived in groups or tribes or villages. Most are not loners, and their overall emotional health and well-being depends on the way they see themselves through the responses of others towards them.

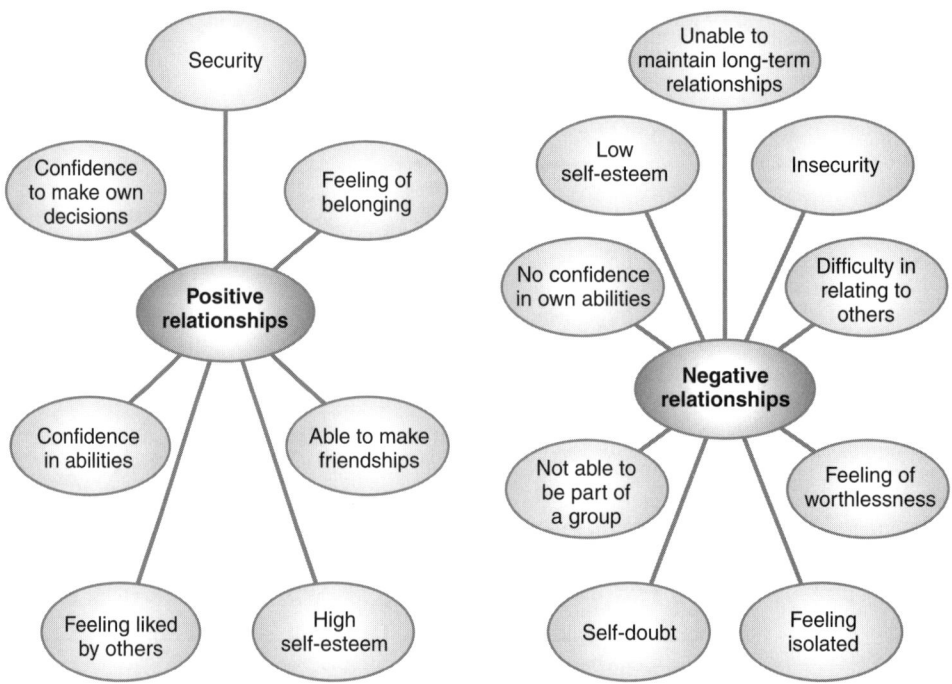

Features of positive relationships   Features of negative relationships

Self-concept and self-image

There is often confusion between self-concept and self-image. They are different and are most easily remembered in the following way:

- Self-concept is how we see ourselves.
- Self-image is how we value ourselves.

Both self-concept and self-image are influenced by the relationships we have throughout our lives. Self-concept is based on our understanding of ourselves and the factors which have influenced our development. Self-concept is based on our cultural background and our values and beliefs. Self-image results from the way in which we have been treated by others and the effect this has on the way we feel about ourselves. Positive relationships tend to encourage a positive self-image and a feeling of confidence and self-belief. Negative relationships can lead to seeing ourselves as being of little value and having no confidence and no self-belief. This is because most of our self-image is formed by the way others make us feel. Someone in a relationship where they are constantly undermined and belittled is likely to feel they are of little value as a person and so have little confidence in their own abilities. This is because they have been exposed to the negative effects of the relationship.

Self-Concept

I am not the sort of person who breaks the law

I am an honest person

I like being part of a family

I have clear values

I am good with children

I believe in equal rights

I am quite clever

I like other people

I care about others

I am a friendly person

I am fairly bright

These are some of the ways we can see ourselves

These are some of the ways we can value ourselves

Difficulties which can surround relationships when they go wrong

Many of the people you care for will have problems in maintaining relationships which matter to them. Relationships can become difficult for various reasons:

- Divorce
- Custody arrangements
- Relationships which have become abusive
- Relationships which are stressful – e.g. a former friend who has become very demanding or difficult
- Relationships with people who have moved away
- Relationships where communication difficulties have made the relationship hard to maintain – e.g. where an individual has had an illness or injury, such as a stroke or brain injury, which has changed their means of communication
- One-sided relationships where only one of the people involved wishes to continue. This could be your client or it could be the other person involved.

- Relationships which are determined by a court order – such as an access or contact order for a parent and children following a divorce.

How to support clients in making decisions about relationships

The basic principles of how you can offer support to clients in difficult relationships are the same regardless of the reasons for the problems. You need to establish the level of help they need from you. As in all your work with clients, you should ensure you are offering help at a level which they say they require and not at a level which you think they need. Once you have established in discussion with the client what help and support you are able to offer and the limits of what you can do, you need to draw up and agree a plan with them. This then should make it clear to the client what actions you will be able to take and what is outside of your role and responsibilities.

For example, a client may ask you to make contact with an ex-partner because they wish to resume a relationship. You need to explain that this is not an appropriate role for you to undertake, but that you would be happy to assist them by providing information on how to locate someone and by providing any necessary support that they may need in writing letters, making telephone calls, sending e-mails, or any other help they may require in order to make contact. It is not appropriate for you to become a 'go-between' in a relationship, and you may have to work hard to convince your client that this is not something you are in a position to do for them. Alternatively, you may be asked to arrange for a meeting with somebody with whom contact is prohibited by a court order. You must point out that you are unable to assist your client in any way to break the law or to deliberately fail to comply with any order of the court.

Other situations may not be as clear cut. For example, you may be asked by a client to assist them in maintaining a relationship with someone who you are aware has caused problems or difficulties for the client in the past. The client could be someone who is receiving support and medication to assist with their mental health problems and it is known that the person they wish to contact has been a contributory factor in the deterioration of their mental health and well-being in the past. This is a difficult situation which you would need to discuss with the care team and to take an agreed view of the level of assistance and support that you would feel able to provide.

Unless there are court orders preventing contact, decisions about contact, even with people who may have a detrimental effect, ultimately have to be made by the client. However, you or an agreed team member should discuss the potential effects that such contact may have and should be very clear that any decisions the client makes are made after full discussion and full consideration of the possible consequences.

Keys to good practice

- Always agree the level of support with the client.
- Do not agree to become directly involved in a client's relationship.
- Do not agree to support a client in flouting or ignoring a court order.
- Ensure that the client has considered the consequences of a potentially damaging relationship.
- Remember that you cannot prevent or forbid any legal relationship a client wishes to develop.

Case study

V has MS and uses a wheelchair for mobility. She had a relationship with S, who was not disabled, which lasted for about a year. This finally broke up about nine months ago. V was very dependent on S, who encouraged her dependency and did everything for her. V's independence was seriously affected during her relationship and this undermined her ability to undertake even the most straightforward of tasks for herself. Since the break up, which was initiated by S, V, although she was initially very upset, has been able to develop a far greater degree of independence and has been re-taking control of her life. She has recently started to receive direct payments and has now established a good team of carers who are able to meet her needs. V has begun working again, which she had stopped doing when she was with S because he thought it was too much for her, and has developed a new circle of friends.

S had now contacted V again and wishes to re-start the relationship. V was distressed by the break up, and is keen to get involved again. She has told you very excitedly about this. As her key worker, you are very concerned at this prospect because of the way S made her so dependent previously. You feel that such behaviour was clearly more about meeting S's own needs than out of any genuine concern for V. You also dislike S and find it difficult to view him in a positive way.

1 How would you respond to V when she told you about this development?
2 Do you feel that you should share your concerns with V?
3 If so, how would you go about it?
4 Would there be any justification for speaking to S?
5 What factors are likely to influence your approach?
6 List the difficulties you would face in dealing with this situation.

Barriers to relationships

There are barriers that can make it difficult for people to start or maintain relationships. To help and support clients in overcoming barriers to relationships you must discuss with them the type of help they want from you.

Language

If there are language barriers then the use of translators can be considered; if there are difficulties with speech communication, then options such as the use of electronic or written means of communicating can be explored. It may also be possible for you to support a friend or relative of your client in learning the communication system that your client uses.

Access

If a client is experiencing access difficulties, either because of distance or because of the physical limitations of the environment, then you should explore some of the alternative options with them.

Transport

Transport can often be a barrier to relationships, sometimes in the same way as access is. You are likely to be able to help with this if the client wants you to.

Communication

Communication can be a problem for clients with particular communication needs, and who are keen to maintain or begin a relationship with someone who may or may not have particular communication needs themselves. In such a case you need to explore with the client the communication needs of the other person in the relationship. You will need to look at ways in which any differences can be overcome.

Environment

The environment can be a barrier to relationships. For example, a client living in an environment with a minimal amount of privacy, perhaps in residential accommodation, may find it difficult to develop or maintain a personal relationship. You may need to consider ways in which they can have access to quiet and personal time where they will have a chance to develop a close personal relationship with someone else.

Overcoming barriers to maintaining relationships

Apart from face-to-face contact (through visits or meetings) there are various other ways to overcome barriers in order to maintain relationships. These include:

- Letter
- Telephone
- Camcorder
- E-mails
- Video

Barriers fall into four broad categories: physical, legal, emotional and communication. Below are just a few examples of the kind of situations you may have to deal with and some suggestions of ways to respond.

Type of barrier	Example	Ways to overcome barriers
Physical	1 Wheelchair user wishes to maintain contact with a friend or relative who lives in a high-rise block of flats which has lifts that are too small to take a wheelchair.	1 The relative or friend comes to visit your client in their location or a meeting is arranged in a location where there is suitable access for both parties.
	2 The friend or relative living in the high-rise block is house-bound and unable to leave their own flat.	2 Discuss alternative ways of maintaining a relationship. Relationships do not have to be conducted face to face – if they did families and friends who moved to different parts of the country or different parts of the world would soon lose touch with each other!
Legal	Your client's contact with his children is limited to one day every other month, and must be supervised by a support worker.	Provide the support and supervision, try to make the contact sessions as pleasant as possible for the children and your client. Arrange for some contacts to take place at different venues (provided the court order does not specify). Be as unobtrusive as possible.

Emotional	Your client has a long-standing disagreement with a sibling; they have not spoken for years. The sibling now wants to heal the split. Your client is reluctant to forgive and forget.	Provide emotional support, use counselling skills to allow your client to explore the reasons for the problem. Assist them to look at the positive and negative aspects of the relationship and to make an informed and considered decision.
Communication	Your client's mother has suffered a stroke, she now has difficulty speaking. Your client is distressed by not being able to communicate.	Help your client to explore other means of communication such as flash cards, written word, etc.

Active knowledge

Look at the types of barriers to relationships experienced by the clients you work with. Choose one client and list all their relationships. Next, note down how each one is maintained, and note any barriers which have been overcome. Then note any relationships which have been abandoned or not developed because the barriers were not overcome. Think about ways in which you could have dealt with the barriers and what resources would have been needed.

Issues around contact with others

The term 'contact' is usually linked to relationships regulated in some way by the law, as in the case of the access and contact of a relationship with children, other relatives or family members being laid down by a court of law.

Mental Health Act

You may come across the issue of contact if you work with clients who are subject to the requirements of the Mental Health Act 1983. Depending on their circumstances, they may or may not have received compulsory treatment or may have been detained compulsorily in hospital under the Mental Health Act, thus limiting the contact they are able to have with others who are important to them. You may find you have a client whose contact with certain other people has been restricted under the Act by a court order, or who the courts may have placed under the guardianship of a social services department, which may or may not include limiting access or contact with certain people.

The Mental Health Act is currently under review by the government. New proposals are likely to include the provision of compulsory treatment for mental health problems in people's own homes rather than compulsorily treating them in hospital as they currently are. This will also increase the need for reviewing any decisions which impose compulsory orders of any kind on individuals, who will also have greater access than they do now to review tribunals for any decisions made.

If you are working with clients who have restrictions imposed on them, then you will need to ensure that you work within the legal framework but support them in dealing with the inevitable frustrations and difficulties they will face. This can be extremely taxing for both you and the client, but it is essential that they understand the terms of the order which restricts them and the consequences of not complying with the order. Clients who persistently break the terms of a requirement under the Mental Health Act risk having a greater degree of restriction imposed on them. For example, they may have to move from living in the community to living in a hostel, or from there into a supervised hostel, or ultimately into hospital.

You may need to frequently re-state the possible consequences of their actions and to regularly review their actions and provide them with the opportunity to express their anger and frustration. Along with the rest of the care team, you will need to look at ways in which a client's anger and frustration can be managed by using therapeutic activities and opportunities for expression. If a client is having issues with managing their frustrations, it is important this is discussed in a review and appropriate plans made for dealing with them.

Court orders

You may also need to support clients whose access to others is limited by a court order. The order may be a result of divorce or an injunction or an order under the Children Act which either prevents them contacting their children or former partners or limits the extent to which they can contact them. Or it may be that it is their former partner or their parents who are subject to limited access or contact with them. It is important that the whole team is aware of the restrictions and aware of the precise legal position so that compliance can be ensured. You may have an important role in assisting or supervising access and contact. This could be as a requirement of the court or it may be at the request of the client. In either case you should ensure that you work closely with the client and discuss with them exactly what arrangements need to be put in place, and make clear what your role will be.

For example, if you are asked to provide a supervised access environment for a client and their children, then you must make it clear that your role is to supervise the access and not to become involved in any arguments or disputes with an ex-partner over custody arrangements. You will need to be very clear about this so that your client has no doubts about your role.

Frequently parents who are in dispute over access custody of children will use them to try to gain an advantage over one another. You may be told:

> *'He says he doesn't want to go back to his Mum's because he doesn't like her new boyfriend. Will you be my witness that he doesn't want to go back and I'm keeping him here?'*

Your response must be:

> *'If you want to change the access or custody arrangements you must speak to your solicitor and ask for an emergency court hearing. You cannot take matters into your own hands. I cannot agree to provide any sort of witness evidence for you.'*

Your response to an allegation that the other parent is abusing a child must be:

> *'I will refer this to the duty social worker and the whole matter will have to be investigated. You may or may not be able to keep your child with you, but this will be decided by the police and social services after investigations. I cannot agree to you taking any action without the agreement of the court or the child protection agencies.'*

These are matters for solicitors, police and statutory social workers. However, you may be able to support your client in accessing the appropriate legal advice if they have problems doing so. The key points when working to support clients in maintaining relationships are the following:

Keys to good practice

- Your role is to support clients in their decisions – not to make decisions for them.
- You must ensure that the basis on which you are able to offer support is clear and the client knows the limits of your role.
- Ensure that you comply with any legal restrictions and requirements.
- Research the consequences of your client not complying with the particular court decision.
- Clearly explain to the client the consequences of them failing to comply with legal requirements of court orders.
- Always ensure that you have taken every possible step to overcome barriers which are creating difficulties for clients.

Recording decisions

As with any decisions taken about working with your clients, decisions regarding relationships and contact must be recorded clearly so that any other team members are aware of what decisions have been taken and what agreements have been reached. Use the following checklist to help you remember what and how to record.

Checklist for recording decisions

- Copies of any court orders should be obtained from the relevant agencies, and details of the consequences of failure to comply should be recorded.
- Plans for supervised contact visits should be noted carefully, so that the client will not be disappointed if someone has to take over from you and the plans change.
- Agreements reached about assistance to overcome physical barriers to relationships should be noted, and will need team discussion if they involve resources.
- Make a note of discussions – not the detail, just the outcomes – which you have about the emotional factors around relationships and the difficulties clients may have had. It is important that others in the team know the issues.

Active knowledge

Choose a set of case notes for one of your clients. Check how many entries provide information about relationships. Think about how much you know about your client's relationships that is not in the case notes. Work out how much you could find out about your client's relationships if they were a new client to you. Asking the following questions will help:

- Who are the people who are important in this client's life?
- Who are the people with difficult relationships?

- What are the plans for approaching the difficulties?
- Are there any court orders or other restrictions?
- What are the consequences of failure to comply?

Transfer notes from what you know into the case notes!

Support clients in maintaining and evaluating contact in difficult or potentially difficult relationships

WHAT YOU NEED TO LEARN

- Your role in supporting contact.
- How clients' conditions can affect contact.
- Ways to provide support.
- Recording contact information.

Your role in supporting contact

Once it has been established that your client is to make contact with someone who is important to them but the relationship is difficult or could be difficult, you may need to provide help and support to your client in maintaining that relationship and in dealing with any difficulties that they may experience as a result of it. As always you will need to discuss carefully with your client the level of support they need and what is appropriate. Depending on the circumstances, your role can be hugely varied. For example:

Your role	Key practice points
You may be asked to be present throughout a meeting with the relative or friend in question.	• You are there to support not to run the meeting. • You are not there to become involved or take sides. • Agree in advance what you will and will not say and do – and stick to it. • Concentrate on what is happening – be prepared to offer feedback if you are asked.
Another client may simply want some help from you in setting up the contact by assisting with finding an appropriate location for a face-to-face meeting.	• Agree the level of help required. • Provide any necessary contact information. • Relay any messages clearly without interpreting or changing them. • Double check any booking or travel arrangements.

Your role	Key practice points
You need to provide reassurance before a potentially difficult meeting or some support and discussion afterwards.	• Set aside sufficient time for the discussion. • Ensure that the environment is appropriate. • Use your communication and counselling skills. • Do not attempt to direct or control.
Assist if the contact is to be by telephone or by using an electronic means such as e-mail.	• Act as an intermediary if needed to relay information by telephone or e-mail. • Relay any messages clearly without interpreting or changing them. • Provide access to specially adapted electronic or telephone communication, if necessary.

It is always important to clarify with your client exactly what help they are expecting you to provide. You must ensure that the expectations are realistic and you are not being asked to do anything which exceeds your job role or which may break any conditions which have been laid down in respect of the particular contact or meeting. You should always try to make sure that your job role and its limits are clearly understood (see Element W5.1 about legal restrictions and the limits of your role).

How clients' conditions can affect contact

The client's physical or emotional condition or current mental health can affect relationships or the potential for relationships. For example, if you are working with a client with a degenerative condition and they are attempting to re-establish contact with someone they have not met for a long time, then it may be important to discuss with your client whether or not they wish to prepare the person they want to contact for any changes in their condition.

The same applies if your client has mental health problems. The person they wish to contact may not be familiar with their condition, or may be unaware of the effect their mental health problems has had on their behaviour. Or the person they wish to contact may only have known your client during periods when their mental health problems were difficult, and may be concerned and anxious about meeting them again. In such a case this has to be addressed in order to allow a meeting to take place.

Active knowledge

Try to think of an occasion where you have been apprehensive about meeting someone you have not seen for a long time, or where your meeting was difficult on the last occasion. It may be a school reunion or a college get together. It could be a meeting with a relative or a family member with whom you argued on the last occasion you met, or it could be with a senior manager in your organisation whose last contact with you involved a disciplinary matter. There are a wide range of possibilities. Try to think of one or two and make some notes about how you felt and also whether the meeting justified the nervousness that you felt in advance.

Ways to provide support

If your client has asked you to be present to support them during a meeting then you need to be clear about the role you are being asked to play. If your role is simply to provide support for your client, who may feel more confident and relaxed simply because you are there, then you may not need to take an active role in the meeting itself. However, if your client has asked you there to play a role as an advocate, then you should be very clear in explaining the limitations of that role and how you handle it. As a general rule, if you are undertaking advocacy on your client's behalf it would be at the request of the client because it was something they were unable to undertake for themselves, either because they are physically or emotionally unable to do so or because of other significant barriers preventing them doing so.

The role of an advocate is to put forward the views of the person they represent. However, be careful that you are not drawn into being asked to provide advocacy where the meeting involves a personal dispute between your client and the person they are meeting. Generally, your advocacy role should be limited to occasions when clients are unable to undertake the role themselves. You should not allow yourself to be in a position where a client is trying to use you to back up or support their point of view.

Support before or after a meeting

If you are not attending a contact meeting to support your client, because you have not been asked or it isn't appropriate, you may need to provide support before or after your client has made contact with the other person in their relationship. The support you give can range from straightforward reassurance and information to relieve anxiety and apprehension to using basic counselling skills to resolve some of the questions, issues and concerns which may have resulted from a meeting. If you find yourself having to offer extensive support to your client, you should talk to your supervisor or line manager if you feel you need advice or guidance before you undertake the task; otherwise make sure you do the following:

- You must follow basic procedures of good communication. Remember to talk to your client in an appropriate environment where they can be relaxed and comfortable.
- Remember that you are doing the listening, not the talking.
- Listen actively to what your client tells you and prompt by nodding and using encouraging words.
- You may need to mirror what your client has said to show that you have understood.
- Paraphrasing may also show your client that you are listening to what they are telling you.
- Try to avoid giving direct advice if at all possible, but try to get the client to understand for themselves what has happened to them and to look at the options for their next course of action.
- Review the work you did for Units CL1 and CL2 to ensure that you are using good communication skills.

Support for you

Never underestimate how hard it can be to be involved in someone else's difficult relationship. As a care worker there may be times when you feel distressed, concerned or worried by a situation you have become involved in. You may be concerned about the work you have been asked to do or because you feel a relationship is potentially dangerous, either for your client or for someone else involved in it. Or it could be that the work has been emotionally traumatic. For whatever reason, you should ensure that you get support for yourself. In the first place, you should go to your supervisor or line manager. They may be able to help or they may refer you for support outside your workplace. Remember, this is not a reflection on your abilities; in fact it is a positive reflection that you are able to recognise your own need for support and to do something about it, rather than attempt to continue, which can result in extreme stress and difficulties in maintaining your own standards of good practice.

Case study

D is 24 years old. He lives with his parents and has used a wheelchair since a serious road accident three years ago. D suffered serious head and facial injuries in the accident but has, apart from mood swings, recovered well from his brain injuries. He has been left with a changed appearance following his facial injuries.

D has been communicating by e-mail with a woman he met through an internet chat room. The communication has been going on for a couple of months and D has now made plans to meet the young woman. His parents have expressed their concerns but D flies into a rage when he is challenged. D's support worker has spoken to him at length about the intended meeting and has discovered that D has not prepared the young woman in any way for the meeting; she is unaware that D uses a wheelchair and is also unaware of the effect that the accident has had on his appearance. D's support worker is aware of the fact that he will need to attempt to bring about some change in D's intended course of action in order to avoid a potentially difficult situation.

1 How would you tackle the issue of this meeting?
2 What action can the support worker take if D proves to be adamant?
3 What advice should be given to D's parents?
4 What steps should the worker take
    a before the meeting
    b after the meeting?
5 What are the potential difficulties for D which could follow?

Recording contact information

It is important that information on a client's contacts are kept up to date in your client records. The rest of the members of the care team will need to know if any information has changed, such as contact details for people who are important to the client, or the arrangements for meeting and contacts with others, or if the legal position has altered. These should be recorded clearly and immediately. It is no good you knowing that your client's mother, whom she sees every week, has changed address if you are off work sick and nobody else knows about the change, which may mean that visiting arrangements break down.

Your role is vital to your clients in maintaining relationships that they wish to or are required to. You also need to support them when they make decisions about relationships which are, or could be, difficult to handle. The role is not an easy one, and it may not be one which you have to undertake on a regular basis. However, it is important. When you do have to take it on the demands and amount of time can be quite significant. You will need to be prepared and to have considered the implications of what you will need to do to fulfil this role.

Unit test

1   What are the different types of relationships?

2   What are the main features of relationships?

3   How are families structured in different ways?

4   What are the factors that affect how we see ourselves?

5   What are the factors that affect how we value ourselves?

6   How do relationships affect self-image?

7   How can relationships be affected by legislation?

8   What is the range of roles that a care worker may be asked to undertake in respect of client relationships?

9   What are the conditions that can affect a client's relationship with others?

10   Why is it important to record information about clients' contacts?

Unit X2 Prepare and provide agreed individual development activities for clients

Activities are important for a wide range of clients and can serve a different purpose for each individual. Well planned and supported activities are about much more than giving people something to do. Activities can support development and can provide a valuable way for individuals to promote various aspects of development which may have been impaired, delayed or interrupted. There are several key stages to providing development activities: you will need to learn about how clients are assessed, how to plan activities, the best ways to support clients when activities are taking place, and how to evaluate the effectiveness of the activities you have been involved with.

Being involved in activities with clients, whether individually or in a group, can be thoroughly enjoyable and good fun, depending on the activity of course! It gives you a really good chance to get to know your clients well and enables you to use the time well to build and develop relationships as well as supporting clients to further their development.

Element X2.1 Contribute to the assessment of clients' abilities and needs

WHAT YOU NEED TO LEARN

- Why clients have to be assessed.
- Ways of assessing clients.
- How to involve clients in assessments.
- How to record assessments.

Why clients have to be assessed

Before any activities can be planned or undertaken, first you have to know:

- if your client needs any development support
- what the developmental needs are
- what your client can already do.

The assessment process should give you this information. If you started planning a series of developmental activities without carrying out an assessment, it is possible you could be involving the client and yourself in something which is inappropriate, unnecessary, and a complete waste of time. Not because it was badly planned or prepared, or because it was badly administered, but because it was not the right activity and it was not pitched at the right level of development for the particular client.

Think about any activity you undertake, for example riding a horse. If you have never ridden a horse before, it would be counterproductive for you to be given the largest horse and be told to ride over a series of large jumps. You would simply fall off and not learn anything! On the other hand, if you are a highly skilled and experienced chess player, you would not learn much from playing in the local 'Chess for beginners' class!!

Assessment is also important because it allows you to measure the development levels of particular individuals. Regardless of the client group you are working with, it is important to measure and record development progress. Measuring development and recording data for an individual is an important part of the assessment. Remember, measuring is different from finding out about needs, or how much support someone needs. In order to measure anything, there must be something to measure against. The most obvious is measuring length or height, which cannot be done without some form of measuring instrument. The instrument can be as simple as a ruler or tape measure or as complex as a fine electronic measuring device used by engineers. If measurements are not accurate, all kinds of problems can develop.

Anything can go wrong if your measurements are not accurate

Active knowledge

Think about the sort of things you measure frequently, for example the ingredients for a recipe, how tall your children have grown, your weight, all of which are measured against an agreed and accepted scale. You can easily obtain the tools you need to carry out the measuring, such as scales, rulers or tape measures, and these will enable you to measure against an agreed scale which is universally accepted.

There are a range of abilities you may need to measure, depending on your client group and the individual concerned. You may need to measure the degree of sensory impairment, by looking at the results from a range of different tests and observations which have been carried out by the relevant professional, or you may need to carry out some of the measurements and observations yourself. You may need to measure the extent to which someone can participate in an activity according to their level of mobility. You might have to make a judgement about the likely benefits of an activity given a client's current mental health issues, or their likely level of understanding. Some of the abilities you need to assess may be relatively easy to measure because of the formal tests which have been established and which are generally accepted as giving you the necessary information.

Ways of assessing clients

There are many specific assessment programmes and tests which have been devised to measure specific conditions; doctors and psychologists for example use a wide range of tests to measure conditions ranging from cerebral palsy to autism and from dyslexia to sensory impairment. These are called Standardised Tests, because that is what they are. They measure against an agreed standard, so that the results are comparable for all those being assessed. Formal assessments are usually administered by the relevant professional depending on the condition being assessed and will provide a clear set of measures and a system for making judgements – often using a scoring system. Well known examples of formal assessment are:

The Snellen eye chart is one way of testing the eyesight of clients

- An IQ test, which asks a series of questions or gives problems to solve, the results being measured against a scale, and an IQ score being given. IQ tests are usually administered and scored by psychologists or, occasionally, teachers.
- An eye test, which is the basic test of reading letters on a card. This provides an optician, or a doctor, with some basic information about your sight from which they can go on to find out more by using a series of other tests.

You may also know about other tests, for example:

- Portage workers undertake an assessment of a child, along with the parents, using a checklist. This checklist is used to measure a child's abilities in six areas: infant stimulation, social development, communication, speech and language, self-help, cognitive development and motor development.
- Health visitors can do a preliminary test called CHAT (Checklist for Autism in Toddlers) which can identify potential autism in toddlers as young as 18 months. This is a questionnaire which the health visitor will ask parents, followed by observations which the health visitor, or other primary care worker (such as the GP), needs to make. Both sections of the test are scored and the results give an indication that the child may be at risk of developing a social-communication disorder such as autism. The questionnaire asks a series of questions such as:
  - Does your child ever PRETEND, for example, to make a cup of tea using a toy cup and teapot, or pretend other things?
  - Does your child ever use his/her index finger to point, to indicate INTEREST in something?

Observations also need to be made, such as:

- Get child's attention, then point across the room at an interesting object and say 'Oh look! There's a (name of toy!).' Watch child's face. Does the child look across to see what you are pointing at?
- Get the child's attention, then give child a miniature toy cup and teapot and say 'Can you make a cup of tea? Does the child pretend to pour out tea, drink it, etc.?

- Say to the child 'Where's the light?', or 'Show me the light'. Does the child POINT with his/her index finger at the light?

This last test is a mixture of a questionnaire and observation, but is still a formal means of assessing with a standard scoring system. It is also likely that you will use more informal systems which may use some of the same techniques, but will use the outcomes in a different way.

Sometimes assessments will need specialised equipment for carrying them out, for example testing a client's fine motor skills may involve them in being asked to pick up and move small objects, or to draw or fill in outlined objects. Standardised psychological tests will have scoring charts and documentation to interpret the results. Tests designed to measure sensory impairment are likely to use advanced technology, as will many of the tests designed to measure physical levels of functioning. If you are involved in the administration of these formal assessments, you must be sure that you have all the necessary equipment you will need prepared and ready before the start of the assessment. It is not good practice to interrupt an assessment because you have forgotten a vital piece of equipment or an essential chart, so check, and then check again!

Informal assessment

Informal assessment does not use a formal system of scoring results against a set of agreed measures in the same way as standardised tests, however you will need to make professional judgements based on what you learn from observations, interviewing clients or using a checklist. For example, you may make a judgement about whether or not someone with learning difficulties is able to benefit from an activity you are planning around using ICT as an aid to daily living, or whether a group of clients who have poor concentration as a result of depressive illnesses will benefit from a memory game designed to improve concentration.

In your workplace, you may have drawn up a checklist of factors you need to take into account for clients before decisions are taken as to whether or not they will benefit from an activity. If not, you will need to work with other members of the care team to develop one. Your checklist will, of course, be specific to your workplace and your particular group of clients. The checklist for the technology activity is likely to include the following areas for consideration:

- Familiarity with technology
- Ability to follow instructions
- Ability to retain information and repeat actions
- Likelihood of direct benefit from using technology
- Problem-solving skills
- Interest in technology

You may also discuss with the client the possibility of them being involved with this type of activity, and you would judge from their response the level of enthusiasm and interest. A discussion would also give you the chance to deal with any questions or concerns they may have, all of which will feed into the assessment process. If the client is one you work with regularly, you will also have other valuable insights to feed into the assessment process. For example, you will know whether or not there are family members or friends who are likely to be supportive and interested in activities based around technology, and you will know the clients' previous responses in situations where they have been involved in something new. For discussions or interviews, you will need to use your communication skills, see Units CL1 and CL2.

Keys to good practice

Interviews/discussions

- Make sure you are sitting in a warm, well lit, comfortable environment.

- Check that the client is comfortably seated, does not have sun in their eyes, etc.

- Use any communication support necessary in order to deal with any differences between the client's communication style and yours.

- Lean slightly forward in your seat to indicate that you are interested.

- Use open questions to promote communication.

- Use your body language to indicate your interest in what is being said.

- Use encouraging nods and sounds to promote the client's responses.

- Remember you are there to listen, observe and encourage, not to talk!

Active knowledge

Check out the arrangements in your workplace for undertaking assessments. Look at the different factors which are taken into account for different types of activities. Make a list of activities and note down one particular factor you would take into account for each activity on your list.

Observation

Another skill you will use is observation. Observation is about much more than simply looking at someone or something. In order to observe, you will need to know in advance what you are looking for, and to watch carefully and note down details of the relevant observations you make. For example, you may decide after careful observation of a client who has been depressed, that they seem to respond better to some clients in the group rather than others. The information gained from this observation could be useful if you are designing activities which involve interacting with others. In another case, you may have observed that a particular client with learning difficulties has a noticeable improvement in motor control when he is transplanting small seedlings. This could be valuable information if you are thinking about the types of activities which could improve his motor skills, and you could try developing horticulturally based activities!

The value of good observation is a key part of assessment. Although observation can be a specific, planned assessment tool, it can also be spontaneous and part of your everyday work. Remember, good observations involve the following:

- Be unobtrusive – do not sit and stare!
- Always be alert to what is happening around you.
- Observe details such as people's body language and non-verbal communication.
- Look at people's reaction to their environment and others around them.
- Make notes about what you observe – you will not remember the detail.

Observation of clients involves much more than just looking at them

Ways to involve clients in assessments

Remember this is the client's assessment. It is about them, and they are the most important person in the process. So it is essential that the client feels that they are involved and not that the assessment is something which is being 'done to' them.

This is not always easy, particularly if the assessment is a standardised test or a formal process. These are often not designed in a way which encourages clients to feel they are gaining something from the process. It is easy for people to feel they are being tested or experimented on, a bit like a laboratory animal. So it is your job to make sure that your clients are clear about:

- What is to happen
- Why it is happening
- How it will be carried out
- What they need to do
- How to stop it if they are unhappy.

You should tell your client things using their preferred method of communication. In the case of a new client you will need to find out how they need to communicate. For those you are familiar with you will know which method to use to communicate with them and how to make sure that the support is available. For example, if a client uses sensory aids you need to make sure these are available and can be used if necessary. You should always check that devices such as hearing aids are working correctly. There is no point in giving a client a carefully thought out explanation of the assessment you are about to undertake, only to discover their hearing aid had no working batteries and they haven't heard a word you said!

It is also important for the assessment that all sensory and other equipment is in working order, otherwise you risk not getting an accurate picture of the client's level of development and the needs which they have. If you attempted to undertake an assessment for a client who normally wears glasses, but who did not wear them for the assessment, you are likely to find that you have made an inaccurate judgement about what size print you need to use or the extent to which activities based on visual participation will be of value.

Remember to check:

> ## Checklist of aids
> - Glasses – check and clean if necessary
> - Hearing aids – check batteries and clean if necessary
> - Speaking aids, such as voice synthesisers – check and obtain technical help if necessary
> - Prosthesis
> - Any implants related to mobility or sensory function
> - Mobility aids

If you do a check like this, you can make sure that the information you are sharing with the client gives them the opportunity to fully understand it. Most assessments require and certainly benefit from client co-operation. In order to obtain maximum possible co-operation, you must be sure that clients understand:

- why the assessment is being done
- what exactly is going to happen
- what you have found out when the assessment is complete
- what the results mean in terms of the activities which will follow.

Obtaining agreement

Only by carefully explaining the purpose and process of the assessment can you ensure the client agrees with the assessment going ahead. Clients must be able to make an informed decision. Do not proceed with an assessment without the client's agreement. An assessment is no different to any other procedure you are carrying out, so consent must always be given. Provided that the purpose of the assessment is understood and that a client, or their advocate, can see how the assessment and subsequent activities are linked to their agreed plan of care, you are unlikely to experience any difficulties with obtaining agreement. However, if agreement is refused, you must not proceed with the assessment and will need to refer back to your manager and the rest of the care team for further discussion.

Your workplace will have a protocol relating to consent for assessments. It is unlikely to involve the signing of a written consent form, as assessments are not usually invasive procedures, however you will have to comply with the procedure in your workplace for obtaining consent. It is most likely that a verbal indication of agreement is sufficient. The most common form of agreement you are likely to come across is, ' …so that's how it will work – OK? Yes, that's fine.'

Active knowledge
Find out your workplace protocol for consent for assessment – see if it varies depending on the type of assessment, or if it is always verbal or always written. Check how this relates to the overall policy regarding consent for other procedures. Is there a difference ? Try to find out the reason and justification for the difference.

How to record assessments

Recording both the process and the results of assessments is important in the overall care of the client. If you are using a formal assessment method, the assessment process is likely to include a scoring or record sheet. This will need to be completed in order to obtain the results of the assessment, and is then usually kept in the client records for future reference. If you have carried out an assessment based on more informal methods, such as observation or interviews, you will need to make sure that you have recorded the results in the client's notes in the normal way. This will provide useful information for other members of the care team, and will mean that future plans will be able to make use of the assessment results you have obtained and recorded. All recordings which are not on a formal record sheet accompanying the assessment should be clear and readily usable by others. In order for assessment records to be of the maximum possible use, they need to include:

- The date, length and place of the assessment
- The purpose of the assessment
- Who was present
- The methods used for the assessment
- The client's view of the assessment
- The results
- The implications of the results
- The activities which are planned as a result of the assessment.

They also need to be readily accessible and be understood by colleagues, in order to be of most use. Records should not be too long, or include too much detail.

Case study

P is 27 years old. She lives with her two children aged 3 and 5. She has a hearing impairment for which she is supposed to wear a hearing aid, but doesn't wear it as she says she never sees anyone, so doesn't see the point.

P has not been outside the house since her youngest child was born and P suffered severe post-natal depression. P does not have a partner since he left because he was unable to cope with her post-natal depression. Transport is provided to take the children to nursery and school and P does most of her shopping from the mobile shop, or she has a friend who will shop for her.

If P attempts to leave the house, she experiences severe panic attacks. These have distressed her so much that she is now afraid to go out. However, P recognises that she needs to address some of the issues around her fears of going out, and has been working with a counsellor. She is keen to become involved in any activities which may help her.

1 What factors need to be taken into account when assessing P?
2 What do you consider may be the most appropriate method of assessing P?

Element X2.2 Plan and prepare agreed development activities for clients

WHAT YOU NEED TO LEARN

- Development activities.

- How to plan for activities.
- Ways to prepare for activities.

Development activities

Activities carried out for the specific purpose of improving the health or well-being of a client can be classed as development activites. It is the *purpose* not the *type* of activity which decides whether it qualifies as a developmental activity. For example, a commercial artist painting a picture because they have been commissioned to do so is doing something with a different purpose to the person who has mental health issues and is using the medium of art as a means of expressing many of the complex emotions and feelings they are attempting to deal with.

Another example is that of a group of older people chatting about the good times they remember from their youth and the way life used to be. This is different from a group of older people being encouraged to reminisce in order to help them to communicate, or when reminiscence is being used as part of a life review therapy for those who are terminally ill. The activity is the same, but the purpose if different.

Active knowledge

Think about activities which you undertake in your own life which may be repeated, but have a different purpose. For example, reading a magazine to look at the latest bathrooms or hairstyles or cars and reading a magazine because there is an article in it that your NVQ assessor has told you to read – by tomorrow! Then think about activities you carry out in your workplace. When does talking to someone stop being just chatting or communicating and start being a development or therapeutic activity? Discuss this with your supervisor or assessor.

A wide range of activities can be carried out with the purpose of promoting the development of an individual. Some of these may be undertaken by a specialist professional such as a physiotherapist, occupational therapist, art or music therapist, or other activities may be carried out by the client alone, or with support from professional carers in the care setting. You could be involved in planning and preparing for many different activities depending on the client group you work with and their assessed needs. The sorts of activities which may need to be planned in your workplace could be:

Development activities for the workplace	
Type of activity	**Examples of possible development or therapeutic value**
Social activities – e.g. birthday parties, social events, joint events with local community, visits to places of interest, luncheon, family outings, etc.	Prevents isolation, opportunity to have variety in life, promotes joy/happiness, provides support, companionship, improves health and well-being, helps meet emotional and social needs, maintains contact with outside activities, provides opportunities to maintain/increase social contacts, provides interest and stimulation

Intellectual activities – e.g. word games, chess, current events, using Internet and other IT, academic classes, health care groups, etc.	May help to improve verbal ability, stimulates thought processes, stimulates those with cognitive impairment, provides intellectual challenges, maintains contact with the outside world, helps orientation level, maintains intellectual/cognitive level
Spiritual activities – e.g. attending religious service, attending prayers, shabbat, shalom, nature sounds and sights, etc.	Meets need for pastoral/spiritual care, improves comfort level, maintains religious/cultural beliefs, helps with mood and behaviour, self-esteem, provides opportunities to socialise
Specialty activities – e.g. sensory integration, re-motivation, 24-hour reality orientation, handwriting classes, etc.	Maintains or increases alertness, decreases anxiety, improves or maintains orientation, increases motivation, helps with mood, maintains or improves skills, prevents withdrawal/regression, increases attention span, increases independence
Creative activities – e.g. resident council craft/art/poetry/creative writing classes, knitting, needlework, woodwork, etc.	Maintains or improves cognitive skills, improves self-esteem, improves motor control/co-ordination, provides intellectual stimulation
Physical activities – e.g. walking, exercise programmes, competitive sports, swimming, gardening, golf	Maintains or improves cardiovascular fitness, tones muscles, promotes feeling of well-being, improves self-esteem, maintains/improves mobility

How to plan for activities

Planning for the individual

The examples above show some of the activities which may be implemented in your workplace with some general suggestions about the therapeutic value they may have. However, the value is only realised for each individual if the activities are planned in response to the assessment of needs of the particular individual. An exercise programme which could provide a first-rate cardiovascular workout for a fit and active sixty-five-year-old could have dire consequences for an overweight, unfit forty-year-old!

In the first element of this unit, you looked at the ways in which assessments are undertaken. The planning of activities is the next step and is always based on the results of the assessment process. Depending on the type of activity, the planning may be undertaken by the relevant professional – for example a programme of muscular exercises for someone recovering from a stroke may be planned by a physiotherapist, or a programme of activities to support speech improvement may be planned by a speech therapist. Alternatively, those carers supporting the client may be asked to develop a programme of activities designed to promote and meet social, intellectual or emotional needs. This could include:

- Discussions
- Games
- Relaxation
- Outings
- Exercises
- Work experience

Planning process

In order for planning to be effective in promoting development goals, it needs to be about far more than just making sure that the timetable works or that you don't forget a vital piece of equipment! Of course, these things are important, but good planning is as much a part of the final benefit as the activity itself. Planning is part of a process which begins with assessment, and the two are closely linked. The assessment will have identified the client's needs and their ability to participate in any developmental activity. An assessment will also have identified the likely activities which are appropriate and will benefit the client. It is important that any planning takes all of these assessments into account. The plan is a means of achieving what the assessment has identified as being needed.

Setting goals, or aims

All plans must be moving towards a clearly identified goal, or goals. Without this, a plan is just a list of a series of actions which are not focussed and are without direction. Imagine a football team who took to the field without a game plan – everyone would be running everywhere without any clear idea of what they were doing. Something similar can happen to a care team who work without planning clear goals!

Goals can take all kinds of forms depending on the needs of the individual. There will be an overall aim for the client which will have been agreed by the client and the care team. The goals must all be aimed at achieving the overall aim – see the example in the case study below.

Case study

J is a young woman 27 years old. She has Down's syndrome and has always lived with her parents. J has attended a local day centre since she left school, but has always been very dependent on her parents and reluctant to meet new people or to try new experiences. She has always got on well with older people and seems to have a real rapport with them.

Her support worker has arranged for J to spend time as a volunteer at a local residential care home. Although shy at first, J has recently been increasing the time she has spent working as a volunteer. She makes tea and lays tables for the residents, she enjoys talking with the residents and now wants to learn how to improve her skills. J is hopeful that she may eventually be able to get a job at the residential home and is now asking for information about how she can increase her independence by moving out of home and into supported accommodation.

J's parents are now in their early seventies and have always been concerned about what will happen to her if they can no longer care for her. They are supportive of her wish to become more independent, and have requested that the care team look for ways to encourage J to be more independent.

Q: What is the aim for J?

A: To increase her ability to live as independent a life as possible.

Q: What are the goals for J?

Think about goals as the steps on the way to achieving the overall aim of the client. However, setting goals is all very well, achieving them is essential. In order for clients to be able to achieve the goals they have agreed with you, the goals must be realistic and achievable. There is no quicker way to demoralise and de-motivate an individual than to set unrealistic expectations which they constantly fail to meet. Goals are better to be small and achievable than large and out of reach. Goals must be related to an assessment of both need and ability. For example, someone who has a panic attack every time they leave their front door, is unlikely to achieve a goal of managing a Saturday afternoon shopping in Oxford Street! However, a goal of being able to walk as far as the front gate, or the bus stop, may be something they can manage. All of your communication skills may be needed to walk the fine line between aiming too low and contributing to a feeling of worthlessness or aiming too high and setting someone up to fail.

Setting the pace

The time-scales and pace of activities is also an important part of planning. As with the setting of goals, the speed at which goals need to be achieved is also a key as to how realistic it is for the individual concerned. The client, as always, should be

You are more likely to achieve your goals if you set yourself smaller ones to achieve over a relatively short period of time

involved in agreeing a reasonable time-scale for the achievement of their goals. You may find that you need to encourage and support individuals in thinking about what is realistic for their own circumstances and history. For example, someone with a long history of stress-related illness may decide that they want to be able to be off medication and back in full-time work in six weeks. However, a more realistic time-scale may be six months, or even twelve months. Asking anyone to work towards something so far away is unlikely to meet with success – smaller goals which can be achieved over relatively short periods of time are more likely to be achieved.

Remember, nothing succeeds like success – achievement makes people grow in confidence and therefore more likely to go on achieving.

Getting clients to participate in planning

Making sure that clients are involved in the planning process is one of your vital roles. Clients have a right to decide what they want to achieve and how they want to go about it to the best of their ability. They should be taking control of the process to whatever extent they are able. Having been involved throughout the assessment process, clients must be a part of planning any development activities which follow on.

The methods you use to encourage participation will vary depending on the setting in which you work and the level of ability of the individual concerned. If you work in a residential setting, participation could be on two levels: the individual may decide their own programme of activities, and a residents group may also have an overall plan for group activities for the setting as a whole.

Any of the following methods could be helpful in encouraging participation:

- One-to-one planning
- Involvement in the review process
- Discussions with significant carers, relatives or friends
- Preparing written plans for comments
- Taking the client to see activities to provide examples and ideas
- Asking client to prepare own plans.

Active knowledge

In your own workplace, find out the method for agreeing and recording goals for individual clients. Check if decisions are made by the care team, or by key workers, and what the process is for involving clients in decisions about activities. Discuss with your supervisor the basis for the procedures which are in place.

Ways to prepare for activities

Preparing for your role

You could be supporting, organising or participating in a wide range of activities and your role will be different depending on the client involved and the assessment of their level of need and ability. The extent to which you are directly involved or participate in the activity is also likely to vary, partly because of the activity, but also because of the individual needs of the client. In some activities you may be taking part alongside the client, in others you may need to demonstrate what needs to be done, and sometimes you may only be needed in order to set up the activity and give any advice and support.

Activities and roles

Type of activity	Likely role
Swimming	Participation/demonstration
Assertiveness group	Participation
Relaxation	Advice and instruction
Outings and visits	Participation
Art/craft group	Demonstration
Gardening	Demonstration/participation

Preparing equipment

Depending on the activity, you may need to have equipment or materials ready. Nothing is more guaranteed to make people become irritated and lose enthusiasm and interest than equipment being missing or you having to constantly disappear to get the missing items!

As part of the planning process, it is useful to make a list of any materials or equipment you will need and to make sure that it is ready, working and available. For example, if you are planning to run a relaxation session, you will need relaxing sounds or music CD or tape – and something to play it on. Your checklist may look something like this:

Checklist of activities items

- Numbers participating ☐
- Music CD ☐
- CD player ☐
- Check where power socket is ☐
- If no power socket – use batteries ☐
- Spare batteries ☐
- Check room warm ☐
- Individual mats or towels ☐
- Soft and warm floor covering ☐
- Check lighting – use lamps if too harsh ☐
- Privacy – curtains/blinds ☐

You can add tick boxes like the above to your checklist and tick off the items as you collect them together.

Your list for a visit to a theatre or gallery, designed to promote social and intellectual development, will look very different, and will include items such as tickets, guidebooks or programmes and transport arrangements.

If the activity is a craft session designed to develop motor and intellectual skills, such as making a collage, you may have prepared some materials in advance. You could have already cut up pieces of material and torn out magazine pages. Your list of materials in this case may be lengthy and will need to include items such as glue, scissors and paper. Access to water for cleaning up afterwards will be important as will good lighting and sufficient tables and chairs – all of these things will need to form part of your checklist.

If you are preparing for a board games session with a group, in order to improve concentration, intellectual and communication development, you may need to think about the games you are going to use and check that they are all available and are complete – Scrabble with half the letters missing, or Monopoly without a dice or Park Lane is not much fun!

You must make sure that all the items are available for clients when they engage in activities

As with all the planning and preparation process, the needs of the client or client group must take priority. There is little point in planning a relaxation session which involves lying on the floor with a group of clients who will have difficulty getting up and down! Similarly, material and equipment you are planning to use for your activities will need to be useable by the group or individual for whom the activity is designed. For example,

- If you are going to plan a craft session using glue, can the handles of the brushes be gripped by the clients who will be participating?
- If you are planning a games session, can everyone in the group see/read the cards and dice?
- If you are planning a discussion group, does anyone in the group need support in hearing what is going on?

Case study

M works at a busy day centre for people with mental health problems. He has only been working in the job for six months, but he loves the work and is starting his NVQ. He was asked to organise a small group for people who wanted to discuss issues around employment. All those who were participating had previously had issues with working, either because they presented challenging behaviour in the workplace or because they found workplaces threatening or stressful. Group members were all at the stage where they had decided they wished to get back into work, but wanted support and the opportunity to discuss concerns and fears in a group.

All the group rooms were in use on the day allocated for the first meeting, so J decided to use a room in the nearby council building. He left a message on the voicemail of the person responsible for booking rooms. Prior to the meeting J collected up-to-date information about employment opportunities and possible opportunities for work experience. He explained the aims of the group to the local job centre and agreed to keep them informed of developments.

On the day of the group meeting, everyone was ready and sitting in the main coffee area, and J explained that the meeting was to take place in the council building down the road. When they arrived, reception had no record of the room booking, however there was a room available and after about 10 minutes of negotiation J was able to book it. The room needed to have extra chairs brought in which made it a bit hot and squashed, but the group did eventually get started.

1 What was J's first mistake?
2 What should he have done?
3 What preparation did he miss?
4 What preparation did he do well?
5 How do you think group members were feeling by the time the group began?
6 How well do you think the group will progress towards meeting their goals?
7 What does J need to do next?

Element X2.3   Support clients in individualised development activities

WHAT YOU NEED TO LEARN

- How to ensure that clients are willing to participate in activities.
- Ways to give clients information about activities.
- Ways to give feedback and encouragement.

How to ensure that clients are willing to participate in activities

Establishing a client's consent

Gaining the client's consent for joining an activity is as essential as for a medical procedure. Be wary of assuming that the client is willing to participate without actually asking them. Because you may have been involved throughout the process of assessment and planning, it could have slipped your attention that no one has actually asked the client if this is something they wish to do!

Consent may not always have to be formal, such as signing a consent form, although some activities may require this. Your workplace will probably have clear policies regarding when specific consent is required – for example, if you were planning to take someone hang-gliding or hot-air ballooning you are likely to need to have formal consent!! On the other hand, if you are going for an outing to the local supermarket with someone who is about to move into semi-independent living, you are unlikely to need to get any forms signed to do this.

Active knowledge

Check out your workplace's policy on obtaining consent for activities. See if you can work out the basis for the policy. Is it based on the potential risk of the type of activities, or is it based on cost or level of involvement. If you are unsure, ask your supervisor.

If there are no requirements for formal consent for the activity you are planning, then you should still ensure that the client is a willing partner by checking directly with them. You will need to explain exactly what is planned, what will happen and the reasons for the activity so that you can be sure that they are giving informed consent. It is not enough to say, 'We'll go for a swim tomorrow OK?', unless this is a regular part of an ongoing programme which the client has already given consent to.

Ways to give clients information about activities

You will need, generally, to give more information, such as:

> 'You know you agreed at the last planning meeting that you wanted to take more physical exercise, well, I have checked out the times at the new pool and they have an adults-only session at 10am tomorrow. That means that it should be fairly quiet and not too much splashing. If you would like to go, we could get there at about 10 and stay for about half-an-hour. Allowing time to get changed, that should get us back here for about 11. Would that suit you?'

Providing clients with information can be done verbally, as in the example above, or it could be in a written format giving details of the plans. This could be an individual note, or, if it is something which is undertaken regularly, there may be a leaflet or poster giving information.

For some clients, it may also be appropriate to provide information to their carers – with the client's agreement of course. This may be particularly relevant where a client has poor memory recall or where the carer is likely to be involved in the activity or in the

This is one way of providing clients with information

consequences of the activity. For example, if a client is participating in a basic computer skills group and is likely to have some 'homework' to do, the carer may be needed to provide support at home. It is also generally good practice to involve carers in all aspects of a client's care, including activities and plans for promoting development. Where there is agreement carers should be a part of the process throughout.

Ways to give feedback and encouragement

Nothing is much worse than doing something, especially something new or something you are unsure about, and getting no information about how you are doing. Many of you will have taken a driving test. One of the most difficult aspects of the test is that you have no feedback while it is going on, you only know at the end how well (or otherwise!) you have done. Throughout the activities you should make sure that you provide feedback and encouragement to clients.

Feedback should always be constructive. If you need to offer criticism, it should always be positive and offer alternatives. Negative feedback is very destructive and de-motivating. For example:

> 'Lucy, you are relaxing much better now, if you keep going on the breathing pattern you'll find it will work even better.'

> 'Frank, that spreadsheet is so good – I think we could use it in the office if there was a date column added.'

> 'Liz, the way you have made contributions in the group recently has been fantastic. I'd love to see how well you can use your listening skills to help others to join in.'

These are all really positive ways of saying.

> 'Lucy, you won't ever relax properly unless you get your breathing right.'

> 'Frank, you've missed out the date column.'

> 'Liz, you need to not talk so much and give others a chance to get a word in edgeways.'

Active knowledge

Think of occasions when you have been put down by negative criticism. Try to remember how you felt. Make a list with two columns: one for negative and one for positive feedback. Use the examples above and add to them. For each one give the positive and negative versions. Over a period of about a week, make a note each time you make a criticism of how you could have done it more positively.

element X2.4   Evaluate agreed development activities with other members of the care team

WHAT YOU NEED TO LEARN

- How to measure progress towards goals.
- How to share information with the care team.

How to measure progress towards goals

The goals which were set during the planning process are the basis for evaluation. You will need to measure progress towards these goals. Some goals are easier to measure than others. If, for example, the goal was to walk unaided to the end of the corridor, its achievement, or progress, can be measured and recorded.

If, on the other hand, the goal was to become more assertive, that is more difficult to measure because it is largely about how people feel, however some examples can be used to illustrate progress.

Example 1:

John walked two-thirds of the way along the corridor unaided. This is excellent progress towards his goal and the exercise programme should continue.

Example 2:

Asher feels that the assertiveness group has helped him in changing his behaviour. He explained to his colleague this week that he was not able to do any extra work to cover for him again as he needed to leave work on time. He also sent back a meal at a restaurant because it was not what he ordered.

The judgement about the extent to which goals have been met must be made by the client along with the care team. In many cases it is the client's feelings which are being measured. It is often at the point of evaluation that goals can be changed. For example, a client may have wanted to live independently and move out of their parent's home. However, after developing more assertive behaviour they may have found there was a change in the relationship with their family which means that they no longer feel the need to leave.

Goals may also be reviewed and changed to be more demanding. Someone whose previous goal was to be able to leave the house without having a panic attack may now want to move the goal on to planning a visit to the supermarket.

A list of questions can be useful in supporting clients to think through what they have achieved and what they are looking for next. Each work setting will be different, and every client will need their own list, however something like this may help:

List of questions on achieving goals

1 What did you want to achieve?
2 Did you achieve it fully, partly, not at all?
3 How do you feel about your progress?
4 Has your goal changed?
5 If so, what is your goal now?
6 Do you think the way you set about achieving your goal worked?
7 If not, why not?
8 What do you want to do next?
9 How will this help towards your goal?

Depending on their circumstances and levels of ability, clients may prefer to think about this independently, some may wish to work it through with their carer, family or friends, and others may want their key worker to work with them. Whatever method they choose, you will also need to undertake your own evaluation of the progress towards the agreed goals and the effectiveness of the activities and approaches chosen.

How to share the information with the care team

Other members of the care team will need to be able to participate in the evaluation process, either because they may have their own contribution to make, or because they have an interest in the progress of the client. The most obvious time to discuss and share progress reports and evaluations is at a regular review meeting. Depending on your work setting these may be held at regular intervals, or when there is something to discuss. The process will usually involve all the professionals involved with a particular client, the client themselves and their carer. Review meetings give an excellent chance for everyone to make a contribution and develop the next stage of any care plan or programme.

Other workplaces may not operate in quite the same way and evaluation may be on a smaller scale and just involve the key worker and client, along with carers or family, and then the information may be passed on to the other members of the team. Regardless of the method, it is important that all progress and evaluations are recorded and any changes are clearly made in the client's care plans. There is detailed information about the review and evaluation process in Unit SC3.

Unit test

1 Why are development activities important?

2 List at least three purposes of developmental activities.

3 What types of activities can be useful for improving development?

4 What are the important aspects of planning?

5 Why is careful preparation important?

6 How can you support clients during activities?

7 What are the most effective ways of giving feedback?

8 Why is evaluation important?

9 How can you share information with the care team?

Unit Y2

Enable individuals to find out about and use services and facilities

In this unit you will have the opportunity to think about how you pass information to your clients and how you help them to gain access to the most useful services and facilities. Regardless of your role and area of work, you will at some point need to provide information to those you care for or to their relatives or friends. It is important that you understand how to access and update that information and how you can assist people, not only to consider services but to use them where they need support.

Information is knowledge and knowledge makes a huge contribution towards empowering people. Information and a familiarity with services and facilities which are available and accessible will provide the service users with the opportunity to increase their level of independence by being able to know about and use services without having to ask others to do it for them.

Element Y2.1 · Enable individuals to find out about services and facilities

WHAT YOU NEED TO LEARN

- How to establish the services clients need.
- How to obtain accurate information.
- How to provide information.

How to establish the services clients need

The key word in the heading for this section is 'clients'. You need to be sure that you establish what your client needs and wants in the way of services and facilities. You also need to know what is available so that you can help individuals to live independently.

This is not about what you think would be best for your client, tempting as it may be to try persuade your client to use a facility you think would benefit them. This is not your role – even if they would benefit enormously! Your role is to find out what your clients want and need and to give them the information to help them reach their own conclusions.

Do not assume your clients will necessarily be in a position to directly ask for the information they need. This is not as odd as it sounds. To be able to ask for what you need, you have to know the right questions to ask and you have to know that something exists. To establish the services that a client needs you may have to ask quite a few questions. You will not be able to rely on them being able to identify what it is they want. How can someone ask about when the local wheelchair archery club meets if they don't know it exists? How can an individual ask about how they can employ a carer using the direct payment scheme if they have never heard of the scheme?

Finding out clients' wants and needs

You will need to use your listening skills to pick up what it is that clients are looking for. It can also help if you ask some prompting questions. This may help point clients in the general direction of a service or facility they would like to use. The sort of questions are those that begin, 'Would you like…?', 'Would it help if …?', 'Would you enjoy…?' To allow your client the maximum possible independence in reaching their decisions, it may be better to phrase your questions generally, so 'Would you enjoy some company for lunch once or twice a week?' may be better than 'Would you like to go to the luncheon club at the community centre once or twice a week?' Posing a question in this way allows your client to gradually get used to the idea and to think about their preferences. It also allows people to stop at the point where they feel they have made sufficient commitment for the present. To continue with our elderly client and the luncheon club, it may be sufficient in a first conversation for them to establish they would like some company. It may take a little more time for them to decide they would like to join a group of other people rather than arrange for somebody to come and join them once or twice a week. The general question has allowed them, first of all, to make a decision about the idea of company. Later questions and discussion can establish exactly the form and the setting in which they would welcome the company. If you had begun the discussion by providing the full details of the luncheon club and the community centre, you may have received a negative response from the client, who actually would welcome company, but may not be totally convinced about meeting a lot of strangers or going to a strange building with which they were unfamiliar. However, with time and thought and full information, decisions can be taken at a pace which suits the client.

In order to live more independently clients need up-to-date information. It is part of your role to inform them what is available, so widening the options, to enable them to decide for themselves what they want to do

Of course, you may not always be in the position of gradually widening the options for your client. There may be circumstances where you are faced with the opposite. For example, you may have a young enthusiastic client with learning difficulties, or a disability, who wants to know a range of information about a wide choice of opportunities and facilities with which they can become involved. In such a case you may have to carefully help them to take a realistic view of how many things they are able to undertake at any one time. The golden rule is to make sure that you are going at the client's pace, whatever that may be, and that you are providing the information they require about the services they consider to be important. Be careful not to limit the information you provide or the ways in which you provide it because you believe that particular facility or service is unsuitable for your client. It is for them to decide once they have the information whether or not a particular service meets their needs or not.

Keys to good practice

- Get to know your client's interests and needs.
- Go at the client's pace.
- Do not impose your views about suitability or appropriateness.
- Be realistic about what is available.
- Keep your information accurate and up to date.

If you have worked with a client for a period of time and have got to know them, it will be much easier for you to know their interests and the sorts of services and facilities they are likely to need and make use of. It is then much easier to regularly talk to them and raise questions about any new facilities or services they may wish to try.

You also need to take care you do not provide clients with unrealistic expectations about any services and facilities available to them in the local area. When you are asking questions about services and facilities they would like to use, take care you only provide positive and definite information about those of which you are certain. If you have any doubts whether a service or facility is provided in your local area or is unavailable or restricted due to lack of resources, then you should advise your client that you will find out more information for them and let them know if such a service is possible, rather than indicating that the service is definitely available.

It may be useful to have a regular list which you check in respect of all of your clients about the sorts of services and facilities which may interest them and be of value to them. Facilities vary greatly from area to area and from setting to setting. However, the following table gives a general picture of the sorts of services and facilities which clients may find useful and which you should be able to provide information about. It may help if you think of it as the 'What, Who, and Where list'.

Services and facilities checklist

What	Who	Where
Meals	Social services or voluntary organisation	Social services department
Home-help	Social services or independent provider	Social services department
Family support	Social services or independent sector	Social services department

What	Who	Where
Shopping	Local voluntary organisations	Library, Citizens Advice Bureau, social services department, local church
Lunch or social clubs	Social services or local voluntary organisations	Social services department, library, Citizens Advice Bureau, local church
Holidays	Specialist travel companies, e.g. Saga, Winged Fellowship, etc. social services, specialist voluntary organisations, e.g. Royal National Institute for the Blind, Mencap, Scope, Age Concern, etc.	Social services department, library, Citizens Advice Bureau, Internet, travel agent
Pensions/Benefits	Benefits Agency, social services, Welfare Rights Centres	Welfare Rights Centre, Claimant's Union, Benefits Agency, Citizens Advice Bureau
Sports and leisure facilities	Leisure services department, National Organisation for Sport for the Disabled, International Paraolympic Committee, Riding for the Disabled, etc.	Town hall, Citizens Advice Bureau, library, Internet
Mobile library	Libraries/leisure department	Town hall
Cinema, theatre and entertainment	Leisure services department, theatres and cinemas	Town hall, library, Internet, What's on Guide

Case study

J was a young man in his mid-twenties who used a wheelchair following a spinal injury. J was provided with 24-hour care and had a team of support workers. Recently J had appeared to be very fed up and somewhat unhappy. He said that he was bored and wanted something more exciting to do. His support worker suggested a range of options, including visiting the cinema, the theatre, going to a social club or visiting an art gallery – all of which were interests of J's. However, every suggestion was rejected without J giving any clear reason why.

A few days later a different support worker decided to approach matters in a different way and, through questioning, established that J would very much like to take up any of the suggestions made earlier, but had made the assumption that to do any of them he needed to take a taxi to get to them and this was something he felt unable to afford. J had not liked to say he could not afford the taxi and so had simply refused any of the suggestions.

The second support worker was able to explain to J that the local authority operated a dial-a-ride service with a small bus specially adapted for wheelchairs and that J could book this service and use it for a nominal charge. J was delighted and began to make plans for a range of visits and activities.

What may have happened if the second support worker had not spoken to J?

How to obtain accurate information

No one expects you to have your head full of information that you can pass on to your clients! However, you do need to know where to find information and what are the best and most effective ways of doing it. You also need to know how to keep that information so that you have easy access to it whenever you need to use it and update it. We now live in an information society. Masses of information is available, on more subjects then you ever knew existed. The trouble is that it is easy to become confused and end up with information which is irrelevant and will not serve a useful purpose for your clients.

Local sources of information

One of the most useful sources of information is the 'one stop shop' approach of organisations such as the Citizens Advice Bureau. You may also find in your area that your local council's voluntary services or your local authority may have an information point. These are often located in libraries, town halls, civic centres, or other easily accessible places. At these points you can usually obtain leaflets and information and there are staff available to find out more for you and to offer advice on specific areas of need. Most advice centres will find information for you, if they do not already have it to hand. You may be looking for specific information in response to a client's request or you may be generally updating your own information so that you are ready to deal promptly with any information requests from your clients. Whatever your information needs, any of these facilities is a very good starting point.

Special interest groups

Other excellent sources of information are specific issue interest groups, such as Age Concern, the Alzheimers Society, Mencap, Scope, etc. These provide information about facilities and services specifically related to those with a particular condition. The contact addresses and telephone numbers for these organisations will be found at your starting point advice centre, whether it be a Citizens Advice Centre or your local library or your council's voluntary services.

The Internet

One of the best sources of information is the Internet, if you have access to it. To use this you will need access to a computer which is connected to the Internet. You will also need instructions in how to use the various search engines in order to locate sites of the organisations you are interested in. The information you can obtain from the Internet is almost unlimited and covers every possible subject you could imagine. However, you must be aware that information on the Internet is not subject to verification or control, and therefore its accuracy is not always possible to confirm. If you are finding information from the Internet to pass on to clients you would be advised to obtain it primarily from official web sites of relevant organisations, either for the particular area of interest or the particular area reflecting your clients' needs. Other useful web sites are official government sites and those of universities and research establishments. Using the World Wide Web via the Internet can be a very quick and easy way of getting very accurate and up-to-date information, often before it has appeared in print or is readily accessible in other ways.

The Internet can also provide many people with the opportunity to network with others who have similar interests and issues to their own. This can help to broaden the social contacts of individuals who may otherwise find themselves with limited opportunities for social contact. Where clients with whom you are working are particularly vulnerable, you should ensure that they are aware of the basic precautions which should be taken when entering any Internet-based network:

- Always use a pseudonym.
- Never give out your address.
- Do not give out your telephone number.
- Do not arrange to meet people you have contacted via the Internet.

The Internet can also provide useful opportunities for learning using 'online' learning materials. This can make learning more accessible and may offer the chance for new knowledge and understanding which may not have been available through traditional teaching approaches.

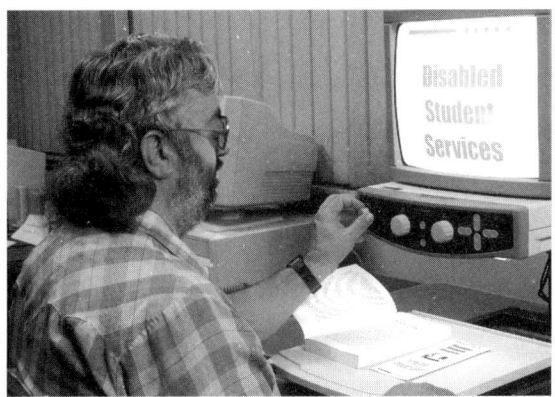

One way for clients to find out information for themselves is through the Internet

Providing the opportunity for clients to access information for themselves through the Internet can be useful and can motivate them to go on looking for more information and to explore the huge potential of using the Internet. There are an increasing number of opportunities for people without computers to access the Internet. Cyber cafés and many libraries, local town halls, colleges and universities have facilities for public access to the Internet, usually for a small fee. You might encourage your clients to do this where appropriate and it may lead to clients taking an interest in the Internet and pursuing information through it. As always the best approach to take, if possible, is to support your client to be self-managing and to find out information for themselves rather than rely on you. Once you have obtained information for your client or to update your knowledge, you need to be sure that you can store this information in an accessible way.

Storing information

You may remember that you can locate information in the Citizens Advice Bureau or Welfare Rights Centre, and what information is available there, but you will not be able to recall the individual addresses, telephone numbers or detailed information about the services provided. So it is a good idea to create an information store for yourself, where you can keep leaflets, notes, telephone numbers, cuttings from newspapers or magazine advertisements, all of which relate to areas you believe may be of interest either to your current clients or to others in the future. A simple filing system, organised alphabetically or by subject and stored in a concertina file or in a filing drawer, is probably the easiest way to do this. A small library of information is very useful provided it is maintained and kept up to date. It is important to regularly go through it, perhaps every three months, and discard outdated information and replace it with the most current. You could store information electronically on a computer. It could be stored where you record the website and e-mail addresses of relevant services. It is also useful to keep important websites in the 'favourites' menu so they are easily accessible.

Active knowledge

Collect information and prepare an information store for yourself either in hard copy or on a computer. File the information under clearly distinguishable headings or alphabetically, and make sure you can find any information you require easily and accurately. Make plans to revisit your sources of information or the relevant websites at least once every three months and update any information, discarding anything which has become outdated. Make a note of how many times you refer to your information store during the first three months of use.

How to provide information

Once you establish what your client's needs are and referred to your own store of information or made other enquiries to find out further details or established new facts, then you have to provide information to your client in a way which they are going to find useful. Providing people with information isn't just a matter of telling them what it is. You need to give careful thought to:

- The needs of the person receiving the information.
- The nature of that information.

The needs of the client

You need to give information in a way which can be understood by your client. Your client may need to be communicated with in specific ways. For example, they may require the information in a particular form, such as in large print or in braille, or to be written or provided in sign language. There are many other considerations. You will also need to consider the circumstances of giving somebody information on a particular service or facility. For example, you would not communicate information about social clubs and outings to a man whose wife had just died. He is unlikely to be interested or ready to receive such information at this time, but would be in a few weeks or months. Though this an extreme example, the point it makes can be applied in other less extreme circumstances. You also need to take into account the client's state of health and any planned or current medical treatment they may be undertaking.

There is also a right way and a right time for giving information. From work on communication skills, you will remember that in communicating effectively it is important that you do not rush or hurry what you say and that clients are more receptive if they are comfortable and at ease. Do not pass on something to a client as you are rushing out of the door. A client may not remember your hurried 'Oh Betty, I did check and there is a painting class on Tuesday afternoons at 2.30, or Thursday mornings at 10.30, and you can go along to either of them if you just phone the library first.'

How well you use your skills to communicate information to your clients has an effect on what they know and can do

The nature of the information

For many clients it can be beneficial to write down information or to give them an information leaflet relevant to their needs. This may be sufficient for many clients, who may undertake the next stages of information search for themselves. Many others, however, may want you to do further research for them. For most people it is important to have information in a form they can refer to again while they consider it or commit it to memory.

Before meeting a client always prepare the information in the form, written or recorded, that is appropriate for passing on to that client.

Element Y2.2 — Enable individuals to use services and facilities

WHAT YOU NEED TO LEARN

- How to encourage clients to use services.
- Potential barriers to accessing services and how to overcome them.
- How to support clients in using services.

How to encourage clients to use services

The range of services your clients may want to use is large and varied. By no means all the services and facilities which clients will want to take advantage of are those provided by the health and care services. Many other services and facilities provided by the world of commerce, industry, entertainment and retail will also be services that clients may wish to access and enjoy.

Home services

Depending on clients' individual circumstances, they may wish to take advantage of services which can be supplied to them in their own home setting rather than having to travel to the service. If you have a client who is unable or unwilling to travel to a service then you will need to find out and establish whether or not it is possible for them to receive the service in their own home. There are many services with facilities to provide an off-site service. Examples are mobile shops, mobile libraries, many firms of solicitors and all of the services provided by a social services department. Using the Internet service, many banks and building societies provide services on-line, as do many large and small retail shopping facilities. Home delivery take-away food is readily available in most areas, as is access to films via rented videos or through satellite or cable television.

There are many services that clients can have access to that enable them to do things for themselves, e.g. Internet banking and ordering food from the supermarket and having it delivered

Travelling to services

Clients will have to travel if they want to participate in many forms of entertainment and culture, such as the theatre, concerts, art galleries, or sporting events. They will also have to travel to make essential appointments, such as an appearance in court or a visit to the hospital. When you are encouraging clients to make maximum use of services you may need to discuss with them arrangements to access these services if they need to travel to reach them.

Providing information on services

Many clients may need to be encouraged to use services by you providing information so they can make an informed choice or reassuring them about particular services or facilities. However, you must be careful not to cross the boundary between encouraging them and pressurising them into using a particular facility or service. Everyone has a right to choose or not to choose to take up services and facilities available to them. You are unlikely to pressurise somebody into reading a particular book or seeing a particular film, simply because you thought that it was good, even if you really felt they would enjoy it. You are unlikely to go beyond simply telling them how enjoyable you found the book or film and strongly recommending that they read it or go see it.

However, it is easy to step over the boundary when you believe the client needs to be encouraged to use a service in their interests. For example, receiving additional support services, attending a physiotherapy session or making a claim for additional benefit. All these are services you may genuinely feel would be of great benefit to your client. However, your role is limited to providing the information they need to make an informed choice. You should avoid exercising undue pressure on them to take a particular course of action. Similarly, you should not attempt to prevent a client from following a particular course of action simply because you believe it is risky or unsuitable for them. This can create major problems for carers whose clients insist in acting in ways which may expose them to undue risk of injury or other dangers. There is a fine line between neglect and restriction and it is one which is easy to overstep. Most of those working in health and care are likely to err on the side of overcaution. Although this concern for the safety of clients is well-intentioned, it results in restricting the rights of the clients to fully enjoy facilities and services available to them.

Case study

E has lived in a residential facility for people with learning difficulties since she was 5 years old. She is now 25 and although perfectly able to live in supported group accommodation in the community, she has chosen to remain in the same residential facility in which she has grown up. Because of her unique circumstances of having been there since she was a young child, a decision has been taken that E can remain in the residential facility even though all the present residents require a much higher degree of care than E does. All the former residents who functioned in the way that E does have long since moved on into group homes out in the community.

E helps a great deal at the residential home and carries out simple tasks to support members of staff. She also still requires a considerable degree of protection herself as she has an extremely naïve understanding of the world and has no understanding of any risk to her personal safety.

E is extremely sociable and has recently decided that she wishes to make regular visits to a local nightclub. This arose after she became friendly with some local young people and started to visit the local pub with them, and then decided she would like to take up their invitations to join them on nights out further afield. Staff at the residential home are concerned that E will be at risk in an unsupervised social environment because she has little or no understanding of the personal safety or sexual risks to which she could be exposed. They are therefore considering whether or not they are able to, or ought to, restrict or refuse permission for E to go on these outings to nightclubs.

1 Do the staff have any legal right to stop E going to a nightclub?
2 Do the staff have any moral right to stop E going to a nightclub?
3 How do you think this situation should be handled?
4 To what extent should E be allowed to make her own choices?
5 Would the circumstances and your views be any different if E were living in group accommodation in the community rather than in a residential setting?
6 Was the decision to allow E to remain in the residential setting the right one?

Potential barriers to accessing services and how to overcome them

There are many barriers which can restrict or prevent people from accessing facilities or services. These tend to fall into three categories: environmental, communication, psychological. These are general indicators only, so the circumstances of a particular client may mean they will experience particular barriers.

Environmental barriers

These are the most common barriers, and include:

- lack of wheelchair access
- lack of disabled toilet facilities
- no ramps
- no lifts
- narrow doorways
- high risk or threatening location, e.g. A Well Woman Centre situated across the road from a busy pub or parade of shops which is a known hang-out for gangs of young men
- lack of transport or lack of access by transport.

Communication barriers

These barriers can be:

- lack of information in an appropriate language or format
- lack of loop system

- poor quality communication skills from staff at the facility, e.g. The unhelpful and obstructive receptionist
- lack of translators or interpreters
- lack of information or publicity about the service or facility.

Psychological barriers

These barriers are:

- fear of anxiety
- unfamiliarity
- unwillingness to accept help
- concern at loss of independence
- lack of confidence.

How to overcome the barriers

Your role is encouraging your client to make maximum use of services and facilities available to them is likely to involve you in making plans to overcome whatever barriers are standing in the way of them doing this. For example, you may need to search out alternative facilities if the ones you originally intended to use do not have wheelchair access, as in the case of a local theatre which does not have wheelchair access, forcing you to make arrangements for your client to travel to one which does. Of course, you would raise the issue with the local theatre and encourage them to improve their access for people with disabilities. If there are problems getting suitable transport then it may be necessary to provide transport facilities by accessing local transport with provision for your particular client group or by using taxi or public transport facilities which have the necessary adaptations. Most train companies, for instance, have support services for people with disabilities by way of providing ramps and a porter service to enable people to get on and off the trains. However, many trains that do provide portage and ramps do not have readily accessible toilets for the disabled. You may need to arrange or to assist the client to arrange for translators or interpreters.

Before you agree any particular arrangements with a facility to provide access for a client, you must ensure that you have agreed this with the client. If a client has to make an important visit to a particular location which cannot be changed or substituted and there is no wheelchair access through the main entrance, it may be suggested that the client use a back entrance or goods entrance and the goods lift to reach the appropriate facility. You should always check with a client before agreeing to this type of arrangement, as your client may not be prepared to access a building through a rear or goods entrance. In such a case, you may need to arrange for the visit to take place at a different location. It is essential you never compromise the right of a client to choose their own means of access and to set their own boundaries as to what is acceptable to them in terms of their own personal space and dignity.

Active knowledge

Choose three different types of facility which clients may wish to access in your locality. They should each be located in a different part of your area. For each, list the potential barriers to access and the ways in which you would begin to tackle the barriers for each one.

How to support clients in using services

The level of support which you need to provide to a client will vary depending on their circumstances. Your support can range from handing them an information leaflet to making all the arrangements for them to use a service and accompanying them to use it. Between these extremes there is a wide range of alternatives. Some clients may simply need you to make the initial contact for them. Others may need you to accompany them on a first visit to a new support facility or to meet a new group of people, and then to gradually withdraw your support as they grow in confidence in using the service. On other occasions your role may be to enlist the support of other people who are either better qualified or more experienced or who have the resources, time or experience, to provide a better or more consistent level of service for the client.

It is important you encourage clients to dispense with your support as soon as they feel able to manage independently. You should do this when you notice them becoming more confident in using the facility or the service, and you should do it by gradually and appropriately reducing the level of support. You may have accompanied a client on their first visit to a Welfare Rights Advice Centre. They needed you with them because they were unfamiliar with the service and they did not understand the benefit system to be able to clearly explain what their problem was. However, as the visits continue and the work of the Welfare Rights Advice Centre is underway you may be able to withdraw from accompanying the client as they become more familiar with the workers in the Advice Centre. Your involvement perhaps may be then limited to driving the client to the centre, or maybe holding a support session when the client returns from their visit.

It may take clients longer to adjust with confidence to new social situations. For instance, if a client has been supported by you accompanying them to a new day centre or social club, it may take a few visits before they are confident enough to go on their own, in the certainty they will find enough friendly and familiar faces there. As always your role is to do the minimum and to allow clients the maximum opportunities to make their own lives and to be as independent as possible.

Unit test

1 What are the main sources of information about services and facilities for clients?

2 How would you go about collecting and storing a general information bank?

3 What are the key factors to take into account when providing clients with information?

4 What are the potential pitfalls in the way that information is provided?

5 What are the effective ways of encouraging clients to use services?

6 Name six potential barriers to accessing services and facilities.

7 How could these barriers be overcome?

8 What are the different ways in which you could offer support to clients using services?

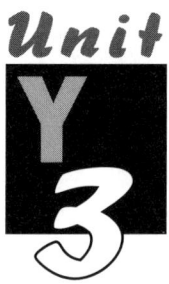

Unit Y3

Enable individuals to administer their financial affairs

In this unit you will learn about ways of supporting a range of clients in managing their finances in the most independent way possible. This unit is most likely to be of importance to those working in the community supporting clients in their own homes, however many supported living environments and some types of residential setting provide for clients to have a significant degree of financial independence. Even within a residential setting it is important that you are aware of some of the financial regulations in case you are asked questions by clients or their relatives.

Clients will need to access and manage money for a wide range of purposes; the obvious needs such as managing bills and household expenses, saving and putting money into pensions for the future. There are also other opportunities which will require clients to have sufficient money or savings to enjoy, such as holidays, new cars, socialising and buying new clothes.

Element Y3.1   Enable individuals to make payments

WHAT YOU NEED TO LEARN

- Ways of establishing payments clients need to make.
- Methods of making payments.
- Ways of recording payments made.
- Ways of dealing with potential conflicts.

Ways of establishing payments clients need to make

Much of what you need to do to establish the payments which are due will depend upon your client. You could be carrying out this sort of task for a wide range of clients, each with varying levels of ability to manage their own financial affairs. The first thing that you should do in any situation where a client has requested financial management assistance is to make sure exactly what level of assistance they need and how much information they feel comfortable with you having about their financial affairs. For example, some clients may be happy for you to collect their pension or to pay their TV licence or gas bill, but would not consider showing you their bank

When a client is having trouble handling their financial affairs, you may need to support them to cope alone

statement. This is the kind of level of involvement that you must establish and must ensure is agreed with the client.

It is important that you establish the difference between a client who needs support to manage their own financial affairs and one who is not capable of managing their financial affairs. It is one thing to agree a level of support you will provide for a client and quite another to take over the administration of their affairs completely, because they are incapable. Administering totally the entire financial affairs of another person is not part of your role and if you feel that you are working with a client who is not capable of understanding their financial affairs then this must be reported to your supervisor at once. The appropriate legal steps to protect the client can then be taken. There are a range of legal provisions in place to ensure that those who are unable to make financial decisions for themselves are protected from the possibility of being exploited. This process is likely to involve either a member of the family or a solicitor assuming the **power of attorney** in respect of the client's financial affairs. In some cases, depending on the circumstances, the law provides for the social services department to assume responsibility under guardianship arrangements. You could find in working with a client for several years, perhaps helping them in managing their finances, that as they deteriorate you are doing more and more. It is important that from time to time, particularly where you have a client with a degenerative condition such as Alzheimer's disease, that you check their level of understanding of what is happening to their finances and that you report any concerns as soon as possible.

Establishing the level of help and support

One of the best ways to work out with your client the level of support they require is to look at the reasons why they need assistance to make their payments. Is it because:

- they are specifically unable to make payments
- they are confused and forget to make payments

- they are unsure what payments they have to make
- they are unlikely to be able to motivate or organise themselves to make payments on time
- they do not recognise the importance of making payments.

Once you have established the reasons why they need support and help, it is then much easier to agree a level with them. For example, if your assistance is required simply because somebody is physically unable to write a cheque or to walk to the post office or the bank, then it may be quite sufficient for you to write cheques for them or take things to the post office. There may be no need for you to assist with the process of identifying payments which are due or becoming involved in any financial planning.

If your client is unable to make payments because they are confused or unable to recognise the importance of making payments of bills when they become due, for a wide range of reasons, then they may be happy for you to become involved at a more detailed level in their financial budgeting and planning.

Encouraging clients to be self-managing

One of the keys to working effectively with clients, whatever your role, is that you should always encourage clients to take as much active responsibility for their own lives and actions as is possible. Never assume that they will always require assistance at the level you currently provide. You should always review progress and wherever possible, either because their condition has improved or because they have learned from working with you, the client should resume or take on as much responsibility as possible for their financial planning, budgeting and payments.

Keys to good practice

- Always begin by asking the client to do as much as possible of the preparation for planning their finances.

- Find out what the client can do first, then support where necessary.

- Always check back with the client on everything which you are doing and ask 'What do you think?'

- Always make a regular review time for any financial support plan for a client. This could be three or six months, depending on their circumstances. At this stage you should review your level of support to see if the client's needs have changed.

- If you notice changes in between reviews, for example bills which have not been paid which the client used to deal with themselves, then you should follow this up and make changes if necessary.

- If your client is beginning to take more of an interest in thier finances and making suggestions, check if they would like to take more responsibility themselves and reduce your involvement.

Range of payments

We all have our own range of payments to make, either regularly or as one-offs. Whilst everyone has different financial demands made on their income there are some types of payments which are more likely to occur for most of the clients you work with. When you are looking at the payments which need to be made by any particular client, you should first ask them to identify, if they are able, which payments they need to make. It can be helpful to have a written checklist which you can use to try to make sure no payments have been forgotten. The following list is a suggestion only and it will obviously vary for each individual.

Checklist of payments

Regular payments (which could be weekly/monthly/annually):

- Rent
- Council tax
- Water
- Repair or maintenance charges
- TV licence
- Catalogue payments
- Hire purchase or loan payments

- Mortgage
- Heating and lighting
- Insurance
- Telephone
- TV/video/satellite rental
- Credit card payments

Occasional payments:

- Food
- Furniture

- Clothes
- Holidays

If a client is having trouble sorting out the payments they have to make, you could suggest they make up a checklist to make it simpler to remember

Such a checklist can be used for any client with whom you are working. Additional items may need to be added to meet the circumstances of any given individual. Once you have identified all of the payments which your client needs to make, then you should discuss with them which payments they wish you to undertake and which payments they will continue to undertake themselves. At this stage it is also useful to discuss methods of payment with your client and to look at the advantages and disadvantages of the range of payment methods available.

Methods of making payments

The following table lists the different methods of payment for goods and services and the advantages and disadvantages of these.

Method	Advantages	Disadvantages
Cash	<ul><li>Easy for those who receive wages or benefits in cash.</li><li>Easily understood.</li><li>Allows people to see exactly their financial position.</li></ul>	<ul><li>Safety – keeping cash represents a serious burglary risk.</li><li>Loss – cash is easy to lose, particularly if a client is confused or forgetful.</li><li>Inconvenience – cash cannot be sent in the post, so cash payments have to be made direct or through a bank, and this can mean having to make arrangements to visit the offices or the bank of the payee.</li></ul>
Cheque	<ul><li>Convenient – can be sent by post.</li><li>More secure than cash.</li><li>Generally accepted (with a cheque guarantee card).</li></ul>	<ul><li>Requires bank account.</li><li>Can incur considerable bank charges.</li><li>Becoming less used with the advent of electronic bank cards.</li><li>Cheque book can be lost or stolen.</li><li>Cheques can be misused.</li></ul>
Electronic bank card, e.g. Switch or Delta	<ul><li>Convenient, generally accepted.</li><li>Easy to carry and convenient.</li><li>Easy to stop if stolen.</li></ul>	<ul><li>Requires bank account.</li><li>May confuse some clients.</li><li>Can be stolen and misused.</li></ul>
Standing order – set up by client	<ul><li>Regular payments made by bank.</li><li>No action needed by client.</li><li>Makes payments direct.</li></ul>	<ul><li>Requires bank account.</li><li>Client needs to remember to alter if payments change.</li><li>Incurs bank charges.</li></ul>
Direct debit – set up by payee	<ul><li>Regular payments made by bank.</li><li>No action needed by client.</li><li>Makes payments direct.</li></ul>	<ul><li>Requires bank account.</li><li>Can incur bank charges.</li></ul>
Credit card	<ul><li>Makes payments even if temporarily short of money.</li><li>Convenient.</li></ul>	<ul><li>Can accumulate large amounts of debt.</li><li>Has higher interest charges.</li><li>Is easily stolen and misused.</li><li>Not accepted for all types of payment.</li></ul>

Armchair/On-line banking	• Can be used by clients who have bank accounts with access via telephone/Internet/satellite TV. • Can be used without leaving the house. • Does not require any permanent set up arrangement. • Is safe and secure.	• Only available to those with the necessary hardware and level of technological understanding to use the equipment.

Active knowledge

If you are not currently working with a client that involves assisting with finances, you could carry out this exercise on your own personal finances. Make a list, as above, of all of the payments that you make and look at the range of methods you use to pay. Check which items you pay using which methods. If you include grocery and general household shopping, you may find that the balance of methods you use alters. Similarly, if you look at methods of payments for large items you may also find that this alters the balance of the different types of payments you use. Review the payment methods that you currently use and see how you could benefit by changing any of them in order to either save on charges, interest rates or to improve the convenience or safety.

Case study

P has suffered from severe depression since the birth of her third child, now one year old. Her other children are aged two and four. Her husband left six months ago as he felt unable to cope with her depressed state. P has been receiving medication from her GP for her depression which helps to some extent, but she finds it very difficult to cope on a day-to-day basis. She was referred for support by her health visitor who was concerned about her motivation and her seeming lack of ability to organise the basic requirements of living for herself and her three children. P had neglected to pay the mortgage on their house, not because of a lack of income but because she had not been motivated to make the required arrangements to transfer the payments after her husband left. She was now being threatened with repossession of the house, and as she had not paid recent utility bills and there were various threatening letters from the companies.

A support worker began to work with P and her family, and following agreement with her made arrangements for all of her utility bills and mortgage payments to be made via direct debit. The support worker negotiated with the building society to extend the mortgage period by the missing six months and negotiated with the utility companies to allow P to pay off the excess amounts over a period of time.

P kept up the payments to the utility companies and managed to meet the mortgage payments. There was never any money left over, but the children were clothed and fed and P used a detailed budget to keep control of her weekly outgoings.

1 What could have been the consequences for P and her family had the support worker not begun to work with them?

2 What alternative ways could have been used to resolve P's problems?

3 What other effects might you reasonably expect to see from the improvement in P's financial situation?

4 What skills would the support worker need to have used in order to improve P's circumstances?

Budgeting

Where you are working with a client who has found managing their financial affairs difficult and who is experiencing financial difficulty, either because of problems with management and organisation or because of **low income**, then doing some budget planning with them could be extremely valuable. This can only be done with the agreement of the client. If your client agrees you should be careful not to impose your own values and beliefs on them. For example, if you have always been brought up to believe that you should never owe money and that you should always 'pay your way' and pay all bills as they fall due, then you may find it difficult to accept the philosophy of a client who never pays bills until the bailiffs arrive at the doorstep, or who is happy to allow debts to mount and bills to go unpaid. However, if a client wants to work to resolve financial difficulties or simply wants to organise their finances better and is happy to plan a budget with your assistance, there are various ways in which you can do this, however the following approach is simple, easy to understand and works in most circumstances.

An 'income and expenditure budget' chart

These are the steps you can take in filling in the income and expenditure budget chart that follows on page 282.

Step 1 List the income that your client has from whatever source. The headings clearly cover the individual circumstances of a wide range of clients, so you should simply select the sources of income which are appropriate for the client with whom you are working.

Step 2 List expenditure. Similarly, the expenditure is designed to cover the circumstances of a wide range of clients and you should simply list those which relate to your client. There are advantages in completing the weekly, monthly and yearly columns. This means that you are less likely to miss any payments which occur less frequently and it also allows an overview of the client's complete financial position.

Step 3 This allows you to see the financial position by looking at the total of the yearly income and taking away the total yearly expenditure. It will show you whether the client is able to live within the income they currently receive. If they are not and the expenditure is greater than their income, then you need to look at ways of either increasing their income or reducing their expenditure. This may be through claiming additional benefits or, if they are working, they may wish to consider whether it is possible to work additional hours or to explore the possibility of finding additional sources of income. For those on a low income, make sure they are receiving all the government support to which they are entitled. If your client is dependent upon income from pensions and savings they may wish to consider whether to move savings into an account which will provide a higher rate of interest. If this is a step to be considered then you must strongly advise the client to consult a financial

Income and expenditure budget chart			
Step 1 – Income	**Weekly**	**Monthly**	**Yearly**
Salary/wage			
Other income			
Pension			
Jobseekers allowance			
Income support			
Housing benefit			
Other benefits			
Interest on savings			
Total			
Step 2 – Expenditure			
Mortgage or rent			
Second mortgage/secured loan			
Council tax			
Water rates			
Ground rent			
Repairs & maintenance charges			
Buildings insurance			
Contents insurance			
Gas			
Electricity			
Telephone			
Food			
Clothing			
TV rental and licence			
Prescriptions			
Health insurance			
Car tax and insurance			
Petrol/diesel			
Car repairs and servicing			
Public transport			
School fees, uniform, etc.			
Holidays			
Credit cards and loans			
Maintenance payments			
Contribution to pension			
Reserve for emergencies			
Regular savings			
Total			
Step 3 – Financial position			
Total income			
Total expenditure			
Financial position			

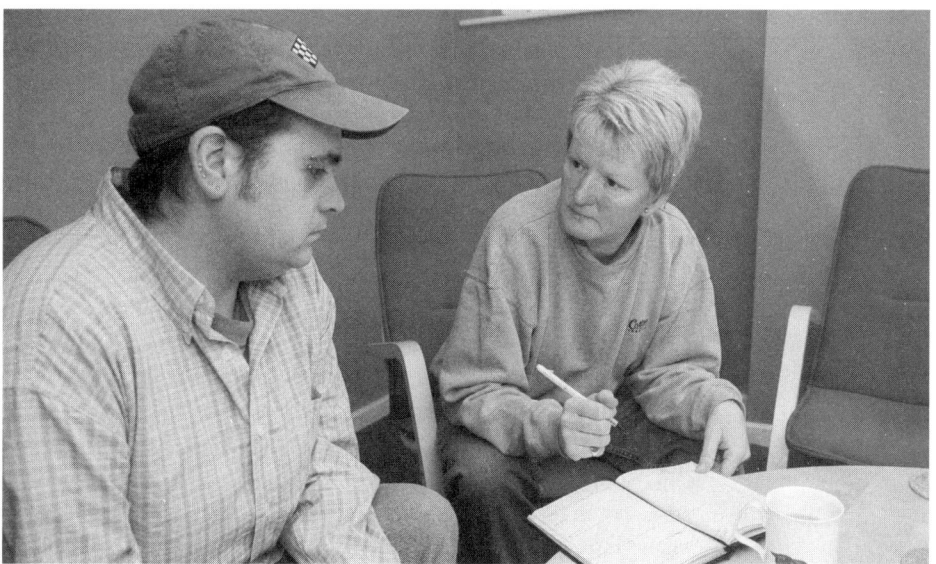

Those who want to take charge of their finances and clear their debts could get help from a debt counsellor at a Citizens Advice Bureau or a local Money Advice Centre

adviser before making such a decision. You should not, under any circumstances, offer financial advice of this nature unless you are qualified to do so.

The other alternative for any client whose expenditure exceeds their income is to review expenditure and to examine where reductions can be made.

Dealing with debt

If you are supporting a client who is in debt then you should encourage them to enlist the support of an experienced debt counsellor. These are available through the **Citizens Advice Bureau**, **Welfare Rights Advice Centres** and local **Money Advice Centres**. However, it is useful if you understand the steps that a debt counsellor will take in order to resolve the client's problems.

The first thing that the debt councillor will do is establish the nature of the debts which the client has. Debts are defined **as priority debts** and **non-priority debts**.

Priority debits include:
- mortgage or rent
- council tax
- water charges
- gas
- electricity
- payments ordered by courts
- maintenance payments also ordered by courts or the Child Support Agency.

Non-priority debts include:
- hire purchase debts.

The difference between the two kinds of debts is that failure to pay priority debts could mean the loss of a client's home or having to live without heat or light if services are disconnected. The consequences of failure to meet non-priority debts, whilst unpleasant are not as serious. The repossession of goods by a hire purchase company may make life awkward but does not make it impossible. If a television or satellite system is repossessed the family may be bored, whereas the failure to purchase a TV licence could result in a large fine and an even higher amount of debt to be repaid.

Once the debt counsellor has established the level of income, and they may work it out on both a weekly and a monthly basis, they will then look at basic expense levels – those required for the basics of living, such as food and essential clothing. They will then identify priority debts. They will look at the amount of debt that there is and what that represents in terms of repayments over a period of time. They will concentrate on ensuring that the priority debts are met in the first instance.

Once a debt counsellor has this information they will then negotiate with all of the creditors involved and agree a schedule of repayments. Creditors are usually happy to agree deferred payments of outstanding debts as this is preferable to not receiving any payment at all from the debt. Debt counsellors are trained and experienced in this type of debt management and you should encourage your client to make use of their services if necessary. However, if they are unwilling to do so and wish you to carry out the negotiations or to do it themselves, then you may wish to consult your local Citizens Advice Bureau or a Money Advice Centre for any further information or guidance before you begin negotiation with creditors.

It is important that you encourage your client to abide by any arrangements which have been made for the repayment of their debt. It frequently happens that once arrangements have been negotiated for repayment the client believes that the problem has somehow 'gone away' and they no longer need to concern themselves with it.

It could be worse

Budget repayment plan for those in debt

Here is an example of how to budget the repayment of debt.

Income/expenses	Weekly	Monthly
List income per week/month		
List basic expense per week/month		
Deduct basic expenses from income		
Total money for debt repayment plan		
List priority debts		
Deduct priority debts from repayment plan		
Total money for other debt repayment		

Did you know?

The reason that many clients and families are in debt is because they receive such a low income. In the UK today 25 per cent of the population, one person in four, lives in poverty. Poverty is officially defined as 50 per cent or less of average national income after housing costs. One in three, or 34 per cent, of children live in poverty.

Being aware of the benefits

When identifying and supporting clients in making payments you should also ensure you are aware of any benefits or concessions they can receive on those payments. For example, are you aware of the latest information on the Disabled Person's Tax Credit? From 1 April 2000 people who are registered blind received a 50 per cent reduction in the cost of their television licence. If you are working with a client who lives in sheltered housing or other supported living, you should check whether it is a scheme which qualifies for a concessionry licence. Many older people, people with disabilities and people on low incomes are entitled to concessions for travel, use of local leisure facilities and libraries. There are also reductions in council tax for people who live alone and for people who have severe disabilities. It is important that you are aware of these concessions and reductions and that you encourage your clients to take full advantage of them. You should keep your knowledge updated through regular contact with local advice centres and Citizens Advice Bureaux.

Ways of recording payments made

All payments made for any goods or services require a receipt. It is important that you encourage your clients to always obtain and keep receipts for any payments they make. By doing this it will always be possible to resolve any disputes about the time and amount of payments which have been made and it avoids confusion over which bills have and have not been paid.

If you are making payments on behalf of a client then it is essential you obtain a receipt and keep a copy in the client's case notes or receipts file. This protects you and the client if any question about the payment is ever raised. Receipts can come in a range of formats. Payments made via a bank will be recorded on a bank statement, so an individual receipt will not be needed. However, payments made by cheque, debit card or credit card need a receipt of individual transactions, which are kept until the transactions appear on either the bank statement or credit card statement. This makes it easy to identify any unexpected or unauthorised payments which appear on the statement. Also a transaction receipt helps to easily resolve any dispute over the transaction.

Receipts should be maintained in a system where they are easily accessible – the sideboard draw does not qualify as easily accessible! A simple filing system where receipts are identified as utility bills, food, TV licence, clothing, holidays, etc. may be

A client's sense of independence can be increased by showing them how to make and record the payments they make for goods and services and to take control of their finances

the easiest way of locating them when they are needed. Receipts should not be kept indefinitely and the system will have to be maintained. Receipts for any item under guarantee should be kept at least for the life of the guarantee. Other payment receipts should be kept until the payment itself shows on an overall statement of that particular account. Many clients do not see the importance of keeping receipts or may forget where they have put them or may lose them. You should try to obtain the client's agreement to set up a system which they can use or if that is beyond what they feel able to undertake initially, then to hand over their receipts to you until they become more familiar with the system. This is likely to prove the most effective way of recording your client's financial transactions.

Ways of dealing with potential conflicts

You may be faced with a dilemma if clients ask you to make payments in certain situations or tell you they intend not to make certain payments. This could involve:

- making payments for illegal items
- making payments for items of which you personally disapprove
- a client telling you they intend to avoid making payments which are due.

Illegal payments

If a client asks you to make a payment which you know to be illegal, for example to pay for stolen goods or any other illegal items, then you should explain that it will not be possible for you to assist them and that it is inappropriate for them to ask you to undertake this. If you become aware that your client is involved in criminal activity then you must report this to your line manager and follow your agency's policies and procedures.

Payments of which you disapprove

A client may ask you to assist them with making payments for an activity which is in conflict with your own beliefs and values. An example would be a client asking you, who are strongly opposed to gambling, to place a bet with a bookmaker on their behalf. In such a case you must be sure that you do not allow your own beliefs and values to influence the level of service which you provide for your client.

The intention not to make payments

If your client advises you that they are not going to make payments for goods or services or

You have to remember that a client's beliefs and values are crucial to their sense of independence, so you must not allow what you believe and think influence the service you provide to them to meet their legal requirements, then you can find yourself in a difficult position. For example, a client advises you during the budgeting process not to include an allowance for a TV licence as they do not intend to purchase one. In this situation you should advise the client of the consequences of their actions and of the levels of fines which are imposed on those who fail to purchase a TV licence. You are not, however, in a position to insist on a certain action or to override your client's wishes. You are only able to advise them and ensure that any decisions they make about failing to maintain or make payments are based on an informed choice. You should record this information and advise your line manager accordingly. You must explain to your client that you are doing this. You should never actively condone or encourage clients to avoid making payments which they are required to make. Be careful that you do not give the appearance of encouragement by failing to comment. You do have a responsibility to ensure that a client is informed of the potential consequences of any actions.

Active knowledge

Make a two-column list, one with all the payments which your client has to make, the other with the consequences in each case of failure to pay. This should enable you to clearly see which payments need to take priority because of the consequences for the client.

Element Y3.2   Enable individuals to claim benefits and allowances

WHAT YOU NEED TO LEARN

- How to find out about benefits and allowances for your client.
- How to help clients apply for benefits and allowances.

How to find out about benefits and allowances

As always your initial step is to establish with the client the level of help they are going to need. It is always preferable to encourage and enable clients to find out as much information for themselves as possible. You should only directly intervene in the provision of information when the client is unable to do so and it is not possible for you to empower them. Sources of information about benefits and allowances are extremely varied throughout the country and whether or not you are working in a rural or urban area. The most comprehensive advice and information is available at centres such as the local Citizens Advice Bureau, at a Welfare Rights Centre or a Money Advice Centre. Citizens Advice Bureau is a national organisation with branches in most towns and cities throughout the UK. It also has a comprehensive website and telephone advice lines. The Welfare Rights Centres and Money Advice Centres are often run by local authorities, so your local council should be able to tell you the nearest location of these. The local library is always a good source of information about the location of advice centres and they will also be able to advise on the nearest Citizens Advice Bureau. The Benefits Agency provides a benefits

Knowing their entitlement to benefits and allowances helps to increase client's independence

helpline where information about specific allowances and benefits can be obtained. However, this only relates to state benefits. Any broader or more general advice will need to be obtained from a Citizens Advice Bureau or a Money Advice Centre.

There is a wide range of reasons why a client may need assistance and support to find out about benefits and allowances, and in many circumstances you will find that offering some additional support may be all that is required to allow a client to assess their own information. Below is a list of why people need help and ways of finding out what can be done.

Possible difficulty	Assistance which could be offered
Mobility	Arrange transport, check in advance of access to information centre, library, etc.
Lack of confidence	Offer to accompany client to find out information.
Unable to use telephone	Explore use of telephone adaptations if appropriate.
No access to Internet	Arrange support to visit library, cyber café, and computer centre to access the website information.

Client's entitlements

Depending on their circumstances your client may be eligible for a number of state benefits or allowances. However, state benefits are not the only source of income that you may need to assist your client with. If your client has been in employment they may have access to a company or private pension scheme or they may be eligible for financial support from a charity or benevolent fund specifically for retired or former members of particular occupations. The *Charity Digest*, a copy of which should be available in your local library, gives information about every charity in the country and explains the help provided by each charitable organisation.

Clients may be entitled to other sorts of help in addition to any particular benefits. Some of these may be 'passported' because the clients are eligible for a particular allowance (e.g. income support). Or they may be entitled because of age or level of disability. These benefits can make a significant difference to a client's financial situation, so it is important that you ensure that clients obtain information about their entitlements. You don't have to have full knowledge of welfare rights and all the allowances available for your clients. However, it is an advantage for you know in general terms what a client may be eligible to receive, and more importantly that you can advise them where to obtain further information.

General information on benefits

Pensions

Women over 60 and men over 65 are entitled to the state retirement pension. This basic pension is paid to people who have reached pensionable age and who have sufficient National Insurance contributions. People who do not have sufficient National Insurance contributions made or credited throughout their working life may get a reduced pension or possibly no pension at all. Married women, if they do not have sufficient contributions of their own, can claim a pension based on their husband's contributions. In 2002 the full basic pension is £75.50 for an individual. The reduced rate for married women whose claims are based on their husband's contributions is £45.20.

Help with residential or nursing home fees

People wishing to enter residential or nursing home care will have their care needs assessed by their local authority. Assistance with nursing home fees will be provided on a sliding scale after a financial assessment or means test is carried out. Any potential resident who has more than £16,000 in savings will have to pay the full cost of their residential or nursing home care.

Prescription charges

People over 60 are entitled to free prescription charges and free sight tests regardless of their level of savings or their income.

Transport

Most local authorities offer free or reduced bus/train fares to local older people. These vary so you should ask your local council what the provisions are. Many rail companies give reductions on national rail fares to people aged 60 or over, and some of the national bus companies provide similar discounts.

Attendance allowance

This allowance is designed for people who need assistance with washing, dressing, mobility or feeding, or who need supervision so they are not a risk to themselves. In 2002 this is paid at two different rates: one is a weekly rate of £37,65 for clients who need help during the day or night and the other, higher rate, is currently £56.25 for help needed round the clock. Clients are eligible to claim for attendance allowance regardless of their living circumstances. They can claim even if they live alone. The requirement is that the client needs help. They do not actually have to be getting help in order to qualify for the allowance. As a general rule clients must meet the conditions for the allowance for a period of at least six months before it is payable. However, special rules apply for clients who are terminally ill.

Rates of benefit from 1946 to date

Family allowance date rate

06/08/46	5s a week for each child other than the first child
02/09/52	8s a week for each child other than the first child
02/10/56	10s a week for the third and each subsequent child
24/10/67	15s a week for the fourth and each subsequent child
09/04/68	15s a week for the second child, 17s a week for the third and each subsequent child
08/10/68	18s a week for the second child, £1.00 a week for the third and each subsequent child
08/04/75	£1.50 a week for the second and each subsequent child

Child benefit/One parent benefit

Date	Eldest child	Other children	OPB
05/04/77	£1.00	£1.00	0.50
24/11/80	£4.75	£4.75	£3.00
25/11/85	£7.00	£7.00	£4.55
09/04/90	£7.25	£7.25	£5.60
10/04/95	£10.40	£8.45	£6.30
12/04/99	£14.40	£9.60	N/A

Child benefit

Child benefit – called Family Allowance until 1977 – is payable as a universal benefit, regardless of income or savings, to the mothers of all children who are in full-time education. It is interesting to see how since its introduction in 1946 child benefit has risen from 5 shillings (25p) a week for each child after the first one to £1 a week in 1977, when it began to be paid for the first child as well as others, to the present rate of £15.75 for the first child and £10.55 for the second and subsequent children.

Benefits for those on low incomes

All the benefits designed to support people with low incomes are based on a means test which includes savings and income. Some of these benefits are related to the amount of National Insurance contributions.

Income support (also called minimum income guarantee)

This benefit is widely claimed by older people but is available to those who are both under 60 and are ill or who are carers and are not registered as unemployed.

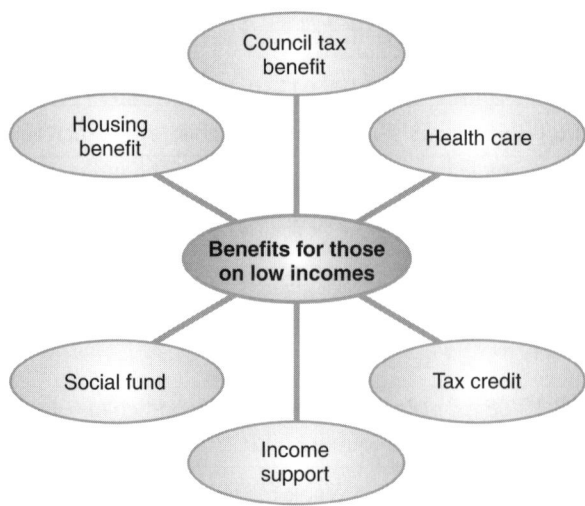

People on low incomes are eligible for certain benefits

Did you know?

That 70 per cent of pensioner households depend on state benefits for at least 50 per cent of their income. That 13 per cent of pensioner households receive all their income from state benefits and over 1.7 million people aged 60 or over are receiving income support because of their low income. Income support is available for people who have no more than £8,000 in savings. It has been announced that this level will increase to £12,000 in 2001 for people aged 60. The level of income support is set by Parliament. Income and savings are taken into account along with allowances for items such as housing costs, and these are then deducted from the amounts which Parliament has set down as being the minimum amount required to live on. Full details of the current income support rates can be obtained from the Benefits Agency or any of the advice centres.

Housing benefit and council tax benefit

Housing benefit provides assistance towards the rent of those on a low income, and council tax benefit provides support for the payment of council tax. Both these benefits are only available to claimants with less than £16,000 in savings. A broad guide is that if a client is eligible for income support they are also likely to be entitled to housing benefit and council tax benefit. As in the case of income support, the circumstances of an individual are taken into account, including income, savings, how many in the family, level of disability and so on. There are also schemes which provide a reduction in council tax for people who live alone and for those who live with another person who has a low income. Those in receipt of income support will automatically be sent the appropriate forms to complete for housing and council tax benefit. Otherwise the forms will be available from the local authority.

Health costs

People in receipt of income support will receive free prescriptions, free dental treatment, help with travel costs for hospital visits, free sight tests and help towards the purchase of glasses. Those who do not receive income support, and do not have more than £8,000 worth of savings, can still get some help towards these costs by completing a form which is available from their dentist, optician or the hospital.

Social fund

The social fund can provide lump sum cash payments to cover extra expenses which cannot be met from normal weekly incomes. For example, the purchase of large furniture items such as beds and cookers, or to cover funeral costs. The social fund can also make loans in a crisis or an emergency but it is important to take into account that these loans must be repaid.

Working families tax credit

This is a tax credit to ensure that low-income families who are working will receive an income which meets the minimum income guarantee regardless. Further information on this benefit, which is dependent upon levels of wages, allowances for housing and other costs, and the number of dependant children, can be obtained from the Benefits Agency.

Benefits for people with disabilities and for carers

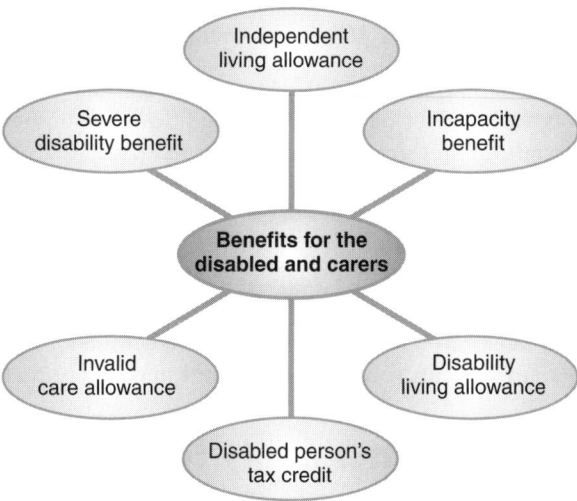

There are a range of benefits that disabled people can claim

Disability living allowance

This is a benefit for those who are disabled and require the same sort of care and assistance that qualifies people for the attendance allowance. It provides benefit for those unable to walk or have great difficulty walking outdoors, and have a mobility element included. The rates at which it is paid are complex. Information should be obtained from the Benefits Agency or a local advice centre.

Invalid care allowance

This is paid to carers who are unable to work full time because of the care they are giving to someone else. Carers are eligible to claim this allowance if the person they are caring for qualifies for an attendance allowance or disability living allowance. To qualify carers must be under 65 when they first apply for the allowance and must not be earning more than £50 a week. Carers who are getting other benefits may not be able to get invalid care allowance.

Incapacity benefit (previously called invalidity benefit)

This is paid to people who cannot work because they are sick or disabled. It is based on the National Insurance contributions paid. The rates at which it is paid depends on the length of time that a person is unable to work. Incapacity benefit stops when a person reaches pensionable age.

Severe disablement allowance

This is benefit is paid to severely disabled people who cannot work but do not have sufficient contributions to get incapacity benefit. It is only applicable to disabled people aged under 65. A medical examination by the Benefits Agency is also required and there are strict guidelines as to the definition of severely disabled. The rate is the same as income support but it is not means tested, and so is applicable to people with a severe disability regardless of income or savings they have.

Independent living fund

This helps severely disabled people who need to pay for care or support in order to remain living at home. Local authorities can also make payments as an alternative to providing community care services, thus enabling a disabled individual to make their own arrangements for care and support. Payments are not age restricted and are available to anyone aged over 16 who is severely disabled.

Disabled person's tax credit

This benefit is designed for people with disabilities who are in work but earn a low income. Through the **tax credit** they are able to ensure that their income does not fall below the minimum income guarantee level.

All this information is intended only to provide you with a guide as to the range of benefits which may be available for any individual client you are working with. It is not an exhaustive list, so it is vitally important for your client's benefit that you obtain information from expert sources, either at advice centres or direct from the Benefits Agency, about any benefits to which your client may be entitled.

How to help clients apply for benefits and allowances

A client may choose not to claim benefits to which they are entitled. This can be extremely frustrating if you are trying to support them in surviving on a limited income. And it can often be difficult to encourage people to claim their entitlements. Many people, particularly older people, may feel that claiming benefit is a form of charity and something they are not prepared to contemplate. Others may feel it is an admission of failure or defeat that they are unable to provide their own income through working. Some find it hard to acknowledge that a change in their circumstances or the development of a disability means they are no longer able to earn a living independently. For many in these circumstances the claiming of a benefit seems like the final admission and acknowledgement of their disability or illness. You should also be aware that a client may have literacy difficulties if there appears to be no logical explanation as to why they are refusing to claim a benefit. If you suspect this is the case, and that the client is too embarrassed to discuss the problem with you, then you need to try to overcome the difficulty. You could offer to complete the relevant application form for the client, perhaps on the grounds that the forms are lengthy to complete, or you could advise them that there is a telephone application line for people who do not wish to complete a written form. If you find that the client responds positively to such suggestions, you should consider that your client may have literacy problems. If you establish this, then you could find a way of finding out if they want support and help to improve their literacy.

Did you know?

The Benefits Agency estimates that between 27 per cent and 37 per cent of pensioners entitled to income support, and up to 12 per cent of those entitled to housing benefit and somewhere between 20 per cent and 30 per cent of those entitled to council tax benefit do not claim it.

Despite the frustrations that it may cause you as a worker attempting to support a client who does not want to claim benefits, you must be prepared to support them in their decision. This does not mean you should not try to encourage them to claim the benefit and to ensure they have all the necessary information, however you should recognise the point at which encouragement becomes harassment or bullying and allow your client to make their informed decision. Once the decision has been made then you must support them to manage their finances on the level of income they have. This does not mean decisions cannot be periodically reviewed and revisited and this is something you should encourage your client to do from time to time in the hope they may have changed their views. If they do change their views on claiming a particular benefit you should offer an appropriate level of support in assisting them to make the claim.

Case study

Mrs F had lived alone since her husband died 25 years ago. She kept her small house neat and clean and had always been very independent doing all her own shopping, gardening and cleaning. She has a son in another part of the country who she sees about twice a year, she is friendly with her neighbours and attends her local church where she has a wide circle of friends. Mrs F has been finding it increasingly difficult to manage on her single state pension. Until she was admitted to hospital for investigations for a bowel condition she had no idea that she may have been entitled to additional support. Despite having a wide circle of friends and contacts in the local church she never considered discussing her personal financial circumstances with anyone outside her family, and on the rare occasions when she saw her son even then she did not want to burden him with discussions of her financial circumstances. It was a passing comment she made to one of the support workers at the hospital about the quality of hospital food being a considerable improvement on what she could afford at home that prompted a few further questions to Mrs F, and to the discovery of the amount of pension she was receiving.

Mrs F who advised about what she could claim and was supported to make a claim for income support. As a result she received additional income, bringing her weekly income to the guaranteed minimum level. This made a huge difference to Mrs F, who was now able to run her home and do her shopping without the sort of worry and anxiety that she had endured for so many years.

1 What steps could have been taken to have provided Mrs F with this information much earlier?

2 How would you organise an information campaign for people like Mrs F?

3 What sources would you have targeted for information to help people such as Mrs F?

Filling in forms to claim for benefits may seem to some clients a time-consuming and tedious task. However, if it means they will increase their independence through extra financial support, you should encourage them to do it and help in whatever way you can

Completing the paperwork

Benefit claim forms are usually very long. However, great improvements have been made in the way they have been structured to make them much simpler to understand and easier to know what information is required. Nevertheless, it is often the length of these forms that inhibit people from filling them in. For example, the claim form for income support is 20 pages long. Actually completing the forms is not as arduous as it appears, as for the vast majority of people large parts of the forms will not require filling in. These are the sections asking about savings, property owned and other sources of income. Even so, the mere appearance of the form makes some people feel that they are unable to complete it.

The Benefits Agency has a system of filling them in over the telephone and sending them to clients for checking and completing. This is a valuable service for many people and ensures the information is filled in correctly and in the correct places on the form. However, for clients who do not want to do this by telephone you may be asked to support and assist them in completing application forms. This does not mean you would take over the filling in of the forms, however the client may ask you to check that the form they have completed has been filled in correctly. It is important to make sure that a client with no income or no savings writes 'none' in the appropriate boxes.

You may need to make sure that a client making a claim fills in the form legibly. This is important as any difficulty in marking out the filled in details may cause a delay in processing the claim. Also the information could be interpreted wrongly and the wrong decisions made in respect of the benefit. If a client's writing legibility is a problem, you will need to handle this with tact and care. A client may be offended if you imply they cannot complete a form legibly. If a client has literacy problems then you could either offer to assist them or complete the form on their behalf. Another course is to encourage them to use the telephone application line.

You may have to deal with a client who refuses to complete the whole form because they feel it is too long and complex or because they are not willing to provide all the information the form asks for, such as information about their finances. You can only explain to them what the consequences will be of not providing that information. For example, if the client is claiming a means tested benefit then the claim will not be considered unless the financial information is provided. The client must be aware of the consequences of their actions in order to make an informed decision about whether or not they wish to pursue the claim for a particular benefit and to provide all of the necessary information.

Potential difficulties

If you are aware that a client is attempting to make a deliberately fraudulent claim for a benefit or is making a deliberate attempt to mislead an agency providing a benefit about their circumstances then you must:

- explain that you cannot support them in this action and that you will be unable to assist them in making the claim
- make it clear that if they persist in making a fraudulent or misleading claim then you will have to record the matter and report it to your agency
- report the matter to your line manager who will advise you as to your agency's policy.

Section 2
Your claim for *Incapacity Benefit*

Please read through **Section 1** of this form. Your employer has filled in **Section 1** to tell you why you cannot get Statutory Sick Pay (SSP).
Statutory Sick Pay (SSP) is money paid by employers to employees who are away from work for 4 days or more in a row because they are sick. If you disagree with the decision, ask your employer to explain it to you. If you still disagree with the decision, ask the Inland Revenue (NI contributions) office for advice. You may be able to ask for an Inland Revenue officer's decision. You can contact them by phone, their phone number and address are in the phone book under **Inland Revenue**. Leaflet **NI244** *Statutory Sick Pay – check your rights* tells you more about this. You can get this leaflet from any social security office.
Please fill in the rest of this form if you want to claim Incapacity Benefit.
If you need help filling in this form, get in touch with your social security office. If you cannot fill in this form yourself, you can ask someone else to fill it in for you.

Part 1 **About you**

Benefit you can get because of this claim can be paid more quickly if you
- answer all the questions on this form that apply to you and
  your partner, if you have one
- send us all the documents we ask for.
If you cannot do this, get in touch with us, but benefit you can get because of this claim may be delayed.

Surname or family name	Mr/Mrs/Miss/Ms
All other names – in full	
All other surnames or family names you have been known by or are using now. Please include maiden name, all former married names and all changes of family name.	
Address	
	Postcode
Daytime phone number	Code Number
Date of birth	/ /

National Insurance (NI) number
You can find the number on your NI numbercard, letters from social security or payslips.

Letters   Numbers   Letter
☐ ☐   ☐ ☐ ☐ ☐ ☐ ☐   ☐

If you do not know your NI number, have you ever had one or used one at any time?
No ☐
Yes ☐

Marital status
married ☐   widow or widower ☐   separated ☐
single ☐   divorced ☐

Please tell us about any other personal details you think we should know about in **Part 18** Other information. For example, other names or recent previous addresses.

Copyright, Department of Social Security 2000
Page from the application form for Statutory Sick Pay and Incapacity Benefit

Active knowledge

Obtain a copy of a benefits claim form (e.g. income support). Check it through to familiarise yourself with its style.

Element Y3.3 — Enable individuals to collect benefits and allowances

WHAT YOU NEED TO LEARN

- Methods of collecting benefits and allowances.
- Ways of ensuring clients keep their money safe.

Methods of collecting benefits and allowances

Payment into bank account

You really must trust a bank to look after your money for you. It will be safer there.

You may need to convince a client that a bank is a safer option for keeping their money than keeping it at home

You will need to discuss and agree with your client the best way you can support them in collecting any benefits or allowances to which they are entitled. State benefits and many other payments from private pensions or employer pensions are now paid directly into clients' bank accounts. If your client does not have a bank account then it may be helpful if you can explain to them the value of having one, and give them information on how their benefit could be paid directly into it and how relatively easy it is to access it.

Payment by giro cheque

The Benefits Agency pays some state benefits direct by a regular giro cheque, which can be cashed at the local post office. This requires the client to attend the post office in person and to produce some identity. Where people are ill or unable to attend the post office it is possible for a cheque to be cashed on their behalf provided that appropriate identity and authority is produced.

Payment by order book

Many regular payments, such as income support, child benefit and the state retirement pension, are paid through a regular order book. In these cases the client

How clients budget their money can have an effect on their independence if they can make it last until their next payment, so that they don't need further support

collects their benefit each week (or month) from the post office where the appropriate counterfoil is stamped and removed from their book and the cash is paid to them. Cash is welcomed by a many people on low incomes. It gives them immediate access to their money, so there is no need to go to the bank to access it. Also, this avoids the additional expense of bank charges for writing cheques or making payments with a debit card. However, it means that people on a low income who are totally dependent on receiving cash each week have no emergency funds and often experience severe difficulties after they have spent all their money and have to wait for the next cash payment.

Help may be needed

If clients are physically unable to visit a post office to collect their benefit or allowance because of temporary illness or disability, then you can arrange to collect their benefits for them by them signing the appropriate sections on the back of the payment counterfoil in their order book. If you do collect a client's payments in this way it is essential for your protection and theirs that they sign for the receipt of the money as soon as you hand it over to them. You could use a simple form for this. All you need is a record of the amount of money which you have given to them, the date on which it was handed over and a record of the client's signature.

Record of Monies Collected	
Date	*25 May 2000*
Received from	*A N Other*
The sum of	*£75.50*
Pension collected by	*Mary P – Support worker*
Signature	

It is also important you record in the client's case notes or records that you have collected and handed over any benefits to them. If the client is collecting their own benefits you should encourage them to check that the amount they are given is correct and if there are any problems they should immediately report them. Where payments are being made directly into a client's bank account, you should encourage them to check their bank statements regularly to make sure that all the necessary payments are being recorded in their account.

If you are dealing with money for clients in residential care your work setting will have its own form of recording what money is received on behalf of each resident and how much is spent. This will have to be recorded, as well as any payments which are made into any bank accounts which are held in the client's name.

Ways of ensuring clients keep their money safe

In settings where you are working with vulnerable clients, whether they are residential or in the client's own home, it is necessary to discuss with your client the subject of the safety and security of any money they have. Many vulnerable people who continue to live in their own homes, particularly those who are elderly or with disabilities, are at high risk of being robbed if they keep cash in the house. Elderly people are more likely to keep large amounts of cash in the house and you should discourage this wherever possible. They and their money will be much safer if they can be persuaded to put the money into a bank, building society or post office savings account.

Clients continuing to lead an independent life should do what they can to avoid putting this at risk, such as by not keeping large amounts of money at home

In a residential setting there will be arrangements for the safe keeping of clients' valuables and money. They should be encouraged to use this facility rather than keep money in their room or handbag or wallet. If a client refuses to use the safe-keeping facility provided by the residential establishment, then it is likely they will be asked to sign a disclaimer form to acknowledge they have been offered the facility but have chosen to take care of their valuables themselves. You will explore this in more detail when you do Unit CU1.

If you are aware of any cash being lost or stolen from your client you must immediately report the loss – to your line manager if you are in a residential setting or to the police if you are working with clients in their own homes. Clients are likely to be distressed by the loss of valuables, so you will need to offer them a lot of support during this time.

Managing finances is an important part of the lives of all adults. People will need your support to a greater or lesser degree in order to be able to manage their finances effectively. You will need to have a broad and general understanding of how finances work and the sort of support and benefits to which your clients may be entitled. Above all you will need to know where to obtain advice and guidance for clients on all financial matters.

Active knowledge

Check out the system for recording clients' finances in your workplace. Think about how it could be improved, in terms of ease of use and its suitability. If you feel improvements could be made to update, simplify or extend it, then have a go at designing a new system of recording. When you have done this you may want to discuss it with your line manager. You never know, it might be brought into use in your work setting!

Unit test

1 Where can information be obtained about benefits and allowances? Name at least three sources.

2 List the different ways in which payments can be made.

3 List the different ways in which benefits and allowances can be received.

4 Identify four reasons why people may refuse to claim benefits to which they are entitled.

5 What would be the general areas of benefit that you would advise people over 60 to consider?

6 What would be the general areas of benefit that you would advise families on a low income to consider?

7 What would be the general areas of benefit that you would advise people with a disability to consider?

8 What are the ways in which the benefit system can contribute to the independence of individuals?

9 Think about the ways in which you feel the benefit system could be improved.

10 What other sources of income could you explore other than state benefits and allowances?

Support individuals in undertaking health care

Individuals who are undertaking their own health care, or who are having their health care administered by a carer rather than a health care professional, are taking control of a key aspect of being independent. Being able to retain or regain control over health care makes a huge contribution to individuals being empowered and in control of their own lives.

Being able to provide support, advice and guidance to those who are undertaking their own health care or to carers who are providing health care for friends or relatives is an important and key role for workers in health and social care. There are many situations in which the ability to deliver health care in the community contributes to the key factors in enabling clients to remain in their own homes. The additional support provided by a health or care worker to a client or their carer can ensure that a plan of care can be developed and undertaken successfully to provide the maximum possible benefit for the client.

Element Y4.1   Support individuals in undertaking procedures, treatments and dressings

WHAT YOU NEED TO LEARN

- Ways to ensure clients have all they need for their health care.
- The range of procedures clients may need to undertake.

Ways to ensure clients have all they need for their health care

You need to establish with clients the level of support they are happy for you to provide. This may involve you in directly supporting a carer rather than the client, so you may need to discuss with them the level of support they need. The support you could be asked to provide includes:

- assisting in the ordering or collection of the supplies and equipment needed
- providing explanations and guidance on carrying out the health care procedures
- demonstrating the correct techniques and procedures to be followed
- observing and offering advice
- being present in order to offer emotional support and reassurance
- providing advice, information or assistance in the disposal of waste.

Level of support

You need to discuss carefully with your client and their carers, if any, the level of support they need you to provide, taking into account the degree of independence your clients wants in managing their own health care. If you have been working with a client for some time, you will be aware of the degree of independence they want and level of support needed. However, if you have a new client or a job in which your role involves short periods of support to clients, then you need to discuss with your client or clients the type and level of support they require. You need to remember that your client may not be aware of the types of help available to them and the supplies and equipment which could be provided to improve and extend their level of independence. So, you must take a proactive role in providing this information and making sure that your client has the maximum possible information about what is available, so they can make an informed decision about how much they feel able to undertake for themselves.

Equipment and supplies

Once you have decided with the client the level of support you will provide, the next stage is to make sure they have all of the equipment and supplies which they need to carry out their treatments. The client may have a list of the supplies they need. This may have been given to them by their GP, district nurse, hospital doctor or nurse, or by a specialist health care professional. If they do not have a list of supplies, then check with the care team responsible for the health care of the client exactly what supplies will be needed and check the quantities needed at any one time to ensure that storage recommendations are complied with.

The supplies are likely to be obtained through a pharmacy or possibly from the health centre or specialist hospital clinic, depending on the treatments to be undertaken. However, it is unlikely that large quantities would be supplied from a hospital, as NHS prescribing is usually only available for in-patients receiving care or treatment. All prescribing, including supplies, is undertaken by the GP in the community and supplied through a local pharmacy. It can be useful to check the following list to make sure your client has all of the necessary equipment and supplies:

1 **Source of supply**. This needs to be checked with the local GP for any medications or supplies subject to a prescription. You need to check or get the client to check that there is a facility for a regular repeat prescription when needed. If the supplies do not require a prescription, you should ensure that the local pharmacy always has an adequate supply and work out with your client how often the supplies will need to be renewed.

2 **Storage facilities**. Many items needed for health care require special storage. All items need to be stored in a place not subject to extreme temperatures. Damp or excessively hot or cold places can contaminate or spoil medical supplies, equipment and medication. All medications and sterilised items will have an expiry date. Clients should be encouraged to set up a regular system of reviewing their supplies and returning any which are outdated to the pharmacy for proper disposal. Never use outdated medications or medical supplies. If special storage requirements are needed, for example insulin has to be kept in a refrigerator, then it is essential to follow the instructions. Failing to do this could result in medication becoming ineffective or even dangerous.

3 **Ability to understand and comply with instruction**. You must stress to your clients the need to store medications correctly and you must satisfy yourself they have understood this. If you are concerned a client has not understood or is not able or willing to comply with storage requirements for medical supplies or medication, then you should refer the matter immediately to the care team and your line manager. Alternative arrangements for administering medication will need to be considered.

Medical equipment and supplies should be stored correctly and kept up to date.

The range of procedures clients may need to undertake

Many clients can undertake their own health care in their home setting. Some may require the support of their carer, if they have one, to carry out health care procedures at home. Whether you are supporting a client or a carer or a combination of both, you could be involved in making sure they are able to undertake any health procedures, including dealing with dressings for lesions such as ulcers or pressure sores or other wounds which have been stitched.

Dressing a wound or lesion

If a client is doing this in their home setting, they will need supplies of sterile dressing packs, which contain gauze packs, cotton wool and sterile cotton wool balls, tweezers and a dish. They will also need small packs of saline solution (Normasol). The type of dressing used will vary depending on the individual client and their particular condition. This could be a standard gauze dressing, an artificial skin (Tagaderm) or other specialist dressing which may be impregnated with particular substances. The length of time between changing dressings will vary, depending on the nature of the wound or lesion. For example, in some surgical wounds which have been sutured the dressing will not be changed until the sutures are removed. It has been found that a lower incident of post-operative wound infection occurs if dressings are left untouched in most cases.

Following a clean procedure

Dressing and cleaning an area will need to follow a clean procedure. You need to make sure your client understands the importance of thoroughly washing their hands before dealing with any dressing. Although the risk of cross-infection is obviously less if the individual concerned is carrying out their own personal health care, it is still essential they wash their hands before and after completing the procedure. The steps they should take are:

1 Wash hands.

2 Open dressing pack.

3 Remove old dressing and place in a bag for disposal.

4 Use cotton wool balls held with tweezers and dipped in saline solution to clean the affected area.

5 Apply any medication required.

6 Pick up new dressing with tweezers, place on the affected area and hold in place with adhesive tape (Micropore).

This is a general guide only and specific procedures may need to be followed for a particular individual. It is essential that you and/or the client check with the district nurse or the hospital the exact procedure which will be necessary. You should refer to Unit Z7 for details of how to deal with lesions caused by pressure sores.

Catheters and stoma care

Clients are likely to manage catheters and stoma care in their own home setting. Detailed instructions for changing a catheter and stoma appliances are given below. The processes for changing stoma appliances are the same whether they are being changed by a carer or by the individual client. The same level of hygienic practice carried out by a health care worker must be observed by the individual client. Many people who need stoma care prefer to do it themselves if possible, as they find it embarrassing having someone else do it.

Stoma care

Stoma care is the care of clients who have had surgery to provide an additional means of eliminating waste from their bodies, either faeces or urine. The most usual stoma care is given to clients who have a colostomy. This is the result of providing an additional surgical opening for clients who are unable, either on a temporary or permanent basis, to use their bowel in the normal way. This can be the result of colon cancer, ulcerative colitis or a series of other diseases. Following a colostomy faeces are collected in a special stoma bag which needs to be changed regularly. Many clients are able to do this for themselves, but it may be necessary to provide stoma care for them in the early days after the colostomy has been performed or because the client is ill or becoming frail.

It is likely you would only be asked to provide stoma care for a client who has an established colostomy and therefore likely to be familiar with the procedure. However, you should still check that they are happy for you to change their appliance and that they understand the procedure you are about to undertake. This is what you must do to carry out the procedure:

1 Wash hands.

2 Ensure the client understands the procedure and that you have provided for privacy.

3 Expose the appliance, the stoma bag. Place a towel over the client's abdomen and a protector on the client's bed to keep the bed clean.

4 Make sure you have all the necessary equipment and put on gloves.

5 Gently remove the old pouch and the wafer, which is the thin layer that provides the seal between the pouch or bag and the client.

6 Measure the contents of the bag, note any changes from normal to the contents and then dispose of it in accordance with the policy of your work setting.

7 Wipe the skin around the stoma using a warm cloth to ensure that any faeces are removed. Dry the area with a towel.

8 Prepare the new wafer by cutting it to fit over the stoma. There should not be any visible skin between the stoma and the wafer.

9 Apply the new wafer to the skin, make sure there are no air pockets under the wafer, and hold it in place for 30 seconds to help the adhesive to work.

10 Apply the stoma pouch or bag to the flange on the wafer, and make sure that the bag is sealed.

11 Remove the protectors and clean the area.

12 Wash your hands.

13 Record the procedure in the client's care plan or case notes.

Catheter care

Clients who have an indwelling catheter, which is likely to be a Foley's catheter, may need support in ensuring that the risk of infection is reduced as far as possible. Clients with catheters are prone to infections, and hygiene and sterile techniques must be observed to minimise the risk. In order to maintain hygiene the site at which the catheter enters the client's body should be cleaned regularly. You should follow procedures laid down for your workplace, which may vary slightly but are generally likely to be:

1 Wash hands.

2 Take universal precautions.

3 Ensure that the client understands the procedure and that you have provided for privacy.

4 Using a sterile technique, prepare a tray with either saline or savlon or any other medium identified in your workplace procedures.

5 Using swabs, dip one swab into the solution and wipe in one direction around one side of the entry site.

6 In a female client you should ensure that you wipe away from the rectal opening in one direction only.

7 Discard the swab after one wipe and take a fresh swab to wipe the other side of the entry site.

8 Discard that swab.

9 Continue using fresh swabs for each wipe until the area is clean.

10 Do not wipe the area excessively as this can lead to irritation and introduce infection. It should be sufficient for one wipe each side of the entry site.

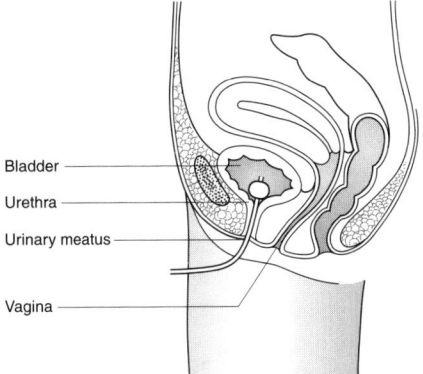

11 Dispose of the used swabs and tray in accordance with the procedures for your workplace for disposal of contaminated waste.

12 Remove your gloves.

13 Wash your hands.

14 Record the procedure in the client's care plan or case notes.

Indwelling urinary catheter in place in female body

You are unlikely to be involved in the insertion or removal of catheters as this is undertaken by a qualified clinical practitioner, although you may be asked to assist under direction on occasions.

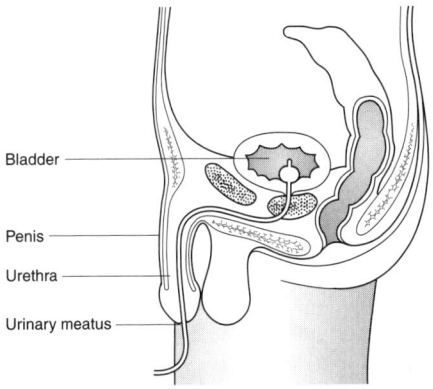

Indwelling urinary catheter in place in male body

Diabetes

Clients and carers could undertake treatments and health care at home for other conditions, such as the control of diabetes. This depends on the type of diabetes. The treatment may consist of insulin injections which the client needs to take on a regular, prescribed basis. Insulin needs to be stored in a refrigerator and a supply of insulin syringes must be kept. It is essential to regularly check the supply to ensure the client does not run short. Diabetics have close contact with a specialist diabetic nurse at the local hospital and most diabetics are well-informed of the care they must provide to control their illness, and of the consequences of failure to do this. If you become aware that a client with diabetes is failing to follow the prescribed treatment, then you must contact an appropriate member of the care team, as the consequences can be extremely serious. Not all diabetes is controlled by the injection of insulin. Type II diabetes, which has its onset later in life, is controlled through diet rather than through medication. This will be indicated in the plan of care for the particular client.

Drainage or feeding tubes

Clients having ongoing treatment for a chronic condition may have drainage or feeding tubes or shunts in place. The sites of these will need to be maintained. Any client with an implanted appliance receives a comprehensive set of instructions about how to maintain it. This needs to be included in the care plan for the individual client and you must ensure that care is undertaken as identified in the instructions. If there is anything about which you are unclear, then you must refer to the appropriate specialist member of the care team.

Monitoring the clients

One of your key roles is to be aware of the potential for adverse reactions to particular treatments or procedures and to report these without delay to the appropriate care team member. Where lesions, sores or wounds are being dressed check for any signs of potential infection such as reddening, swelling or excessive heat in the area. You also need to report any pain, discomfort, nausea or clamminess, sweating or fever experienced by clients who are undertaking any health care procedures at home.

Safe disposal of waste

Most health care procedures leave some element of waste. This could be used dressings or empty syringes or emptied catheter bags. All waste of this nature must be disposed of appropriately. Waste should not simply be placed in a dustbin, it should be carefully bagged and ideally incinerated. If incineration is not possible then it must be placed in a sealed bag before disposal. Used syringes or other glass containers must never be placed in a dustbin. They should be put into a special sharps box, which you can get from your health centre, pharmacy or hospital. The sharps box is a rigid container which ensures that syringes do not put anyone at risk of a needle stick injury. Sharps boxes can be collected from the individual or arranged for collection through the local health centre.

Active knowledge

Identify a client for whom you provide support in undertaking health care. If you do not currently work in this way, use a relative or friend as your example.

Make a detailed list of:

- the medical/pharmaceutical supplies needed
- where they can be obtained
- where they would be stored
- how any waste will need to be disposed of.

Support individuals in obtaining specimens and taking physical measurements

WHAT YOU NEED TO LEARN

- How to ensure that clients understand how to obtain specimens.
- How to identify the level of support clients need.

How to ensure that clients understand how to obtain specimens

Individuals managing their own medical conditions while remaining at home may need to take a variety of different measurements and to obtain specimens on a regular basis to monitor their current state of health.

Measurements of health can be:

- Blood pressure.
- Samples of urine.
- Blood samples.
- Peak flow readings.
- Height/weight ratio readings.

Some of these will be obtained by taking physical measurements and others through the analysis of specimens. Where specimens are required, see below for detailed instructions on how to obtain these.

Taking specimens

Any client who needs to take specimens as part of a monitoring process will also receive very specific instructions by the appropriate member of the care team about how the specimen should be obtained and how, if appropriate, it should be analysed. The commonest condition requiring an analysis of specimens at home is diabetes. However, there are many other conditions where clients may need to test their urine on a regular basis to ensure that their body systems are functioning correctly. The following contains detailed information on how to analyse both blood and urine.

Urine

It is easiest to take a sterile urine specimen from a client who has a catheter and to obtain it from the catheter line. To collect this you should:

1 Wash your hands.

2 Explain to the client what you are going to do and answer any questions they may have.

3 Make sure you have collected all the equipment you need and put on your gloves.

4 Clamp the catheter line below the port by folding the tubing in half and apply the clamp.

A catheter line

5 Wait for a small amount of urine to collect in the tubing above the port.

6 Insert a sterile syringe gently into the port. Make sure you do not pierce the tubing itself.

7 Withdraw approximately 10cc of urine into the syringe.

8 Empty the syringe into the sterile specimen container.

9 Make sure you do not contaminate the insides or the lid of the container.

10 Unclamp the catheter tubing and make sure the urine is freely flowing.

11 Label the container and complete the documentation for your workplace and send it to the laboratory following the procedures for your own work setting.

12 Record in the case notes or care plan the fact you have taken the specimen.

Withdrawing a urine specimen

Clients who do not have a catheter should be supplied with the appropriate equipment to provide a **mid-stream sample of urine (MSSU)**. The equipment consists of a funnel and a sterile urine container. The funnel and container should come in a sterile pack and the client should be asked to pass urine into the funnel and fill the pot.

Equipment for obtaining mid-stream sample of urine

Testing urine

The condition of a client's urine can provide a great deal of information about their state of health. There are simple tests which can be carried out on urine and you may be asked to undertake some of these. However, it is important before carrying out any tests that you follow some basic observations which will provide you with an initial indication of any problems.

Healthy urine should be clear, pale yellow and not have an offensive smell. If urine smells offensive, is cloudy, has particles in it, has blood in it, is a bright orange colour, or any other colour apart from clear pale yellow, then these are the first signs of concern. You should also check with your client whether they have experienced any pain or burning when they pass urine as either of these could be indicators of more serious underlying conditions. These simple observations are indicators of further problems but are insufficient on their own to establish that there really are problems. It is necessary to carry out further tests on the client's urine in order to find out more detailed information about their state of health.

Urine tests

There are two methods of testing urine. It can be sent to a laboratory, which would normally be a specialist **uro-genital bacteriology** section, where extensive testing and the growing of cultures can be carried out. However, if an initial indication of any possible underlying problems is required the most normal method is to use **urine-analysis sticks**. These are short flexible sticks a few inches long containing sensitive material which changes colour depending on the substances they come into contact with in the urine. It is possible to test for a range of factors in urine by using urine-analysis sticks. The following table shows some examples.

Test for	Indications
1 Leucocytes, ((white blood cells), an indicator of infection)	Change of colour – sticks range from white through to dark purple
2 Protein (another indicator of infection)	Colour changes from light green through to dark green
3 Blood	Colour changes from white to dark blue
4 Glucose (high blood sugar)	Colour changes from light blue to yellow

Urine storage

If you need to store urine prior to testing, it is important that it should be in a tightly sealed sterile container. It should be kept in a separate specimen fridge, *never* in a fridge which is used for storing ordinary food stuff. It must also be clearly labelled with the:

- client's name
- type of specimen
- date the specimen was collected.

Blood

There are two ways of obtaining blood samples. One is through a finger prick using a small lancet blade and the other is through **venipuncture**, which involves using a needle and syringe to take blood from a client's vein.

Blood which is obtained from a finger prick is obtained from capillary vessels, which are the tiny blood vessels near the surface of the skin. The blood from there is squeezed onto the testing apparatus. The most commonly used method is using testing strips for testing blood sugar levels, or the **phenylketonuria (PKU) test**, which is done by pricking the heels of babies during the first few days of life. Where larger amounts of blood are required for more extensive tests, then it is necessary to understand where to find the relevant veins in the arm and hand.

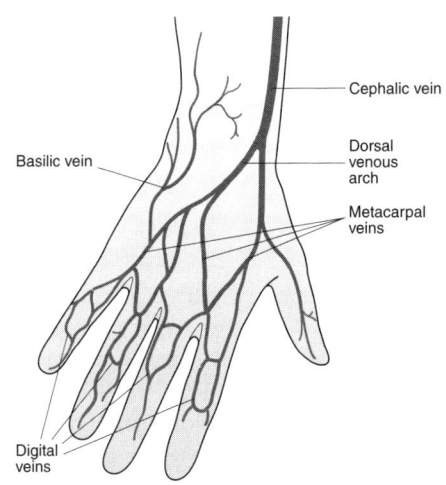

Blood samples can be taken from these veins in the fingers, hands and forearm

You need to be specially trained to take blood from a client. There are courses that provide this training. The information in this unit will give you some guidance and assistance, however it will not enable you to have the skill to undertake the procedure on clients. You should never attempt to carry out this procedure without the specific agreement and under the instructions of a medical practitioner or your supervisor, unless you have been trained by your workplace to carry out these procedures.

Obtaining blood samples by finger prick

Blood sugar levels are tested on a regular basis (often daily) for clients who are diabetic. The most usual method is to prick the side of the finger using a small lancet and then read the results with a blood glucose meter. There are many different types of meters so you should make sure you are familiar with the one which is used in your work setting. In order to test a client's blood sugar level, you should do the following:

1 Wash your hands.

2 Explain to the client if necessary what the process involves. However, if the client has been a diabetic for some time they are likely to be very familiar with the procedure and many carry it out for themselves. If you do need to undertake the procedure for them you should ensure that you have their consent.

3 Assemble the equipment that you will need, which is:
   - gloves
   - meter
   - test strips
   - lancet.

4 Check that the test strips are the appropriate ones for the meter, remove a test strip from the container, then close the container. Do not touch the white area on the strip.

5 Place the end of the lancet firmly on the side of the client's finger, press the button on the top of the lancet in order to pierce the skin.

6 Squeeze the finger gently to obtain a large drop of blood.

7 Apply the blood sample to the test strip.

8 Wait the indicated amount of time for the result to appear on the meter.

9 Clean the meter and dispose of the strips in accordance with procedures in your workplace.

10 Document and record and results in the client's care plan or case notes.

Obtaining blood sample by finger prick

Testing blood for sugar

Blood probably can tell more about the health and well-being of a client than any other bodily fluid. Most blood tests are carried out in laboratories. However, you may be asked to carry out a blood sugar analysis. This is a test used regularly for clients who are diabetic and who need to ensure that their medication or diet regime is maintaining their blood sugar at an appropriate level.

Diabetes is the disorder caused by the body's inability to use insulin properly or to provide sufficient insulin to convert sugar into energy, which is the normal role of insulin. When this happens the levels of sugar within the client's blood becomes abnormally high or low and results in potentially dangerous symptoms.

Hyperglycemia is an excessively high level of blood sugar and **hypoglycemia** is an abnormally low level of blood sugar. The symptoms of hyperglycemia are heavy and laboured breathing, nausea, vomiting, increased thirst, increased urination, loss of appetite and sweet-smelling breath. The symptoms of hypoglycemia are excessive sweating, hunger, feeling of faintness, trembling, blurred vision and headaches.

You should observe your client carefully for any of these signs or symptoms and immediately obtain medical assistance if any of them are present, or if your client reports any of them to you.

Taking physical measurements

Physical measurements, such as blood pressure and peak flow, may be an important part of ongoing health care for a great many clients. High or low blood pressure is symptomatic of many medical conditions and can give an early warning about a client's health. Similarly, regular peak flow readings enable people with respiratory diseases, such as asthma, bronchitis or emphysema, to monitor lung function and identify any cause for concern about their health. It can also be useful in identifying any potential change or adaptation in the use of medication. Detailed information on the taking of physical measurements and the normal range of expected results from these is found below. It is essential you are aware of the normal range of measurements expected from your client and their condition. This information should be included in the plan of care and you will need to become familiar with it so that you can report any changes to the appropriate member of the care team.

Temperature

Temperature is a useful indicator of health or illness. Temperature rises when a client has an infection, or possibly following injury or trauma, whereas a low temperature indicates a serious condition such as hypothermia. Temperature can be taken with a traditional thermometer containing mercury. The mercury rises up the glass tube of the thermometer and indicates the client's temperature on the gauge printed on the tube. This type of thermometer has increasingly been replaced by a thermometer which operates with a battery and has a liquid crystal display which shows the client's body temperature. Many health and care settings now use a disposable

Mercury thermometer

Thermodot

LCD thermometer

thermometer which records the client's temperature on a series of dots which will change colour to indicate temperature.

The normal temperature of the human body is 37° Centigrade, 98.4° Fahrenheit. Any significant variation from this must be reported immediately. Temperature should be recorded on a temperature chart (see Unit CU5).

Pulse

Taking a pulse is a way of establishing a client's heart rate by measuring the beats of the heart through a main artery, usually in the wrist. It is possible to take a client's pulse at various other points in the body.

To take a pulse manually, place your first two fingers lightly on the client's wrist directly below the heel of the thumb.

The pulse points in the human body – neck, wrists, groin, ankles

Through your fingers you will then feel the client's pulse in their brachial artery. You will need to use your first two fingers to feel the pulse. You cannot feel somebody else's pulse through your thumb because you have a pulse in your own thumb. When you can feel a pulse you should then count the number of beats you can feel for a period of 30 seconds. You will need to look at your watch whilst you count the pulse. You then multiply the number of beats by two, which will give you a pulse rate of beats per minute.

Taking a pulse from the wrist

Pulse can also be taken by a **pulseoximeter** which fits onto the client's finger and records the pulse electronically. If you take any exercise in a gym or use an exercise bike you may well have seen a pulseoximeter.

Pulse can also be taken as part of a combined reading with blood pressure on an instrument called a **dynomap**. Normal pulse rate is around 70 beats per minute, although this can be raised by illness, anxiety or exercise. People who are extremely fit will have a lower pulse rate; some athletes have pulse rates as low as 50. You will need to know if your client takes regular exercise as this could explain a low pulse rate.

Respiration

A client's respiration is measured in breaths per minute. You will need to observe the number of times that the chest rises and falls per minute. A rise and fall constitutes one respiration. You will need to time your observations for 30 seconds and then multiple by 2 to obtain the number of respirations per minute. A sudden increase or decrease in a client's respiration rate can indicate a deterioration or change in condition and should immediately be reported to a qualified clinical practitioner as giving cause for concern.

Blood pressure

Blood pressure indicates the pressure at which blood is being pumped around the body from the heart. It is important that blood pressure remains within a defined area of measurement. Excessively high or low blood pressure can indicate illness or disease and can directly cause a health problem. Blood pressure is measured with a sphygmomanometer and a stethoscope. The process is as follows:

1 Attach the blood pressure cuff to the client's upper arm.

2 Ensure that you can feel the client's brachial pulse at the inner elbow.

3 Put a stethoscope at the point of the inner elbow where you feel the brachial pulse.

4 Pump up the cuff until the pulse disappears (this is aproximately at a measurement of 180–200 on the sphygmomanometer).

5 Then, decrease the air in the cuff slowly, letting it out using the valve on the sphygmomanometer until you can hear the pulse through the stethoscope.

Taking blood pressure

6 Note the reading on the sphygmomanometer at this point.

7 This will provide you with your **systolic** (upper) reading. This is normally around 120.

8 Continue letting the air out of the cuff and listen until the pulse disappears. Note the reading at this point.

9 This will give you your **diastolic** (lower) reading, which should be around 80.

There can be many reasons for blood pressure being higher or lower than 120/80 and there is a fairly wide acceptable range, which can alter with age. However, you should ensure that all measurements of blood pressure are recorded and any significant variations are reported.

Height and weight

A person's weight in relation to their height can indicate the extent to which their health is being put at risk by them being excessively underweight or overweight.

Weight and health

Underweight The health of clients who are severely underweight could be adversely affected. This could be as a result of illness or as a result of deliberate over-dieting, which is also dangerous to health. Excessive dieting can lead to eating disorders, such as anorexia nervosa or bulimia, caused by clients not getting sufficient nutrients to remain healthy. However, most clients who are underweight are likely to be suffering from some illness.

Overweight, very overweight and obese. The risk to health associated with being overweight or obese grows with the increase in weight. Excess weight can increase the risk of cardiovascular disease, diabetes, arthritis and other weight associated complications.

Note: There is quite a wide range of accepted weights for height which will not represent any threat to the client's health.

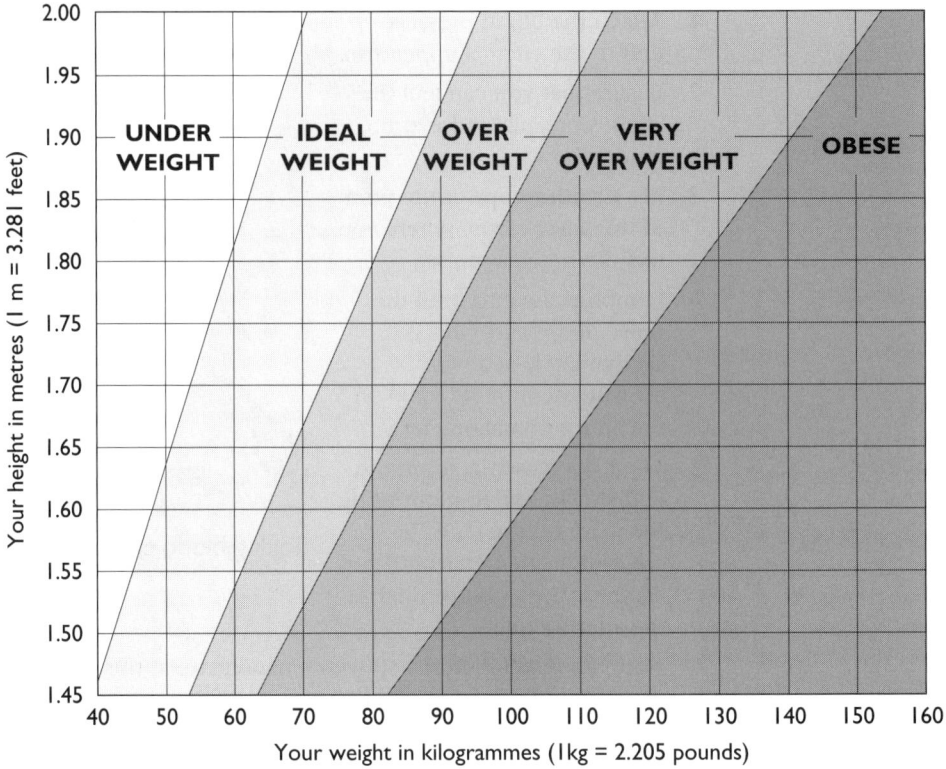

A height/weight chart

There are ideal weights for heights which have been calculated to present the least risk to health. This can be identified in a height/weight chart.

Measuring weight

Where possible clients should be able to stand on a set of scales for the measurement to be taken. Heavy items of clothing such as shoes and outdoor coats should be removed. Clients should stand on the scales and the weight adjusted until the scales balance. A client's weight should be read in kilograms and recorded in their case notes or care plan.

Where clients are unable to stand safely on a set of weighing scales then a scale which provides a seat should be used and the weight recorded in the same way.

Measuring height

Height should be measured using a fixed height ruler which should be attached to the wall of an examination room, or a portable fixed height rule should be used. The client should be asked to stand against the wall with their heels back against the door and stand as straight as they can. The height-measuring bar should be lowered until it rests gently on the top of their head. The resulting height should then be read from the upright ruler. The height, which is likely to be in metres and centimetres, should be recorded in the client's case notes or care plan.

Measuring girth

This should be done around the middle of the client's torso in approximately the waist area. A tape measure should be placed around the waist area and read at the point where both ends meet comfortably without over tightening. The measurement in centimetres should be recorded in the client's case notes or care plan.

Body mass index

Another way to measure a person's weight is to measure and calculate their **body mass index (BMI)**:

$$BMI = \frac{\text{Weight (kg)}}{\text{Height (m}^2)}$$

The result obtained from this calculation indicates whether a person is underweight, at normal weight, overweight or obese:

BMI < 20 kg   underweight
BMI 20–25 kg   normal
BMI 25–30 kg   overweight
BMI > 30 kg   obese
BMI > 40 kg   severely obese

How to calculate BMI

A person weighs 16 stone and is 5 ft 6 ins tall. What is their BMI?

- For the top line (weight):
  Convert 16 stones to kilograms
  There are 2.2 lbs to 1 kg.
  Convert 16 stones to pounds
  16 stone is 16×14 lb = 224 lbs
  224 lbs divided by 2.2 = 102 kg

- For the bottom line (height squared – m^2 means the height is squared, i.e. multiplied by itself):
  Convert 5 ft 6 inches to metres
  There are 39.5 inches to 1 metre. Convert 5 feet to inches
  $5\,ft = 5 \times 12\,ins = 60 + 6\,ins = 66\,ins$
  Then convert inches to metres
  66 divided by 39.5 = 1.67 m
  The height squared is $1.67 \times 1.67 = 2.79$ m
  So,

$$BMI = \frac{102\,kg}{2.79\,m} = 36.6$$

(If you are able to measure weight in kilograms and measure height in metres this will save doing any conversions).

This value indicates that the person's health is at risk and that they would benefit from losing weight. We should all aim to be in the 20–25 kg range as this represents least risk to health.

Did you know?

That up to 56 per cent of men and 45 per cent women in the United Kingdom are classified as being overweight (this is identified as having a BMI of more than 25).

The table shows the percentage of males and females who have excess weight at certain ages.

	Age (years)					
	16–24	25–34	35–44	45–54	55–64	All ages
Males Total with excess weights (%)	31	50	62	68	69	56
Females Total with excess weights (%)	28	38	45	44	64	45

Peak flow

Peak flow measures lung capacity. This is a useful indicator of illness or lung damage. A reduced peak flow is evident in people who are asthmatic or have any chronic respiratory disease. A peak flow meter, a hollow plastic tube about eight inches long, is used to measure peak flow. It has a small gauge on the top and a disposable cardboard blow pipe is inserted into one end. The client should be asked to blow a short, sharp breath into the tube and this will then register on the gauge. The normal rate of lung capacity should be around about 500. In asthmatics or people with chronic lung disease, such as emphysema, a peak flow can be as low as 150 or 200.

A peak flow meter

Fluid balance

The **fluid balance** is the amount of fluid is taken in and excreted out from the body. It is a very important indicator of health. If more fluid is excreted than is taken in then a client can become dehydrated. Conversely if they retain too much fluid in their body this can result in swelling, oedema and ultimately heart failure.

Intake and output is measured by keeping a record of the volume of fluids in and out. This is recorded on a fluid balance chart.

Input

In order to keep an accurate record of input and output of fluid, all fluid which the client takes into their body, either through the mouth or through an intravenous drip. must be measured. If drinks are left for the clients to pour for themselves, you should measure the drinks in the jug and constantly check how much has been used. Explain to the client that they should not take any drinks from anywhere unless they are recorded on the chart.

FLUID CHART (ADULT)															PLEASE SEE REVERSE SIDE FOR NOTES ON USE OF THIS CHART

A fluid balance chart

Output

All fluid output should be measured. The urine in a catheter bag or in a bedpan or commode should be measured before disposal. All vomit should also be measured and its volume recorded.

Maintaining a fluid balance chart

Maintaining a fluid balance chart is not difficult provided you carry out the basic sums correctly! You will need to be sure you have done the addition and subtraction so that the balance of fluid for your client is clearly recorded. Each individual is different as to the amount of fluid they take in and excrete from their bodies but, broadly speaking, everyone should have a positive fluid balance, that is they should put out slightly more fluid than they take in.

Active knowledge

1 Take your own height and weight and then using the calculations in this element work out your own body mass index. Try to do this for two or three other friends or family members until you are confident with the calculations.

2 Work out the fluid balance for the following figures and calculate whether or not this client is maintaining a positive fluid balance.

Intake
0800: IV Therapy – Hartman's 1000 ml
1200: Hartman's discontinued
1300: T 250 ml
1400 : Juice 250 ml
1630 : T 250 ml
Output
1230: 300 ml urine
1600: 500 ml urine; 100 ml vomit
1830: 600 ml urine

How to identify the level of support clients need

Many clients become familiar and comfortable with routines involved in monitoring a long-term health condition. They often know in detail about their own condition and the factors likely to cause improvement or deterioration, and they can identify very quickly alterations in measurements and the steps which need to be taken. In such cases your role will be restricted to offering any support they feel will be useful to them. On the other hand, a client who is concerned or anxious about their condition, possibly because it is newly diagnosed or a new development for them, may not feel confident enough to recognise the implications of the measurements they are taking. So, you may need to have a more proactive role in monitoring the results of measurements and specimens in order to identify early indications of potential problems.

Through discussion and agreement with your client you need to establish the level of intervention and activity you should undertake and precisely the nature of your role. All the key principles concerning your level of involvement are the same if the health care procedures are being undertaken for the client by a carer. In this case you would take into account when deciding on your role the carer's level of familiarity with the procedures and their confidence in undertaking them. Many people who spend a long time caring for someone with a chronic medical condition develop a high level of expertise in obtaining the necessary specimens and measurements and interpreting them accurately. This should be recognised and acknowledged and your role limited to those areas the carer has identified as requiring support.

However many carers may feel concerned or have little confidence in their ability to maintain an extensive monitoring regime. Or they may be under extreme stress and find the level of care too much. In this case more extensive support may be welcomed and it may be appropriate for you to extend your role to provide some relief for the carer.

Active knowledge

Use an example of a client where you provide support for obtaining specimens, or use a friend or relative. Imagine you were leaving detailed instructions for a colleague who was to carry out your role. Make sure you have given enough information on the specimen/measurement to be obtained to enable them to undertake the task effectively.

Element Y4.3 — Support individuals to administer the client's own medication

WHAT YOU NEED TO LEARN

- The regulations and procedures for administering medicines.
- The correct methods of administering medicines.
- How to ensure safe practice.

Regulations and procedures for administering medicines

The handling and use of medicines, drugs and poisons is governed by a series of Acts and Regulations of Parliament. The main ones are:

- The Medicines Act 1968 – which regulates the manufacture, distribution, import, export, sale and supply of medicinal products and medications.

- The Misuse of Drugs Act 1971 – which controls the availability of drugs which could be misused.

- The Misuse of Drugs Regulations 1985 – which enables specified health care professionals to possess, supply, prescribe and/or administer controlled drugs in their practice.

Misuse of Drugs Act

The Misuse of Drugs Act is designed to check and reduce the unlawful use of the kinds of drugs which could produce dependence, if they are misused. These drugs are referred to as **controlled drugs** and they include cocaine, diamorphine (heroin), methadone, levorphanol, morphine, opium, pethidine, amphetamine, dexamphetamine, dihydrocodeine injection, mephentermine, methylphenidate.

Controlled drugs may be prescribed by medical practitioners and registered dentists.

> **A prescription must clearly show:**
> - patient's name and address.
> - date.
> - signature of the prescriber.
> - total quantity to be supplied in words or figures.

Every GP or dentist is required to keep a record of all the controlled drugs which are issued. Hospital pharmacies also have controls over the supply of controlled drugs and they are administered under strict control in a hospital setting. The regulations which govern the administration of controlled drugs are:

- A special cupboard must be used for storing controlled drugs and it should be clearly marked 'Controlled Drugs Cupboard'.

- The cupboard is locked and the key must be held by a state registered nurse or midwife who is in charge of the setting in which the drugs cupboard is kept.

- The supplies of controlled drugs can only be obtained on the signature of a medical practitioner and the drugs can only be administered to patients if there are written instructions from a medical practitioner.

- Each dose of controlled drugs administered must be entered into the special register with the date, the patient's name and the time the dose was given.

- The practitioner who gives the drugs and who checks the drugs must sign the entry.

- In most hospitals the doses must be checked by two people, one of whom should be a state registered nurse or midwife.

- The person checking should see the bottle from which the drug is taken and check the dose with the written prescription.

- All bottles or packages containing controlled drugs must be clearly labelled.

- The nurse or midwife in charge of the ward needs to check the controlled drugs and the accompanying records every seven days.

Medicines Act 1968

The Medicines Act covers all substances used as medical products or ingredients in medicinal products. This Act divides medicines into three categories:

1 **Prescription only medicine (POM)**. This includes controlled drugs, although they are subject to the additional regulations discussed above. These may be prescribed for a patient and subsequently supplied by a pharmacist.

2 **Pharmacy medicine (P)**. This is supplied by a pharmacist but can be dispensed without a prescription.

3 **General sale list (GSL)**. This need not be obtained through a pharmacist.

The prescription only medicines are those which can only be obtained from a GP or a dentist. They include the majority of medicines which are used to control or relieve the symptoms of a wide range of diseases. They may or may not include controlled drugs, but where they do they are subject to the regulations.

The pharmacy medicines will include items such as very strong painkillers, some forms of cold or flu remedies and a wide range of specialist preparations which are designed to alleviate the symptoms of common illnesses.

The general sale list includes mild painkillers and preparations designed to cause temporary alleviation of symptoms of some mild common illnesses, such as throat lozenges and those designed to clear congestion.

In hospital or nursing home settings all drugs are kept in lockable cupboards, freezers or fridges; and even portable drugs trolleys need to be lockable. Normally, in a home setting drugs are not required to be kept in locked containers or cupboards, however they should wherever possible be kept in a secure cupboard and must be kept out of the reach of children.

Doctors and dentists may administer or supply prescription only medicines directly to the patient. Nurses and other health care workers can only supply medicines under the direction of the doctor, however midwives may administer specified controlled drugs under certain conditions. When prescription drugs are supplied by a pharmacist they must be labelled and the name and the label must show the name of the patient, the date of the prescription, the name of the drug, the quantity in the container, the dosage to be taken, any specific instructions about how to take the medication, and the name of the pharmacist supplying the medication. If the drugs are supplied for someone who is in hospital the label is also likely to show their unit number, their date of birth and the name of their consultant.

The correct methods of administering medicines

Medicines on prescription will be accompanied by instructions for how they are to be taken. This could be a short instruction on the label or there may be more detailed instructions contained within the packaging of the medication. Instructions should be carefully read and followed. The label on the medication will also show the dosage. It is absolutely essential that the correct dose of a medicine is always taken. If a client is unwilling to take the required dose or wishes to stop taking the medicine prescribed because they feel it is having unwanted side-effects, then you should refer them to the appropriate member of the care team. They should be discouraged from stopping the medication until they have discussed the problems they are experiencing with their medical practitioner. It is likely that an alternative medication or a different dosage can be prescribed.

It is useful to keep a check on the levels of medication remaining in bottles or packages, particularly where clients are vulnerable or maintain their medication without support of a carer. If you have reason to suspect that a client has exceeded the prescribed dose you must take immediate action to seek medical assistance.

Dosage instruction will be on the label of the medication. Instructions are written now in English although some doctors and other health care professionals still write in the abbreviations, taken from instructions in Latin. The abbreviations you may occasionally see and should be aware of are:

Abbreviation	Latin	English
a.c.	Ante cibum	Before food
Ad lib.	Ad libitum	To the desired amount
b.d. or b.i.d.	Bis in die	Twice a day
c.	Cum	With
o.m.	Omni mane	Every morning
o.n.	Omni nocte	Every night
p.c.	Post cibum	After food
p.r.n.	Pro re nata	Whenever necessary
q.d.	Quaque die	Every day
q.d.s.	Quarter die sumemdum	Four times daily
q.i.d.	Quarter in die	Four times a day
q.q.h.	Quarter quaque hora	Every four hours
R	Recipe	Take
s.o.s.	Si opus sit	If necessary
Stat.	Statim	At once
t.d.s.	Ter die sumendum	Three times a day
t.i.d.	Ter in die	Three times a day

Types of medication

All medications have specific ways of being taken or administered. These will be detailed in instructions with the medication but they are likely to follow a general pattern.

Oral medicines

Tablets or capsules are one of the commonest ways of taking medicines. Not only is the content of the tablet or capsule important, very often the structure and the materials used for the tablet or capsule will react only in certain environments. This often means that the coating on a capsule will dissolve or react in a particular way at a particular point in the digestive system, depending on the environment in that particular part of the system. This is why instructions are often given to take before food, take after food, or take with a hot or cold drink. These instructions are important to ensure that medicines are absorbed into the metabolism in the correct way.

Failure to follow instructions and take medicine in the way in which it has been prescribed can result in it being less effective or having different effects from those intended. If there are no specific instructions about taking tablets or capsules, then they should be taken at specific times each day to comply

Medication box

with the dosage requirements and are usually better swallowed with liquid, such as water, which is unlikely to have any effect. For clients who are managing their medication without the support of a carer, the pharmacist can supply boxes designed for keeping the required doses of medication, with each compartment within the box labelled with a specific day and number of doses. In this way it is easier for a client who may be likely to forget to keep track of which dose of their medication they have taken, and it reduces the risk of an accidental overdose. Most pharmacists will supply these boxes ready filled with the client's medication in the correct compartments at the correct times of each day.

Medication spoon and cup

Liquid is the other common form of oral medication. Many of these are in suspension and will need to be shaken before being taken. All oral liquid medicines come supplied with a 5ml plastic spoon, or with a small medicine cup which is marked at different dose levels, usually 2.5ml, 5ml and 10ml. Having the correct dose of medicine is important and the correct spoon must be used for administering medicines. A teaspoon from the kitchen drawer is not adequate as they differ in size and can result in either too small a quantity of medicine being ingested or an accidental overdose. You should encourage your client to wash the spoon after each dose of medicine so that it is ready to be used for the next dose.

Inhaled medicines

Those who have chronic respiratory conditions, such as asthma and chronic bronchitis, are likely to be prescribed inhalant medicines. These are usually in the form of an aerosol puff inhaler, though they can be in the form of a 'spinhaler', which works on the inhalation of breath. The principles of all of these inhaled medications is the same. The client needs to breathe out and then insert the inhaler in the mouth, take a puff and breathe inwards deeply for the required dosage. The dosage for all inhaled medicines is measured in the number of puffs.

There is a range of inhaled medicines available which serve different purposes. A

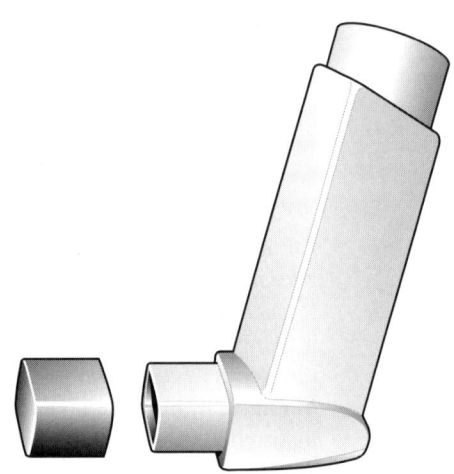

Asthmatic inhaler

client may be prescribed several different inhalers, some of which will be used to relieve symptoms and some of which will be for long-term daily use for preventive medication. It is important that the client understands that inhalers serve different purposes and that they must comply with the instructions for the number of times they need to be used.

Clients with severe respiratory conditions may also require a nebuliser. This is a machine which pumps air through a chamber containing the drug. A fine must of the drug then passes into the face mask worn by the client, who inhales the drug. This needs to be used when symptoms are severe.

Administering eye preparations

Eye preparations

Clients are most likely to be prescribed eye drops or eye ointment at some time. The method of administration is largely the same. The lower eyelid should be pulled downwards and the correct number of drops inserted in the 'pocket'. Some clients find it easier to tip the head back slightly to achieve this, however it should not be necessary to tip the head right back, as it is almost impossible to self-administer eye drops if the head is tipped too far backwards. Eye ointment should be applied in a similar way. As with the administration of all medications, you should encourage the client to wash their hands both before and after administering eye drops or ointment.

Nasal preparations

Nasal medication is likely to be prescribed in one or two forms, either as drops or as spray. Nasal sprays should be applied by placing the spray bottle into the end of one nostril while holding the other nostril closed. The client should be encouraged to breath deeply through their nose while spraying. This process should then be repeated for the other nostril.

Nasal drops, in order to be effective, should be taken with the head tipped as far forward as possible. Ideally, the client should kneel on the floor and bend over until they are resting the top of their head on the floor and then apply the nasal drops. This way the drops have the most effect on the nasal passages.

Administering nasal preparations

Alternatively, the same angle can be achieved by lying on a bed or across a stool with the head hanging over the edge. Unless otherwise advised, nasal drops should not be applied by tipping the head backwards. In this position the drops will run down the back of the client's throat and so will be less effective in the nasal area where they are intended. If a client is unable to achieve the optimum position for applying nasal drops because of lack of flexibility or mobility, you may need to discuss this with the prescribing doctor. They may reconsider the type of preparation they have prescribed.

Ear drops

Ear drops are likely to be supplied in an applicator bottle, so there is no requirement to use a separate applicator for them. The required number of drops should be dropped into the ear, being careful not to insert the applicator inside the ear

Administering ear drops

and risk causing damage. It may be helpful to keep the head tipped over slightly while inserting the drops and for a few seconds afterwards to ensure they have run inside the ear as intended. Unless directed otherwise by the prescribing doctor, it is not generally necessary or advisable to insert cotton wool into the ear after administering eardrops.

Vaginal and rectal preparations

Clients may wish to administer these themselves and it will depend on their degree of mobility and flexibility whether they are able to achieve this. If vaginal and rectal preparations are being self-administered by somebody who has the required level of fitness and mobility, then the simplest administration involves placing one foot on a chair or low stool and inserting the preparation. This is likely to be in pessary form or it may be a cream or vaginal spray. A similar procedure is likely to be effective for the application of pessaries or ointment into the rectal passage. It is more likely that vaginal and rectal preparations will be administered by a carer, in which case the optimum positions for achieving this are likely to be:

- For vaginal preparations, the client should lie on a bed with their legs bent at the knees and slightly apart to allow easy access to the vagina. Clients should be encouraged to relax whilst the preparation is inserted.

Administering vaginal preparations

- For rectal preparations, the client should lie on one side with their knees drawn up towards their chest. This allows the most straightforward access for inserting preparations into the rectal passage.

Administering rectal preparations

It is essential that proper hand washing is undertaken by the client or the carer administering these preparations both before and after administration. If these are being administered by a carer then gloves should be worn. Surgical gloves for carers use at home can be obtained from the pharmacy.

Topical preparations

Where clients have been prescribed specific ointments or creams for particular areas, these should be applied in the dosage and with the frequency prescribed. They should be applied with clean, gloved hands and gently spread over the affected area. They should not be rubbed in unless specifically instructed. Most ointments or creams are designed to be gradually absorbed and rubbing may cause damage or infection in the affected area.

How to ensure safe practice

Adverse reactions and side-effects

Many drugs have side-effects, so the prescribing doctor should explain the possibility of the effects on a client taking the medication. Also, a leaflet identifying the potential side-effects is likely to accompany the medication. The client may

Applying topical preparations

find the side-effects acceptable if they are counterbalanced by the benefits of taking the medication, and they may tolerate some of the milder side-effects that medication can cause, for example dry mouth, drowsiness, etc. However, if side-effects cause serious disruption to a client's daily life or make the client feel worse than not taking the medication, then they must contact the prescribing doctor and discuss the difficulties they are having. They should be discouraged from simply stopping the medication.

It is important to recognise the difference between side-effects and adverse reactions. Side-effects are relatively minor and do not interfere seriously with a client's general state of health. An adverse reaction to a medication can indicate an allergy or other serious side-effect. This could take the form of swelling of the hands or face, blotchiness of the skin, reddening of the skin in any part of the body, sweating or clamminess, shivering or becoming faint. If any of these conditions occur you must immediately summon medical assistance as adverse or allergic reactions to medication can be extremely rapid and extremely serious, even fatal in some cases. One other thing you should consider when you observe a client showing serious symptoms is that they could be reacting to medication equipment, particularly that which includes latex or rubber, for example gloves and some clinical tubing. The effects of an allergic reaction to latex can be extremely serious and require immediate medical attention.

Your role

Your support can be a key factor in ensuring that clients are able to manage their medical conditions safely and effectively in the community. It may also make it possible for carers to feel more confident and able to continue caring for their friend or relative knowing that support and advice is readily available to them. A central part of your role will be to ensure that there is regular liaison and contact with other members of the care team, particularly those responsible for prescribing and those who are responsible for maintaining health services to clients in the community, such as district nurses and other members of the primary care team.

Active knowledge

Check the procedures in your workplace for the administration of medication.

Make sure that you know:

- who are the people who have access to controlled drugs
- who is allowed to check drugs
- how many people have to check controlled drugs
- where drugs are kept.

Unit test

1   What are the main Acts which govern drug administration?

2   What essential preparations must be made before administering any drugs or medication?

3   Why is it important to follow the instructions on how drugs should be taken?

4   What are the essentials of safe and effective drug storage in the home?

5   How does this differ from drugs storage in a hospital or nursing home?

6   How should blood samples be obtained?

7   How should urine samples be obtained?

8   What are the likely testing methods which clients at home would use?

9   Why is it important to regularly check the levels of medication remaining in bottles or packaging?

10 Who are the key members of the care team in respect of maintaining a drug regime for clients at home?

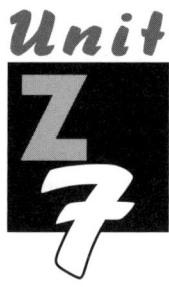

Unit Z7 Contribute to the movement and handling of individuals to maximise their physical comfort

The achievement of independence is relative to the circumstances of each individual. Everyone is entitled to be comfortable and to be as free from irritation, pain and discomfort as possible. Even where individuals require assistance to achieve this, they have achieved a considerable degree of independence if they are in control and are able to direct those helping them as to the way they want the support carried out.

This unit is primarily concerned with those individuals with whom you work who are most dependent upon your assistance. The level of assistance they need can vary from needing help to get out of a chair to being completely dependent on others to move them, to turn them over and to alter their position in any way, for example if they are unconscious or paralysed. When individuals require this degree of care it is essential that they are moved and handled in the most sensitive and safe way. This is also vital for you as a worker – the commonest causes of people being unable to continue to work in health or care are that they suffer injuries, usually back injuries, from lifting and moving individuals. It is possible to minimise the risk to both you and the individuals for whom you provide care by following the correct procedures and using the right equipment.

The first element is about preparing individuals for being moved. In the second element you will need to learn about how to carry out the move and to ensure that you know the way to carry it out correctly and safely, and offer all the support which is needed to the individual. The final element deals with pressure sores, which are painful, debilitating and a serious potential risk of infection for an individual. Understanding the causes of pressure sores and methods of avoiding them is very important – they take so long to heal that steps should be taken to prevent them, as far as possible.

Element Z7.I Prepare individuals and environments for moving and handling

WHAT YOU NEED TO LEARN

- How to assess risks.
- How to encourage independence.

How to assess risks

As you may remember from Unit CU1 your employer has a responsibility under health and safety legislation to examine and assess all procedures which take place in your working environment involving risk. All risks must be noted, assessed and steps taken to minimise them as far as possible. Your employer is required to provide adequate equipment for such tasks as moving and handling individuals who require assistance.

The risk assessments your employer carries out are, however, general risks for your work environment. Each time *you* move or lift any individual, you too must make an assessment of the risks involved in carrying out that particular manoeuvre. Even if you have moved this individual every day for the past six months, you should still assess the risks on each occasion before you put anything into practice. No two lifts are ever the same – there are always some factors that are different. These factors could be to do with the individual and his or her mood or health on that particular day, they could be about the environment, or they could be about you and your current physical condition.

You should run through the same checklist each time before you carry out any activity which involves you in physically moving a person from one place to another. A suggested checklist is shown below. You may need to adapt it to fit your own place of work and the circumstances in which you work.

Checklist

1	Is individual weight-bearing?	Yes	☐
		No	☐
2	Is individual unsteady?	Yes	☐
		No	☐
3	What is the general level of mobility?	Good	☐
		Poor	☐
4	(a) What is the individual's weight?	_____	
	(b) What is the individual's height?	_____	
	(c) How many people does this lift require?	_____	
	(Work this out on the scale devised by your workplace.)		
7	What lifting equipment is required?	Hoist	☐
		Sling	☐
		Trapeze	☐
		Transfer board	☐
8	Is equipment available?	Yes	☐
		No	☐
9	If not, is there a safe alternative?	Yes	☐
		No	☐
10	Are the required number of people available?	Yes	☐
		No	☐
11	What is the purpose of the move?		
	_____		
12	Can this be achieved?	Yes	☐
		No	☐

A checklist for assessing risks before moving an individual

You also need to consider carefully the environment when you are assessing risk. You should take into account all of the following factors:

- Is the floor surface safe? Are there wet or slippery patches?
- Are you wearing appropriate clothing – low-heeled shoes, tunic or dress which has enough room to stretch and reach?
- Is the immediate area clear of items that may cause a trip or a fall, or items which could cause injury following a fall?
- Is all the equipment, both to carry out the lift and the place to which the individual is to be moved, ready?
- Does the individual have privacy and can his or her dignity be maintained during the move?
- Is there anyone you could ask for help, for example a porter or member of the ambulance service?

Working with the individual to be moved

The individual who is going to be moved is the key person to be actively involved, as far as possible, in decisions about the best way to carry out the move. Unless the person concerned is unconscious or semi-conscious or so confused as to be unable to contribute to any discussion about the best way to proceed, then it is important that you discuss with the person the way that he or she would feel most comfortable with. Many people who have a long-standing disability will be very experienced in how to deal with it. They are the best people to ask for advice as they know the most effective ways for them to be lifted, avoiding pain and discomfort as far as possible.

Active knowledge

Your workplace probably uses an assessment form similar to the one on the next page. Find the one your workplace uses and make sure you know how to fill it in. It may be similar to the checklist on page 330.

ASSESSMENT FORM FOR PATIENTS WHO REQUIRE MANUAL HANDLING

Name: _Mr K_ Weight: _8 stone 8 lbs_

Height: _5 3_

Any relevant physical disabilities: _Congenital foot deformity_

Patient's mental ability and comprehension: _Sometimes aggressive_

History of falls? Yes No _when being dealt with_

Yes	No
	✓

Any equipment used by patient

> _The hoist must be used at all timed when moving and handling due to his inability to bear weight._

Handling constraints

Skin	_Dry_
Pain	_occasionally on movement._
Infusions	_-_
Catheters, etc.	_-_
Other	_-_

Abilities in following situations

Walking	_Unable - needs wheelchair to mobilise_
Standing	_Unable to bear weight - needs hoist_
Toiletting	_Use toiletting sling and hoist_
Transferring in/out of bed	_Use of hoist and quick fit deluxe sling_
Transferring in/out bath	_Use of ambulift bathchair_

TO BE COMPLETED WITHIN 24 HOURS OF ADMISSION AND THE RELEVANT INFORMATION WRITTEN INTO THE CARE PLAN. UPDATE THE ASSESSMENT FORM AND CARE PLAN AS NECESSARY.

Assessor's signature

Grade _Officer in charge_

Date _1.5.98_

A risk assessment form for manual handling

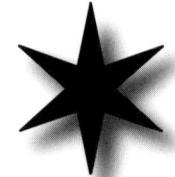

Remember

Your first port of call for advice on how to carry out a lift, after you have checked out the safety aspect and the risk factors, should be the individual himself or herself.

Once you have carried out all of the necessary assessments, you should explain carefully to the individual exactly what you intend to do and what his or her role is in contributing to the effectiveness and safety of the move. This will vary according to the person's ability, but nonetheless most individuals will be able to participate to some extent. Even where individuals are unconscious or appear to have no understanding of what is going on, you should still explain exactly what you are doing and why you are doing it and what the effects will be. We have a limited understanding of what a state of unconsciousness means to the person experiencing it. *Every* individual has the same right to be treated with dignity and respect and to have procedures explained rather than simply having things done to him or her by care workers who believe that 'they know best'. Each stage of the proposed move should be explained in detail before it is carried out, and it is essential to obtain the individual's consent before you move or handle him or her in any way. If you move an individual without his or her consent this could be construed as an assault. So you should always be sure that you are carrying out the individual's wishes before you commence any move.

Keys to good practice

- Assess risks to the individual and to yourself before starting any lift or move.
- Ask the individual about the best way of moving, or assisting, him or her.
- Explain the procedure at each stage, even where it may not be obvious that you are understood.
- Explain how the equipment operates.
- Check that you have the agreement of the person you are moving.
- Stop immediately if the individual does not wish you to continue – you may not move a person without his or her consent.

Your clothing

The type of clothing you wear when you are moving individuals is very important. It can make the difference between carrying out a procedure safely and doing it with difficulty and possible risk of injury. Footwear should be supportive and flat, with soles that grip firmly.

Recent recommendations in respect of uniforms are that dresses should have a pleat in the skirt and a similar pleat in the sleeves. These are to allow you to move so that you do not find that your own movements are restricted by your clothing, possibly forcing you to lift in an awkward way. It may be necessary, for example, to place one knee on a bed in certain types of manoevres. This is impossible if you are wearing a dress with a straight skirt. Even if not totally impossible, it can be very difficult to manage at the same time as maintaining dignity – yours, not the client's!

If you are in a situation where you do a great deal of lifting and handling, it is a good idea to wear trousers with a tunic top, which also has plenty of room in the sleeves and shoulders to allow free movement. Your employer should have carried out a risk assessment and ensured that the clothing that is provided for you to wear is appropriate and complies with current best practice and requirements in terms of lifting and handling.

Equipment

In your work you may use many different types of equipment, including several types of lifting and moving equipment. It is important that you check every time you use a piece of equipment that it is safe and that it is fit for use for that particular individual.

If you do find equipment has become worn, damaged or appears to be unsafe in any way, you should immediately stop using it, take it out of service and report it to your supervisor. You must do this even if it means having to change your handling assessment for the individual you were about to move. Under no circumstances is it acceptable to take a risk with equipment which may be faulty. It is better that the

Work clothing should allow for free movement when handling individuals.

individual waits a little longer for a move or is moved in an alternative way rather than being exposed to risks from potentially unsafe equipment.

Make sure that you have read the instruction manual for each piece of equipment you use. It should give you a safety checklist – make sure you follow it.

Active knowledge

Find out the procedure in your workplace for reporting faulty equipment. Check whether there is a file or a book where you need to record the fault. You may only need to make a verbal report, or you may have to enter the details of the fault into a computer. Make sure that you know what the correct procedure is.

How to encourage independence

There are many ways in which an individual can assist and co-operate with care workers who are lifting or moving him or her. It is important that this is encouraged and that individuals are not made to feel as though they are simply being transported from place to place like 'a piece of meat'. Co-operation from the individual is invaluable, both for maintaining his or her own independence and for assisting those who have to carry out the lift. For example, you may be transferring an individual from a bed to a wheelchair. The first part of the process – getting to the edge of the bed and sitting on it – may well be possible for the individual to accomplish if he or she follows a correct set of instructions, rather than having to be moved by carers.

Any independence which can be achieved is vitally important in terms of the individual's self-esteem and sense of well-being. A person may be able to transfer himself or herself from a wheelchair to a chair, to a car seat or into bed, either by the use of transfer boards or by simply being able to use sufficient upper body strength to slide across from chair to wheelchair, and vice versa, once the arm is removed.

You may wish to employ techniques such as bridging when you need to give an individual a bed pan. Rather than having to lift the person manually, he or she can be encouraged, with some simple instructions, to bend the knees and raise the bottom to allow the bed pan to be slid underneath him or her (see pages 340-341).

Techniques like this involve the active co-operation of the individual. Obviously they are not suitable for use where individuals are unable to co-operate, either because of their state of consciousness or because they have almost total paralysis. Some individuals may not be able to co-operate for emotional reasons – they may lack the confidence to make any moves for themselves because of fear of falling or fear of pain or discomfort. Where the plan of care has identified that the individual is capable of co-operation in moving and handling, this should be gently encouraged and the reasons for his or her reluctance to co-operate should be explored with the individual.

Good preparation is the key to a successful lift or transfer. Where the individual and the worker are working together, there is likely to be the maximum safety and minimum risk, pain and discomfort.

Element Z7.2   Assist individuals to move from one position to another

WHAT YOU NEED TO LEARN

- Equipment for moving and handling.
- Methods for manual moving and handling.
- Recording and passing on information.

Equipment for moving and handling

There is a wide range of equipment available and technological advances are being made continuously in the field of medical equipment. Regardless of the individual products and improvements which may be made to them, lifting and handling equipment broadly falls into the following categories:

- hoists, slings and other equipment, which move the full weight of an individual
- equipment designed to assist in a move and to take some of the weight of individual, such as transfer boards
- equipment designed to assist the individual to help himself or herself, such as lifting handles positioned above a bed to allow individuals to pull themselves up. This category also includes grab handles, raised toilet seats, and lifting seat chairs.

Depending on the setting in which you work, you may have to use some or all of the equipment shown below. If you work with individuals in their own homes, your access to equipment may be more limited, although there is now an extensive range of equipment that can be used very effectively within an individual's own home, often removing the need for residential care.

Using equipment

Each piece of equipment will have an instruction manual. You must read this and be sure that you follow the instructions for its use. There are some general points about how to use particular types of equipment, but you must know how to use the particular type of equipment in your workplace.

Hoists

- Make sure that you use the correct sling for the hoist and for the weight of the client.
- Most slings are colour-coded. Check that you have the right one for the weight of the client.
- Ensure that the seams on the hoist are facing outwards, as they can be rough and can easily damage the skin.
- Only attempt to manoeuvre a hoist using the steering handles – do not try to move it with the jib, as it can overbalance.
- Place the sling around or under the client. Lower the bed to its lowest position. *Then* lift the client. It is only necessary to have a small clearance from the bed or chair – there is no need to raise the client a great distance.

Equipment for moving and handling

You cannot learn to use a hoist safely by reading a book – you must familiarise yourself with the hoists in your workplace and ask to be shown how to operate them.

Transfer boards/sheets

These require at least two people standing on opposite sides of the bed. They allow people to be moved from bed to trolley and vice versa. They can be used regardless of the level of consciousness of the individual.

They all work on the same principles. They are made of friction-free material which is placed half under the person and half under the sheet he or she is lying on. One worker then pulls and the other pushes. The sheet, complete with person, then slides easily from one to the other. There are several types available: 'Pat-slide', 'Easy-glide' and 'Easy-slide' are amongst the most common.

Slideboards

The slideboard is a small board placed between a bed and a chair or wheelchair. It is designed for use by clients who are able to be quite active in the transfer and only require assistance. The board allows the client to slide from bed to chair, and vice versa, with some assistance in steadying and some encouragement.

Monkey pole or lifting handle

This is a handle which is fixed above a bed, and swings from a metal frame. It is designed to allow people to assist themselves. They have to pull on the bar to lift the upper part of the body off the bed. This can enable people to help themselves to sit up, turn over and change position without having to call for assistance.

When you are assessing how to assist a person to move and which equipment to use, you need to consider:

- the potential risks
- what the person can do to help himself or herself to move, and what he or she cannot do – remember that it is important to encourage as much independence as possible
- what the person knows from experience to be the best method, or the method he or she prefers.

If the person's preference conflicts with safe practice, you should tactfully explain this, pointing out the potential risks and suggesting the best method. Reassure the person, if necessary. If there is still a problem, you will need to tell your supervisor immediately.

Remember

You should never move anyone without his or her agreement.

Active knowledge

Investigate the equipment available in your workplace for moving and handling. Make sure you know where different items are kept and how they work. Make notes to refer to when necessary.

Methods for manual moving and handling

There are very few situations in which manual lifting should be carried out. Unless it is an emergency or a life-threatening situation, there should be no need to move anyone without the correct equipment. Manual handling should only be carried out in situations which do not involve lifting all, or most, of a person's weight.

This means that even shoulder lifts are no longer considered to be safe. There is no safe weight limit for lifting, so the only workplaces where lifting should now take place are units caring for babies and small children. Even there, it is important to ensure that risk assessments are carried out to avoid the likelihood of injury.

If you need to move someone manually in order to change his or her position or to provide assistance, you should follow the principles of effective manual moving and handling:

- The procedures should be well-planned and assessed in advance. Technique rather than strength is what is important.
- The procedure should be comfortable and safe for the individual – creating confidence that being moved is not something to be anxious about and that he or she can relax and co-operate with the procedure.
- The procedure should be safe for the workers carrying it out. A worker who is injured during a badly planned or executed transfer or move is likely in turn to injure the individual he or she is attempting to move. Similarly, an individual who is injured during a move is likely to cause an injury to those who are moving him or her.

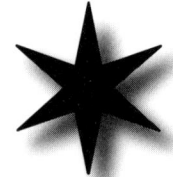

Remember

The interests and safety of the individual and the workers are so closely linked that you must consider them both together.

Active knowledge

Find out what the rules for manual handling are in your workplace. Make a note of them for your portfolio.

Team work

Most moving procedures, whether manual or assisted, are carried out by more than one person. If you are to work successfully as part of a team, you need to follow some simple rules:

- Decide who is going to 'shout'.
- That person will check that everyone is ready.
- He or she will say '1-2-3 lift' or '1-2-3 move' or (depending on familiarity with American TV) 'on my count 1-2-3'.
- Everyone must follow the count of the person who shouts.

Transfer

If you are assisting an individual to transfer from a bed or chair to a wheelchair, this can be done with one person providing assistance to steady the person as he or she uses the transfer board, providing that there are no complicating factors such as an individual who is particularly heavy or tall or who has serious disabilities. In that case, they should be moved using a hoist or a turntable.

Rolling or turning

If you need to roll or turn someone who is unable to assist, either because of paralysis, unconsciousness, seriously illness or confusion, you should:

- always carry this out with at least two workers

- roll the person using a transfer sheet or board, or use the bottom sheet to roll the person onto his or her side
- support the person with pillows or packing.

When the person needs to be turned again, remove the pillows, lower him or her onto the back and repeat the other way.

Overcoming 'pyjama-induced paralysis'

One of the key factors in a safe handling policy is to encourage people to help themselves. There is a great temptation for people to believe that they can do far less than they are capable of. This is often encouraged by staff who find it quicker and easier to do things rather than wait for people to help themselves.

If you encourage individuals to make their own way out of bed, for example, then they would need to follow the simple set of instructions shown in the diagram below.

Instructions for getting out of bed

1 Roll towards the edge of the bed

2 Swing your legs over the side of the bed whilst continuing to lie the top half of your body on the bed.

3 Push with your hands and sit upright.

The legs act as a counter balance and help to pull the individual upright on the edge of the bed.

You may wish to encourage an individual to roll over in the bed, rather than having to be manually rolled by a care worker. This could be necessary to allow changing of bedding, a bed bath or to change clothes. The instructions for achieving this are quite simple, and can be carried out by all but the most severely ill or disabled individuals, as shown in the diagram below.

Instructions for rolling over in bed

1 Turn to face the direction in which you are rolling

2 Bend the leg of the other side and keep your foot flat on the bed

3 Reach across your body with the opposite arm. This uses the counter weight of moving the arm across the upper body to assist with the movement of achieving a roll.

If you need to get someone to raise his or her bottom from the bed in order to give a bedpan, or to prepare for rolling or turning (known as bridging), then you should ask the person to follow the instructions below.

Instructions for bridging

1 Bend both knees

2 Keep your feet flat on the bed and push up on your feet and hands, so that your bottom is raised.

Even in community settings, where previously it was unusual for carers to be using equipment, it is now much more common to see domiciliary services carrying out risk assessments for their carers and support workers, and insisting that unless equipment like hoists are made available it is not possible to continue to provide a service without putting the care workers at risk of injury.

Recording and passing on information

Information about the most effective ways of moving someone, or techniques which have proved effective in encouraging a person to assist himself or herself, should be recorded in the plan of care.

The plan of care should contain information on the moving needs of each individual, and it is important that these are followed. However, you may notice a change in behaviour or response. This could be:

- a person finding movement more painful
- a loss of confidence in a particular technique
- an improvement in how much assistance a person can give
- a changed reaction following being moved.

Any of these changes, or anything else you notice, are significant and must be reported to your supervisor. Any changes may be indications of overall changes in the person's condition and should never be ignored.

The information you record should be:

- clear
- easily understood
- a good description of the person's needs.

NURSING CARE PLAN

Date	No.	PATIENT'S NURSING NEEDS/PROBLEMS AND CAUSES OF PROBLEMS (N.B. Physiological, Psychological, Social and Family Problems)	Objectives	Nursing Instructions	Review On/By	Date Resolved
1.5.98	8	Mobility:			8.5.98	
					15.5.98	
		Due to suffering from	To prevent	a) Encourage Mr. K to be as	22.5.98	
		a congenital foot	complications of	independent as possible.	29.5.98	
		deformity, Mr. K	immobility and	b) Always give clear, concise	5.6.98	
		is unable to bear weight	maintain Mr. K's	instructions when moving and	12.6.98	
		and needs the hoist	safety as far	handling to gain client's full	19.6.98	
		to be used when	as is reasonably	co-operation.	26.6.98	
		moving and handling	practicable.	c) The hoist must be used at all	3.7.98	
				times with either the Quickfit	10.7.98	
				deluxe sling or the toiletting sling –	17.7.98	
				depending upon circumstances.	24.7.98	
				d) Ensure safe practice maintained	31.7.98	
				when moving and handling client.	7.8.98	
				e) Observe for any problems and		
				reassess appropriately.		
				f) Review problem weekly.		

An example of notes on an individual's mobility in his plan of care

Case study

Shireen is the carer for Mrs G, who is 39 and has rheumatoid arthritis. Shireen needs to move Mrs G from a bed into a chair. Mrs G is only able to assist a little as she has very painful joints and is unable to bear weight. She weighs 16 stones (101.6 kg).

1 What would you expect to see in Mrs G's care plan in respect of moving procedure? Give reasons.
2 What factors should Shireen take into account before starting to move Mrs G?
3 What should Shireen say to her?

When you are carrying out a moving procedure, it may be necessary to move items of furniture so that you can work safely. Whether you are working in a care setting or in an individual's own home, it is important that furniture is returned to its original position afterwards, so the individual can easily locate personal items in their usual places and feel reassured by the familiar surroundings.

Element Z7.3   Assist individuals to prevent and minimise the adverse effects of pressure

WHAT YOU NEED TO LEARN

- How pressure sores can happen.
- How to prevent pressure sores.
- How to treat pressure sores.

How pressure sores can happen

Pressure sores are the result of an interruption to the blood supply, which causes the tissue in that particular area to break down. The interruption to the blood supply is caused by various types of pressure, exerted in different ways, but the effect is the same - it causes the tissue in the affected area to die and to degenerate into a sore. Every one of us would get pressure sores if we were not able to move regularly each night whilst we were asleep. For individuals who are unable to change their own position regularly, whether that is lying down or sitting in a wheelchair, the pressure can result in a sore. There are some areas which are particularly vulnerable:

- back of the head
- shoulders
- sacrum (the bottom of the back)
- buttocks
- backs of legs and calves
- heels.

The diagram on page 343 shows the most common sites of pressure sores.

Compression

There are several ways in which pressure sores are caused, but one of the commonest is compression, where the weight of a part of the skeleton presses through the flesh and skin against a relatively hard surface, such as a bed or a chair.

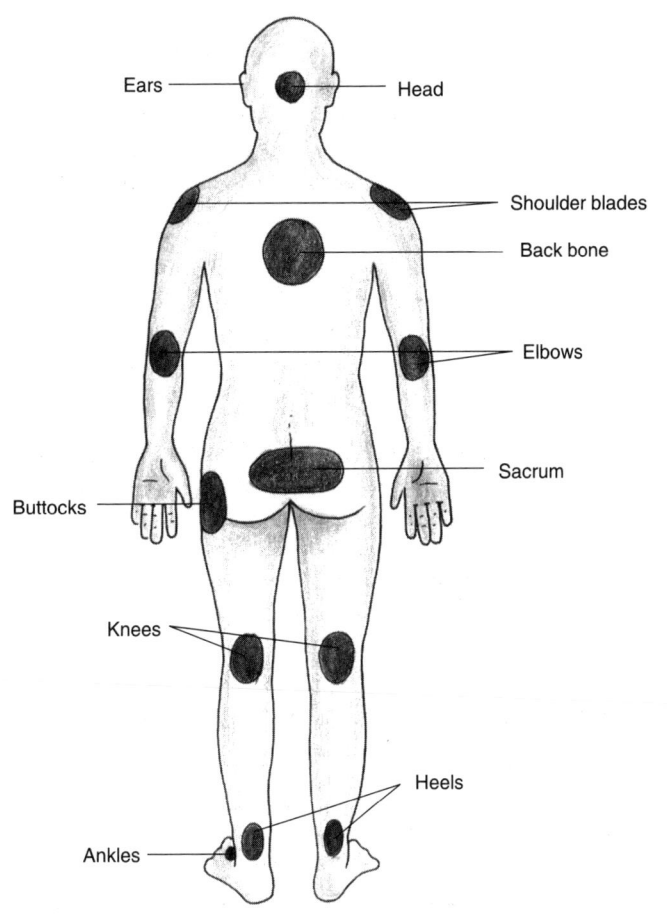

Common sites of pressure sores

This compression causes the blood supply to be cut off to that area of tissue, which then dies and degenerates into a sore. This is commonly seen in people who are confined to a chair or a wheelchair. These sores develop on the buttocks because of the weight of their skeleton on their buttocks and against the chair. It also happens where people are confined to bed and are not able to move their position regularly and here other pressure points, such as shoulder blades, elbows, the back of the head and the heels, are all likely to suffer sores as a result of compression.

Shearing

Shearing

Another way in which pressure sores can be caused is called shearing. This is when an individual is left in a half lying, propped up position in bed and the downward pressure, which gradually slides him or her down in bed, drags the skin across the surface of the bed and grazes it, damaging the small blood vessels (see the diagram on page 343). These pressure sores are commonly seen on the sacrum (bottom of the back) and the heels.

Friction

Pressure sores can also be caused by friction when two areas rub against each other. This can often be seen with rumpled nightclothes or when crumbs or other debris are left in the bed, or when there is a wet area around the buttocks and sacrum caused by incontinence.

Assessing risk of pressure sores

There has been considerable research into the care of pressure areas and several different assessment scales have been developed to judge the people who are most likely to be at risk from pressure sores and for whom preventive action can be taken at an early stage. The commonest assessment score is called the Norton Score (shown below). The lower the score a person has, the greater the chance of developing sores.

The Norton Score for pressure sore risk assessment

Physical condition		Mental state		Activity		Mobility		Incontinence	
Good	4	Alert	4	Ambulant	4	Full	4	Not	4
Fair	3	Apathetic	3	Walks with help	3	Slightly limited	3	Occasionally	3
Poor	2	Confused	2	Chair-bound	2	Very limited	2	Usually urine	2
Very bad	1	Stuporous	1	Bedfast	1	Immobile	1	Double	1

How to prevent pressure sores

It is always better to work on preventing pressure sores, rather than having to treat them once they have already developed. The best way to ensure that pressure sores do not develop is to keep people as active as possible, so that they are less likely to remain in one position. It is also important for individuals who are confined to bed or a chair to have a special mattress or cushion (such as a Roho cushion), which is designed to distribute weight more evenly so that the downward pressure from the skeleton is evenly spread and does not concentrate pressure in one area.

You should also ensure that individuals eat a good balanced diet with a significant protein content, as protein is required for cell renewal – this is a significant way of reducing the risk of tissue breakdown and the development of pressure sores.

It is vital to ensure that clients who are incontinent are never left sitting in wet clothes or incontinence pads which have become soaked. The effect of wet, urine-soaked clothing on skin is to render it very likely to develop sores in the pressure areas.

Sheepskin or artificial sheepskin is another useful way of preventing the development of pressure sores. This tends to be used particularly on heels where sheepskin booties are used. It has the effect of relieving the pressure and spreading the weight of the joint more easily. Some individuals are comfortable with an artificial sheepskin under their shoulders or their buttocks or to sit on one in their wheelchair. Increasingly, these are now being replaced by the more technologically advanced forms of mattresses and cushions which use a combination of specially devised air pockets or, in some cases, water to spread the pressure more evenly across areas of the body.

Cushions

Sheepskin pads

Aids to prevent pressure sores

Reporting and recording

Just as the plans for moving and handling should be in a person's care plan, so should information on any pressure area care. There should be notes about any sore places which may be developing, and any changes in the skin, such as reddening or grazes, must be reported at once. Skin becomes very fragile as people get older, and it can be easily injured. It is these apparently minor skin injuries which often develop into sores that can take months to heal.

Keys to good practice

- Move people regularly.
- Turn an unconscious or paralysed person every two hours.
- Use aids such as a Roho cushion, a special mattress or fleece pads.
- Check that the person's diet contains adequate protein.
- Change wet clothes and bedclothes immediately.
- Report any changes you notice in a person's skin.

Active knowledge

Try to sit in a propped up position without moving for as long as possible without altering your position. You will find that before very long you will begin to feel uncomfortable, and after a fairly short period of time it is painful to remain without moving. Imagine how that feels for somebody who is totally unable to move.

How to treat pressure sores

Pressure sore treatments are constantly being developed and improved, so you should seek advice from a qualified medical or nursing practitioner about the latest developments. Current practice is to use dressings which will allow moist healing of the sore. At one time it was believed that pressure sores should be dried and were best allowed to heal in their dry state. There is now little argument that all wounds including pressure sores heal far better in a warm, moist environment.

There are various dressings available which adhere very closely to the skin and will allow oxygen through but no moisture, enabling the wound to retain any moisture to assist healing. As long as a wound is not infected, these types of dressings, such as Op-site, appear to achieve quite good results.

Did you know?

The benefits of moist wound healing were first demonstrated almost 30 years ago However, in a recent study carried out in a large hospital, less than 50 per cent of the people questioned knew about the procedure.

An individual's care plan will identify the treatment regime which needs to be used for his or her particular pressure sores, and the treatment will be supervised by a qualified practitioner. Treatments today will not include practices such as massaging the area or washing with soap and water, which were common some years ago. There is no evidence to support the theory that massaging the area will play any part in healing the sore and, in fact, it is likely to aggravate the situation.

The key to effective treatment of pressure sores is to attempt, where possible, to increase the general health of the individual – people who are malnourished or debilitated because of an illness or long periods of neglect are unlikely to heal pressure sores effectively until their general state of health has been considerably improved. The care plan should include arrangements for the individual to receive, if possible, a high protein, high carbohydrate diet.

Pressure sores are extremely unpleasant, but they are avoidable. Good practice and good levels of care can prevent pressure sores from occurring and can speed the healing of any which existed before the individual received care.

Did you know?

When the Egyptian pyramids were investigated, evidence was found that some of the people mummified within the tombs had suffered with pressure sores. This makes it very clear that the problem of pressure sores has always existed.

Unit test

1 Name three factors you would take into account when assessing the risk of carrying out a lift.

2 In what sort of circumstances would you consider asking an individual to move him or herself across the bed?

3 What type of clothing is most suitable for carrying out lifting?

4 What steps should you take if you have concerns about the safety of equipment?

5 What are the three categories of lifting and handling equipment?

6 Describe how the following are used:

   a a hoist
   b a transfer board or sheet
   c a slideboard
   d a monkey pole.

7 What are the three principles of effective manual handling?

8 Describe the procedures for:

   a bridging
   b rolling or turning
   c transfer.

9 Why should information and changes regarding mobility be recorded and passed on?

10 Which areas are most likely to suffer from pressure sores?

11 Name two ways of relieving pressure sores.

12 What are the best ways of preventing an individual from developing pressure sores?

13 Which individuals are likely to be the most vulnerable to pressure sores?

14 How can you contribute to increasing the independence of an individual by the way you assist them?

Glossary

Abuse	Treating someone or something in a way that causes harm. Abuse may be directed at oneself (self-harm), at others, or at things. It may be emotional, financial, physical, psychological or sexual.
Aims and objectives	Targets and ways of achieving them.
Alcohol hand rub	Can be used to clean and disinfect hands where there is no access to soap and water.
Anaphylactic shock	A severe reaction to a substance touching or entering the body.
Assumption	An acceptance that something is true although there is no real proof of it.
Barium enema	Used to diagnose abnormalities in the stomach or intestines.
Burches colposuspension	A surgical procedure for women which creates a 'sling' to support the pelvic floor. Can be effective in dealing with stress incontinence caused by weak pelvic muscles.
Care setting	The context for health and social care services. These include hospitals, residential settings, day-care facilities, clinics and domiciliary settings.
Care team	All those with a formal or informal responsibility for care, whether paid or unpaid. The care team includes the client/patient.
Carer	A person who is delivering care in an informal capacity. A carer is someone who is responsible for supporting an individual through the provision of some form of care, be it physical, emotional or financial. The carer is usually a partner, relative or friend.
Cascading	A method of sharing knowledge, usually in a workplace, by one person accessing information and passing it on to colleagues.
Charter	A statement which sets out the rights and entitlements of users of a particular service.
Client/patient	The terms 'client' and 'patient' are used to describe the person who is the focus of health and social care activity and cover individuals of all ages. The term 'patient' is used only in matters specifically related to health care.
Clinical activity	Any treatments or investigations carried out by health professionals.
Clinical procedures	Clinical activities in which health care workers may be involved.
Communicate	Share information, ideas, views and emotions with people by speaking, writing, body language or through the use of equipment.
Confidentiality	The principle of only sharing information about individuals with those who have a need to know it in order to benefit the individual or when the safety of others may be at risk.

Consent	Agreement by the client, after being given information, for any procedure or clinical activity to be undertaken.
Data	The raw information obtained from any process of research or investigation.
Development plan	A document which includes targets and timescales for the planning and direction of your education, training and future career.
Discrimination	The practice of treating one person or group of people less well or less fairly than other people or groups.
Diversity	The different skills, abilities, language, culture, religion, values and beliefs which provide a rich and varied society.
Dynamap	Instrument for reading blood pressure and pulse.
Enable	To act in such a way that others will be able to do something through the provision of resources, information, encouragement or help.
Environment	The surrounding in which services are delivered, particularly the intangible aspects.
Equal opportunities	Offering services, without discrimination on the basis of race, sex, religion, disability, etc., which aim at ensuring everyone has equal access and equal treatment.
Ethics	Moral principles about right and wrong behaviour. An ethic of a particular kind is an ideal or moral belief that influences the behaviour, attitudes and philosophy of a group of people.
Facilitate	To make something easier or more likely to happen.
Feedback	Valuable information gained from others, such as supervisors, colleagues or clients on the way in which you carry out your work.
Group	A set of people who come together because they have something in common.
Hazardous waste	Medical, biological and human body waste, or waste from chemical and industrial processes which could cause a risk to human health.
Health and social well-being	All aspects of social, physical, intellectual and emotional/psychological health which contribute to one's health and social well-being.
Human Rights Act	Act of Parliament passed in 1998 but largely enacted in October 2000. The Act establishes a legal right to the provisions of the European Convention on Human Rights.
Individual	Any person who may be the focus of the activity concerned. This may be the person who is in receipt of the services but also may be other workers, managers or those in the vicinity.
Inequality	Different levels of opportunities to access the rights, benefits and routes to achievement.
Infringement of rights	An action or situation that interferes with someone's rights and freedom.
Internet	The interface between technology, e.g. computers, digital televisions, digital telephones, and the information on the World Wide Web.
Invasive clinical procedure	A treatment or investigation which involves putting instruments or equipment inside the body through the skin or through a natural opening.

Key worker	The person who has the main responsibility for relating to a client and is the main point of contact.
Life stage	Human development levels such as baby, infant, toddler, child, adolescent, adult, old age.
Manager	The person with direct managerial responsibility for the worker in the sense of allocating, co-ordinating and evaluating her/his work.
Materials and equipment	All types of supplies, consumables, sundries, instruments, equipment and machines. These may be clinical or non-clinical. 'Materials' refers to items which have a short life or single use. 'Equipment' refers to items which may be used many times.
Monitoring	The process of keeping a regular check to ensure that any significant changes are noticed.
MRSA (Methicillin-Resistant Staphylococcus aureus)	The most serious nosocomial infection which is resistant to all the common antibiotics.
MSSU (mid-stream sample of urine)	A urine sample which is obtained by asking the client to stop, or slow, their flow of urine and then restart into the collection vessel.
Mucocutaneous exposure	When potentially infected body fluids come into contact with mucous membranes such as eyes or nose.
Non-hazardous waste	Waste which does not pose a risk to human health.
Non-pathogenic	Micro-organisms which do not cause infection to humans.
Norm	Within the commonly accepted or usual boundaries.
Nosocomial infections	Infections which are prevalent in hospitals.
Package of care	The set of measures brought together to meet a person's needs.
Pathogenic	Micro-organisms which do cause infection to humans.
Percutaneous exposure	When potentially infected body fluids enter through the skin either because of injury, such as a 'needle stick' or broken skin.
Phenylketonuria (PKU) test	A test which can show the lack of an essential enzyme for breaking down phenylalanine. If undetected, this can lead to severe brain damage.
Plan of care	An outline of an individual's present and future needs and the ways in which these needs will be met.
Policy	Protocols, procedures and requirements to which the worker must adhere. Policies may be set at international, national, local or agency level.
Power of attorney	A legal process which gives one person, usually a relative or legal or financial professional, the power to conduct someone's financial and legal affairs. This power is only granted when someone is incapable of managing their own affairs.
Practice guidelines	Recognised good practice within agencies, including codes of good practice and recognised methods of working.
Pulseoximeter	An instrument for taking pulse.

Records	Electronic, written, diagrammatic, photographic or other information kept about an individual while in receipt of services.
Referral	The act of forwarding a case or issue to a person who is authorised or better qualified to deal with it. Referrals may be between workers in the same agency or across agencies.
Reflective practitioner	One who considers and thinks about their own practice, skills and abilities and takes steps to improve and develop their working skills.
Sharps	Instruments which could cause a penetrating injury such as needles, syringes, scalpels, razors etc.
Social stratification	A means of identifying society into different groupings according to income, occupation and lifestyle.
Socioeconomic deprivation	Consequences of low income and poor environmental conditions such as bad housing, education and local facilities.
Sphygmomano-meter	A traditional instrument for reading blood pressure, which uses mercury and is being phased out of use.
Standard precautions	See **Universal precautions**
Stereotype	A fixed general image believed to represent a particular type of person or thing. If you stereotype people you form a fixed idea of them so that you assume they will behave in a particular way.
Sterile field	A treatment area which has had all pathogens removed.
Team leader	A person who is heading a team of workers to achieve common outcomes.
Universal precautions	Preventive measures which should be taken before being exposed to possible contamination by body fluids.
Values	The moral principles and beliefs that are considered important.
Venipuncture	The process of taking blood from a vein using a needle.
Visitors	Someone who goes to see a person or place who does not usually work there, live there or attend there.
World Wide Web	Almost unlimited source of information, accessible using information technology such as computers, digital televisions and digital telephones.

Index

blood sampling
    blood sugar test 311-13
    finger prick 312
    frequent 312
    phenylketonuria test 311
    venipuncture 311
body fluids and waste
    disposal 78
body mass index [BMI] 317
body temperature 313-14
bronchitis 313
budgeting 281-3
burns and scalds 93-4

Caldecott Guardians 32, 33, 36
Caldecott Principles 31-36
cardiac arrests 87-8, 93
care environments, definition 126
care packages
    carers 213-14
    changes 216-17
    clients 213-14
    direct payments 214-15
    evaluating effectiveness 215-16
    monitoring 207-15
    reviewing 217-22
care planning meetings
    clients at 110-111, 114-15
    preparation 109
    proposals
        client agreement 117-18
        communicating 116
        imposition 118
    recording 114-15, 119
    stereotyping 112
care plans
    abuse 136-7
    changing needs 122
        implementing 123
    mobility 341
    monitoring provision 120-21
    review processes 124
carers
    barriers 213-14
    benefits 293-4
    development activities 254-5
    feedback 210-11
    support 239-40
    support for 302-3
cash, security of 298, 300
catheters
    client procedures 305

hygiene 306
indwelling 306
latex allergy 327
urine specimen collection 309-10
cerebral palsy 153, 160
Charters
    Benefits Agency 17
    Long-term Care 17
    Patients 17
Child Benefit [formerly Family Allowance] 291
children
    abuse 127, 131, 132, 147
        signs of 138-9
    records of 106
Children Act [1989] 9, 235
choice, importance of 40-1
choking 91-2
Citizens Advice Bureaux 283, 288-9
clean techniques
    clients 304-5
client participation
    development activities 254
client procedures
    catheters 305
    diabetes 307
    drainage/feeding tubes 308
    monitoring 308
    stoma care 305-6
    waste disposal 308
    wound dressing 304-5
clinical procedures
    protective clothing see universal precautions
clinical waste see hazardous waste
clothing
    health and safety 80, 333-4
colleagues
    discrimination by 25
    unacceptable behaviour by 46-9, 133
Commission for Racial Equality 26
communication
    choosing methods of 173
    cultural differences 153, 160-1
    dementia 153, 163
    effective 263-4
    encouraging 59, 163-4
    good practice 52, 57-8
    hearing impairment 55, 152, 157-8, 163
    interaction 43, 60-1
    language differences 56, 152, 156-7, 163
    learning difficulties 153, 160, 163
    and listening 58-9
    non-verbal 50-2, 162

eye, nose and ear 325-6
inhaled 324
oral 323-4
prescription 321-2
regulations 321-3
side-effects 327
storage 321
topical 326-7
vaginal and rectal 326
dynomaps 314
dysphasia 153, 159-60

ear drops 325-6
electrocution 94-5
emergencies
bleeding 86-7
burns and scalds 93-4, 95
cardiac arrests 87-8, 95
choking 91-2
electrocution 94-5
epileptic seizures 91
fractures 92
hospitals 85
loss of consciousness 89-90
poisoning 94
reporting 96
residential settings 86
shock 88
emergency services, calling 96
emphysema 313, 318
epilepsy 91
Equal Opportunities Commission 13, 14, 26
Equal Pay Act [1970] 14
equipment
client lifting and moving 66, 67, 333-4
hoists 336
monkey poles/lifting handles 337
slideboards 337
transfer boards/sheets 336-7
instructions 303
sources 303
storage 303
ethnicity 27-8
evacuation, buildings 69
evaluating
care packages 215-16
development activities 259-61
expectations, clients' 100-1
eye tests 290
eyes
medications 325

family
relationships 224
structures 226-7
feedback
carers 210, 211
clients 210-11, 213-14
development activities 259
families 211
health professionals 211
service providers 212
feeding/drainage tubes 308
filing rules 181
financial affairs
benefits 285-6, 289-94, 294-7
budgeting 281-3
cash security 298, 300
debts 383-5
payments
checklist 278
illegal 287
methods 279-80
recording 286-7
self-management 277
support level 275-6
fire safety
building evacuation 69
extinguishers 68
procedures 67-8
fluid balance 318
charts 319
input 318
output 319
footwear
health and safety 80, 333
fractures 92
Freedom of Information Bill 30
friendships 225

girth, measurement 316
gloves
body fluid protection 81
goals/aims
development activities 252-3, 260-61

hair, safety 82
handling and lifting *see* lifting and handling
handwashing
infection control 81
methods 81-2
reasons for 81-2
hazardous waste
body fluids and waste 78

two-way exchange 173
written 173
sharing
development activities 260-61
injections 307
instruments
reusable 78
insulin *see* diabetes
interaction
stages 60-1
understanding 43
Internet
services and agencies 266-7
intruders 65, 69-70
Invalid Care Allowance 293

language differences
communication 56, 152, 156-7, 163
interpreters 56, 156
non-verbal communication 156-7
latex, allergy to 327
learning difficulties 153, 160, 164
legislation
and monitoring 209
and relationships 234-5
lifting and handling clients
client consultation 331-3
client help 84, 332, 334-5
clothing 333, 334
equipment 66, 67, 333-4, 335-7
manual 66, 84, 337-8
rolling/turning 338-9
transfer 338
recording needs 341
regulations 66
risk assessments 330-1, 332
listening
abuse disclosures 140
active 58-9
literacy difficulties 294-5
Long-term Care Charter 17
low incomes 281
benefits 291-3
Council Tax 292
health costs 292-3
Housing Benefit 293
Income Support 291
Social Fund 293
Working Families Tax Credit 293
lung capacity 318

Manual Handling Operations Regulations [1993]
66

measuring
goals/aims 260-61
medical records, access 106-7, 176
Medicines Act [1968] 322
medicines/medications *see* drugs and medicines
Mental Health Act [1983] 106, 133, 209, 234-5
mid-stream sample of urine [MSSU] 310
Misuse of Drugs Act [1971] 321
Money Advice Centres 283, 288-9
monitoring
carers 210
importance of 208-9
legislation and guidelines 209
methods 121-2
resources 209
monitoring, by
carers and families 211
clients 210-11, 213-15
health care professionals 211
service providers 212
monkey poles/lifting handles 337
motivation, teams 189-90, 191
motor neurone disease [MND] 153, 160
moving clients *see* lifting and handling clients

nasal medications 325
needles *see* sharps
needs, assessing clients' 99-101, 262-5
non-verbal communication
facial expression 51, 52
gestures 51, 162
language differences 156-7
and physical disability 55
posture 51, 52
Norton Scale, pressure sore risk assessments 344

obesity 315, 316

Patients' Charter 17
payments by clients
avoidance of obligations 287-8
checklist 278
debts 283
disapproved 287
illegal 287
payments to clients
benefits
methods 298-301
receipts for collected 299-300
methods 279-80
recording 286-7
peak flow meters 289, 313, 318

Other titles of interest
Coming August 2003 – 2nd Edition

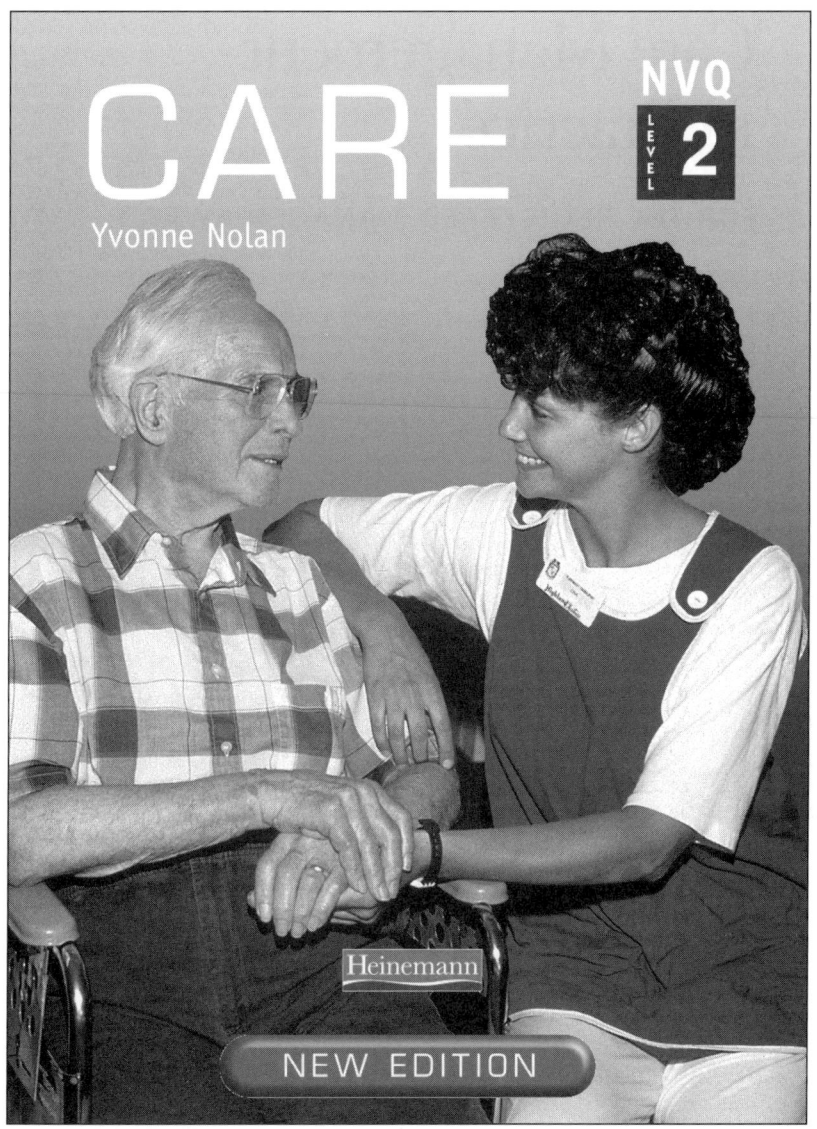

The best-selling book for success in S/NVQ Level 2 in Care
1st Edition ISBN 0435 45224 X, currently available
2nd Edition ISBN 0435 45221 5, available in August 2003.

TEL: 01865 888080

FAX: 01865 314029

E-MAIL: orders@heinemann.co.uk

WEB: www.heinemann.co.uk

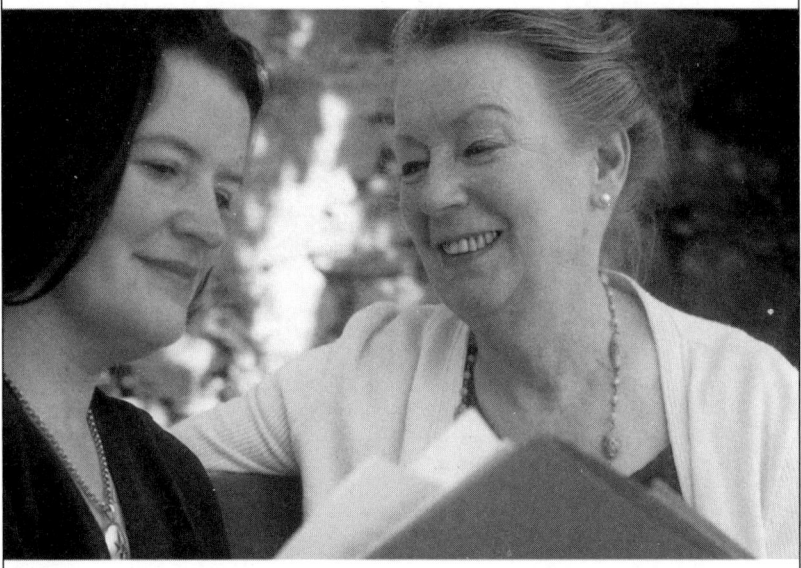

Care Management in Practice

FOR THE REGISTERED MANAGER AWARD

Dr. Andrew Thomas
Lynda Mason and Sharon Ford

Heinemann

Inspiring generations

A comprehensive resource to help you succeed in your Registered Manager Award qualification.
ISBN 0435 40159 9

TEL: 01865 888080
FAX: 01865 314029

E-MAIL: orders@heinemann.co.uk
WEB: www.heinemann.co.uk